Web Application Architecture

Principles, protocols and practices

Leon Shklar
Richard Rosen

Dow Jones and Company

John Wiley & Sons, Ltd

Other Wiley Editorial Offices

John Wiley & Sons Inc., 111 River Street, Hoboken, NJ 07030, USA

Jossey-Bass, 989 Market Street, San Francisco, CA 94103-1741, USA

Wiley-VCH Verlag GmbH, Boschstr. 12, D-69469 Weinheim, Germany

John Wiley & Sons Australia Ltd, 33 Park Road, Milton, Queensland 4064, Australia

John Wiley & Sons (Asia) Pte Ltd, 2 Clementi Loop #02-01, Jin Xing Distripark, Singapore 129809

John Wiley & Sons Canada Ltd, 22 Worcester Road, Etobicoke, Ontario, Canada M9W 1L1

Wiley also publishes its books in a variety of electronic formats. Some content that appears in print may not be available in electronic books.

Library of Congress Cataloging-in-Publication Data

Shklar, Leon.
  Web application architecture : principles, protocols, and practices /
Leon Shklar, Richard Rosen.
    p. cm.
Includes bibliographical references and index.
 ISBN 0-471-48656-6 (Paper : alk. paper)
 1. Web sites—Design. 2. Application software—Development. I.
Rosen, Richard. II. Title.
 TK5105.888.S492 2003
 005.7′2—dc21

                                2003011759

British Library Cataloguing in Publication Data

A catalogue record for this book is available from the British Library

ISBN 0-471-48656-6

Typeset in 10/12.5pt Times by Laserwords Private Limited, Chennai, India
Printed and bound in Great Britain by Antony Rowe Ltd., Chippenham, Wiltshire
This book is printed on acid-free paper responsibly manufactured from sustainable forestry
in which at least two trees are planted for each one used for paper production.

Contents

Acknowledgements

I would like to thank my wife Rita and daughter Victoria for their insightful ideas about this project. I also wish to thank my mother and the rest of my family for their support and understanding.

Leon Shklar

Thanks to my wife, Celia, for tolerating and enduring all the insanity associated with the writing process, and to my parents and the rest of my family for all they have done, not only in helping me finish this book, but in enabling Celia and me to have the most fantastic wedding ever in the midst of all this.

Rich Rosen

We would both like to acknowledge the following people for their guidance and assistance:

- Karen Mosman and Jill Jeffries at John Wiley & Sons, Ltd for getting this book off the ground,

- Our editor, Gaynor Redvers-Mutton, and her assistant, Jonathan Shipley, for lighting the fire underneath us that finally got us to finish it.

- Nigel Chapman and Bruce Campbell for taking the time to review our work and provide us with valuable insights and advice.

- And finally, our friends and colleagues from the glory days of Pencom Web Works—especially Howard Fishman, Brad Lohnes, Dave Makower, and Evan Coyne Maloney—whose critiques, comments, and contributions were as thorough, methodical, and nitpicky (and we mean that in a *good* way!) as an author could ever hope for.

1 Introduction

1.1 THE WEB IN PERSPECTIVE

A little more than a decade ago at CERN (the scientific research laboratory near Geneva, Switzerland), Tim Berners-Lee presented a proposal for an information management system that would enable the sharing of knowledge and resources over a computer network.

The system he proposed has propagated itself into what can truly be called a *World Wide Web*, as people all over the world use it for a wide variety of purposes:

- Educational institutions and research laboratories were among the very first users of the Web, employing it for sharing documents and other resources across the Internet.

- Individuals today use the Web (and the underlying Internet technologies that support it) as an instantaneous international postal service, as a worldwide community bulletin board for posting virtual photo albums, and as a venue for holding global yard sales.

- Businesses engage in *e-commerce*, offering individuals a medium for buying and selling goods and services over the net. They also communicate with other businesses through *B2B* (business-to-business) data exchanges, where companies can provide product catalogues, inventories, and sales records to other companies.

The Web vs. the Internet

There is an often-overlooked distinction between the Web and the Internet. The line between the two is often blurred, partially because the Web is rooted in the fundamental protocols associated with the Internet. Today, the lines are even more blurred, as notions of 'the Web' go beyond the boundaries of pages delivered to Web browsers, into the realms of wireless devices, personal digital assistants, and the next generation of Internet appliances.

1.2 THE ORIGINS OF THE WEB

Tim Berners-Lee originally promoted the World Wide Web as a virtual library, a document control system for sharing information resources among researchers. Online documents could be accessed via a unique document address, a *Universal Resource Locator* (URL). These documents could be cross-referenced via *hypertext links*.

Hypertext

Ted Nelson, father of the Xanadu Project, coined the term 'hypertext' over 30 years ago, as a way of describing 'non-sequential writing—text that branches and allows choice to the reader.' Unlike the static text of print media, it is intended for use with an interactive computer screen. It is open, fluid and mutable, and can be connected to other pieces of hypertext by 'links'.

The term was extended under the name hypermedia to refer not only to text, but to other media as well, including graphics, audio, and video. However, the original term hypertext persists as the label for technology that connects documents and information resources through links.

From the very beginnings of Internet technology, there has been a dream of using the Internet as a universal medium for exchanging information over computer networks. Many people shared this dream. Ted Nelson's *Xanadu* project aspired to make that dream a reality, but the goals were lofty and were never fully realized. Internet file sharing services (such as *FTP* and *Gopher*) and message forum services (such as *Netnews*) provided increasingly powerful mechanisms for this sort of information exchange, and certainly brought us closer to fulfilling those goals.

However, it took Tim Berners-Lee to (in his own words) "marry together" the notion of hypertext with the power of the Internet, bringing those initial dreams to fruition in a way that the earliest developers of both hypertext and Internet technology might never have imagined. His vision was to connect literally *everything* together, in a uniform and universal way.

> **Internet Protocols are the Foundation of Web Technology**
>
> It should be noted that the Web did not come into existence in a vacuum. The Web is built on top of core Internet protocols that had been in existence for many years prior to the Web's inception. Understanding the relationship between 'Web technology' and the underlying Internet protocols is fundamental to the design and implementation of true 'Web applications'. In fact, it is the exploitation of that relationship that distinguishes a 'Web page' or 'Web site' from a 'Web application'.

1.3 FROM WEB PAGES TO WEB SITES

The explosively exponential growth of the Web can at least partially be attributed to its grass roots proliferation as a tool for *personal publishing*. The fundamental technology behind the Web is relatively simple. A computer connected to the Internet, running a *Web server*, was all that was necessary to serve documents. Both CERN and the National Center for Supercomputer Applications (NCSA) at the University of Illinois had developed freely available Web server software. A small amount of *HTML* knowledge (and the proper computing resources) got you something that could be called a *Web site*.

> **Primitive Web Sites from the Pre-Cambrian Era**
>
> Early Web sites were, in fact, just loosely connected sets of pages, branched off hierarchically from a home page. HTML lets you link one page to another, and a collection of pages linked together could be considered a 'Web site'. But a Web site in this day and age is more than just a conglomeration of Web pages.

Granted, when the Web was in its infancy, the only computers connected to the Internet and capable of running server software were run by academic institutions and well-connected technology companies. Smaller computers, in any case, were hardly in abundance back then. In those days, a 'personal' computer sitting on your desktop was still a rarity. If you wanted access to any sort of computing power, you used a *terminal* that let you 'log in' to a large server or mainframe over a direct connection or dialup phone line.

Still, among those associated with such organizations, it quickly became a very simple process to create your own Web pages. Moreover, all that was needed was a simple text editor. The original HTML language was simple enough that, even without the more sophisticated tools we have at our disposal today, it was an easy task for someone to create a Web page. (Some would say *too* easy.)

"Welcome to My Home Page, Here Are Photos of My Cat and A Poem I Wrote"

In those pioneer days of the Web, academic and professional organizations used the Web to share information, knowledge, and resources. But once you got beyond those hallowed halls and cubicle walls, most people's Web pages were personal showcases for publishing bad poetry and pictures of their pets. The thought of a company offering information to the outside world through the Web, or developing an intranet to provide information to its own employees, was no more than a gleam in even the most prophetic eyes.

There is a big difference between a Web page and a Web *site*. A Web site is more than just a group of Web pages that happen to be connected to each other through hypertext links.

At the lowest level, there are *content-related* concerns. Maintaining thematic consistency of content is important in giving a site some degree of identity.

There are also *aesthetic* concerns. In addition to having thematically-related content, a Web site should also have a common look and feel across all of its pages, so that site visitors know they are looking at a particular Web site. This means utilizing a common style across the site: page layout, graphic design, and typographical elements should reflect that style.

There are also *architectural* concerns. As a site grows in size and becomes more complex, it becomes critically important to organize its content properly. This includes not just the layout of content on individual pages, but also the interconnections between the pages themselves. Some of the symptoms of bad site design include links targeting the wrong frame (for frame-based Web sites), and links that take visitors to a particular page at an *appropriate* time (e.g. at a point during the visit when it is impossible to deliver content to the visitors).

If your site becomes so complex that visitors cannot navigate their way through it, even with the help of site maps and navigation bars, then it needs to be reorganized and restructured.

1.4 FROM WEB SITES TO WEB APPLICATIONS

Initially, what people shared over the Internet consisted mostly of static information found in files. They might edit these files and update their content, but there were few truly *dynamic* information services on the Internet. Granted, there were a few exceptions: search applications for finding files found on FTP archives and Gopher servers; and services that provided dynamic information directly, like the weather, or the availability of cans from a soda dispensing machine. (One of the first Web applications that Tim Berners-Lee demonstrated at CERN was a gateway for looking up numbers from a phone book database using a Web browser.)

However, for the most part the information resources shared on the Web were static documents. Dynamic information services—from search engines to CGI scripts to packages that connected the Web to relational databases—changed all that.

With the advent of the *dynamic web*, the bar was raised even higher. No longer was it sufficient to say that you were designing a 'Web site' (as opposed to a motley collection of 'Web pages'). It became necessary to design a *Web application*.

Definition of a Web Application

What is a 'Web application?' By definition, it is something more than just a 'Web site.' It is a *client/server* application that uses a Web browser as its client program, and performs an interactive service by connecting with servers over the Internet (or Intranet). A Web site simply delivers content from static files. A Web application presents dynamically tailored content based on request parameters, tracked user behaviors, and security considerations.

1.5 HOW TO BUILD WEB APPLICATIONS IN ONE EASY LESSON

But what does it mean to design a *Web application*, as contrasted to a Web *page* or a Web *site*? Each level of Web design has its own techniques, and its own set of issues.

1.5.1 Web page design resources

For Web page design, there is a variety of books available. Beyond the tutorial books that purport to teach HTML, JavaScript, and CGI scripting overnight, there are some good books discussing the deeper issues associated with designing Web pages. One of the better choices is *The Non-Designer's Web Book* by Robin Williams (*not* the comedian). Williams' books are full of useful information and guidelines for those constructing Web pages, especially those not explicitly schooled in design or typography.

1.5.2 Web site design resources

When it comes to Web sites, there are far fewer resources available. *Information Architecture for the World Wide Web,* by Louis Rosenfeld and Peter Morville, was one of the rare books covering the issues of designing Web *sites* as opposed to Web pages. It is unfortunately out of print.

1.5.3 Web application design resources

When we examined the current literature available on the subject of *Web application development*, we found there were three main categories of books currently available.

- *Technical Overviews.* The first category is the *technical overview*. These books are usually at a very high level, describing terminology and technology in broad terms. They do not go into enough detail to enable the reader to design and build serious Web applications. They are most often intended for 'managers' and 'executives' who want a surface understanding of the terminology without going too deeply into specific application development issues. Frequently, they attempt to cover technology in huge brushstrokes, so that you see books whose focus is simply 'Java', 'XML', or 'The Web.'

   Such books approach the spectrum of technology so broadly that the coverage of any specific area is too shallow to be significant. Serious application developers usually find these books far too superficial to be of any use to them.

- *In-Depth Technical Resources.* The second category is comprised of in-depth technical resources for developing Web applications using specific platforms. The books in this category provide in-depth coverage of very narrow areas, concentrating on the 'how-to's' of using a particular language or platform without explaining what is going on 'under the hood.' While such books may be useful in teaching programmers to develop applications for a specific platform, they provide little or no information about the underlying technologies, focusing instead on the platform-specific implementation of those technologies. Should developers be called upon to rewrite an application for another platform, the knowledge they acquired from reading these books would rarely be transferable to that new platform.

   Given the way Web technology changes so rapidly, today's platform of choice is tomorrow's outdated legacy system. When new development platforms emerge, developers without a fundamental understanding of the inner workings of Web applications have to learn their inner workings from the ground up, because they lacked an understanding of first principles—of what the systems they wrote *really* did. Thus, the ability to use fundamental technological knowledge across platforms is critical.

- *Reference Books.* These form a third category. Such books are useful, naturally, as references, but not for the purpose of *learning* about the technology.

What we found lacking was a book that provides an in-depth examination of the *basic concepts* and *general principles* of Web application development. Such a book would cover the core protocols and technologies of the Internet in depth, imparting the principles associated with writing applications for the Web. It would use examples from specific technologies (e.g. CGI scripts and servlets), but would not promote or endorse particular platforms.

Why is Such a Book Needed?

We see the need for such a book when interviewing job candidates for Web application development positions. Too many programmers have detailed knowledge of a particular API (*Application Programming Interface*), but they are lost when asked questions about the underlying technologies (e.g. the format and content of messages transmitted between the server and browser). Such knowledge is not purely academic—it is critical when designing and debugging complex systems.

Too often, developers with proficiency *only* within a specific application development platform (like *Active Server Pages, Cold Fusion, PHP*, or *Perl* CGI scripting) are not capable of transferring that proficiency directly to another platform. Only through a fundamental understanding of the core technology can developers be expected to grow with the rapid technological changes associated with Web application development.

1.5.4 Principles of web application design

What do we mean when we discuss the *general principles* that need to be understood to properly design and develop Web applications?

We mean the core set of protocols and languages associated with Web applications. This includes, of course, *HTTP* (*HyperText Transfer Protocol*) and *HTML* (*HyperText Markup Language*), which are fundamental to the creation and transmission of Web pages. It also includes the older Internet protocols like *Telnet* and *FTP*, protocols used for message transfer like *SMTP* and *IMAP*, plus advanced protocols and languages like *XML*. Additionally, it includes knowledge of *databases* and *multimedia* presentation, since many sophisticated Web applications make use of these technologies extensively.

The ideal *Web application architect* must in some sense be a 'jack of all trades'. People who design Web applications must understand not only HTTP and HTML, but the other underlying Internet protocols as well. They must be familiar with JavaScript, XML, relational databases, graphic design and multimedia. They must be well versed in application server technology, and have a strong background in information architecture. If you find people with all these qualifications, please let us know—we would love to hire them! Rare is the person who can not only architect a Web site, but also design the graphics, create the database schema, produce the multimedia programs, and configure the e-commerce transactions.

In the absence of such a Web application superhero/guru/demigod, the best you can hope for is a person who at least understands the issues associated with designing Web applications. Someone who understands the underlying languages and protocols supporting such applications. Someone who can understand the mechanisms for providing access to database and multimedia information through a Web application.

We hope that, by reading this book, you can acquire the skills needed to design and build complex applications for the World Wide Web. No, there is no 'one easy lesson' for learning the ins and outs of designing Web applications. However, this book will hopefully enable you to design and build sophisticated Web applications that are scaleable, maintainable, extensible, and reusable.

We examine various approaches to the process of Web application development—starting with the CGI approach, looking at template languages like *Cold Fusion* and *ASP*, and working our way up to the *Java Enterprise* (*J2EE*) approach. However, at each level, we concentrate not on the particular development platform, but on the considerations associated with designing and building Web applications regardless of the underlying platform.

1.6 WHAT IS COVERED IN THIS BOOK

The organization of this book is as follows:

- **Chapter 2: TCP/IP**— This chapter examines the underlying Internet protocols that form the basis of the Web. It offers some perspectives on the history of TCP/IP, as well as some details about using several of these protocols in Web applications.

- **Chapter 3: HTTP**— The HTTP protocol is covered in detail, with explanations of how requests and responses are transmitted and processed.

- **Chapter 4: Web Servers**— The operational intricacies of Web servers is the topic here, with an in-depth discussion of what Web servers must do to support interactions with clients such as Web browsers and HTTP proxies.

- **Chapter 5: Web Browsers**— As the previous chapter dug deep into the inner workings of Web servers, this chapter provides similar coverage of the inner workings of Web browsers.

- **Chapter 6: HTML and Its Roots**— In the first of our two chapters about markup languages, we go back to SGML to learn more about the roots of HTML (and XML as well).

- **Chapter 7: XML**— This chapter covers XML and related specifications, including XML Schema, XSLT, and XSL FO, as well as XML applications like XHTML and WML.

- **Chapter 8: Dynamic Web Applications—** After covering Web servers and Web browsers in depth, we move on to Web applications, describing their structure and the best practices for building them, so that they will be both extensible and maintainable. In providing this information, we refer to a sample application that will be designed and implemented in a later chapter.

- **Chapter 9: Approaches to Web Application Development—** This chapter contains a survey of available Web application approaches, including CGI, Servlets, PHP, Cold Fusion, ASP, JSP, and frameworks like Jakarta Struts. It classifies and compares these approaches to help readers make informed decisions when choosing an approach for their project, emphasizing the benefits of using the Model-View-Controller (MVC) design pattern in implementing an application.

- **Chapter 10: Sample Application—** Having examined the landscape of available application development approaches, we decide on Jakarta Struts along with the Java Standard Tag Library (JSTL). We give the reasons for our decisions, and build the *Virtual Realty Listing Services* application (originally described in Chapter 8) employing the principles we have been learning in previous chapters. We then suggest enhancements to the application as exercises to be performed by the reader.

- **Chapter 11: Emerging Technologies—** Finally, we look to the future, providing coverage of the most promising developments in Web technology, including Web Services, RDF, and XML Query, as well as speculations about the evolution of Web application frameworks.

BIBLIOGRAPHY

Berners-Lee, T. (2000) *Weaving the Web: The Original Design and Ultimate Destiny of the World Wide Web.* New York: HarperBusiness.

Nelson, T. H. (1982) *Literary Machines 931.* Sausalito, California: Mindful Press.

Rosenfeld, L. and Morville, P. (1998) *Information Architecture for the World Wide Web.* Sebastopol, California: O'Reilly & Associates.

Williams, R. and Tollett, J. (2000) *The Non-Designer's Web Book.* Berkeley, California: Peachpit Press.

2   Before the Web: TCP/IP

As mentioned in the previous chapter, Tim Berners-Lee did not come up with the World Wide Web in a vacuum. The Web as we know it is built on top of core *Internet protocols* that had been in existence for many years before. Understanding those underlying protocols is fundamental to the discipline of building robust Web applications.

In this chapter, we examine the core Internet protocols that make up the *TCP/IP protocol suite*, which is the foundation for Web protocols, discussed in the next chapter. We begin with a brief historical overview of the forces that led to the creation of TCP/IP. We then go over the layers of the TCP/IP stack, and show where various protocols fit into it. Our description of the client-server paradigm used by TCP/IP applications is followed by a discussion of the various TCP/IP application services, including Telnet, electronic mail, message forums, live messaging, and file servers.

2.1 HISTORICAL PERSPECTIVE

The roots of Web technology can be found in the original Internet protocols (known collectively as TCP/IP), developed in the 1980s. These protocols were an outgrowth of work done for the United States Defense Department to design a network called the *ARPANET*.

The ARPANET was named for *ARPA*, the *Advanced Research Projects Agency* of the United States Department of Defense. It came into being as a result of efforts funded by the Department of Defense in the 1970s to develop an open, common, distributed, and decentralized computer networking architecture. There were a number of problems with existing network architectures that the Defense Department wanted to resolve. First and foremost was the centralized nature of existing networks. At that time, the typical network topology was *centralized*. A computer network had a single point of control directing communication between all the systems belonging to that network. From a military perspective, such a topology had a critical flaw: Destroy that central point of control, and all possibility of communication was lost.

Another issue was the *proprietary* nature of existing network architectures. Most were developed and controlled by private corporations, who had a vested interest both in pushing their own products and in keeping their technology to themselves. Further, the proprietary nature of the technology limited the interoperability between different systems. It was important, even then, to ensure that the mechanisms for communicating across computer networks were not proprietary, or controlled in any way by private interests, lest the entire network become dependent on the whims of a single corporation. Thus, the Defense Department funded an endeavor to design the protocols for the next generation of computer communications networking architectures.

Establishing a *decentralized, distributed network topology* was foremost among the design goals for the new networking architecture. Such a topology would allow communications to continue, for the most part undisrupted, even if any one system was damaged or destroyed. In such a topology, the network 'intelligence' would not reside in a single point of control. Instead, it would be distributed among many systems throughout the network.

To facilitate this (and to accommodate other network reliability considerations), they employed a *packet-switching* technology, whereby a network 'message' could be split into packets, each of which might take a different route over the network, arrive in completely mixed-up order, and still be reassembled and understood by the intended recipient.

To promote *interoperability*, the protocols needed to be *open*: be readily available to anyone who wanted to connect their system to the network. An infrastructure was needed to design the set of agreed-upon protocols, and to formulate new protocols for new technologies that might be added to the network in the future. An *Internet Working Group* (INWG) was formed to examine the issues associated with connecting heterogeneous networks together in an open, uniform manner. This group provided an open platform for proposing, debating, and approving protocols.

The Internet Working Group evolved over time into other bodies, like the IAB (Internet Activities Board, later renamed the Internet Architecture Board), the IANA (Internet Assigned Numbers Authority), and later, the IETF (Internet Engineering Task Force) and IESG (Internet Engineering Steering Group). These bodies defined the standards that 'govern' the Internet. They established the formal processes for proposing new protocols, discussing and debating the merits of these proposals, and ultimately approving them as accepted Internet standards.

Proposals for new protocols (or updated versions of existing protocols) are provided in the form of *Requests for Comments*, also known as RFCs. Once approved, the RFCs are treated as the standard documentation for the new or updated protocol.

2.2 TCP/IP

The original ARPANET was the first fruit borne of this endeavor. The protocols behind the ARPANET evolved over time into the *TCP/IP Protocol Suite*, a layered taxonomy of data communications protocols. The name TCP/IP refers to two of the most important protocols within the suite: TCP (*Transmission Control Protocol*) and IP (*Internet Protocol*), but the suite is comprised of many other significant protocols and services.

2.2.1 Layers

The protocol layers associated with TCP/IP (above the 'layer' of physical interconnection) are:

1. the *Network Interface* layer,

2. the *Internet* layer,

3. the *Transport* layer, and

4. the *Application* layer.

Because this protocol taxonomy contains layers, implementations of these protocols are often known as a *protocol stack*.

The *Network Interface layer* is the layer responsible for the lowest level of data transmission within TCP/IP, facilitating communication with the underlying physical network.

The *Internet layer* provides the mechanisms for intersystem communications, controlling message routing, validity checking, and message header composition/decomposition. The protocol known as IP (which stands, oddly enough, for Internet Protocol) operates on this layer, as does *ICMP* (the *Internet Control Message Protocol*). ICMP handles the transmission of control and error messages between systems. *Ping* is an Internet service that operates through ICMP.

The *Transport layer* provides message transport services between applications running on remote systems. This is the layer in which TCP (the *Transmission Control Protocol*) operates. TCP provides reliable, connection-oriented message transport. Most of the well-known Internet services make use of TCP as their foundation. However, some services that do not require the reliability (and overhead) associated with TCP make use of *UDP* (which stands for *User Datagram Protocol*). For instance, streaming audio and video services would gladly sacrifice a few lost packets to get faster performance out of their data streams, so these services often operate over UDP, which trades reliability for performance.

The *Application layer* is the highest level within the TCP/IP protocol stack. It is within this layer that most of the services we associate with 'the Internet' operate.

These Internet services provided some degree of information exchange, but it took the birth of the web to bring those initial dreams to fruition, in a way that the earliest developers of these services might never have imagined.

OSI

During the period that TCP/IP was being developed, the International Standards Organization (ISO) was also working on a layered protocol scheme, called 'Open Systems Interconnection', or OSI. While the TCP/IP taxonomy consisted of five layers (if you included the lowest physical connectivity medium as a layer), OSI had seven layers: Physical, Data Link, Network, Transport, Session, Presentation, and Application.

There is some parallelism between the two models. TCP/IP's Network Interface layer is sometimes called the Data Link layer to mimic the OSI Reference Model, while the Internet layer corresponds to OSI's Network layer. Both models share the notion of a Transport layer, which serves roughly the same functions in each model. And the Application layer in TCP/IP combines the functions of the Session, Presentation, and Application layers of OSI. But OSI never caught on, and while some people waited patiently for its adoption and propagation, it was TCP/IP that became the ubiquitous foundation of the Internet as we know it today.

2.2.2 The client/server paradigm

TCP/IP applications tend to operate according to the *client/server* paradigm. This simply means that, in these applications, *servers* (also called *services* and *daemons*, depending on the language of the underlying operating system) execute by (1) waiting for requests from *client* programs to arrive, and then (2) processing those requests.

Client programs can be applications used by human beings, or they could be servers that need to make their own requests that can only be fulfilled by other servers. More often than not, the client and server run on separate machines, and communicate via a connection across a network.

Command Line vs. GUI

Over the years, the client programs used by people have evolved from command-line programs to GUI programs. Command-line programs have their origins in the limitations of the oldest human interfaces to computer systems: the teletype keyboard. In the earliest days of computing, they didn't have simple text-based CRT terminals—let alone today's more sophisticated monitors with enhanced graphics capabilities! The only way to enter data interactively was through a teletypewriter interface, one line at a time.

As the name implies, these programs are invoked from a command line. The command line prompts users for the entry of a 'command' (the name of a program) and its 'arguments' (the parameters passed to the program). The original DOS operating system on a PC, as well as the 'shell' associated with UNIX systems, are examples of command-line interfaces.

Screen mode programs allowed users to manipulate the data on an entire CRT screen, rather than on just one line. This meant that arrow keys could be used to move a 'cursor' around the screen, or to scroll through pages of a text document. However, these screen mode programs were restricted to character-based interfaces.

GUI stands for 'Graphical User Interface'. As the name implies, GUI programs make use of a visually oriented paradigm that offers users a plethora of choices. For most, this is a welcome alternative to manually typing in the names of files, programs, and command options. The graphics, however, are not limited to just textual characters, as they are in screen mode programs. The GUI paradigm relies on WIMPS (Windows, Icons, Mouse, Pointers, and Scrollbars) to graphically display the set of files and applications users can access.

Whether command-line or GUI-based, client programs provide the interface by which end users communicate with servers to make use of TCP/IP services.

Early implementations of client/server architectures did not make use of open protocols. What this meant was that client programs needed to be as 'heavy' as the server programs. A 'lightweight' client (also called a *thin client*) could only exist in a framework where common protocols and application controls were associated with the client machine's operating system. Without such a framework, many of the connectivity features had to be included directly into the client program, adding to its weight.

One advantage of using TCP/IP for client/server applications was that the protocol stack was installed on the client machine as part of the operating system, and the client program itself could be more of a thin client.

Web applications are a prime example of the employment of thin clients in applications. Rather than building a custom program to perform desired application tasks, web applications use the web browser, a program that is already installed on most users' systems. You cannot create a client much thinner than a program that users have already installed on their desktops!

How Do TCP/IP Clients and Servers Communicate with Each Other?

To talk to servers, TCP/IP client programs open a socket, which is simply a TCP connection between the client machine and the server machine. Servers listen for connection requests that come in through specific ports. A port is not an actual physical interface between the computer and the network, but simply a numeric reference within a request that indicates which server program is its intended recipient.

There are established conventions for matching port numbers with specific TCP/IP services. Servers listen for requests on well-known port numbers. For example, Telnet servers normally listen for connection requests on port 23, SMTP servers listen to port 25, and web servers listen to port 80.

2.3 TCP/IP APPLICATION SERVICES

In this section, we discuss some of the common TCP/IP application services, including Telnet, electronic mail, message forums, live messaging, and file servers.

2.3.1 Telnet

The Telnet protocol operates within the Application layer. It was developed to support Network Virtual Terminal functionality, which means the ability to 'log in' to a remote machine over the Internet. The latest specification for the Telnet protocol is defined in Internet RFC 854.

Remember that before the advent of personal computers, access to computing power was limited to those who could connect to a larger server or mainframe computer, either through a phone dialup line or through a direct local connection. Whether you phoned in remotely or sat down at a terminal directly connected to the server, you used a command-line interface to log in. You connected to a single system and your interactions were limited to that system.

With the arrival of Internet services, you could use the Telnet protocol to log in remotely to other systems that were accessible over the Internet. As mentioned earlier, Telnet clients are configured by default to connect to port 23 on the server machine, but the target port number can be over-ridden in most client programs. This means you can use a Telnet client program to connect and 'talk' to *any* TCP server by knowing its address and its port number.

2.3.2 Electronic mail

Electronic mail, or *e-mail*, was probably the first 'killer app' in what we now call cyberspace. Since the net had its roots in military interests, naturally the tone of electronic mail started out being formal, rigid, and business-like. But once the body of people using e-mail expanded, and once these people realized what it could be used for, things lightened up quite a bit.

Electronic *mailing lists* provided communities where people with like interests could exchange messages. These lists were closed systems, in the sense that only subscribers could post messages to the list, or view messages posted by other subscribers. Obviously, lists grew, and list managers had to maintain them. Over time, automated mechanisms were developed to allow people to subscribe (and, just as importantly, to unsubscribe) without human intervention. These mailing lists evolved into *message forums*, where people could publicly post messages, on an *electronic bulletin board*, for everyone to read.

These services certainly existed before there was an Internet. Yet in those days, users read and sent their e-mail by *logging in* to a system directly (usually via telephone dialup or direct local connection) and running programs on that system (usually with a command-line interface) to access e-mail services. The methods for using these services varied greatly from system to system, and e-mail connectivity between disparate systems was hard to come by. With the advent of TCP/IP, the mechanisms for providing these services became more consistent, and e-mail became uniform and ubiquitous.

The transmission of electronic mail is performed through the SMTP protocol. The reading of electronic mail is usually performed through either POP or IMAP.

SMTP

SMTP stands for *Simple Mail Transfer Protocol*. As an application layer protocol, SMTP normally runs on top of TCP, though it can theoretically use any underlying transport protocol. The application called 'sendmail' is an implementation of the SMTP protocol for UNIX systems. The latest specification for the SMTP protocol is defined in *Internet RFC 821*, and the structure of SMTP messages is defined in *Internet RFC 822*.

SMTP, like other TCP/IP services, runs as a *server, service*, or *daemon*. In a TCP/IP environment, SMTP servers usually run on port 25. They wait for requests to send electronic mail messages, which can come from local system users or from across the network. They are also responsible for evaluating the recipient addresses found in e-mail messages and determining whether they are valid, and/or whether their final destination is another recipient (e.g. a forwarding address, or the set of individual recipients subscribed to a mailing list).

If the message embedded in the request is intended for a user with an account on the local system, then the SMTP server will deliver the message to that user by appending it to their *mailbox*. Depending on the implementation, the mailbox can be anything from a simple text file to a complex database of e-mail messages. If the message is intended for a user on another system, then the server must figure out how to transmit the message to the appropriate system.

This may involve direct connection to the remote system, or it may involve connection to a *gateway* system. A gateway is responsible for passing the message on to other gateways and/or sending it directly to its ultimate destination.

Before the advent of SMTP, the underlying mechanisms for sending mail varied from system to system. Once SMTP became ubiquitous as the mechanism for electronic mail transmission, these mechanisms became more uniform.

The applications responsible for transmitting e-mail messages, such as SMTP servers, are known as MTAs (Mail Transfer Agents). Likewise, the applications responsible for retrieving messages from a mailbox, including POP servers and IMAP servers, are known as MRAs (Mail Retrieval Agents).

E-mail client programs have generally been engineered to allow users to both read mail and send mail. Such programs are known as MUAs (Mail User Agents). MUAs talk to MRAs to read mail, and to MTAs to send mail. In a typical e-mail client, this is the process by which a message is sent. Once the user has composed a message, the client program directs it to the SMTP server. First, it must *connect* to the server. It does this by opening a TCP socket to port 25 (the SMTP port) of the server. (This is true even if the server is running on the user's machine.)

Client/Server Communications

Requests transmitted between client and server programs take the form of command-line interactions. The imposition of this constraint on Internet communication protocols means that even the most primitive command-line oriented interface can make use of TCP/IP services. More sophisticated GUI-based client programs often hide their command-line details from their users, employing point-and-click and drag-and-drop functionality to support underlying command-line directives.

After the server acknowledges the success of the connection, the client sends commands on a line-by-line basis. There are single-line and block commands. A block command begins with a line indicating the start of the command (e.g., a line containing only the word 'DATA') and terminates with a line indicating its end (e.g., a line containing only a period). The server then responds to each command, usually with a line containing a response code.

A stateful protocol allows a request to contain a sequence of commands. The server is required to maintain the "state" of the connection throughout the transmission of successive commands, until the connection is terminated. The sequence of transmitted and executed commands is often called a session. Most Internet services (including SMTP) are session-based, and make use of stateful protocols.

HTTP, however, is a stateless protocol. An HTTP request usually consists of a single block command and a single response. On the surface, there is no need to maintain state between transmitted commands. We will discuss the stateless nature of the HTTP protocol in a later chapter.

As shown in Figure 2.1, the client program identifies itself (and the system on which it is running) to the server via the 'HELO' command. The server decides (based on this identification information) whether to accept or reject the request. If the server accepts the request, it waits for the client to send further information.

One line at a time, the client transmits commands to the server, sending information about the originator of the message (using the 'MAIL' command) and each of the recipients (using a series of 'RCPT' commands). Once all this is done, the client tells the server it is about to send the actual data: the message itself. It does this by sending a command line consisting of only the word 'DATA'. Every line that follows, until the server encounters a line containing only a period, is considered part of the message body. Once it has sent the body of the message, the client signals the server that it is done, and the server transmits the message to its destination (either directly or through gateways).

Having received confirmation that the server has transmitted the message, the client closes the socket connection using the 'QUIT' command. An example of an interaction between a client and an SMTP server can be found in Figure 2.1.

```
220 mail.hoboken.company.com ESMTP xxxx 3.21 #1 Fri, 23 Feb 2001
13:41:09 -0500
HELO ubizmo.com
250 mail.hoboken.company.com Hello neurozen.com [xxx.xxx.xxx.xxx]
MAIL FROM:<rrosen@neurozen.comt>
250 <rrosen@neurozen.com> is syntactically correct
RCPT TO:<shklar@cs.rutgers.edu>
250 <shklar@cs.rutgers.edu> is syntactically correct
RCPT TO:<rr-booknotes@neurozen.com>
250 <rr-booknotes@neurozen.com> is syntactically correct
DATA
354 Enter message, ending with "." on a line by itself
From: Rich Rosen <rrosen@neurozen.com>
To: shklar@cs.rutgers.edu
Cc: rr-booknotes@neurozen.com
Subject: Demonstrating SMTP

Leon,

Please ignore this note.  I am demonstrating the art of connecting to
an SMTP server for the book. :-)

Rich
.
250 OK id=xxxxxxxx
QUIT
```

Figure 2.1   Example of command line interaction with an SMTP server

Originally, SMTP servers executed in a very open fashion: anyone knowing the address of an SMTP server could connect to it and send messages. In an effort to discourage spamming (the sending of indiscriminate mass e-mails in a semi-anonymous fashion), many SMTP server implementations allow the system administrator to configure the server so that it only accepts connections from a discrete set of systems, perhaps only those within their local domain.

When building web applications that include e-mail functionality (specifically the *sending* of e-mail), make sure your configuration includes the specification of a working SMTP server system, which will accept your requests to transmit messages. To maximize application flexibility, the address of the SMTP server should be a parameter that can be modified at run-time by an application administrator.

MIME

Originally, e-mail systems transmitted messages in the form of standard ASCII text. If a user wanted to send a file in a non-text or 'binary' format (e.g. an image or sound file), it had to be encoded before it could be placed into the body of the message. The sender had to communicate the nature of the binary data directly to the receiver, e.g., 'The block of encoded binary text below is a GIF image.'

Multimedia Internet Mail Extensions (MIME) provided uniform mechanisms for including encoded attachments within a multipart e-mail message. MIME supports the definition of boundaries separating the text portion of a message (the 'body') from its attachments, as well as the designation of attachment encoding methods, including 'Base64' and 'quoted-printable'. MIME was originally defined in Internet RFC 1341, but the most recent specifications can be found in Internet RFCs 2045 through 2049.

It also supports the notion of content typing for attachments (and for the body of a message as well). MIME-types are standard naming conventions for defining what type of data is contained in an attachment. A MIME-type is constructed as a combination of a top-level data type and a subtype. There is a fixed set of top-level data types, including 'text', 'image', 'audio', 'video', and 'application'. The subtypes describe the specific type of data, e.g. 'text/html', 'text/plain', 'image/jpeg', 'audio/mp3'. The use of MIME content typing is discussed in greater detail in a later chapter.

POP

POP, the *Post Office Protocol*, gives users direct access to their e-mail messages stored on remote systems. *POP3* is the most recent version of the POP protocol. Most of the popular e-mail clients (including Eudora, Microsoft Outlook, and Netscape Messenger) use POP3 to access user e-mail. (Even proprietary systems like Lotus Notes offer administrators the option to configure remote e-mail access through POP.) POP3 was first defined in *Internet RFC 1725*, but was revised in *Internet RFC 1939*.

Before the Internet, as mentioned in the previous section, people read and sent e-mail by logging in to a system and running command-line programs to access their mail. User messages were usually stored locally in a mailbox file on that system. Even with the advent of Internet technology, many people continued to access e-mail by Telnetting to the system containing their mailbox and running command-line programs (e.g. from a UNIX shell) to read and send mail. (Many people who prefer command-line programs still do!)

Let us look at the process by which POP clients communicate with POP servers to provide user access to e-mail. First, the POP client must connect to the POP server (which usually runs on port 110), so it can identify and authenticate the user to the server. This is usually done by sending the user 'id' and password one line at a time, using the 'USER' and 'PASS' commands. (Sophisticated POP servers may make use of the 'APOP' command, which allows the secure transmission of the user name and password as a single encrypted entity across the network.)

Once connected and authenticated, the POP protocol offers the client a variety of commands it can execute. Among them is the 'UIDL' command, which responds with an ordered list of message numbers, where each entry is followed by a unique message identifier. POP clients can use this list (and the unique identifiers it contains) to determine which messages in the list qualify as 'new' (i.e. not yet seen by the user through this particular client).

Having obtained this list, the client can execute the command to retrieve a message ('RETR *n*'). It can also execute commands to delete a message from the server ('DELE *n*'). It also has the option to execute commands to retrieve just the header of a message ('TOP *n* 0').

Message headers contain *metadata* about a message, such as the addresses of its originator and recipients, its subject, etc. Each message contains a message header block containing a series of lines, followed by a blank line indicating the end of the message header block.

```
From: Rich Rosen <rr-booknotes@neurozen.com>
To: Leon Shklar <shklar@cs.rutgers.edu>
Subject: Here is a message...
Date: Fri, 23 Feb 2001 12:58:21 -0500
Message-ID: <G987W90B.D43@neurozen.com>
```

The information that e-mail clients include in message lists (e.g. the 'From', 'To', and 'Subject' of each message) comes from the message headers. As e-mail technology advanced, headers began representing more sophisticated information, including MIME-related data (e.g. content types) and attachment encoding schemes.

Figure 2.2 provides an example of a simple command-line interaction between a client and a POP server.

As mentioned previously, GUI-based clients often hide the mundane command-line details from their users. The normal sequence of operation for most GUI-based POP clients today is as follows:

1. Get the user id and password (client may already have this information, or may need to prompt the user).

2. Connect the user and verify identity.

3. Obtain the UIDL list of messages.

4. Compare the identifiers in this list to a list that the client keeps locally, to determine which messages are 'new'.

5. Retrieve all the new messages and present them to the user in a selection list.

6. Delete the newly retrieved messages from the POP server (optional).

Although this approach is simple, there is a lot of inefficiency embedded in it. All the new messages are always downloaded to the client. This is inefficient because some of these messages may be quite long, or they have extremely large attachments.

```
+OK mail Server POP3 v1.8.22 server ready
user shklar
+OK Name is a valid mailbox
pass xxxxxx
+OK Maildrop locked and ready
uidl
+OK unique-id listing follows
1 2412
2 2413
3 2414
4 2415
.
retr 1
+OK Message follows
From: Rich Rosen <waa-booknotes@neurozen.com>
To: Leon Shklar <shklar@cs.havers.edu>
Subject: Here is a message...
Date: Fri, 23 Feb 2001 12:58:21-0500
Message-ID: <G987W90B.D43@neurozen.com>

The medium is the message.
   --Marshall McLuhan, while standing behind a placard
      in a theater lobby in a Woody Allen movie.
.
```

Figure 2.2   Example of command line interaction with a POP3 server

Users must wait for *all* of the messages (include the large, possibly unwanted ones) to download before viewing any of the messages they *want* to read. It would be more efficient for the client to retrieve *only* the message headers and display the header information about each message in a message list. It could then allow users the option to selectively download desired messages for viewing, or to delete unwanted messages without downloading them. A web-based e-mail client could remove some of this inefficiency. (We discuss the construction of a web-based e-mail client in a later chapter.)

IMAP

Some of these inefficiencies can be alleviated by the *Internet Message Access Protocol (IMAP)*. IMAP was intended as a successor to the POP protocol, offering sophisticated services for managing messages in remote mailboxes. IMAP servers provide support for multiple remote *mailboxes* or *folders*, so users can move messages from an incoming folder (the 'inbox') into other folders kept on the server. In addition, they also provide support for saving sent messages in one of these remote folders, and for multiple simultaneous operations on mailboxes.

IMAP4, the most recent version of the IMAP protocol, was originally defined in *Internet RFC 1730*, but the most recent specification can be found in *Internet RFC 2060*.

The IMAP approach differs in many ways from the POP approach. In general, POP clients are supposed to download e-mail messages from the server and then delete them. (This is the default behavior for many POP clients.) In practice, many users elect to leave viewed messages on the server, rather than deleting them after viewing. This is because many people who travel extensively want to check e-mail while on the road, but want to see *all* of their messages (even the ones they've seen) when they return to their 'home machine.'

While the POP approach 'tolerates' but does not encourage this sort of user behavior, the IMAP approach eagerly embraces it. IMAP was conceived with 'nomadic' users in mind: users who might check e-mail from literally anywhere, who want access to all of their saved *and* sent messages wherever they happen to be. IMAP not only allows the user to leave messages on the server, it provides mechanisms for storing messages in user-defined folders for easier accessibility and better organization.

Moreover, users can save sent messages in a designated remote folder on the IMAP server. While POP clients support saving of sent messages, they usually save those messages locally, on the client machine.

The typical IMAP e-mail client program works very similarly to typical POP e-mail clients. (In fact, many e-mail client programs allow the user to operate in either POP or IMAP mode.) However, the automatic downloading of the content (including attachments) of *all* new messages does not occur by default in IMAP clients. Instead, an IMAP client downloads only the header information associated with new messages, requesting the body of an individual message only when the user expresses an interest in seeing it.

POP vs. IMAP

Although it is possible to write a POP client that operates this way, most do not. POP clients tend to operate in 'burst' mode, getting all the messages on the server in one 'shot.' While this may be in some respects inefficient, it is useful for those whose online access is not persistent. By getting all the messages in one burst, users can work 'offline' with the complete set of downloaded messages, connecting to the Internet again only when they want to send responses and check for new mail.

IMAP clients assume the existence of a persistent Internet connection, allowing discrete actions to be performed on individual messages, while maintaining a connection to the IMAP server. Thus, for applications where Internet connectivity may not be persistent (e.g. a handheld device where Internet connectivity is paid for by the minute), POP might be a better choice than IMAP.

Because the IMAP protocol offers many more options than the POP protocol, the possibilities for what can go on in a user session are much richer. After connection and authentication, users can look at new messages, recently seen messages, unanswered messages, flagged messages, and drafts of messages yet to be sent. They can view messages in their entirety or in part (e.g. header, body, attachment), delete or move messages to other folders, or respond to messages or forward them to others.

IMAP need not be used strictly for e-mail messages. As security features allow mailbox folders to be designated as 'read only', IMAP can be used for 'message board' functionality as well. However, such functionality is usually reserved for message forum services.

2.3.3 Message forums

Message forums are online services that allow users to write messages to be posted on the equivalent of an electronic bulletin board, and to read similar messages that others have posted. These messages are usually organized into categories so that people can find the kinds of messages they are looking for.

For years, online message forums existed in various forms. Perhaps the earliest form was the *electronic mailing list*. As we mentioned earlier, mailing lists are closed systems: only subscribers can view or post messages. In some situations, a closed private community may be exactly what the doctor ordered. Yet if the goal is open public participation, publicly accessible message forums are more appropriate.

Although message forums were originally localized, meaning that messages appeared only on the system where they were posted, the notion of distributed message forums took hold. Cooperative networks (e.g. FIDONET) allowed systems to share messages, by forwarding them to 'neighboring' systems in the network. This enabled users to see all the messages posted by anyone on any system in the network.

The Internet version of message forums is *Netnews*. Netnews organizes messages into *newsgroups*, which form a large hierarchy of topics and categories. Among the main divisions are *comp* (for computing related newsgroups), *sci* (for scientific newsgroups), *soc* (for socially oriented newsgroups), *talk* (for newsgroups devoted to talk), and *alt* (an unregulated hierarchy for 'alternative' newsgroups). The naming convention for newsgroups is reminiscent of domain names in reverse, e.g. *comp.infosystems.www*.

Usenet and UUCP

Netnews existed before the proliferation of the Internet. It grew out of Usenet, an interconnected network of UNIX systems. Before the Internet took hold, UNIX systems communicated with each other over UUCP, a protocol used to transmit mail and news over phone lines. It has been suggested, only half in jest, that the proliferation of UNIX by Bell Laboratories in the 1980s was an effort by AT&T to increase long distance phone traffic, since e-mail and Netnews were being transmitted by long distance calls between these UNIX systems.

Today, Netnews is transmitted using an Internet protocol called *NNTP* (for *Network News Transfer Protocol*). NNTP clients allow users to read messages in newsgroups (and post their own messages as well) by connecting to NNTP servers. These servers propagate the newsgroup messages throughout the world by regularly forwarding them to 'neighboring' servers. The NNTP specification is defined in *Internet RFC 977*.

Netnews functionality is directly incorporated into browsers like Netscape Communicator, which includes the functionality into its Messenger component, which is responsible for accessing electronic mail. It is also possible to create web applications that provide Netnews access through normal web browser interactions. One site, deja.com (now a part of Google), created an entire infrastructure for accessing current as well as archived newsgroup messages, including a powerful search engine for finding desired messages.

2.3.4 Live messaging

America Online's *Instant Messaging* service may be responsible for making the notion of *IM*-ing someone part of our collective vocabulary. But long before the existence of AOL, there was a *talk* protocol that enabled users who were logged in to network-connected UNIX systems to talk to each other.

A *talk* server would run on a UNIX machine, waiting for requests from other *talk* servers. (Since *talk* was a bi-directional service, servers had to run on the machines at both ends of a conversation.) A user would invoke the *talk* client program to communicate with a person on another machine somewhere else on the network, e.g. *elvis@graceland.org*. The *talk* client program would communicate with the local *talk* server, which would ask the *talk* server on the remote machine whether the other person is on line. If so, and if that other person was accepting *talk* requests, the remote talk server would establish a connection, and the two people would use a screen mode interface to have an online conversation.

Today, the vast majority of Internet users eschew command-line interfaces, and the notion of being logged in to a particular system (aside from AOL, perhaps) is alien to most people. Thus, a protocol like *talk* would not work in its original form in today's diverse Internet world. Efforts to create an open, interoperable Instant Messaging protocol have been unsuccessful thus far. Proprietary 'instant messaging' systems (such as AOL's) exist, but they are exclusionary, and the intense competition and lack of cooperation between instant messaging providers further limits the degree of interoperability we can expect from them.

2.3.5 File servers

E-mail and live messaging services represent fleeting, transitory communications over the Internet. Once an instant message or e-mail message has been read, it is usually discarded. Even forum-based messages, even if they are archived, lack a certain degree of permanence, and for the most part those who post such messages tend not to treat them as anything more than passing transient dialogues (or, in some cases, monologues).

However, providing remote access to more persistent documents and files is a fundamental necessity to enable sharing of resources.

For years before the existence of the Internet, files were shared using *BBS*'s (electronic *Bulletin Board Systems*). People would dial in to a BBS via a modem, and once connected, they would have access to directories of files to download (and sometimes to 'drop' directories into which their own files could be uploaded). Various file transfer protocols were used to enable this functionality over telephone dialup lines (e.g. Kermit, Xmodem, Zmodem).

To facilitate this functionality over the Internet, the *File Transfer Protocol* (*FTP*) was created.

FTP

An FTP server operates in a manner similar to an e-mail server. Commands exist to authenticate the connecting user, provide the user with information about available files, and allow the user to retrieve selected files. However, e-mail servers let you access only a preset collection of folders (like the inbox), solely for purposes of downloading message files. FTP servers also allow users to traverse to different directories within the server's local file system, and (if authorized) to upload files into those directories.

The FTP specification has gone through a number of iterations over the years, but the most recent version can be found in Internet RFC 959. It describes the process by which FTP servers make files available to FTP clients.

First, a user connects to an FTP server using an FTP client program. FTP interactions usually require *two* connections between the client and server. One, the *control connection*, passes commands and status responses between the client and the server. The other, the *data connection*, is the connection over which actual data transfers occur. User authentication occurs, of course, over the control connection.

Once connected and authenticated, the user sends commands to set transfer modes, change directories, list the contents of directories, and transfer files. Whether or not a user can enter specific directories, view directory contents, download files, and/or upload files depends on the security privileges associated with his/her user account on the server. (Note that the root directory of the FTP server need not be the same as the root directory of the server machine's local file system. System administrators can configure FTP servers so that only a discrete directory subtree is accessible through the FTP server.)

FTP servers can allow open access to files without requiring explicit user authentication, using a service called anonymous FTP. When an FTP server is configured to support anonymous FTP, a user ID called 'anonymous' is defined that will accept any password. 'Netiquette' (Internet etiquette) prescribes that users should provide their e-mail address as the password. The system administrator can further restrict the file system subtree that is accessible to 'anonymous' users, usually providing read-only access (although it is possible to configure a 'drop' folder into which anonymous users can place files). Most of the FTP archives found on the Internet make use of anonymous FTP to provide open access to files.

Other file server protocols have come into being over the years, but none has achieved the popularity of FTP. With the advent of next generation distributed file-sharing systems such as the one used by Napster, we can expect to see changes in the file server landscape over the next few years.

2.4 AND THEN CAME THE WEB...

While FTP provided interactive functionality for users seeking to transfer files across the Internet, it was not a very user-friendly service. FTP clients, especially the command-line variety, were tedious to use, and provided limited genuine interactivity. Once you traversed to the directory you wanted and downloaded or uploaded your files, your 'user experience' was completed. Even GUI-based FTP clients did not appreciably enhance the interactivity of FTP.

Other services sought to make the online experience more truly interactive. *Gopher* was a service developed at the University of Minnesota (hence the name— Minnesota is the 'gopher state') that served up *menus* to users. In Gopher, the items in menus were not necessarily actual file system directories, as they were in FTP. They were logical lists of items grouped according to category, leading the user to other resources. These resources did not have to be on the same system as the Gopher menu. In fact, a Gopher menu could list local resources as well as resources on other systems, including other Gopher menus, FTP archives, and (finally) files.

Again, once you reached the level of a file, your traversal was complete. There was 'nowhere to go', except to retrace your steps back along the path you just took.

Gopher only caught on as a mainstream Internet service in a limited capacity. Over time, for a variety of reasons, it faded into the woodwork, in part because a better and more flexible service came along right behind it.

That system married the power of the Internet with the capabilities of *hypertext*, to offer a medium for real user interactivity.

Of course, as you have already figured out, that system is the one proposed by Tim Berners-Lee in the late 1980s and early 1990s, known as the World Wide Web.

2.5 QUESTIONS AND EXERCISES

1. Find and download the RFC's associated with the POP3, SMTP and FTP protocols.
2. What kind of traffic is sent over ICMP?

3. What is the main difference between TCP and UDP? What kinds of traffic would be suitable for each? What kinds of traffic would be suitable for both? Provide examples.

4. If you get your e-mail from a provider that offers POP3 service, use a 'telnet' client program to connect to your POP3 server. What POP3 commands would you use to connect, authenticate, and check for mail? What command would you use to read a message? To delete a message? To view message headers?

5. Assume you are implementing an e-mail application (MUA) for a handheld device that does not have a persistent connection to the Internet. Which protocol would you use for reading e-mail? For sending e-mail?

6. Which mode of FTP is used at public FTP sites? How does it differ from 'normal' FTP service?

BIBLIOGRAPHY

Comer, D. (1991) *Internetworking with TCP/IP (Volume 1: Principles, Protocols, and Architecture)*. Englewood Cliffs, NJ: Prentice-Hall.

Davidson, J. (1988) *An Introduction to TCP/IP*. New York: Springer-Verlag.

Hafner, K. and Lyon, M. (1996) *Where Wizards Stay Up Late: The Origins of the Internet*. New York: Simon & Schuster.

Krol, E. (1994) *The Whole Internet User's Guide and Catalog, Second Edition*. Sebastopol, California: O'Reilly.

Stephenson, N. (1999) *In the Beginning Was the Command Line*. New York, NY: Avon Books.

Wood, D. (1999) *Programming Internet Email*. Sebastopol, California: O'Reilly.

3 Birth of the World Wide Web: HTTP

The main subject of this chapter is the *HyperText Transfer Protocol* (HTTP). We begin with a short foray into the history of the World Wide Web, followed by a discussion of its core components, with the focus on HTTP. No matter how Web technology evolves in the future, it will always be important to understand the basic protocols that enable communication between Web programs. This understanding is critical because it provides important insights into the inner workings of the wide range of Web applications.

3.1 HISTORICAL PERSPECTIVE

For all practical purposes, it all started at CERN back in 1989. That is when Tim Berners-Lee wrote a proposal for a hypertext-based information management system, and distributed this proposal among the scientists at CERN. Although initially interest in the proposal was limited, it sparked the interest of someone else at CERN, Robert Cailliau, who helped Berners-Lee reformat and redistribute the proposal, referring to the system as a 'World Wide Web'.

By the end of 1990, Berners-Lee had implemented a server and a command-line browser using the initial version of the *HyperText Transfer Protocol* (HTTP) that he designed for this system. By the middle of 1991, this server and browser were made available throughout CERN. Soon thereafter, the software was made available for anonymous FTP download on the Internet. Interest in HTTP and the Web grew, and many people downloaded the software. A newsgroup, *comp.infosystems.www*, was created to support discussion of this new technology.

Just one year later, at the beginning of 1993, there were about 50 different sites running HTTP servers. This number grew to 200 by the autumn of that year. In addition, since the specification for the HTTP protocol was openly available, others were writing their own server and browser software, including GUI-based browsers that supported typographic controls and display of images.

3.2 BUILDING BLOCKS OF THE WEB

There were three basic components devised by Tim Berners-Lee comprising the essence of Web technology:

1. A markup language for formatting hypertext documents.

2. A uniform notation scheme for addressing accessible resources over the network.

3. A protocol for transporting messages over the network.

The markup language that allowed cross-referencing of documents via hyperlinks was the *HyperText Markup Language* (HTML). We shall discuss HTML in a later chapter.

The uniform notation scheme is called the *Uniform Resource Identifier* (URI). For historic reasons, it is most often referred to as the *Uniform Resource Locator* (URL). We shall cover the fundamentals of the URL specification in Section 3.3.

HTTP is a core foundation of the World Wide Web. It was designed for transporting specialized messages over the network. The simplicity of the protocol does not always apply to HTTP interactions, which are complicated in the context of sophisticated Web applications. This will become apparent when we discuss the complex interactions between HTML, XML, and web server technologies (e.g. servlets and Java Server Pages).

Understanding of HTTP is just as critical in maintaining complex applications. You will realize it the first time you try to analyze and troubleshoot an elusive problem. Understanding the HTTP messages passed between servers, proxies and browsers leads to deeper insights into the nature of underlying problems. The inner workings of HTTP are covered in Sections 3.4–3.6.

3.3 THE UNIFORM RESOURCE LOCATOR

Tim Berners-Lee knew that one piece of the Web puzzle would be a notation scheme for referencing accessible resources anywhere on the Internet. He devised this notational scheme so that it would be flexible, so that it would be extensible, and so that it would support other protocols besides HTTP. This notational scheme is known as the *URL* or *Uniform Resource Locator*.

I Am He As You Are He As URL as We Are All Together

Participants in the original *World Wide Web Consortium* (also known as the *W3C*) had reservations about Berners-Lee's nomenclature. There were concerns about his use of the word 'universal' (*URL* originally stood for '*Universal Resource Locator*'), and about the way a URL specified a resource's location (which could be subject to frequent change) rather than a fixed immutable name. The notion of a fixed name for a resource came to be known as the *URN* or *Uniform Resource Name*.

URNs would be a much nicer mechanism for addressing and accessing web resources than URLs. URLs utilize 'locator' information that embeds both a server address and a file location. URNs utilize a simpler human-readable name that does not change even when the resource is moved to another location. The problem is that URNs have failed to materialize as a globally supported web standard, so for all practical purposes we are still stuck with URLs.

As a matter of convenience, W3C introduced the notion of the *URI* (or *Uniform Resource Identifier*) which was defined as the union of URLs and URNs. URL is still the most commonly used term, though URI is what you should use if you want to be a stickler for formal correctness. Throughout this book, we will favor the more widely accepted term URL for the strictly pragmatic reason of minimizing confusion.

Here is the generalized notation associated with URLs:

```
scheme://host[:port#]/path/.../[;url-params][?query-string][#anchor]
```

Let us break a URL down into its component parts:

- *scheme*—this portion of the URL designates the underlying protocol to be used (e.g. 'http' or 'ftp'). This is the portion of the URL preceding the colon and two forward slashes.

- *host*—this is either the name of the IP address for the web server being accessed. This is usually the part of the URL immediately following the colon and two forward slashes.

- *port#*—this is an optional portion of the URL designating the port number that the target web server listens to. (The default port number for HTTP servers is 80, but some configurations are set up to use an alternate port number. When they do, that number must be specified in the URL.) The port number, if it appears, is found right after a colon that immediately follows the server name or address.

- *path*—logically speaking, this is the file system path from the 'root' directory of the server to the desired document. (In practice, web servers may make use of aliasing to point to documents, gateways, and services that are not explicitly accessible from the server's root directory.) The path immediately follows the server and port number portions of the URL, and by definition *includes* that first forward slash.

- *url-params*—this once rarely used portion of the URL includes optional 'URL parameters'. It is now used somewhat more frequently, for session identifiers in web servers supporting the Java Servlet API. If present, it follows a semi-colon immediately after the path information.

- *query-string*—this optional portion of the URL contains other dynamic parameters associated with the request. Usually, these parameters are produced as the result of user-entered variables in HTML forms. If present, the query string follows a question mark in the URL. Equal signs (=) separate the parameters from their values, and ampersands (&) mark the boundaries between parameter-value pairs.

- *anchor*—this optional portion of the URL is a reference to a positional marker within the requested document, like a bookmark. If present, it follows a hash mark or pound sign ('#').

The breakout of a sample URL into components is illustrated below:

```
http://www.mywebsite.com/sj/test;id=8079?name=sviergn&x=true#stuff

SCHEME          = http
HOST            = www.mywebsite.com
PATH            = /sj/test
URL PARAMS      = id=8079
QUERY STRING    = name=sviergn&x=true
ANCHOR          = stuff
```

Note that the URL notation we are describing here applies to most protocols (e.g. `http`, `https`, and `ftp`). However, some other protocols use their own notations (e.g. `"mailto:richr@neurozen.com"`).

3.4 FUNDAMENTALS OF HTTP

HTTP is the foundation protocol of the World Wide Web. It is simple, which is both a limitation and a source of strength. Many people in the industry criticized HTTP for its lack of state support and limited functionality, but HTTP took the world by storm while more advanced and sophisticated protocols never realized their potential.

HTTP is an *application level* protocol in the TCP/IP protocol suite, using TCP as the underlying Transport Layer protocol for transmitting messages. The fundamental things worth knowing about the HTTP protocol and the structure of HTTP messages are:

1. The HTTP protocol uses the *request/response paradigm*, meaning that an HTTP client program sends an HTTP request message to an HTTP server, which returns an HTTP response message.

2. The structure of request and response messages is similar to that of e-mail messages; they consist of a group of lines containing *message headers*, followed by a blank line, followed by a *message body*.

3. HTTP is a *stateless* protocol, meaning that it has no explicit support for the notion of state. An HTTP transaction consists of a single request from a client to a server, followed by a single response from the server back to the client.

In the next few sections, we will elaborate on these fundamental aspects of the HTTP protocol.

3.4.1 HTTP servers, browsers, and proxies

Web servers and browsers exchange information using HTTP, which is why Web servers are often called HTTP servers. Similarly, Web browsers are sometimes referred to as HTTP clients, but their functionality is not limited to HTTP support. It was Tim Berners-Lee's intent that web browsers should enable access to a wide variety of content, not just content accessible via HTTP. Thus, even the earliest web browsers were designed to support other protocols including FTP and Gopher. Today, web browsers support not only HTTP, FTP, and local file access, but e-mail and netnews as well.

HTTP proxies are programs that act as both servers and clients, making requests to web servers on behalf of other clients. Proxies enable HTTP transfers across firewalls. They also provide support for caching of HTTP messages and filtering of HTTP requests. They also fill a variety of other interesting roles in complex environments.

When we refer to HTTP clients, the statements we make are applicable to browsers, proxies, and other custom HTTP client programs.

3.4.2 Request/response paradigm

First and foremost, HTTP is based on the *request/response paradigm*: browsers (and possibly proxy servers as well) send messages to HTTP servers. These servers generate messages that are sent back to the browsers. The messages sent to HTTP servers are called *requests*, and the messages generated by the servers are called *responses*.

In practice, servers and browsers rarely communicate directly—there are one or more proxies in between. A *connection* is defined as a *virtual circuit* that is

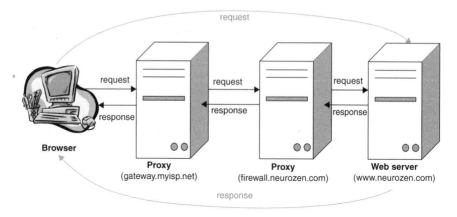

Figure 3.1   The request/response virtual circuit

composed of HTTP agents, including the browser, the server, and intermediate proxies participating in the exchange (Figure 3.1).

3.4.3 Stateless protocol

As mentioned in the previous chapter, HTTP is a *stateless* protocol. When a protocol supports 'state', this means that it provides for the interaction between client and server to contain a sequence of commands. The server is required to maintain the 'state' of the connection throughout the transmission of successive commands, until the connection is terminated. The sequence of transmitted and executed commands is often called a *session*. Many Internet protocols, including FTP, SMTP and POP are 'stateful' protocols.

In contrast, HTTP is said to be 'stateless'. Defining HTTP as a stateless protocol made things simpler, but it also imposed limitations on the capabilities of Web applications. By definition, the lifetime of a connection was a single request/response exchange. This meant that there was no way to maintain persistent information about a 'session' of successive interactions between a client and server. This also meant that there was no way to 'batch' requests together—something that would be useful, for example, to ask a web server for an HTML page and all the images it references during the course of one connection.

Later in this chapter, we discuss the evolution of *cookies* as a mechanism for maintaining state in Web applications. We will also discuss advanced strategies used in HTTP/1.1 to support connections that outlive a single request/response exchange. HTTP/1.1 assumes that the connection remains in place until it is broken, or until an HTTP client requests that it be broken. However, HTTP/1.1 is designed to support persistent connections for the sake of efficiency, but not to support state. We will come back to the technicalities of establishing and breaking HTTP connections when we discuss HTTP/1.1 in detail.

3.4.4 The structure of HTTP messages

HTTP messages (both requests and responses) have a structure similar to e-mail messages; they consist of a block of lines comprising the *message headers*, followed by a blank line, followed by a *message body*. The structure of HTTP messages, however, is more sophisticated than the structure of e-mail messages.

E-Mail Messages vs. HTTP Messages

E-mail messages are intended to pass information directly between people. Thus, both the message headers and the body tend to be 'human-readable'. E-mail messages (at least originally) had message bodies that consisted simply of readable plain text, while their message headers included readable information like the sender address and the message subject.

Over time, e-mail message structure became more sophisticated, in part to provide support for MIME functionality. There were headers added to allow decompression, decoding, and reformatting of message content based on its MIME type. In addition, multi-part messages were supported, allowing messages to have multiple sections (often corresponding to a body and a set of attachments).

When HTTP servers and browsers communicate with each other, they perform sophisticated interactions, based on header and body content. Unlike e-mail messages, HTTP messages are not intended to be directly 'human-readable'.

Another fundamental difference is that HTTP request and response messages begin with special lines that do not follow the standard header format. For requests, this line is called the *request line*, and for responses, it is called the *status line*.

Let us start with a very simple example: loading a static web page residing on a web server. A user may manually type a URL into her browser, she may click on a hyperlink found within the page she is viewing with the browser, or she may select a bookmarked page to visit. In each of these cases, the desire to visit a particular URL is translated by the browser into an HTTP request. An HTTP request message has the following structure:

```
METHOD /path-to-resource   HTTP/version-number
Header-Name-1: value
Header-Name-2: value

[  optional request body  ]
```

Every request starts with the special *request line*, which contains a number of fields. The 'method' represents one of several supported *request methods*, chief among them 'GET' and 'POST'. The '/path-to-resource' represents the *path* portion of the requested URL. The 'version-number' specifies the version of HTTP used by the client.

After the first line we see a list of HTTP *headers*, followed by a blank line, often called a <CR><LF> (for '*carriage return and line feed*'). The blank line separates the request headers from the body of the request. The blank line is followed (optionally) by a *body*, which is in turn followed by another blank line indicating the end of the request message.

For our purposes, let http://www.mywebsite.com/sj/index.html be the requested URL. Here is a simplified version of the HTTP request message that would be transmitted to the web server at www.mywebsite.com:

```
GET /sj/index.html HTTP/1.1
Host: www.mywebsite.com
```

Note that the request message ends with a blank line. In the case of a GET request, there is no body, so the request simply ends with this blank line. Also, note the presence of a Host header. (We discuss headers in request and response messages in greater detail later in this chapter.)

The server, upon receiving this request, attempts to generate a response message. An HTTP response message has the following structure:

```
HTTP/version-number    status-code    message
Header-Name-1: value
Header-Name-2: value

[ response body ]
```

The first line of an HTTP response message is the *status line*. This line contains the version of HTTP being used, followed by a three-digit *status code*, and followed by a brief human-readable explanation of the status code. This is a simplified version of the HTTP response message that the server would send back to the browser, assuming that the requested file exists and is accessible to the requestor:

```
HTTP/1.1 200 OK
Content-Type: text/html
Content-Length: 9934
  ...

<HTML>
<HEAD>
<TITLE>SJ's Web Page</TITLE>
</HEAD>
<BODY BGCOLOR="#ffffff">
<H2 ALIGN="center">Welcome to Sviergn Jiernsen's Home Page</H2>
```

```
    ...
    </H2>
    </BODY>
    </HTML>
```

Note that the response message begins with a *status line*, containing the name and version of the protocol in use, a numeric response status code, and a human-readable message. In this case, the request produced a successful response, thus we see a success code (200) and a success message (OK). Note the presence of header lines within the response, followed by a blank line, followed by a block of text. (We shall see later how a browser figures out that this text is to be rendered as HTML.)

The process of transmitting requests and responses between servers and browsers is rarely this simplistic. Complex negotiations occur between browsers and servers to determine what information should be sent. For instance, HTML pages may contain references to other accessible resources, such as graphical images and Java applets. Clients that support the rendering of images and applets, which is most web browsers, must parse the retrieved HTML page to determine what additional resources are needed, and then send HTTP requests to retrieve those additional resources (Figure 3.2).

Server-browser interactions can become much more complex for advanced applications.

3.4.5 Request methods

There are varieties of *request methods* specified in the HTTP protocol. The most basic ones defined in HTTP/1.1 are GET, HEAD, and POST. In addition, there are the less commonly used PUT, DELETE, TRACE, OPTIONS and CONNECT.

> **Method to Their Madness**
>
> HTTP/1.1 servers are not obligated to implement all these methods. At a minimum, any general purpose server must support the methods GET and HEAD. All other methods are optional, though you'd be hard-pressed to find a server in common usage today that does not support POST requests. Most of the newer servers also support PUT and DELETE methods.
>
> Servers may also define their own methods and assign their own constraints and processing behavior to these methods, though this approach generally makes sense only for custom implementations.

Request methods impose constraints on message structure, and specifications that define how servers should process requests, including the *Common Gateway*

Step 1: Initial user request for "http://www.cs.rutgers.edu/~shklar/"

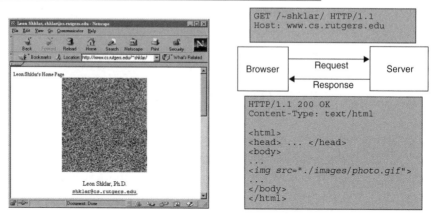

Step 2: Secondary browser request for "http://www.cs.rutgers.edu/~shklar/images/photo.gif"

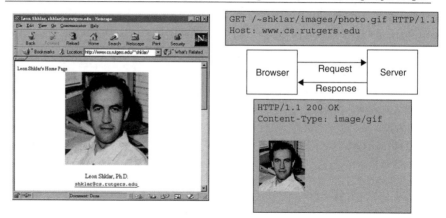

Figure 3.2   Sequence of browser requests for loading a sample page

Interface (CGI) and the *Java Servlet API*, include discussion of how different request methods should be treated.

GET

The simplest of the request methods is GET. When you enter a URL in your browser, or click on a hyperlink to visit another page, the browser uses the GET method when making the request to the web server.

GET requests date back to the very first versions of HTTP. A GET request does not have a body and, until the version 1.1, was not required to have headers. (HTTP/1.1 requires that the Host header should be present in every request in order to support *virtual hosting*, which we discuss later in this chapter.)

In the previous section, we offered an example of a very simple GET request. In that example, we visited a URL, `http://www.mywebsite.com/sj/index.html`, using the GET method. Let's take a look at the request that gets submitted by an HTTP/1.1 browser when you fill out a simple HTML form to request a stock quote:

```
<HTML>
<HEAD><TITLE>Simple Form</TITLE></HEAD>
<BODY>
<H2>Simple Form</H2>
<FORM ACTION="http://finance.yahoo.com/q" METHOD="get">
Ticker: <INPUT SIZE="25" NAME="s">
<INPUT TYPE="submit" VALUE="Get Quote">
</FORM>
<BODY>
</HTML>
```

If we enter 'YHOO' in the form above, then the browser constructs a URL comprised of the 'ACTION' field from the form followed by a *query string* containing all of the form's input parameters and the values provided for them. The boundary separating the URL from the query string is a question mark. Thus, the URL constructed by the browser is `http://www.finance.yahoo.com/q?s=YHOO` and the submitted request looks as follows:

```
GET /q?s=YHOO HTTP/1.1
Host: finance.yahoo.com
User-Agent: Mozilla/4.75 [en] (WinNT; U)
```

The response that comes back from the server looks something like this:

```
HTTP/1.0 200 OK
Date: Sat, 03 Feb 2001 22:48:35 GMT
Connection: close
Content-Type: text/html
Set-Cookie: B=9ql5kgct7p2m3&b=2;expires=Thu,15 Apr 2010 20:00:00 GMT;
path=/; domain=.yahoo.com

<HTML>
<HEAD><TITLE>Yahoo! Finance - YHOO</TITLE></HEAD>
```

```
<BODY>
   ...
</BODY>
</HTML>
```

POST

A fundamental difference between GET and POST requests is that POST requests have a *body*: content that follows the block of headers, with a blank line separating the headers from the body. Going back to the sample form in Section 3.2, let's change the request method to POST and notice that the browser now puts form parameters into the body of the message, rather than appending parameters to the URL as part of a query string:

```
POST /q HTTP/1.1
Host: finance.yahoo.com
User-Agent: Mozilla/4.75 [en] (WinNT; U)
Content-Type: application/x-www-form-urlencoded
Content-Length: 6

s=YHOO
```

Note that the URL constructed by the browser does *not* contain the form parameters in the query string. Instead, these parameters are included after the headers as part of the message body:

```
HTTP/1.0 200 OK
Date: Sat, 03 Feb 2001 22:48:35 GMT
Connection: close
Content-Type: text/html
Set-Cookie: B=9ql5kgct7p2m3&b=2;expires=Thu,15 Apr 2010 20:00:00 GMT;
path=/; domain=.yahoo.com

<HTML>
<HEAD><TITLE>Yahoo! Finance - YHOO</TITLE></HEAD>
<BODY>
   ...
</BODY>
</HTML>
```

Note that the response that arrives from `finance.yahoo.com` happens to be exactly the same as in the previous example using the GET method, but only because designers of the server application decided to support both request methods in the same way.

GET vs. POST

Many Web applications are intended to be 'sensitive' to the request method employed when accessing a URL. Some applications may accept one request method but not another. Others may perform different functions depending on which request method is used.

   For example, some servlet designers write Java servlets that use the GET method to display an input form. The ACTION field of the form is the same servlet (using the same URL), but using the POST method. Thus, the application is constructed so that it knows to display a form when it receives a request using the GET method, and to process the form (and to present the results of processing the form) when it receives a request using the POST method.

HEAD

Requests that use the HEAD method operate similarly to requests that use the GET method, except that the server sends back only headers in the response. This means the *body* of the request is not transmitted, and only the response metadata found in the headers is available to the client. This response metadata, however, may be sufficient to enable the client to make decisions about further processing, and may possibly reduce the overhead associated with requests that return the actual content in the message body.

   If we were to go back to the sample form and change the request method to HEAD, we would notice that the request does not change (except for replacing the word 'GET' with the word 'HEAD', of course), and the response contains the same headers as before but no body.

   Historically, HEAD requests were often used to implement caching support. A browser can use a cached copy of a resource (rather than going back to the original source to re-request the content) if the cache entry was created after the date that the content was last modified. If the creation date for the cache entry is *earlier* than the content's last modification date, then a 'fresh' copy of the content should be retrieved from the source.

   Suppose we want to look at a page that we visit regularly in our browser (e.g. Leon's home page). If we have visited this page recently, the browser will have a copy of the page stored in its cache. The browser can make a determination as to whether it needs to re-retrieve the page by first submitting a HEAD request:

```
HEAD http://www.cs.rutgers.edu/~shklar/ HTTP/1.1
Host: www.cs.rutgers.edu
User-Agent: Mozilla/4.75 [en] (WinNT; U)
```

The response comes back with a set of headers, including content modification information:

```
HTTP/1.1 200 OK
Date: Mon, 05 Feb 2001 03:26:18 GMT
Server: Apache/1.2.5
Last-Modified: Mon, 05 Feb 2001 03:25:36 GMT
Content-Length: 2255
Content-Type: text/html
```

The browser (or some other HTTP client) can compare the content modification date with the creation date of the cache entry, and resubmit the same request with the GET method if the cache entry is obsolete. We save bandwidth when the content does not change by making a HEAD request. Since responses to HEAD requests do not include the content as part of the message body, the overhead is smaller than making an explicit GET request for the content.

Today, there are more efficient ways to support caching and we will discuss them later in this chapter. The HEAD method is still very useful for implementing change-tracking systems, for testing and debugging new applications, and for learning server capabilities.

3.4.6 Status codes

The first line of a response is the *status line*, consisting of the protocol and its version number, followed by a three-digit *status code* and a brief explanation of that status code. The status code tells an HTTP client (browser or proxy) either that the response was generated as expected, or that the client needs to perform a specific action (that may be further parameterized via information in the headers). The explanation portion of the line is for human consumption; changing or omitting it will not cause a properly designed HTTP client to change its actions.

Status codes are grouped into categories. HTTP Version 1.1 defines five categories of response messages:

- *1xx*—Status codes that start with '1' are classified as *informational*.

- *2xx*—Status codes that start with '2' indicate *successful* responses.

- *3xx*—Status codes that start with '3' are for purposes of *redirection*.

- *4xx*—Status codes that start with '4' represent *client request errors*.

- *5xx*—Status codes that start with '5' represent *server errors*.

Informational status codes (1xx)

These status codes serve solely informational purposes. They do not denote success or failure of a request, but rather impart information about how a request can be processed further. For example, a status code of "100" is used to tell the client that it may continue with a *partially submitted request*. Clients can specify a partially submitted request by including an 'Expect' header in the request message. A server can examine requests containing an 'Expect' header, determine whether or not it is capable of satisfying the request, and send an appropriate response. If the server *is* capable of satisfying the request, the response will contain a status code of '100':

```
HTTP/1.1 100 Continue
  ...
```

If it cannot satisfy the request, it will send a response with a status code indicating a client request error, i.e. '417':

```
HTTP/1.1 417 Expectation Failed
  ...
```

Successful response status codes (2xx)

The most common successful response status code is '200', which indicates that the request was successfully completed and that the requested resource is being sent back to the client:

```
HTTP/1.1 200 OK
Content-Type: text/html
Content-Length: 9934
  ...

<HTML>
<HEAD>
<TITLE>SJ's Web Page</TITLE>
```

```
</HEAD>
<BODY BGCOLOR="#ffffff">
<H2 ALIGN="center">Welcome to Sviergn Jiernsen's Home Page</H2>
 ...
</H2>
</BODY>
</HTML>
```

Another example is '201', which indicates that the request was satisfied and that a
new resource was created on the server.

Redirection status codes (3xx)

Status codes of the form '3xx' indicate that additional actions are required to satisfy
the original request. Normally this involves a *redirection*: the client is instructed to
'redirect' the request to another URL.

For example, '301' and '302' both instruct the client to look for the originally
requested resource at the new location specified in the 'Location' header of the
response. The difference between the two is that '301' tells the client that the
resource has 'Moved Permanently', and that it should always look for that resource
at the new location. '302' tells the client that the resource has 'Moved Temporarily',
and to consider this relocation a one-time deal, just for purposes of this request. In
either case, the client should, immediately upon receiving a 301 or 302 response,
construct and transmit a new request 'redirected' at the new location.

Redirections happen all the time, often unbeknownst to the user. Browsers are
designed to respond silently to redirection status codes, so that users never see
redirection 'happen'. A perfect example of such silent redirection occurs when a user
enters a URL specifying a directory, but leaving off the terminating slash. To visit
Leon's web site at Rutgers University, you could enter `http://www.cs.rutgers.`
`edu/~shklar` in your browser. This would result in the following HTTP request:

```
GET /~shklar HTTP/1.1
Host: www.cs.rutgers.edu
```

But "~shklar" is actually a directory on the Rutgers web server, not a deliverable
file. Web servers are designed to treat a URL ending in a slash as a request for
a directory. Such requests may, depending on server configuration, return either
a file with a default name (if present), e.g. index.html, or a listing of the directory's contents. In either case, the web server must first redirect the request, from
`http://www.cs.rutgers.edu/~shklar` to `http://www.cs.rutgers.edu/~`
shklar/, to properly present it:

```
HTTP/1.1 301 Moved Permanently
Location: http://www.cs.rutgers.edu/~shklar/
Content-Type: text/html

...

<html>
<head><title>301 Moved Permanently</title></head>
<body>
<h1>301 Moved Permanently</h1>
The        document        has        moved        <a
href="http://www.cs.rutgers.edu/~shklar/">here</a>.
</body>
</html>
```

Today's sophisticated browsers are designed to react to '301' by updating an internal relocation table, so that in the future they can substitute the new address prior to submitting the request, and thus avoid the relocation response. To support older browsers that do not support automatic relocation, web servers still include a message body that explicitly includes a link to the new location. This affords the user an opportunity to manually jump to the new location.

Remember the Slash!

This example offers a valuable lesson: if you are trying to retrieve a directory listing (or the default page associated with a directory), don't forget the trailing '/'. When manually visiting a URL representing a directory in your browser, you may not even notice the redirection and extra connection resulting from omitting the trailing slash. However, when your applications generate HTML pages containing links to directories, forgetting to add that trailing slash within these links will effectively double the number of requests sent to your server.

Client request error status codes (4xx)

Status codes that start with '4' indicate a problem with the client request (e.g. '400 Bad Request'), an authorization challenge (e.g. '401 Not Authorized'), or the server's inability to find the requested resource (e.g. '404 Not Found'). Although '400', '401', and '404' are the most common in this category, some less common status codes are quite interesting. We have already seen (in the section on 'Informational Status Codes') an example of the use of '417 Expectation Failed'. In another example, the client might use the 'If-Unmodified-Since' header to request a resource only if it has not changed since a specific date:

```
GET/~shklar/HTTP/1.1
Host: www.cs.rutgers.edu
If-Unmodified-Since: Fri, 11 Feb 2000 22:28:00 GMT
```

Since this resource did change, the server sends back the '412 Precondition Failed' response:

```
HTTP/1.1 412 Precondition Failed
Date: Sun, 11 Feb 2001 22:28:31 GMT
Server: Apache/1.2.5
```

Server error status codes (5xx)

Finally, status codes that start with '5' indicate a server problem that prevents it from satisfying an otherwise valid request (e.g. '500 Internal Server Error' or '501 Not Implemented').

Status codes represent a powerful means of controlling browser behavior. There are a large number of different status codes representing different response conditions, and they are well documented in Internet RFC 2616. Familiarity with status codes is obviously critical when implementing an HTTP server, but it is just as critical when building advanced Web applications. Later in this chapter, we will offer additional examples that illustrate how creative use of status codes (and HTTP headers) can simplify application development by quite a few orders of magnitude.

3.5 BETTER INFORMATION THROUGH HEADERS

As we already know, HTTP headers are a form of message metadata. Enlightened use of headers makes it possible to construct sophisticated applications that establish and maintain sessions, set caching policies, control authentication, and implement business logic. The HTTP protocol specification makes a clear distinction between *general headers, request headers, response headers*, and *entity headers*.

General headers apply to both request and response messages, but do not describe the body of the message. Examples of general headers include

- `Date: Sun, 11 Feb 2001 22:28:31 GMT`
  This header specifies the time and date that this message was created.

- `Connection: Close`
  This header indicates whether or not the client or server that generated the message intends to keep the connection open.

- `Warning: Danger, Will Robinson!`
  This header stores text for human consumption, something that would be useful when tracing a problem.

Request headers allow clients to pass additional information about themselves and about the request. For example:

- `User-Agent: Mozilla/4.75 [en] (WinNT; U)`
  Identifies the software (e.g. a web browser) responsible for making the request.

- `Host: www.neurozen.com`
  This header was introduced to support virtual hosting, a feature that allows a web server to service more than one domain.

- `Referer: http://www.cs.rutgers.edu/~shklar/index.html`
  This header provides the server with context information about the request. If the request came about because a user clicked on a link found on a web page, this header contains the URL of that referring page.

- `Authorization: Basic [encoded-credentials]`
  This header is transmitted with requests for resources that are restricted only to authorized users. Browsers will include this header after being notified of an *authorization challenge* via a response with a '401' status code. They consequently prompt users for their credentials (i.e. *userid* and *password*). They will continue to supply those credentials via this header in all further requests during the current browser session that access resources within the same authorization realm. (See the description of the `WWW-Authenticate` header below, and the section on 'Authorization' that follows.)

Response headers help the server to pass additional information about the response that cannot be inferred from the status code alone. Here are some examples:

- `Location: http://www.mywebsite.com/relocatedPage.html`
  This header specifies a URL towards which the client should redirect its original request. It always accompanies the '301' and '302' status codes that direct clients to try a new location.

- `WWW-Authenticate: Basic realm="KremlinFiles"`
  This header accompanies the '401' status code that indicates an authorization challenge. The value in this header specifies the protected realm for which proper authorization credentials must be provided before the request can be processed. In the case of web browsers, the combination of the '401' status code and the `WWW-Authenticate` header causes users to be prompted for ids and passwords.

- `Server: Apache/1.2.5`
  This header is not tied to a particular status code. It is an optional header that identifies the server software.

Entity headers describe either message bodies or (in the case of request messages that have no body) target resources. Common entity headers include:

- `Content-Type: mime-type/mime-subtype`
  This header specifies the MIME type of the message body's content.

- `Content-Length: xxx`
  This optional header provides the length of the message body. Although it is optional, it is useful for clients such as web browsers that wish to impart information about the progress of a request. Where this header is omitted, the browser can only display the amount of data downloaded. But when the header is included, the browser can display the amount of data as a *percentage* of the total size of the message body.

- `Last-Modified: Sun, 11 Feb 2001 22:28:31 GMT`
  This header provides the last modification date of the content that is transmitted in the body of the message. It is critical for the proper functioning of caching mechanisms.

3.5.1 Type support through content-type

So far, we were concentrating on message metadata, and for a good reason: understanding metadata is critical to the process of building applications. Still, somewhere along the line, there'd better be some content. After all, without content, Web applications would have nothing to present for end users to see and interact with.

You've probably noticed that, when it comes to content you view on the Web, your browser might do one of several things. It might:

- render the content as an HTML page,

- launch a *helper application* capable of presenting non-HTML content,

- present such content inline (within the browser window) through a *plug-in*, or

- get confused into showing the content of an HTML file as plain text without attempting to render it.

What's going on here? Obviously, browsers do *something* to determine the content type and to perform actions appropriate for that type.

HTTP borrows its content typing system from *Multipurpose Internet Mail Extensions (MIME)*. MIME is the standard that was designed to help e-mail clients to display non-textual content.

Extending MIME

HTTP has extended MIME and made use of it in ways that were never intended by its original designers. Still, the use of MIME means there is much commonality between web browsers and e-mail clients (which is why it was so natural for browsers to get tightly integrated with email clients).

As in MIME, the data type associated with the body of an HTTP message is defined via a two-layer ordered encoding model, using `Content-Type` and `Content-Encoding` headers. In other words, for the body to be interpreted according to the type specified in the `Content-Type` header, it has to first be decoded according to the encoding method specified in the `Content-Encoding` header.

In HTTP/1.1, defined content encoding methods for the `Content-Encoding` header are `"gzip"`, `"compress"` and `"deflate"`. The first two methods correspond to the formats produced by GNU zip and UNIX compress programs. The third method, `"deflate"`, corresponds to the zlib format associated with the deflate compression mechanism documented in RFC 1950 and 1951. Note that `"x-gzip"` and `"x-compress"` are equivalent to `"gzip"` and `"compress"` and should be supported for backward compatibility.

Obviously, if web servers encode content using these encoding methods, web browsers (and other clients) must be able to perform the reverse operations on encoded message bodies prior to rendering or processing of the content. Browsers are intelligent enough to open a compressed document file (e.g. `test.doc.gz`) and automatically invoke Microsoft Word to let you view the original `test.doc` file. It can do this if the web server includes the `"Content-Encoding: gzip"` header with the response. This header will cause a browser to *decode* the encoded content prior to presentation, revealing the `test.doc` document inside.

The `Content-Type` header is set to a media-type that is defined as a combination of a type, subtype and any number of optional attribute/value pairs:

```
media-type       = type "/" subtype *( ";" parameter-string )
type             = token
subtype          = token
```

The most common example is `"Content-Type: text/html"` where the type is set to `"text"` and the subtype is set to `"html"`. This obviously tells a browser to render the message body as an HTML page. Another example is:

```
Content-Type: text/plain; charset = 'us-ascii'
```

Here the subtype is `"plain"`, plus there is a parameter string that is passed to whatever client program ends up processing the body whose content type is `"text/plain"`. The parameter may have some impact on how the client program processes the content. If the parameter is not known to the program, it is simply ignored. Some other examples of MIME types are `"text/xml"` and `"application/xml"` for XML content, `"application/pdf"` for Adobe Portable Data Format, and `"video/x-mpeg"` for MPEG2 videos.

Since MIME was introduced to support multi-media transfers over e-mail, it is not surprising that it provides for the inclusion of multiple independent entities within a single message body. In e-mail messages, these *multipart messages* usually take the form of a textual message body plus attachments.

This multipart structure is very useful for HTTP transfers going in both directions (client-to-server and server-to-client). In the client-to-server direction, form data submitted via a browser can be accompanied by file content that is transmitted to the server. We will discuss multipart messages used for form submission when we talk about HTML in a later chapter.

In the server-to-client direction, a web server can implement primitive image animation by feeding browsers a multipart sequence of images. Netscape's web site used to include a demo of the primitive image animation technique that generated a stream of pictures of Mozilla (the Godzilla-like dragon that was the mascot of the original Netscape project):

```
GET /cgi-bin/doit.cgi HTTP/1.1
Host: cgi-bin.netscape.com
Date: Sun, 18 Feb 2001 06:22:19 GMT
```

The response is a `"multipart/x-mixed-replace"` message as indicated by the `Content-Type` header. This content type instructs the browser to render enclosed image bodies one at a time, but within the same screen real estate. The individual images are encoded and separated by the *boundary* string specified in the header:

```
HTTP/1.1 200 OK
Server: Netscape-Enterprise-3.6 SP1
Date: Date: Sun, 18 Feb 2001 06:22:31 GMT
Content-Type: multipart/x-mixed-replace; boundary=ThisRandomString
Connection: close

--ThisRandomString
Content-Type: image/gif
```

```
...
--ThisRandomString
Content-Type: image/gif

...
--ThisRandomString
Content-Type: image/gif

...
--ThisRandomString
```

Message typing is necessary to help both servers and browsers determine proper actions in processing requests and responses. Browsers use types and sub-types to either select a proper rendering module or to invoke a third-party tool (e.g. Microsoft Word). Multipart rendering modules control recursive invocation of proper rendering modules for the body parts. In the example above, the browser's *page* rendering module for the multipart message of type 'multipart/x-mixed-replace' invokes the browser's *image* rendering module once per image while always passing it the same screen location. Server-side applications use type information to process requests. For, example, a server-side application responsible for receiving files from browsers and storing them locally needs type information, to separate file content from accompanying form data that defines file name and target location.

3.5.2 Caching control through Pragma and Cache-Control headers

Caching is a set of mechanisms allowing responses to HTTP requests to be held in some form of temporary storage medium, as a means of improving server performance. Instead of satisfying future requests by going back to the original data source, the held copy of the data can be used. This eliminates the overhead of re-executing the original request and greatly improves server throughput.

There are three main types of caching that are employed in a Web application environment: *server-side* caching, *browser-side* caching, and *proxy-side* caching. In this section, we shall deal with browser-side and proxy-side caching, leaving server-side caching for a later chapter.

Take a Walk on the Proxy Side

In the real world, HTTP messages are rarely passed directly between servers and browsers. Most commonly, they pass through intermediate proxies. These proxies perform a variety of functions in the Web application environment, including the relaying of HTTP messages through firewalls and supporting the use of *server farms* (conglomerations of server machines that look to the outside world like they have the same IP address or host name).

Admittedly, proxies sit in the middle, *between* servers and browsers, so it may seem silly to talk about 'proxy-*side*' caching. Even though the wording may seem strange, do not dismiss the notion of proxy-side caching as some sort of anomaly.

When is the use of a cached response appropriate? This is a decision usually made by the server, or by Web applications running on the server. Many requests arrive at a given URL, but the server may deliver different content for each request, as the underlying source of the content is constantly changing. If the server 'knows' that the content of a response is relatively static and is not likely to change, it can instruct browsers, proxies, and other clients to cache that particular response. If the content is so static that it is never expected to change, the server can tell its clients that the response can be cached for an arbitrarily long amount of time. If the content has a limited lifetime, the server can still make use of caching by telling its clients to cache the response but only for that limited period. Even if the content is constantly changing, the server can make the decision that its clients can 'tolerate' a cached response (containing somewhat out-of-date content) for a specified time period.

Web servers and server-side applications are in the best position to judge whether clients should be allowed to cache their responses. There are two mechanisms for establishing caching rules. The first is associated with an older version of the HTTP protocol, version 1.0. The second is associated with HTTP version 1.1. Because there are web servers and clients that still support only HTTP 1.0, any attempt to enable caching must support both mechanisms in what is hopefully a backward-compatible fashion.

HTTP/1.1 provides its own mechanism for enforcing caching rules: the `Cache-Control` header. Valid settings include `public`, `private`, and `no-cache`. The `public` setting removes all restrictions and authorizes both shared and non-shared caching mechanisms to cache the response.

The `private` setting indicates that the response is directed at a single user and should not be stored in a shared cache. For instance, if two authorized users both make a secure request to a particular URL to obtain information about their private accounts, obviously it would be a problem if an intermediate proxy decided it could improve performance for the second user by sending her a cached copy of the first user's response.

The `no-cache` setting indicates that neither browsers nor proxies are allowed to cache the response. However, there are a number of options associated with this setting that make it somewhat more complicated than that. The header may also list the names of specific HTTP headers that are 'non-cached' (i.e. that must be re-acquired from the server that originated the cached response). If such headers *are* listed, then the response may be cached, *excluding* those listed headers.

HTTP/1.0 browsers and proxies are not guaranteed to obey instructions in the `Cache-Control` header that was first introduced in HTTP/1.1. For practical purposes, this means that this mechanism is only reliable in very controlled environments where you know for sure that all your clients are HTTP/1.1 compliant. In the real world, there are still many HTTP/1.0 browsers and proxies out there, so this is not practical.

A partial solution is to use the deprecated `Pragma` header that has only one defined setting: `no-cache`. When used with the `Cache-Control` header, it will prevent HTTP/1.0 browsers and proxies from caching the response. However, this alone may not have the desired effect on clients that are HTTP/1.1 compliant, since the `Pragma` header is deprecated and may not be properly supported in those clients. Thus, a more complete backwards-compatible solution would be to included both `Pragma` and `Cache-Control` headers, as in the following example:

```
HTTP/1.1 200 OK
Date: Mon, 05 Feb 2001 03:26:18 GMT
Server: Apache/1.2.5
Last-Modified: Mon, 05 Feb 2001 03:25:36 GMT
Cache-Control: private
Pragma: no-cache
Content-Length: 2255
Content-Type: text/html

<html>
  ...
</html>
```

This response is guaranteed to prevent HTTP/1.0 agents from caching the response and to prevent HTTP/1.1 agents from storing it in a shared cache. HTTP/1.1 agents may or may not ignore the `Pragma: no-cache` header, but we played it safe in this example to ensure that we do not implement a potentially more restrictive caching policy than intended.

3.5.3 Security through WWW-Authenticate and Authorization headers

HTTP provides built-in support for *basic authentication*, in which authorization credentials (userid and password) are transmitted via the `Authorization` header as a single encoded string. Since this string is simply encoded (not encrypted), this mechanism is only safe if performed over a secure connection.

Many Web applications implement their own authentication schemes that go above and beyond basic HTTP authentication. It is very easy to tell whether an application is using built-in HTTP authentication or its own authentication scheme. When a Web application is using built-in HTTP authentication, the browser brings up its own authentication dialog, prompting the user for authorization credentials, rather than prompting the user for this information within one of the browser's page rendering windows. Application-specific schemes *will* prompt users in the main browser window, as part of a rendered HTML page.

When built-in HTTP authentication is employed, browsers are responding to a pre-defined status code in server responses, namely the '401' status code indicating that the request is not authorized. Let's take a look at the server response that tells the browser to prompt for a password:

```
HTTP/1.1 401 Authenticate
Date: Mon, 05 Feb 2001 03:41:23 GMT
Server: Apache/1.2.5
WWW-Authenticate: Basic realm="Chapter3"
```

When a request for a restricted resource is sent to the server, the server sends back a response containing the '401' status code. In response to this, the browser prompts the user for a userid and password associated with the realm specified in the WWW-Authenticate header (in this case, "Chapter3"). The realm name serves both as an aid in helping users to retrieve their names and passwords, and as a logical organizing principle for designating which resources require what types of authorization. Web server administrative software gives webmasters the ability to define realms, to decide which resources 'belong' to these realms, and to establish userids and passwords that allow only selected people to access resources in these realms.

In response to the browser prompt, the user specifies his name and password. Once a browser has collected this input from the user, it resubmits the original request with the additional Authorization header. The value of this header is a string containing the type of authentication (usually "Basic") and a Base64-encoded representation of the concatenation of the user name and password (separated by a colon):

```
GET /book/chapter3/index.html HTTP/1.1
Date: Mon, 05 Feb 2001 03:41:24 GMT
Host: www.neurozen.com
Authorization: Basic eNCoDEd-uSErId:pASswORd
```

Insecurity

Note that the user name and password are *encoded* but not *encrypted*. Encryption is a secure form of encoding, wherein the content can only be decoded if a unique key value is known. Simple encoding mechanisms, like the Base64 encoding used in basic HTTP authentication, can be decoded by anyone who knows the encoding scheme. Obviously this is very dangerous when encoded (not encrypted) information is transmitted over an insecure connection.

Secure connections (using extensions to the HTTP protocol like Secure HTTP) by definition *encrypt* all transmitted information, thus sensitive information (like passwords) is secure.

It is hard to believe that there are still a large number of web sites—even e-commerce sites—that transmit passwords over open connections and establish secure connections only after the user has logged in!

As a user of the web, whenever you are prompted for your name and password, you should always check whether the connection is secure. With HTTP-based authentication, you should check whether the URL of the page you are attempting to access uses `https` (Secure HTTP) for its protocol. With proprietary authentication schemes, you should check the URL that is supposed to process your user name and password. For example, with a forms-based login you should check the URL defined in the 'action' attribute.

As a designer of applications for the Web, make sure that you incorporate these safeguards into your applications to ensure the security of users' sensitive information.

The server, having received the request with the `Authorization` header, attempts to verify the authorization credentials. If the userid and password match the credentials defined within that realm, the server then serves the content. The browser associates these authorization credentials with the authorized URL, and uses them as the value of the `Authorization` header in future requests to *dependent URLs*. Since the browser does this automatically, users do not get prompted again until they happen to encounter a resource that belongs to a different security realm.

Dependent URLs

We say that one URL 'depends' on another URL if the portion of the second URL up to and including the last slash is a prefix of the first URL. For example, the URL `http://www.cs.rutgers.edu/~shklar/classes/` depends on the URL `http://www.cs.rutgers.edu/~shklar/`. This means that, having submitted authorization credentials for `http://www.cs.rutgers.edu/~shklar/`, the browser would know to resubmit those same credentials within the `Authorization` header when requesting `http://www.cs.rutgers.edu/~shklar/classes/`.

If the server fails to verify the userid and password sent by the browser, it either resends the security challenge using the status code `401`, or refuses to serve the

requested resource outright, sending a response with the status code of 403 Forbidden. The latter happens when the server exceeds a defined limit of security
challenges. This limit is normally configurable and is designed to prevent simple
break-ins by trial-and-error.

We described the so-called *basic* authentication that is supported by both HTTP/1.0
and HTTP/1.1. It is a bit simplistic, but it does provide reasonable protection—as long
as you are transmitting over a secure connection. Most commercial applications that
deal with sensitive financial data use their own authentication mechanisms that are
not a part of HTTP. Commonly, user names and passwords are transmitted in bodies
of POST requests over secure connections. These bodies are interpreted by server
applications that decide whether to send back content, repeat the password prompt or
display an error message. These server applications don't use the 401 status code that
tells the browser to use its built-in authentication mechanism, though they may choose
to make use of the 403 status code indicating that access to the requested resource
is forbidden.

3.5.4 Session support through Cookie and Set-Cookie headers

We've mentioned several times now that HTTP is a stateless protocol. So what do
we do if we need to implement *stateful* applications?

> **10 Items or Less**
>
> The most obvious example of maintaining state in a Web application is the shopping
> cart. When you visit an e-commerce site, you view catalog pages describing items,
> then add them to your 'cart' as you decide to purchase them. When the time comes to
> process your order, the site seems to remember what items you have placed in your
> cart. But how does it know this, if HTTP requests are atomic and disconnected from
> each other?

To enable the maintenance of state between HTTP requests, it will suffice to provide
some mechanism for the communicating parties to establish agreements for transferring state information in HTTP messages. HTTP/1.1 establishes these agreements
through Set-Cookie and Cookie headers. Set-Cookie is a response header sent
by the server to the browser, setting attributes that establish state within the browser.
Cookie is a request header transmitted by the browser in subsequent requests to the
same (or related) server. It helps to associate requests with *sessions*.

Server applications that want to provide 'hints' for processing future requests can
do that by setting the Set-Cookie header:

```
Set-Cookie:    <name>=<value>[;    expires=<date>][;    path=<path>]
             [; domain=<domain name>][; secure]
```

Here, `<name>=<value>` is an *attribute/value pair* that is to be sent back by the browser in qualifying subsequent requests. The *path* and *domain* portions of this header delimit which requests qualify, by specifying the server domains and URL paths to which this cookie applies.

Domains may be set to suffixes of the originating server's host name containing at least two periods (three for domains other than `com`, `org`, `edu`, `gov`, `mil`, and `int`). The value of the domain attribute must represent the same domain to which the server belongs. For example, an application running on `cs.rutgers.edu` can set the domain to `.rutgers.edu`, but not to `.mit.edu`. A domain value of `.rutgers.edu` means that this cookie applies to requests destined for hosts with names of the form `*.rutgers.edu`. The value for the path attribute defaults to the path of the URL of the request, but may be set to any path prefix beginning at '/' which stands for the server root.

For subsequent requests directed at URLs where the domain and path match, the browser must include a `Cookie` header with the appropriate attribute/value pair.

The *expires* portion of the header sets the cutoff date after which the browser will discard any attribute/value pairs set in this header. (If the cutoff date is not specified, this means that the cookie should last for the duration of the current browser session only.) Finally, the *secure* keyword tells the browser to pass this cookie only through secure connections.

Cookie Jars

Browsers and other HTTP clients must maintain a 'registry' of cookies sent to them by servers. For cookies that are intended to last only for the duration of the current browser session, an in-memory table of cookies is sufficient. For cookies that are intended to last beyond the current session, persistent storage mechanisms for cookie information are required. Netscape Navigator keeps stored cookies in a `cookies.txt` file, while Internet Explorer maintains a folder where each file represents a particular stored cookie.

In this example, a server application running on the `cs.rutgers.edu` server generates a `Set-Cookie` header of the following form:

```
HTTP/1.1 200 OK
Set-Cookie: name=Leon; path=/test/; domain=.rutgers.edu
```

The domain is set to `.rutgers.edu` and the path is set to `/test/`. This instructs the browser to include a `Cookie` header with the value `Name=Leon` every time thereafter that a request is made for a resource at a URL on any Rutgers server where the URL path starts with `/test/`. The absence of the expiration date means that this cookie will be maintained only for the duration of the current browser session.

Now let's consider a more complicated example in which we rent a movie. We start with submitting a registration by visiting a URL that lets us sign in to a secure movie rental web site. Let's assume we have been prompted for authorization credentials by the browser and have provided them so that the browser can construct the `Authorization` header:

```
GET /movies/register HTTP/1.1
Host: www.sample-movie-rental.com
Authorization:...
```

Once the server has recognized and authenticated the user, it sends back a response containing a `Set-Cookie` header containing a client identifier:

```
HTTP/1.1 200 OK
Set-Cookie: CLIENT=Rich; path=/movies
...
```

From this point on, every time the browser submits a request directed at `"http://www.sample-movie.rental.com/movies/*"`, it will include a `Cookie` header containing the client identifier:

```
GET /movies/rent-recommended HTTP/1.1
Host: www.sample-movie-rental.com
Cookie: CLIENT=Rich
```

In this case, we are visiting a recommended movie page. The server response now contains a movie recommendation:

```
HTTP/1.1 200 OK
Set-Cookie: MOVIE=Matrix; path=/movies/
...
```

Now we request access to the movie. Note that, given the URL, we are sending back both the client identifier and the recommended movie identifier within the `Cookie` header.

```
GET /movies/access HTTP/1.1
Host: www.sample-movie-rental.com
Cookie: CLIENT=Rich; MOVIE=Matrix
```

We get back the acknowledgement containing access information to the recommended movie for future status checks:

```
HTTP/1.1 200 OK
Set-Cookie: CHANNEL=42; PASSWD=Matrix007; path=/movies/status/
...
```

Note that there are two new cookie values, 'CHANNEL' and 'PASSWD', but they are associated with URL path /movies/status/. Now, the browser will include movie access information with a status check request. Note that the Cookie header contains cookie values applicable to both the /movies/ path and the /movies/status/ path:

```
GET /movies/status/check HTTP/1.1
Host: www.sample-movie-rental.com
Cookie: CLIENT=Rich; MOVIE=Matrix; CHANNEL=42; PASSWD=Matrix007
```

Requests directed at URLs within the /movies/ path but not within the /movies/ status/ path will not include attribute-value pairs associated with the /movies/ status/ path:

```
GET /movies/access HTTP/1.1
Host: www.sample-movie-rental.com
Cookie: CLIENT=Rich; MOVIE=Matrix
```

3.6 EVOLUTION

HTTP has evolved a good deal since its inception in the early nineties, but the more it evolves, the more care is needed to support backward compatibility. Even though it has been a number of years since the introduction of HTTP/1.1, there are still many servers, browsers, and proxies in the real world that are HTTP/1.0 compliant but do not support HTTP/1.1. What's more, not all HTTP/1.1 programs revert to the HTTP/1.0 specification when they receive an HTTP/1.0 message.

In this section, we will discuss the reasoning behind some of the most important changes that occurred between the versions, and the compatibility issues that affected protocol designers' decisions, and the challenges facing Web application developers in dealing with these issues.

3.6.1 Virtual hosting

One of the challenges facing HTTP/1.1 designers was to provide support for *virtual hosting*, which is the ability to map multiple host names to a single IP address. For example, a single server machine may host web sites associated with a number of different domains. There must be a way for the server to determine the host for which a request is intended. In addition, the introduction of proxies into the request stream creates additional problems in ensuring that a request reaches its intended host.

In HTTP/1.0, a request passing through a proxy has a slightly different format from the request ultimately received by the destination server. As we have seen, the request that reaches the host has the following form, including only the *path* portion of the URL in the initial request line:

```
GET /q?s=YHOO HTTP/1.0
```

Requests that must pass through proxies need to include some reference to the destination server, otherwise that information would be lost and the proxy would have no idea which server should receive the request. For this reason, the full URL of the request is included in the initial request line, as shown below:

```
GET http://finance.yahoo.com/q?s=YHOO HTTP/1.0
```

Proxies that connect to the destination servers are responsible for editing requests that pass through them, to remove server information from request lines.

With the advent of HTTP/1.1, there is support for virtual hosting. Thus, we now need to retain server information in all requests since servers need to know which of the virtual hosts associated with a given web server is responsible for processing the request. The obvious solution would have been to make HTTP/1.1 browsers and proxies to always include server information:

```
GET http://finance.yahoo.com/q?s=YHOO HTTP/1.1
```

This would have been fine except that there are still HTTP/1.0 proxies out there that are ready to cut server information from request URLs every time they see one. Obviously, HTTP/1.0 proxies don't know anything about HTTP/1.1 and have no way of making a distinction between the two. Nonetheless, it is worth it to have this as a legal request format for both HTTP/1.1 servers and proxies. (There may come a day when we don't have to worry about HTTP/1.0 proxies any more.)

For now, we need a redundant source of information that will not be affected by any actions of HTTP/1.0 proxies. This is the reason for the `Host` header, which must be included with every HTTP/1.1 request:

```
GET http://finance.yahoo.com/q?s=YHOO HTTP/1.1
Host: finance.yahoo.com
```

Whether this request passes through either an HTTP/1.0 proxy or an HTTP/1.1 proxy, information about the ultimate destination of the request is preserved. Obviously, the request with abbreviated URL format (path portion only) must be supported as well:

```
GET /q?s=YHOO HTTP/1.1
Host: finance.yahoo.com
```

3.6.2 Caching support

In an earlier section, we described the mechanisms through which servers provide information about caching policies for server responses to browsers, proxies, and other clients. If the supplied headers tell the client that caching is feasible for this particular response, the client must then make a decision as to whether or not it should indeed use a cached version of the response that it already has available, rather than going back to the source location to retrieve the data.

In HTTP/1.0, the most popular mechanism for supporting browser-side caching was the use of HEAD requests. A request employing the HEAD method would return exactly the same response as its GET counterpart, but without the body. In other words, only the headers would be present, providing the requestor with all of the response's metadata without the overhead of transmitting the entire content of the response. Thus, assuming you have a cached copy of a previously requested resource, it is a sensible approach to submit a HEAD request for that resource, check the date provided in the Last-Modified header, and only resubmit a GET request if the date is later than that of the saved cache entry. This improves server throughput by eliminating the need for unnecessary extra requests. The only time the actual data need actually be retrieved is when the cache entry is deemed to be out of date.

HTTP/1.1 uses a more streamlined approach to this problem using two new headers: If-Modified-Since and If-Unmodified-Since. Going back to one of our earlier examples:

```
GET /~shklar/ HTTP/1.1
Host: www.cs.rutgers.edu
If-Modified-Since: Fri, 11 Feb 2001 22:28:00 GMT
```

Assuming there is a cache entry for this resource that expires at 22:28 on February 11, 2001, the browser can send a request for this resource with the If-Modified-Since header value set to that date and time. If the resource has *not* changed since that point in time, we get back the response with the 304 Not Modified status code and no body. Otherwise, we get back the body (which may itself be placed in the cache, replacing any existing cache entry for the same resource).

Alternatively, let's examine the following request:

```
GET /~shklar/ HTTP/1.1
Host: www.cs.rutgers.edu
If-Unmodified-Since: Fri, 11 Feb 2000 22:28:00 GMT
```

For this request, we either get back the unchanged resource or an empty response (no body) with the 412 Precondition Failed status code.

Both headers can be used in HTTP/1.1 requests to eliminate unnecessary data transmissions without the cost of extra requests.

3.6.3 Persistent connections

Since HTTP is by definition a *stateless* protocol, it was not designed to support persistent connections. A connection was supposed to last long enough for a browser to submit a request and receive a response. Extending the lifetime of a request beyond this was not supported.

Since the cost of connecting to a server across the network is considerable, there are a variety of mechanisms within many existing network protocols for reducing or eliminating that overhead by creating persistent connections. In HTTP, *cookies* provide a mechanism for persisting an application's *state* across connections, but it is frequently useful to allow connections themselves to persist for performance reasons.

For HTTP applications, developers came up with workarounds involving multipart MIME messages to get connections to persist across multiple independent bodies of content. (We saw an example of this when we discussed image animation using server push via multipart messages.)

Late in the lifecycle of HTTP/1.0, makers of HTTP/1.0 servers and browsers introduced the proprietary Connection: Keep-Alive header, as part of a somewhat desperate effort to support persistent connections in a protocol that wasn't designed to do so.

Not surprisingly, it does not work that well. Considering all the intermediate proxies that might be involved in the transmission of a request, there are considerable difficulties in keeping connections persistent using this mechanism. Just one intermediate proxy that lacks support for the Keep-Alive extension is enough to cause the connection to be broken.

HTTP/1.1 connections are all persistent by default, except when explicitly requested by a participating program via the `Connection: Close` header. It is entirely legal for a server or a browser to be HTTP/1.1 compliant without supporting persistent connections as long as they include `Connection: Close` with every message. Theoretically, including the `Connection: Keep-Alive` header in HTTP/1.1 messages makes no sense, since the *absence* of `Connection: Close` already means that the connection needs to be persistent.

However, there is no way to ensure that all proxies are HTTP/1.1 compliant and know to maintain a persistent connection. In practice, including `Connection: Keep-Alive` does provide a partial solution: it will work for those HTTP/1.0 proxies that support it as a proprietary extension.

HTTP/1.1 support for persistent connections includes *pipelining* requests: browsers can queue request messages without waiting for responses. Servers are responsible for submitting responses to browser requests in the order of their arrival. Browsers that support this functionality must maintain request queues, keep track of server responses, and resubmit requests that remain on queues if connections get dropped and reestablished. We will discuss HTTP/1.1 support for persistent connections in further detail when we discuss server and browser architecture.

3.7 SUMMARY

In this chapter, we have discussed the fundamental facets of the HTTP protocol. This discussion was not intended as an exhaustive coverage of all the protocol's features, but rather as an overview for understanding and working with current and future HTTP specifications from the World Wide Web Consortium. W3C specifications are the ultimate references that need to be consulted when architecting complex applications.

Understanding HTTP is critical to the design of advanced Web applications. It is a prerequisite for utilizing full power of the Internet technologies that are discussed in this book. Knowledge of the inner workings of HTTP promotes reasoning from first principles, and simplifies the daunting task of learning the rich variety of protocols and APIs that depend on its features. We recommend that you return to this chapter as we discuss other technologies.

3.8 QUESTIONS AND EXERCISES

1. Consider the following hyperlink:
   `<a href="http://www.cs.rutgers.edu/~shklar/">`
   What HTTP/1.0 request will get submitted by the browser?
   What HTTP/1.1 request will get submitted by the browser?
2. Consider the example above. Will these requests change if the browser is configured to contact an HTTP proxy? If yes, how?

3. What is the structure of a POST request? What headers have to be present in HTTP/1.0 and HTTP/1.1 requests?

4. Name two headers that, if present in an HTTP response, always have to be processed in a particular order. State the order and explain.

5. How can Multipart MIME be used to implement 'server push'? When is it appropriate? Construct a sample HTTP response implementing server push using Multipart MIME.

6. Suppose that a content provider puts up a 'ring' of related sites:

   ```
   www.site1.provider.hahaha.com
   www.site2.provider.hahaha.com
   www.site3.provider.hahaha.com
   www.site4.provider.hahaha.com
   www.site5.provider.hahaha.com
   ```

   Suppose now this provider wants *unsophisticated* users to remain 'sticky' to a particular site by preventing them from switching to a *different* site in the ring more frequently than once an hour. For example, after a user first accesses www.site4.provider.hahaha.com, she has to wait for at least an hour before being able to access another site in the ring but can keep accessing the same site as much as she wants.

   Hints: Use cookies, and look elsewhere if you need more than two or three lines to describe your solution.

7. Remember the example in which the server returns a redirect when a URL pointing to a directory does not contain a trailing slash? What would happen if the server did not return a redirect but returned an index.html file stored in that directory right away? Would that be a problem? If you are not sure about the answer, come back to this question after we discuss browser architecture.

BIBLIOGRAPHY

Gourley, D. and Totty, B. (2002) *HTTP: The Definitive Guide.* O'Reilly & Associates.
Krishnamurthy, B. and Rexford, J. (2001) *Web Protocols and Practice.* Addison-Wesley.
Loshin, P. (2000) *Big Book of World Wide Web RFCs.* Morgan Kaufmann.
Thomas, S. (2001) *HTTP Essentials.* John Wiley & Sons, Ltd.
Yeager, N. and McGrath, R. (1996) *Web Server Technology.* Morgan Kaufmann.

4 Web Servers

Web servers enable HTTP access to a 'Web site,' which is simply a collection of documents and other information organized into a tree structure, much like a computer's file system. In addition to providing access to static documents, modern Web servers implement a variety of protocols for passing requests to custom software applications that provide access to dynamic content. This chapter begins by describing the process of serving static documents, going on to explore the mechanisms used to serve dynamic data.

Dynamic content can come from a variety of sources. Search engines and databases can be queried to retrieve and present data that satisfies the selection criteria specified by a user. Measuring instruments can be probed to present their current readings (e.g. temperature, humidity). News feeds and wire services can provide access to up-to-the-minute headlines, stock quotes, and sports scores.

There are many methodologies for accessing dynamic data. The most prominent approach based on open standards is the *Common Gateway Interface* (CGI). While CGI is in widespread use throughout the Web, it has its limitations, which we discuss later in this chapter.

As a result, many alternatives to CGI have arisen. These include a number of proprietary template languages (some of which gained enough following to become *de facto* standards) such as *PHP, Cold Fusion*, Microsoft's *Active Server Pages* (ASP), and Sun's *Java Server Pages* (JSP), as well as Sun's *Java Servlet API*.

An ideal approach would allow the processes by which Web sites serve dynamic data to be established in a declarative fashion, so that those responsible for maintaining the site are not required to write custom code. This is an important thread in the evolution of Web servers, browsers and the HTTP protocol, but we have not yet reached this goal.

Later in this chapter, we discuss how Web servers process HTTP requests, and how that processing is affected by server configuration. We also discuss methods for providing robust server security.

4.1 BASIC OPERATION

Web servers, browsers, and proxies communicate by exchanging HTTP messages. The server receives and interprets HTTP requests, locates and accesses requested resources, and generates responses, which it sends back to the originators of the requests. The process of interpreting incoming requests and generating outgoing responses is the main subject of this section.

In Figure 4.1, we can see how a Web server processes incoming requests, generates outgoing responses, and transmits those responses back to the appropriate requestors. The *Networking* module is responsible for both receiving requests and transmitting responses over the network. When it receives a request, it must first pass it to the *Address Resolution* module, which is responsible for analyzing and 'pre-processing' the request. This pre-processing includes:

1. *Virtual Hosting*: if this Web server is providing service for multiple domains, determine the domain for which this request is targeted, and use the detected domain to select configuration parameters.

2. *Address Mapping*: determine whether this is a request for static or dynamic content, based on the URL path and selected server configuration parameters, and resolve the address into an actual location within the server's file system.

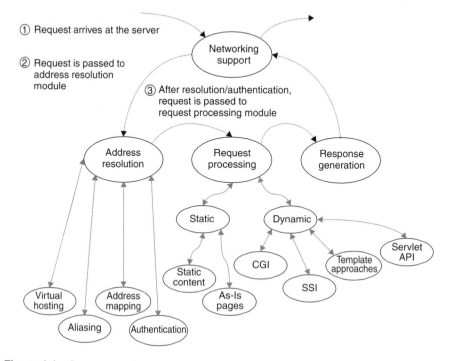

Figure 4.1   Server operation

3. *Authentication*: if the requested resource is protected, examine authorization credentials to see if the request is coming from an authorized user.

Once the pre-processing is complete, the request is passed to the *Request Processing* module, which invokes sub-modules to serve static or dynamic content as appropriate. When the selected sub-module completes its processing, it passes results to the *Response Generation* module, which builds the response and directs it to the *Networking* module for transmission.

It is important to remember that, since the HTTP protocol is stateless, the only information available to the server about a request is that which is contained within that request. As we shall learn later in this chapter, state may be maintained in the form of session information by server-side applications and application environments (e.g. servlet runners), but the server itself does not maintain this information.

4.1.1 HTTP request processing

Let us take a step back and recollect what has to happen for an HTTP request to arrive at the server. For the purposes of this example, we shall examine a series of transactions in which an end-user is visiting her friend's personal web site found at `http://mysite.org/`.

The process begins when the end user tells the browser to access the page found at the URL `http://mysite.org/pages/simple-page.html`. When the browser successfully receives and renders the page (Figures 4.2 and 4.3), the user sees that it has links to two other pages, which contain her friend's 'school links' (`school.html`) and 'home links' (`home.html`). Suppose now that the end user follows the link to her friend's 'school links' page.

> **You Say You Want a Resolution...**
>
> If the links found on the page are *relative URLs* (incomplete URLs meant to be interpreted relative to the current page), then they must be resolved so that the browser knows the complete URL referenced by the link. In the next chapter, we discuss the steps that browsers take to resolve a relative link into an absolute URL in order to construct and submit the request.

```
GET http://mysite.org/pages/simple-page.html HTTP/1.1
Host: mysite.org
User-Agent: Mozilla/4.75 [en] (WinNT; U)
```

Figure 4.2 Browser request to load the *simple-page.html* page

```
<HTML>
<HEAD><TITLE>Simple Page</TITLE></HEAD>
<BODY>
<H2>My Links</H2>
<ul>
<li><a href ="school.html">My school links</a></li>
<li><a href ="home.html">My home links</a></li>
</ul>
</BODY>
</HTML>
```

Figure 4.3 Simple HTML page

Notice that the request in Figure 4.2 does not contain the `Connection: close` header. This means that, if possible, the connection to the server should be left open so that it may be used to transmit further requests and receive responses. However, there is no guarantee that the connection will still be open at the time the user requests `school.html`. By that time, the server, a proxy, or even the browser itself might have broken it. Persistent connections are designed to improve performance, but should never be relied upon in application logic.

If the connection is still open, the browser uses it to submit the request for the school links page (Figure 4.4). Otherwise, the browser must first re-establish the connection. Depending on the browser configuration, it may either attempt to establish a direct connection to the server or connect via a proxy. Consequently, the server receives the request either directly from the browser or from the proxy.

For persistent connections, the server is responsible for maintaining queues of requests and responses. HTTP/1.1 specifies that within the context of a single continuously open connection, a series of requests may be transmitted. It also specifies that responses to these requests must be sent back in the order of request arrival (FIFO).

One common solution is for the server to maintain both the input and output queues of requests. When a request is submitted for processing, it is removed from the input queue and inserted on the output queue. Once the processing is complete, the request is marked for release, but it remains on the output queue while at least one of its predecessors is still there. When all of its predecessors have gone from the output queue it is released, and its associated response is sent back to the browser either directly or through a proxy.

Once the request is picked from the queue, the server resolves the request URL to the physical file location and checks whether the requested resource requires

```
GET http://mysite.org/pages/school.html HTTP/1.1
Host: mysite.org
User-Agent: Mozilla/4.75 [en] (WinNT; U)
```

Figure 4.4 Browser request to load the *school.html* page

authentication (Figure 4.1). If the authentication fails, the server aborts further processing and generates the response indicating an error condition (Section 3.4.3). If the authentication is not necessary or is successful, the server decides on the kind of processing required.

4.1.2 Delivery of static content

Web servers present both *static content* and *dynamic content*. Static content falls into two categories:

1. *static content pages*: static files containing HTML pages, XML pages, plain text, images, etc., for which HTTP responses must be constructed (including headers); and

2. *as-is pages*: pages for which complete HTTP responses (including headers) already exist and can be presented 'as is'.

For dynamic content, the server must take an explicit programmatic action to generate a response, such as the execution of an application program, the inclusion of information from a secondary file, or the interpretation of a template. This mode of processing includes *Common Gateway Interface* (CGI) programs, *Server-Side Include* (SSI) pages, *Java Server Pages* (JSP), *Active Server Pages* (ASP), and Java Servlets, among others.

We shall not attempt to describe all the details of these and other server mechanisms. Instead, we concentrate on describing the most common mechanisms and the underlying principles associated with them. Understanding the operating principles makes it easier to learn other similar mechanisms, and to develop new better mechanisms in the future.

Web servers use a combination of filename suffixes/extensions and URL prefixes to determine which processing mechanism should be used to generate a response. By default, it is assumed that a URL should be processed as a request for a static content page. However, this is only one of a number of possibilities. A URL path beginning with `/servlet/` might indicate that the target is a Java servlet. A URL path beginning with `/cgi-bin/` might indicate that the target is a CGI script. A URL where the target filename ends in `.cgi` might indicate this as well. URLs where the target filename ends in `.php` or `.cfm` might indicate that a template processing mechanism (e.g. PHP or Cold Fusion) should be invoked. We shall discuss address resolution in more detail in the section describing server configuration.

Static content pages

For a *static content page*, the server maps the URL to a file location relative to the server document root. In the example presented earlier in the chapter, we visited a page

```
HTTP/1.1 200 OK
Date: Tue, 29 May 2001 23:15:29 GMT
Last-Modified: Mon, 28 May 2001 15:11:01 GMT
Content-type: text/html
Content-length: 193
Server: Apache/1.2.5

<HTML>
<HEAD><TITLE>School Page</TITLE></HEAD>
<BODY>
<H2>My Links</H2>
<ul>
<li><a href ="classes.html">My classes</a></li>
<li><a href ="friends.html">My friends</a></li>
</ul>
</BODY>
</HTML>
```

Figure 4.5 Sample response to the request in Figure 4.4

on someone's personal web site, found at `http://mysite.org/pages/school.html`. The path portion of this URL, `/pages/school.html`, is mapped to an explicit filename within the server's local file system. If the Web server is configured so that the *document root* is `/www/doc`, then this URL will be mapped to a server file at `/www/doc/pages/school.html`.

For static pages, the server must retrieve the file, construct the response, and transmit it back to the browser. For persistent connections, the response first gets placed in the output queue before the transmission. Figure 4.5 shows the response generated for the HTTP request in Figure 4.4. As we discussed in the previous chapter, the first line of the response contains the status code that summarizes the result of the operation. The server controls browser rendering of the response through the `Content-Type` header that is set to a MIME type. Setting MIME types for static files is controlled through server configuration. In the simplest case, it is based on the mapping between file extensions and MIME types.

Even though desktop browsers have their own mappings between MIME types and file extensions, it is the server-side mapping that determines the `Content-Type` header of the response. It is this header, which determines how the browser should render the response content—*not* the filename suffix, or a browser heuristic based on content analysis.

An Experiment

If you have access to your own Web server, you can try experimenting with your browser and server to see how browser rendering is determined. Within the browser,

> map the file extension .html to text/plain instead of text/html, then visit an HTML page with your browser. You will notice that HTML pages are still rendered as hypertext. Then, try changing the same mapping on the server, map the file extension .html to text/plain. Reload the page in your browser, and you will see the HTML markup tags as plain text.

With all this in mind, it is important that the server set the Content-Type header to the appropriate MIME type so that the browser can render the content properly. The server may also set the Content-Length header to instruct the browser about the length of the content. This header is optional, and may not be present for dynamic content, because it is difficult to determine the size of the response before its generation is complete. Still, if it *is* possible to predict the size of the response, it is a good idea to include the Content-Length header.

We have already discussed HTTP support for caching. Later we come back to this example to discuss the Last-Modified header and its use by the browser logic in forming requests and reusing locally cached content. Note that, even though Last-Modified is not a required header, the server is expected to make its best effort to determine the most recent modification date of requested content and use it to set the header.

As-is pages

Suppose now that for whatever reason you do not want server logic to be involved in forming response headers and the status code. Maybe you are testing your browser or proxy, or maybe you want a quick and dirty fix by setting a special Content-Type for some pages. Then again, maybe you want an easy and convenient way to regularly change redirection targets for certain pages. It turns out there is a way to address all these situations—use the so-called 'as-is' pages. The idea is that such pages contain complete responses and the server is supposed to send them back 'as-is' without adding status codes or headers. That means that you can put together a desired response, store it on the server in a file that would be recognized by the server as an 'as-is' file, and be guaranteed to receive your unchanged response when the file is requested.

Using the 'as-is' mechanism we can control server output by manually creating and modifying response messages. The word 'manually' is of course the key here—whenever you want to change the response, you have to have to go in and edit it. This is convenient for very simple scenarios but does not provide an opportunity to implement even very basic processing logic.

4.1.3 Delivery of dynamic content

The original mechanisms for serving up dynamic content are *CGI* (*Common Gateway Interface*) and *SSI* (*Server Side Includes*). Today's Web servers use more sophisticated and more efficient mechanisms for serving up dynamic content, but CGI and SSI date back to the very beginnings of the World Wide Web, and it behooves us to understand these mechanisms before delving into the workings of the newer approaches.

CGI

CGI was the first consistent server-independent mechanism, dating back to the very early days of the World Wide Web. The original CGI specification can be found at `http://hoohoo.ncsa.uiuc.edu/cgi/interface.html`.

The CGI mechanism assumes that, when a request to execute a CGI script arrives at the server, a new 'process' will be 'spawned' to execute a particular application program, supplying that program with a specified set of parameters. (The terminology of 'processes' and 'spawning' is UNIX-specific, but the analog of this functionality is available for non-UNIX operating systems.)

The heart of the CGI specification is the designation of a fixed set of *environment variables* that all CGI applications know about and have access to. The server is supposed to use request information to populate variables in Table 4.1 (non-exhaustive list) from request information other than HTTP headers.

The server is responsible for always setting the SERVER_SOFTWARE, SERVER_NAME, and GATEWAY_INTERFACE environment variables, independent of information contained in the request. Other pre-defined variable names include CONTENT_TYPE and CONTENT_LENGTH that are populated from Content-Type and Content-Length headers. Additionally, every HTTP header is mapped to an environment variable by converting all letters in the name of the header to upper case, replacing dash

Table 4.1 Environment variables set from sources of information other then HTTP headers

SERVER_PROTOCOL	HTTP version as defined on the request line following HTTP method and URL.
SERVER_PORT	Server port used for submitting the request, set by the server based on the connection parameters.
REQUEST_METHOD	HTTP method as defined on the request line.
PATH_INFO	Extra path information in the URL. For example, if the URL is `http://mysite.org/cgi-bin/zip.cgi/test.html`, and `http://mysite.org/cgi-bin/zip.cgi` is the location of a CGI script, then `/test.html` is the extra path information.
PATH_TRANSLATED	Physical location of the CGI script on the server. In our example, it would be `/www/cgi-bin/zip.cgi` assuming that the server is configured to map the `/cgi-bin` path to the `/www/cgi-bin` directory.
SCRIPT_NAME	Set to the path portion of the URL, excluding the extra path information. In the same example, it's `/cgi-bin/zip.cgi`
QUERY_STRING	Information that follows the '?' in the URL.

with the underscore, and pre-pending the HTTP_ prefix. For example, the value of the User-Agent header gets stored in the HTTP_USER_AGENT environment variable, and the value of the Content-Type header gets stored in both CONTENT_TYPE and HTTP_CONTENT_TYPE environment variables.

It is important to remember that while names of HTTP headers do not depend upon the mechanism (CGI, servlets, etc.), names of the environment variables are specific to the CGI mechanism. Some early servlet runners expected names of the CGI environment variables to retrieve header values because their implementers were CGI programmers that did not make the distinction. These servlet runners performed internal name transformations according to the rules defined for the CGI mechanism (e.g. Content-Type to CONTENT_TYPE), which was a wrong thing to do. These problems are long gone, and you would be hard pressed to find a servlet runner that does it now, but they illustrate the importance of understanding that names of CGI environment variables have no meaning outside of the CGI context.

The CGI mechanism was defined as a set of rules, so that programs that abide by these rules would run the same way on different types of HTTP servers and operating systems. That works as long as these servers support the CGI specification, which evolved to a suite of specifications for different operating systems.

CGI was originally introduced for servers running on UNIX, where a CGI program always executes as a process with the body of the request available as standard input, and with HTTP headers, URL parameters, and the HTTP method available as environment variables. For Windows NT/2000 servers the CGI program runs as an *application process*. With these systems, there is no such thing as 'standard input' (as there is in a UNIX environment), so standard input is simulated using temporary files. Windows environment variables are similar to UNIX environment variables. Information passing details are different for other operating systems. For example, Macintosh computers pass system information through Apple Events. For simplicity, we use the CGI specification as it applies to UNIX servers for the rest of this section. You would do well to consult server documentation for information passing details for your Web server.

Since the CGI mechanism assumes spawning a new process per request and terminating this process when the request processing is complete, the lifetime of a CGI process is always a single request. This means that even processing that is common for all requests has to be repeated every time. CGI applications may sometimes make use of persistent storage that survives individual requests, but persistence is a non-standard additional service that is out of scope of what is guaranteed by HTTP servers.

Perl Before Swine

You probably noticed that CGI programs are frequently called 'CGI scripts.' This is because they are often implemented using a scripting language, the most popular of these being Perl. It is very common to see texts describing the mechanisms of 'Perl/CGI programming.'

While Perl is extremely popular, it is not the only language available for implementing CGI programs. Since Perl is popular, we shall use it in our examples here. There is no reason why you cannot use C or any other programming language, as long as that language provides access to the message body, headers, and other request information in a manner that conforms to the CGI specification.

The advantage of using Perl is that it is portable: scripts written in Perl can execute on any system with a Perl interpreter. The price you pay for using Perl is performance: because Perl scripts are interpreted, they run more slowly than programs written in a compiled language like C.

Figure 4.6 shows a simple HTML page containing a form that lets users specify their names and zip codes. The ACTION parameter of a FORM tag references a server application that can process form information. (It does not make sense to use forms if the ACTION references a static page!)

Figure 4.7 shows the HTTP request that is submitted to the server when the user fills out the form and clicks on the 'submit' button. Notice that the entered information is *URL-encoded*: spaces are converted to plus signs, while other punctuation characters (e.g. equal signs and ampersands) are transformed to a percent sign ('%') followed by two-digit hexadecimal equivalents of replaced characters in the ASCII character set.

Also, notice that the `Content-Type` header is set to `application/x-www-form-urlencoded`, telling the server and/or server applications to expect form data. Do not confuse the `Content-Type` of the response that caused the browser to render this page (in this case `text/html`) with the `Content-Type` associated with the request generated by the browser when it submits the form to the server. Form data submitted from an HTML page, WML page, or an applet would have the same `Content-Type`—`application/x-www-form-urlencoded`.

```
<HTML>
<HEAD><TITLE>Simple Form</TITLE></HEAD>
<BODY>
<H2>Simple Form</H2>
<FORM ACTION="http://mysite.org/cgi-bin/zip.cgi" METHOD="post">
Zip Code: <INPUT SIZE="5" NAME="zip">
Name: <INPUT SIZE="30" NAME="name">
<INPUT TYPE="submit" VALUE="set zip">
</FORM>
<BODY>
</HTML>
```

Figure 4.6 Sample form for submitting user name and zip code

```
POST http://mysite.org/cgi-bin/zip.cgi HTTP/1.1
Host: mysite.org
User-Agent: Mozilla/4.75 [en] (WinNT; U)
Content-Length: 26
Content-Type: application/x-www-form-urlencoded
Remote-Address: 127.0.0.1
Remote-Host: demo-portable

zip=08540&name=Leon+Shklar
```

Figure 4.7 HTTP request submitted by the browser for the zip code example in Figure 4.6

The server, having received the request, performs the following steps:

1. Determines that /cgi-bin/zip.cgi has to be treated as a CGI program. This decision may be based on either a configuration parameter declaring /cgi-bin to be a CGI directory, or the .cgi file extension that is mapped to the CGI processing module.

2. Translates /cgi-bin/zip.cgi to a server file system location based on the server configuration (e.g. /www/cgi-bin/zip.cgi).

3. Verifies that the computed file system location (/www/cgi-bin/) is legal for CGI executables.

4. Verifies that zip.cgi has *execute* permissions for the user id that is used to run the server (e.g. nobody). (This issue is relevant only on UNIX systems, where processes run under the auspices of a designated user id. This may not apply to non-UNIX systems.)

5. Sets environment variables based on the request information.

6. Creates a child process responsible for executing the CGI program, passes it the body of the request in the standard input stream, and directs the standard output stream to the server module responsible for processing the response and sending it back to the browser.

7. On the termination of the CGI program, the response processor parses the response and, if missing, adds the default status code, default Content-Type, and headers that identify the server and server software.

To avoid errors in processing request parameters that may either be present in the query string of the request URL (for GET requests) or in the body of the request (for POST requests), CGI applications must decompose the ampersand-separated parameter string into URL-encoded name/value pairs prior to decoding them.

The example in Figure 4.8 is a function found in a Perl script, which takes a reference to an associative array and populates it with name/value pairs either from

```
sub ReadFormFields
{
        # set reference to the array passed into ReadFormFields
        my $fieldsRef = shift;
        my($key, $val, $buf_tmp, @buf_parm);

        #Read in form contents
        $buf_tmp = " ";
        read(STDIN,$buf_tmp,$ENV{'CONTENT_LENGTH'});
        $buf_tmp = $ENV{QUERY_STRING} if (!$buf_tmp);

        @buf_parm = split(/&/,$buf_tmp);
        #Split form contents into tag/value associative array
        #prior to decoding
        foreach $parm (@buf_parm) {
                # Split into key and value
                ($key, $val) = split(/=/,$parm);

                # Change +'s to spaces and restore all hex values
                $val =~ s/\+/ /g;
                $val =~ s/%([a-fA-F0-9][a-fA-F0-9])/
                   pack("C",hex($1))/ge;

                # Use \0 to separate multiple entries per field name
                $$fieldsRef{$key} .= '\0' if (defined($$fieldsRef
                   {$key}));
                $$fieldsRef{$key} .= $val;
        }
        return($fieldsRef);
}
```

Figure 4.8   Form and Query String processing in CGI code

the request URL's query string (for a GET request) or from the body of the HTTP
request (for a POST request). For forms found in HTML pages, the choice of request
method (GET or POST) is determined by the METHOD parameter in the FORM tag. In
either case, the request parameters consist of ampersand-separated URL-encoded
name/value pairs. In our example, the browser composed the body of the request
from information populated in the form found in Figure 4.6—zip=08540&name
=Leon+Shklar. The CGI script that invokes the ReadFormFields function would
pass it the reference to an associative array. The read command is used to read
the number of bytes defined by the Content-Length header from the body of the
request. Note that read would be blocked when attempting to read more bytes than
available from the body of the request, which will not happen if the Content-
Length header is set properly. Real applications should take precautions to ensure
proper timeouts, etc.

Having read the body of the request into the `$buf_tmp` variable, the next step is to split it into parts using the *ampersand* as the separator, and use the `foreach` loop to split parts into keys and values along the '=' signs. Every value has to be URL-decoded which means that '+' signs need to get turned back into spaces and three-character control sequences (e.g. `%27`) need to get translated back into the original characters. It is very important that keys and values are separated prior to URL-decoding to avoid confusing the splitting operations with '&' and '=' signs that may be contained in the values. (For example, a parameter value may itself contain an encoded equal sign or ampersand, and URL-decoding before separation could cause a misinterpretation of the parameters.)

Figure 4.9 contains a sample CGI program that uses the `ReadFormFields` function to retrieve key/value pairs from request bodies. The `PrintFormFields` function simply prints the `Content-Type` header and the html document with key/value pairs. The empty associative array `fields` is populated by `ReadFormFields` and then passed to the `PrintFormFields` function.

CGI programs may output status codes and HTTP headers but the HTTP server is responsible for augmenting the output to make them legitimate HTTP responses. In the example, the server has to add the status line and may include additional

```perl
#!/usr/local/bin/perl

sub ReadFormFields { ... }

sub PrintFormFields
{
        my $fieldsRef = shift;
        my $key, $value;

        print "Content-Type: text/html\n\n";
        print "<html>\n<head><title>hello</title></head>\n";
        print "<body>\n";
        foreach $key (keys(%$fieldsRef)) {
                $value = $$fieldsRef{$key};
                print "<h3>$key: $value</h3>\n";
        }
        print "</body>\n</html>\n";
}

&ReadFormFields(\%fields);
&PrintFormFields(\%fields);

exit 0;
```

Figure 4.9 Printing parameters in CGI code

HTTP headers including Content-Length, Date, and Server. Most of the time this saves CGI programmers unnecessary hassle but there are situations where you would rather know exactly what is being sent back to the client without letting the server touch the CGI output. Such situations are rare but they do exist and may become a great source of frustration. To avoid this problem, CGI designers introduced the 'no-parse-header' condition, which requires that HTTP servers leave alone the output of CGI scripts with names that start with 'nph-'.

There are many commercial and open source Perl packages, which insulate CGI programmers from the HTTP protocol. There is nothing wrong with using convenience functions, but it is important to understand the underlying data structures and protocols. Without that, finding and fixing problems may turn out to be very difficult. Moreover, understanding HTTP and mappings between the HTTP and CGI specifications simplifies learning other protocols and APIs for building Internet applications.

Finally, you can use any language, not only Perl. CGI specification makes no assumptions about the implementation language, and as long as you access environment variables and standard input (or their equivalents for non-Unix operating systems), you can use any language you want. Nevertheless, the majority of CGI applications are implemented in Perl. It is no surprise, since you would use the CGI mechanism for its simplicity, not performance. The additional overhead of interpreting a Perl program should not matter that much when balanced against the convenience of using an interpreted scripting language.

As a server implementer, you are responsible for detecting CGI requests, starting a new child process for each CGI request, passing request information to the newly initiated process using environment variables and the input stream, and post-processing the response. Response processing that may include adding missing headers and the status code, does not apply to no-parse-header requests.

SSI mechanism

The *Server Side Includes* specification (SSI) dates back almost as far as the CGI specification. It provides mechanisms for including auxiliary files (or the results of the execution of CGI scripts) into an HTML page. The original specification for SSI can be found at http://hoohoo.ncsa.uiuc.edu/docs/tutorials/includes.html.

Let us look at the sample CGI script in Figure 4.9. The PrintFormFields function outputs html tags, and if you want to change html, you have to go back and change the code. This is not at all desirable, since it incredibly complicates maintenance. The most obvious solution is to create partially populated HTML pages, or templates, and fill in the blanks with the output of CGI scripts and, perhaps, other server-side operations. SSI is not a replacement for CGI, but it is an easy way to add dynamic content to pages without a lot of work.

SSI macros must have the following format:

```
<!--#command attr1="value1" attr2="value2" -->
```

The syntax is designed to place SSI commands within HTML comments ensuring that unprocessed commands are ignored when the page is sent to the browser. Valid commands include 'config' for controlling the parsing, 'echo' for outputting values of environment variables, 'include' for inserting additional files, 'fsize' for outputting file size information, and the most dangerous, 'exec', for executing server-side programs. The popular use of the 'exec' command is to invoke CGI scripts as in "exec cgi http://mysite.org/cgi-bin/zip.cgi", but it also may be used to run other server-side programs.

Using SSI to simplify the CGI script in Figure 4.9, we eliminate the need to print out the Content-Type header and the static part of the page. In the SSI example in Figure 4.10, the shorter CGI script is invoked to fill blanks in the page, and the server uses the file extension to set Content-Type. You can refer to the URL of an SSI page in the action attribute of the form tag (e.g. instead of the CGI URL in Figure 4.6), but only if you change the request method to GET. The server will produce an error if you try the POST—not at all surprising, since the CGI specification requires that bodies of POST requests be passed to CGI scripts as standard input. It is not clear what it means to pass the standard input stream to a SSI page. Making it a requirement for the server to pass bodies of POST requests to CGI scripts referenced in SSI pages would have complicated the implementation of the

```
#!/usr/local/bin/perl

sub ReadFormFields { ... }

sub PrintFormFields
{
        my $fieldsRef = shift;
        my $key, $value;

        foreach $key (keys(%$fieldsRef)) {
                $value = $$fieldsRef{$key};
                print "<h3>$key: $value</h3>\n";
        }
}

&ReadFormFields(\%fields);
&PrintFormFields(\%fields);

exit 0;
```

Figure 4.10 Using SSI instead of the CGI program from Figure 4.9

SSI mechanism. Moreover, SSI pages may include many 'exec cgi' instructions, and it is unclear what it means to pass the same input stream to multiple CGI scripts. A sample SSI page is shown below:

```
<html>
<head><title>hello</title></head>
<body>
<!--#exec cgi http://mysite.org/cgi-bin/zip-ssi.cgi -->
</body>
</html>
```

As you no doubt remember, servers do not parse static pages—it is browsers, which are responsible for parsing pages and submitting additional requests for images and other embedded objects. This is not possible for SSI—the server cannot discover and execute SSI macros without parsing pages. In practice, pages containing SSI macros get assigned different file extensions (e.g. .shtml) to indicate the different kind of processing. Later, when we discuss server configuration, we shall look at how different file extensions may be associated with different server-side processing modules.

CGI scripts that are invoked within SSI pages have access to additional context information that is not available in the standalone mode. The context information is passed through environment variables; DOCUMENT_NAME, DOCUMENT_URI, and LAST_MODIFIED describe the SSI page—other environment variables (QUERY_STRING_UNESCAPED, DATE_LOCAL, DATE_GMT) are primarily the matter of convenience. The output of a standalone CGI script is sent to the browser after the server makes its final say in filling up the gaps—default values for required HTTP headers and the status code. When the CGI script is invoked from a SSI page, the server does not perform any error checking on the output. Responses that include the Location header are transformed into HTML anchors, but other than that, response bodies get included in the page no matter what the Content-Type of the response. You have to be careful or you can end up with the horrible GIF binaries mixed up with your HTML tags.

SSI mechanism provides simple and convenient means for adding dynamic content to existing pages without having to generate the entire page. Nothing comes free, and the price of convenience in using SSI is both the additional load on the server and security worries, since fully enabling SSI means allowing page owners to execute server-side programs. The security concerns led server administrators to impose very serious limitations on the SSI mechanism, which in turn limits the portability of SSI pages. If portability and performance are not major concerns, SSI may be a convenient way to implement and maintain applications that collect information from different sources.

4.2 ADVANCED MECHANISMS FOR DYNAMIC CONTENT DELIVERY

Even after you have built a Web server that performs basic tasks discussed in Section 4.1, there is still much to do. In this section, we discuss alternative mechanisms for building server-side applications. In subsequent sections, we discuss advanced features including server configuration and security.

4.2.1 Beyond CGI and SSI

CGI is a simple mechanism for implementing portable server-side applications. It is employed ubiquitously throughout the Web. However, there are a number of problems associated with CGI processing. Its main deficiency is performance. Processing a request that invokes a CGI script requires the spawning of a child process to execute that script (plus another process if the script is written in an interpreted language such as Perl). Moreover, any initialization and other processing that might be common to all requests must be repeated for every single request.

SSI has similar deficiencies when its command processing employs CGI under the hood. It adds the additional performance penalty by requiring servers to parse SSI pages. Most importantly, SSI may represent a serious security risk, especially when not configured carefully by the server administrator. The SSI mechanism is not scaleable, and provides only limited opportunities for reuse.

With this in mind, a number of other approaches to dynamic content processing arose in the Web server environment.

4.2.2 Native APIs (ISAPI and NSAPI)

Efficiency concerns may be addressed by using native server APIs. A *native API* is simply a mechanism providing direct 'hooks' into the Web server's application programming interface. Use of a native API implies the use of compiled code that is optimized for use within the context of a specific Web server environment. NSAPI and ISAPI are two approaches employed by Netscape's Web server software and Microsoft's IIS, respectively.

The problem is that there is no commonality or consistency amongst these native APIs. They are different from each other, and code written for one environment cannot be reused in another. This makes it impossible to implement portable applications.

4.2.3 FastCGI

FastCGI is an attempt to combine the portability of CGI applications with the efficiency of non-portable applications based on server APIs. The idea is simple:

instead of requiring the spawning of a new process every time a CGI script is to be executed, FastCGI allows processes associated with CGI scripts to 'stay alive' after a request has been satisfied. This means that new processes do not have to be spawned again and again, since the same process can be reused by multiple requests. These processes may be initialized once without endlessly re-executing initialization code.

Server modules that enable FastCGI functionality talk to HTTP servers via their own APIs. These APIs attempt to hide the implementation and configuration details from FastCGI applications, but developers still need to be aware of the FastCGI implementation, as the various modules are not compatible with each other. Therein lies the problem: to ensure true portability, FastCGI functionality has to be supported across the board in a consistent and compatible fashion for all different HTTP servers. The failure of FastCGI modules to proliferate to main HTTP servers is the main cause of its eventual disappearance from the server-side application scene. Perhaps it would have worked, except that a much better technology (*servlets*) came along before FastCGI gained universal support, and FastCGI went the way of the dinosaurs.

4.2.4 Template processing

Another approach used to serve dynamic content involves the use of template processors. In this approach, templates are essentially HTML files with additional 'tags' that prescribe methods for inserting dynamically generated content from external sources. The template file contains HTML that provides general page layout parameters, with the additional tags discretely placed so that content is placed appropriately on the rendered page. Among the most popular template approaches are *PHP* (an open source product), *Cold Fusion* (from Allaire/Macromedia), and *Active Server Pages* or *ASP* (from Microsoft).

To some degree, advanced template processing approaches could be considered 'SSI on steroids'. While SSI directives can perform simple tasks such as external file inclusion and the embedding of CGI program output within a page, advanced template processors provide sophisticated functionality. This functionality, which is found in many programming and scripting languages, includes:

- submitting database queries,

- iterative processing (analogous to repetitive 'for-each' looping), and

- conditional processing (analogous to 'if' statements).

The example in Figure 4.11 employs one of the popular template approaches, Allaire/Macromedia's *Cold Fusion*, and demonstrates each of these functions. (Note that Cold Fusion's special tags look like HTML tags, but begin with CF....) The <CFQUERY> block tag describes a database query to be executed. The <CFIF> block

```
<CFQUERY NAME="query1" DATASOURCE="oracle" ...>
   SELECT id, columnX, columnY, columnZ
     FROM TABLE1
    WHERE id = #substitution-parameter#
</CFQUERY>

<CFIF query1.recordcount GT 0>
   <TABLE>
      <CFOUTPUT QUERY="query1">
         <TR>
            <TD>#columnX#</TD>
            <TD>#columnY#</TD>
            <TD>#columnZ#</TD>
         </TR>
      </CFOUTPUT>
   </TABLE>
</CFIF>
```

Figure 4.11   Sample template (Cold Fusion)

tag delimits a section that should only be included in the resulting page if the result set returned from the query was not empty (record count greater than zero). Within that block, the <CFOUTPUT> block tag specifies contents of an HTML table row that should be repeated (with proper value substitution) for each row in the query's result set. (Note that text found within Cold Fusion block tags that is delimited by pound signs indicates a substitution parameter, e.g. #text#). See Figure 4.11.

The advantage of this approach is that, ostensibly, templates can be created and maintained by *page designers*, who have background in HTML and web graphics but are not programmers. Special tags that are 'extensions' to HTML are considered similar enough to SSI tags to put their usage within the grasp of an average page designer. Employing these tags requires less expertise than writing code.

The problem is that the more sophisticated these template approaches get, the more they begin to resemble programming languages, and the more likely it becomes that this perceived advantage of simplicity will not be realized. Some template approaches provide advanced functionality by allowing *scripting* within the template, but this only blurs the line between scripts and templates. It also means that, in all likelihood, two sets of people will need to be responsible for building (and *maintaining*) the template: people with web design skills and people with programming skills.

Separation of Content and Presentation

We hear a lot about the notion of 'separating content from presentation.' It is often taken as an axiom handed down from the mountaintop. However, we should know *why* it is so important.

The example described above provides one reason. When you mix the logic required to retrieve content with the design parameters associated with its presentation, both logic and design elements are contained within the same module. Who is responsible for maintaining this module? A programmer, who may not be skilled in the fine art of page design, or a web designer, who may not be an expert when it comes to programming?

What would be ideal is an approach that explicitly and naturally separates data access logic from presentation. Programmers would maintain the logic component, which encapsulates access to desired data. Designers would maintain the presentation component, though the target format need not be HTML. Designers could create different presentations for different audiences, without affecting the data access logic. Likewise, logic of the data access component could be changed, but as long as it provides the same interface to the data, presentation components do not need to be modified. Moreover, designers and programmers would not "step on each other" while maintaining the same module.

The *model-view-controller* (*MVC*) design pattern provides precisely such an approach. We shall be discussing an approach that can be used to implement this pattern later in the book.

4.2.5 Servlets

A better approach to serving dynamic content is the Servlet API—Java technology for implementing applications that are portable not only across different servers but also across different hardware platforms and operating systems. Like FastCGI, the servlet API uses server application modules that remain resident and reusable, rather than requiring the spawning of a new process for every request. Unlike FastCGI, the servlet API is portable across servers, operating systems, and hardware platforms. Servlets execute the same way in any environment that provides a compliant *servlet runner*. The servlet API generated very strong following; it is widely used in a variety of Web server environments.

Implementers of Java servlets do not need to have any knowledge of the underlying servers and their APIs. Interfacing with the server API is the responsibility of servlet runners, which include a Java Virtual Machine and are designed to communicate with host HTTP servers. The servlet runner does this by talking directly to the server API through the Java Native Interface (JNI), or by running in a stand-alone mode and listening on an internal port for servlet requests that are redirected from general-purpose HTTP servers.

Servlets are Java programs that have access to information in HTTP requests and that generate HTTP responses that are sent back to browsers and proxies. Remember the CGI program that was shown in Figures 4.9 and 4.10? Let us see how the same functionality can be implemented as a servlet (Figure 4.12).

As you can see, methods defined on the `HttpServletRequest` class take care of extracting and decoding parameters and setting response headers. Notice that the `HttpServlet` class has different methods (`doGet()` and `doPost()`) for different HTTP methods. In this example, we want to retrieve parameters passed in both GET and POST requests. We have the luxury of using exactly the same code in both cases—`getParameterNames` and `getParameter` methods adjust their behavior depending on the type of the request and protect programmers from having to know whether to retrieve parameters from the query string or the body of the request.

We shall come back to servlets later in the book. It is worth noting that, unlike CGI scripts, a servlet is capable of handling multiple requests concurrently. Servlets may also forward requests to other servers and servlets. Of course, forwarding a request to another server is accomplished by using HTTP even as programmers stick to method calls that are defined in the servlet API.

4.2.6 Java Server Pages

The Java Server Pages (JSP) mechanism came about as Sun's response to Microsoft's own template processing approach, Active Server Pages. JSP was originally intended to relieve servlet programmers from the tedium of having to generate static HTML or XML markup through Java code. Today's JSP processors take static markup pages with embedded JSP instructions and translate them into servlets, which then get compiled into Java byte code. More precisely, JSP 1.1-compliant processors generate Java classes, which extend the `HttpJspBase` class that implements the `Servlet` interface. What this means is that JSP serves as a pre-processor for servlet programmers. The resulting classes are compiled modules that execute faster than a processor that interprets templates at request time.

In contrast with earlier template approaches, most of which used proprietary tags, JSP instructions are formatted as XML tags, combined with Java code fragments. Together, these tags and code fragments express the logic to transform JSP pages into the markup used to present the desired content.

It is not necessary for all application logic to be included in the page—the embedded code may reference other server-based resources. JSP ability to reference server-based components is similar to SSI support for referencing CGI scripts. It helps to separate the page logic from its look and feel and supports a reusable component-based design.

To illustrate (Figure 4.13), the task of displaying parameters of HTTP requests just got much simpler compared to the servlet example in Figure 4.12. Notice, that we do not have to separately override the `doGet` and `doPost` methods since the `HttpJspBase` class is designed to override the `service` method (`doGet` and `doPost` are invoked from `HttpServlet`'s `service` method).

Unlike servlets, the JSP technology is designed for a much wider audience since it does not require the same level of programming expertise. Moreover, we do not

```
import java.io.*;
import java.util.*;
import javax.servlet.*;
import javax.servlet.http.*;

public class FormServlet extends HttpServlet {
    public void doGet(HttpServletRequest request,
                        HttpServletResponse response)
        throws IOException, ServletException
    {
        response.setContentType("text/html");
        PrintWriter out = response.getWriter();
        out.println("<html>\n<head><title>hello</title></head>");
        out.println("<body>");

        Enumeration e = request.getParameterNames();
        while (e.hasMoreElements()) {
            String name = (String)e.nextElement();
            String value = request.getParameter(name);
            out.println("<h3>" + name + ": " + value + "</h3>");
        }
        out.println("</body>\n</html>");
    }

    public void doPost(HttpServletRequest request,
                        HttpServletResponse response)
        throws IOException, ServletException
    {
        doGet(request, response);
    }
}
```

Figure 4.12 Parameter processing in Servlets

```
<html>
<head><title>hello!</title></head>
<body>
<%@ page import ="java.util.*" %>
<% Enumeration e = request.getParameterNames();
    while (e.hasMoreElements()) {
        String name  = (String)e.nextElement();
        String value = request.getParameter(name);
%>
<h3><%=name%>:<%=value%></h3>
<% } %>
</body>
</html>
```

Figure 4.13 Parameter processing in JSP

have to pay as high a price as we did when using SSI technology instead of CGI scripts. As you remember, using SSI meant additional parsing overhead and issues with security. This is not a problem with JSP pages that are translated into servlets, which, in turn, are compiled into Java byte code.

4.2.7 Future directions

Sun sees the use of servlets and JSP as a next generation approach for web application development. But in and of itself, the combination of servlets with JSPs does not enforce or even encourage a truly modular approach to writing server-side applications. The example described in the previous section does not decouple data access logic from presentation logic, in fact it intermixes them excessively.

Still, this combination *can* be used effectively to implement the *Model-View-Controller* design pattern, which specifically enforces separation of content from presentation in a methodical modular way. Sun refers to this approach as *JSP Model 2*. It involves the use of a controlling 'action' servlet (the *Controller* component) that interfaces with JavaBeans that encapsulate access to data (the *Model* component), presenting the results of this processing through one or more Java Server Pages (the *View* component).

Strict employment of this design pattern ensures that there is true separation of content and presentation. The controlling action servlet routes the request to ensure the execution of appropriate tasks. The JavaBeans (referenced in JSP "useBean" tags) encapsulate access to underlying data. JSPs refer to discrete data elements exposed in Java beans, allowing those data elements to be presented as desired.

Part of the elegance of this approach is the flexibility in the presentation component. The same application can serve data to be presented on a variety of platforms, including HTML browsers running on desktop computers and WML applications running on handheld devices. Different JSPs can tailor the presentation for appropriate target platforms. Multiple view components could be developed for the same target platform to enable personalized/customized presentations.

The *Struts Application Framework* (developed by the *Apache Group* as part of its *Jakarta Project*) provides a set of mechanisms to enable the development of Web applications using this paradigm. Through a combination of Java classes, JSP taglibs, and specifications for action mappings as XML configuration files, Struts provides a means to achieve the goal of truly modular and maintainable Web applications.

The ultimate goal would be a truly declarative framework, where all components could be specified and no coding would be required. Although we are not there yet, existing mechanisms like JSP Model 2 and Struts are moving us further along the path to that goal.

4.3 ADVANCED FEATURES

Historically, server evolution is going hand-in-hand with the evolution of the HTTP protocol. Looking at the changes that were introduced in the HTTP/1.1 specification, some of them are attempts to unify and legitimize proprietary extensions that were implemented in HTTP/1.0 servers, while others are genuinely new features that fill the need for extended functionality. For example, some HTTP/1.0 servers supported the `Connection: Keep-Alive` header even though it was never a part of the HTTP/1.0 specification. Unfortunately, for it to work properly it was necessary for every single proxy in between the server and the browser, and of course the browser itself, to support it as well. As we already discussed in Chapter 3, HTTP/1.1-compliant servers, browsers, and proxies have to assume that connections are persistent unless told otherwise via the `Connection: Close` header. Examples of new features include virtual hosting, chunked transfers, and informational (1xx) status codes.

4.3.1 Virtual hosting

As we already discussed in the section dedicated to HTTP evolution, virtual hosting is the ability to map multiple server and domain names to a single IP address. The lack of support for such feature in HTTP/1.0 was a glaring problem for Internet Service Providers (ISP). After all, it is needed when you register a new domain name and want your ISP to support it.

HTTP/1.1 servers have a number of responsibilities with regard to virtual hosting:

1. Use information in the required `Host` header to identify the virtual host.

2. Generate error responses with the proper `400 Bad Request` status code in the absence of `Host`.

3. Support absolute URLs in requests, even though there is no requirement that the server identified in the absolute URL matches the `Host` header.

4. Support isolation and independent configuration of document trees and server-side applications between different virtual hosts that are supported by the same server installation.

Most widely used HTTP/1.1 servers support virtual hosting. They make the common distinction between *physical* and *logical* configuration parameters. Physical configuration parameters are common for all virtual hosts; they control listening ports, server processes, limits on the number of simultaneously processed requests and the number of persistent connections, and other physical resources. Logical parameters may differ between virtual hosts; they include the location and configuration of the document tree and server-side applications, directory access options, and MIME type mappings.

4.3.2 Chunked transfers

The chances are there were a number of occasions when you spent long minutes sitting in front of your browser waiting for a particularly slow page. It could be because of the slow connection or it could be that the server application is slow. Either way you have to wait even though all you need may be to take a quick look at the page before you move on. HTTP/1.1 specification introduced the notion of *transfer encoding* as well as the first kind of transfer encoding—*chunked*—that is designed to enable processing of partially transmitted messages.

According to the specification, the server is obligated to decode HTTP requests containing the `Content-Transfer-Encoding: chunked` header prior to passing it to server applications. A similar obligation is imposed on the browser, as will be discussed in the next chapter. Server applications, of course, may produce chunked responses, which are particularly recommended for slow applications.

Figure 4.14 demonstrates a sample HTTP response—note the `Content-Transfer-Encoding: chunked` header indicating the encoding of the body. The first line of the body starts with the hexadecimal number indicating the length of the first chunk ('1b' or decimal 28) and is followed with the optional comment preceded by a semicolon. The next line contains exactly 28 bytes, and is followed by another line containing the length of the second chunk ('10' or decimal 16). The second chunk is followed with the line containing '0' as the length of the next chunk, which indicates the end of the body. The body may be followed with additional headers—they are actually called *footers* since they follow the body; their role is to provide information about the body that may not be obtained until the body generation is complete.

It may seem counter-intuitive that a browser request would be so huge as to merit separating it into chunks, but think about file transfer using PUT or POST requests. It gets a bit interesting with POST requests—try defining an HTML form with different input tags at least one of which refers to a file; upon submitting the form the browser creates the request with the `Content-Type` header set to `multipart/form-data`.

```
HTTP/1.1 200 OK
Content-Type: text/plain
Content-Transfer-Encoding: chunked

1b; Ignore this
abcdefghijklmnopqrstuvwxyza
10
1234567890abcdef
0
a-footer: a-value
another-footer: another value
```

Figure 4.14   Chunked transfer

Chunked encoding may not be applied across different body parts of a multipart message but the browser may apply it to any body part separately, e.g. the one containing the file.

Chunked encoding is a powerful feature, but it is easy to misuse it without achieving any benefit. For example, suppose you are implementing a server application that generates a very large image file and zips it up. Even after being zipped up it is still huge, so you think that sending it in chunks may be helpful. Well, let us think about it—the browser receives the first chunk and retrieves the chunk content only to realize that it needs the rest of the chunks to unzip the file prior to attempting to render it. We just wasted all the time to encode and decode the body without obtaining any substantial benefit.

4.3.3 Caching support

Caching is one of the most important mechanisms in building scalable applications. Server applications may cache intermediate results to increase efficiency when serving dynamic content, but such functionality is beyond the responsibility of HTTP servers. In this section, we concentrate our discussion on server obligations in support of browser caching as well as server controls with regard to browser caching behaviors.

Prior to HTTP/1.1, the majority of browsers implemented very simplistic caching policies—cached only pages they recognized as static (e.g. only pages received in response to submitting requests initiated through anchor tags as opposed to forms, and only those with certain file extensions). Once stored, the cache entries were not verified for a fixed period short of an explicit reload request. There were, of course, problems with implementing more advanced caching strategies:

1. On-request verification of cache entries meant doubling the number of requests for modified pages using HEAD requests. As you remember from our earlier HTTP discussion, HEAD requests result in response messages with empty bodies. At best, such responses contained enough information to submit GET requests.

2. HTTP/1.0 servers, as a rule, did not include the Last-Modified header in response messages, making it much harder to check whether cache entries remained current. Verification had to be based on unreliable heuristics (e.g., changes in content length, etc.).

3. There was no strict requirement for HTTP/1.0 servers to include the Date header in their responses (even though most did) making it harder to properly record cache entries.

HTTP/1.1 requires servers to comply with the following requirements in support of caching policies:

1. HTTP/1.1 servers must perform cache entry verification when receiving requests that include `If-Modified-Since` and `If-Unmodified-Since` headers set to a date in the GMT format (e.g. `Date: Sun, 23 Mar 1997, 22:15:51 GMT`). Servers must ignore invalid and future dates and attempt to generate the same response they would in the absence of these headers if the condition is satisfied (content was modified in the case of the `If-Modified-Since` header or not modified in the case of the `If-Unmodified-Since` header). Servers are also responsible for generating proper status codes for failed conditions (`304 Unmodified` and `412 Precondition Failed` correspondingly).

2. It is recommended that server implementers make an effort to include the `Last-Modified` header in response messages whenever possible. Browsers use this value to compare against dates stored with cache entries.

3. Unlike HTTP/1.0, HTTP/1.1 servers are required to include the `Date` header with every response, which makes it possible to avoid errors that may happen when browsers rely on their own clocks.

It is not reasonable to expect servers to implement caching policies for dynamic content—this remains the responsibility of server applications. HTTP/1.1 provides applications with much finer controls than HTTP/1.0 (Section 3.4.2). Depending on the processing mechanism (CGI, Servlet API, etc.), cache control headers may be generated either directly by applications or by the enabling mechanism based on API calls, but the headers are still the same. Understanding what headers are generated when you call a particular method and how these headers affect browser behavior is the best way to get a good intuition for any API. As you know, intuition is invaluable in designing good applications and finding problems.

4.3.4 Extensibility

Real HTTP servers vary in the availability of optional built-in components that support the execution of server-side applications. They also differ in the implementation of optional HTTP methods, which are all methods except `GET` and `HEAD`. Fortunately, they provide server administrators with ways to extend the default functionality (Section 4.4.5). As will be discussed later in this chapter, server functionality may be extended in a variety of ways—from implementing optional HTTP methods to adding custom support mechanisms for building server applications.

4.4 SERVER CONFIGURATION

Web server behavior is controlled by its configuration. While details of configuring a Web server differ greatly between different implementations, there are important common concepts that transcend server implementations. For example, any HTTP server has to be configured to map file extensions to MIME types, and any server has to be configured to resolve URLs to addresses in the local file system. For the purpose of this section, we make use of Apache configuration examples. Note that we refer to Apache configuration as a case study and have no intent of providing an Apache configuration manual, which is freely available from the Apache site anyway. Instead, we concentrate on the concepts and it remains your responsibility to map these concepts to configuring your servers.

4.4.1 Directory structure

An HTTP server installation directory is commonly referred to as the *server root*. Most often, other directories (document root, configuration directory, log directory, CGI and servlet root directories, etc.) are defined as subdirectories of the server root. There is normally the initial configuration file that gets loaded when the server comes up, which contains execution parameters, information about the location of other configuration files, and the location of most important directories. Configuration file formats vary for different servers—from traditional attribute-value pairs to XML formats.

There exist situations when it is desirable to depart from the convention that calls for the most important directories to be defined as subdirectories of the server root. For example, you may have reasons to run different servers interchangeably on the same machine, which is particularly common in a development environment. In this case, you may want to use the same independently located document root for different servers. Similarly, you may need to be able to execute the same CGI scripts and servlets independent of which server is currently running. It is important to be particularly careful when sharing directories between different processes—it is enough for one of the processes to be insecure and the integrity of your directory structure is in jeopardy.

4.4.2 Execution

HTTP server is a set of processes or threads (for uniformity, we always refer to them as *threads*), some of which listen on designated ports while others are dedicated to processing incoming requests. Depending on the load, it may be reasonable to keep a number of threads running at all times so that they do not have to be started and initialized for every request.

Figure 4.15 contains a fragment of a sample configuration file for Apache installation on a Windows machine. The 'standalone' value of the server type indicates that the server process is always running and, as follows from the value of the 'Port' parameter, is listening on port 80. The server is configured to support persistent connections, and every connection is configured to support up to a hundred requests.

```
ServerName demo
ServerRoot "C:/Program Files/Apache Group/Apache"
ServerType standalone
Port 80
KeepAlive On
MaxKeepAliveRequests 100
KeepAliveTimeout 15
MaxRequestsPerChild 200
Timeout 300
```

Figure 4.15   Fragment of a sample configuration file

At the same time, the server is supposed to break the connection if 15 seconds go by without new requests.

Many servers make it possible to impose a limit on a number of requests processed without restarting a child process. This limit was introduced for very pragmatic reasons—to avoid prolonged use that results in leaking memory or other resources. The nature of the HTTP protocol, with its independent requests and responses makes it possible to avoid the problem simply by restarting the process. Finally, the timeout limits processing time for individual requests.

HTTP/1.1 is designed to support virtual hosting—the ability of a single server to accept requests targeted to different domains (this of course requires setting DNS aliases). It is quite useful when getting your favorite Internet Service Provider to host your site. As we have already discussed, this functionality is the reason for requiring the Host header in every request. Every virtual host may be configured separately. This does not apply to operational parameters that were discussed in this section. After all, different virtual hosts still share the same physical resources.

4.4.3 Address resolution

An HTTP request is an instruction to the server to perform specified actions. In fact, you may think of HTTP as a language, HTTP request as a program, and the server as an interpreter for the language. Requests are interpreted largely by specialized server modules and by server applications. For example, the servlet runner is responsible for interpreting session ids in Cookie headers and mapping them to server-side session information. Application logic is normally responsible for interpreting URL parameters, request bodies, and additional header information (e.g. Referer).

The core server logic is responsible for the initial processing and routing of requests. First and most important steps are to select the proper virtual host, resolve aliases, analyze the URL, and choose the proper processing module. In both sample URLs in Figure 4.16, www.neurozen.com is a virtual host. The server has to locate configuration statements for this virtual host and use them to perform address translation.

```
1. http://www.neurozen.com/test?a=1&b2
2. http://www.neurozen.com/images/news.gif
```

```
<VirtualHost www.neurozen.com>
     ServerAdmin          webmaster@neurozen.com
     Alias                /test     /servlet/test
     Alias                /images   /static/images
     DocumentRoot         /www/docs/neurozen
     ServerName           www.neurozen.com
     ErrorLog             logs/neurozen-error-log
     CustomLog            logs/neurozen-access-log common
</VirtualHost>
```

Figure 4.16 Sample URLs and a configuration fragment

In the first URL, /test is defined to be an alias for /servlet/test. The server would first resolve aliases and only then use module mappings to pass the URL to the servlet runner that, in turn, invokes the *test* servlet. In the second URL, /images is defined to be an alias for /static/images, which is not explicitly mapped to a module and is assumed a static file. Consequently, the server translates /static/images to the path starting at the document root and looks up the image with the path /www/docs/neurozen/static/news.gif.

Syntax of configuration fragments in above examples is that of the Apache distribution. Do not get mislead by the presence of angle brackets—this syntax only resembles XML, perhaps it will evolve to proper XML in future versions. Note that almost all configuration instructions may occur within the VirtualHost tags. The exception is configuration instructions that control execution parameters (Section 4.4.2). Instructions defined within the VirtualHost tag take precedence for respective host names over global instructions.

4.4.4 MIME support

Successful (200 OK) HTTP responses are supposed to contain the Content-Type header instructing browsers how to render enclosed bodies. For dynamic processing, responsibility for setting the Content-Type header to a proper MIME type is deferred to server applications that produce the response. For static processing, it remains the responsibility of the server. Servers set MIME types for static files based on file extensions. A server distribution normally contains a MIME configuration file that stores mappings between MIME types and file extensions.

In the example (Figure 4.17), text/html is mapped to two alternate file extensions (.html and .htm), text/xml is mapped to a single file extension (.xml), and video/mpeg is mapped to three alternate extensions (.mpeg, .mpg, and .mpe).

```
text/css                    css
text/html                   html htm
text/plain                  asc txt
text/xml                    xml
video/mpeg                  mpeg mpg mpe
```

Figure 4.17 Sample fragment of the Apache configuration file

There may be reasons for a particular installation to change or extend default mappings. Most servers provide for a way to do this without modifying the main MIME configuration file. For example, Apache supports special *add* and *update* directives that may be included with other global and virtual host-specific configuration instructions. The reason is to make it easy to replace default MIME mappings with newer versions without having to edit every new distribution. Such distributions are quite frequent, and are based on the work of standardization committees that are responsible for defining MIME types.

It is important to understand that MIME type mappings are not used exclusively for setting response headers. Another purpose is to aid the server in selecting processing modules. This is an alternative to path-based selections (Section 4.4.3). For example, a mapping may be defined to associate the .cgi extension with CGI scripts. Such a mapping means that the server would use the .cgi extension of the file name as defined in the URL to select CGI as the processing module. This does not change server behavior in performing path-based selections when MIME-based preferences do not apply. In the example, choosing CGI as the processing module does not have any affect on setting the Content-Type header, which remains the responsibility of the CGI script.

4.4.5 Server extensions

HTTP servers are packaged to support most common processing modules—As-Is, CGI, SSI, and servlet runners. Apache refers to these modules as *handlers*, and makes it possible not only to map built-in handlers to file extensions, but to define new handlers as well. In the example in Figure 4.18, the AddHandler directive is used to associate file instructions with handlers. The AddType directive is used to assign MIME types to the output of these handlers by associating both types and handlers with the same file extension. Further, the Action directive is designed to support introducing new handlers. In the example, the add-footer handler is defined as a Perl script that is supposed to be invoked for all .html files.

According to HTTP 1.0 and 1.1 specifications, the only required server methods are GET and HEAD. You would be hard pressed to find a widely used server that does not implement POST, but many of them do not implement other optional methods—PUT, DELETE, OPTIONS, TRACE, and CONNECT. The set of optional methods

```
AddHandler send-as-is .asis

AddType text /html .shtml
AddHandler server-parsed .shtml

Action add-footer /cgi-bin/footer.pl
AddHandler add-footer .html

Script PUT /cgi-bin/nph-put
```

Figure 4.18   Defining server extensions in Apache

for a server may be extended but custom methods are bound to have proprietary semantics. The SCRIPT directive in the Apache example extends the server to support the PUT method by invoking the nph-put CGI program. As we discussed earlier (Section 4.1.3.1), the "nph-" prefix tells the server not to process the output of the CGI program.

4.5 SERVER SECURITY

Throughout the history of the human race, there has been a struggle between fear and greed. In the context of Internet programming, this tug of war takes the form of the struggle between server security and the amount of inconvenience to server administrators and application developers. Server security is about 80/20 compromises—attempts to achieve eighty percent of desired security for your servers at the cost giving up twenty percent of convenience in building and maintaining applications. Of course, there exist degenerate cases when no security is enough, but that is a separate discussion.

This section is not intended as a security manual, but rather as an overview of the most common security problems in setting up and configuring HTTP servers. We do not intend to provide all the answers, only to help you start looking for them. When it concerns security, being aware of a problem takes you more than half way to finding a solution.

4.5.1 Securing the installation

HTTP servers are designed to respond to external requests. Some of the requests may be malicious and jeopardize not only the integrity of the server, but of the entire network. Before we consider the steps necessary to minimize the effect of such malicious requests, we need to make sure that it is not possible to jeopardize the integrity of the server machine and corrupt the HTTP server installation.

The obvious precaution is to minimize remote login access to the server machine— up to disabling it completely (on UNIX that would mean disabling the *in.telnetd* and *in.logind* daemons). If this is too drastic a precaution for what you need, at least make sure that all attempts to access the system are monitored and logged, and all passwords are crack-resilient. Every additional process that is running on the same machine and serves outside requests adds to the risk—for example, *ftp* or *tftp*. In other words, it is better not to run any additional processes on the same machine. If you have to, at least make sure that they are secure. And do not neglect to check for obvious and trivial problems—like file permissions on configuration and password files. There are free and commercial packages that can aid you in auditing the file system and in checking for file corruption—clear indication of danger. After all, if the machine itself can be compromised, it does not matter how secure the HTTP server is that is running on that machine.

The HTTP server itself is definitely a source of danger. Back in the early days, when the URL string was limited to a hundred characters, everyone's favorite way of getting through Web server defenses was to specify a long URL, and either achieve some sort of corruption, or force the server to execute instructions hidden in the trailing portions of these monster URLs. This is not likely to happen with newer HTTP servers but there are still gaping security holes that occasionally get exposed if server administrators are not careful.

As we already discussed in Section 4.1.3.2, SSI is fraught with dangers. Primarily, this is because it supports the execution of server-side programs. Subtler security holes may be exposed because of buggy parsing mechanisms that get confused when encountering illegal syntax—a variation on ancient monster URLs. In other words, you are really asking for trouble if your server is configured to support SSI pages in user directories. Similar precautions go for CGI scripts—enabling them in user directories is dangerous though not as much as SSI pages. At the risk of repeating ourselves—it is simple security oversights that cause most problems.

4.5.2 Dangerous practices

Speaking of the oversights, there are a few that seem obvious but get repeated over and over again. Quite a number of them have to do with the file system. We mentioned the file permissions, but another problem has to do with symbolic links between files and directories. Following a symbolic link may take the server outside the intended directory structure, often with unexpected results. Fortunately, HTTP servers make it possible to disable following links when processing HTTP requests.

Out of all different problems caused by lack of care in configuring the server, one that stands out has to do with sharing the same file system between different processes. How often do you see people providing both FTP and HTTP access to the same files? The problem is that you can spend as much effort as you want securing your HTTP server but it will not help if it is possible to establish an anonymous FTP connection to the host machine and post an executable in a CGI directory.

Now think of all different dangers of file and program corruption that may let outsiders execute their own programs on the server. It is bad enough that outside programs can be executed, but it is even worse if they can access critical system files. It stands to reason that an HTTP server should execute with permissions that don't give it access to files outside of the server directory structure. This is why, if you look at server configuration files, you may notice that the user id defaults to 'nobody'—the name traditionally reserved for user ids assigned to HTTP servers. Unfortunately, not every operating system supports setting user ids when starting the server. Even less fortunately, system administrators, who log in with permissions that give them full access to system resources, are the ones to start the servers. As a result, the server process (and programs started through the server process) have full access to system resources. You know the consequences.

4.5.3 Secure HTTP

Let us assume for the time being that the server is safe. This is still not enough to guard sensitive applications (e.g. credit card purchases, etc.). Even if the server is safe, HTTP messages containing sensitive information are still vulnerable. The most obvious solution for guarding this information is, of course, encryption. HTTPS is the secure version of the HTTP protocol. All HTTPS messages are the same except that they are transmitted over a Secure Socket Layer (SSL) connection—messages are encrypted before the transmission and decrypted after being received by the server.

The SSL protocol supports the use of a variety of different cryptographic algorithms to authenticate the server and the browser to each other, transmit certificates, and establish session encryption keys. The SSL handshake protocol determines how the server and the browser negotiate what encryption algorithm to use. Normally, the server and the browser would select the strongest possible algorithm supported by both parties. Very secure servers may disable weaker algorithms (e.g. those based on 40-bit encryption). This can be a problem when you try to access your bank account and the server refuses the connection asking you to install a browser that supports 128-bit encryption.

As always, you may spend a lot of effort and get bitten by a simple oversight. Even now, after so many years of Internet commerce, you can find applications that all have the same problem—they secure the connection after authenticating a user but authentication is not performed over a secure connection, which exposes user names and passwords. Next time, before you fill out a form to login to a site that makes use of your sensitive information, check whether the action attribute on that form references an HTTPS URL. If it does not—you should run away and never come back.

4.5.4 Firewalls and proxies

Today, more than a third of all Internet sites are protected by firewalls. The idea is to isolate machines on a Local Area Network (LAN) and expose them to the outside world via a specialized gateway that screens network traffic. This gateway is what is customarily referred to as a *firewall*.

Firewall configurations

There exist many different firewall configurations that fall into two major categories: *dual-homed* gateways and *screened-host* gateways. Dual-homed firewall is a computer with two different interface cards, one of which is connected to the LAN and one to the outside world. With this architecture, there is no direct contact between the LAN and the world, so it is necessary to run a firewall proxy on the gateway machine and make this proxy responsible for filtering network packets and passing them between the interface cards. Passing every packet requires an explicit effort, and no information is passed if the firewall proxy is down. Such configuration is very restrictive and is used only in very secure installations.

Screened-host gateways are network routers that have the responsibility of filtering traffic between the LAN and the outside world. They may be configured to screen network packets based on source and destination addresses, ports, and other criteria. Normally, the router is configured to pass through only network packets that are bound for the firewall host and stops packets that are bound for other machines on the LAN. The firewall host is responsible for running a configurable filtering proxy that selectively passes through the network traffic. The screened-host configuration is very flexible—it is easy to open temporary paths to selected ports and hosts. This comes in handy when you need to show a demo running on an internal machine.

HTTP proxies

It is all well and good to create a firewall but what do you do if you need to make your HTTP server visible to the outside world? The seemingly easy answer—running it on the firewall machine—is not a good one. First, any serious load on the HTTP server that is running on the firewall machine may bring the LAN's connection to the outside world to its knees. After all, the HTTP server and network traffic filters would share the same resources. Secondly, any security breach that exposes the HTTP server could also expose the firewall machine and consequently the entire LAN. At the risk of repeating ourselves—it is a really bad idea to run the HTTP server on the firewall machine, and the reason why we keep repeating it over and over again is because people do it anyway.

An alternative is to take advantage of the flexibility of screened-host gateways and allow network traffic to an internal machine when directed to a certain port (e.g. 80). It is much less dangerous than running the server on the firewall machine but still fraught with problems since you are exposing an unprotected machine albeit in a very limited way. Additionally, this approach has functional limitations—how would you redirect the request to another server running on a different port or on a different machine?

It turns out there exists another solution. Let us go back and think about the reasons why it is not a good idea to run an HTTP server on the firewall machine. The first reason is processing load and the second reason is security. What if we limited the functionality of the HTTP server that is running on the firewall machine, to make it defer processing to machines inside the firewall? This would solve the problem with processing load. How about security? Well, if the HTTP server is not performing any processing on the firewall machine, and passes requests along to an internal machine on the LAN, it is hard to break into this server. The simpler the functionality, the harder it is for malicious outsiders to break in.

This sounds good, but what we are doing is simply passing requests along to another machine that still has to process these requests. Can malicious outsiders break into *that* machine? Well, not so easily—even if they manage to wreak havoc on the HTTP server machine, they cannot access that machine directly and use it as a staging ground for further penetration.

To summarize, the solution is not to run a full-fledged HTTP server on the firewall machine but to replace it with an HTTP proxy that may be configured to screen HTTP requests and forward them to proper internal hosts. Different proxy configurations may be selected depending on a wide range of circumstances but what is important is that no processing is performed on the firewall host and the internal machines are not exposed directly to the outside world.

4.6 SUMMARY

By now, you should have enough information to either build your own HTTP server or extend an existing open source system. We attempted to make a clear distinction between responsibilities of servers and those of server applications. Even if you do not implement your own server or server components, understanding server operation is invaluable when architecting, building, and debugging complex Internet applications. Understanding server operation is also very important in making decisions about configuring a server and securing the server installation.

Implementing server applications was not the focus of this chapter. Instead, we concentrated on the comparative analysis of different application mechanisms, and on passing request and response information to and from server applications. We come back to server-side applications later in this book.

4.7 QUESTIONS AND EXERCISES

1. Describe server processing of a POST request. In case of CGI processing, how does the server pass information to a CGI program (request headers, body, URL parameters, etc.)?
2. What are the advantages and disadvantages in using the SSI mechanism?
3. What are the advantages of Servlet API vs. the CGI mechanism?

4. How does the relationship between CGI and SSI mechanisms differ from the relation-ship between Servlets and JSP?

5. What was the reason for introducing 'Transfer-Encoding: chunked' in HTTP/1.1?

6. Is it possible to use chunked transfer encoding with multipart HTTP messages? Explain.

7. Why was it necessary to introduce the 'Host' header in HTTP/1.1? How is it used to support virtual hosting? Why was it not enough to require that request lines always contain a full URL (as in GET http://www.cs.rutgers.edu/~shklar/ HTTP/1.1)?

8. When (if ever) does it make sense to include HTTP/1.0 headers in HTTP/1.1 responses directed at HTTP/1.1 browsers?

9. HTTP/1.1 servers default to the Keep-Alive setting of the Connection header. Why then do most browsers include Connection: Keep-Alive in their requests even when they know that the target server supports HTTP/1.1?

10. Is it possible for an HTTP/1.1 server not to support persistent connections and still be HTTP-compliant?

11. Name *three* headers that, if present in an HTTP response, always have to be processed in a particular order. State the order and explain. Why did we ask you to name two headers in Chapter 3 but three headers in this exercise?

12. What is the difference between dual-homed gateways and screened-host gateways? Which is safer? Which is more flexible?

13. What functionality would be lost if servers did not know how to associate file extensions with MIME types?

14. Is it a good idea to run an HTTP server on a firewall machine? Explain.

15. Does your answer to the previous question depend on whether the HTTP server is running as a proxy?

16. Implement a mini-server that generates legal HTTP 1.0 responses to GET, HEAD and POST requests. Your program should be able to take the port number as its command-line parameter and listen on this port for incoming HTTP/1.0 requests (remember that back-ward compatibility requirement is part of HTTP/1.0—this means support for HTTP/0.9). Upon receiving a request, the program should fork off a thread for processing the request and keep listening on the same port. The forked off thread should generate the proper HTTP response, send it back to the browser, and terminate. The server should be capable of processing multiple requests in parallel. Pay attention to escape sequences and separa-tors between the key-value pairs in the bodies of POST requests and query strings of GET requests. Make sure the necessary request headers are included in incoming request (e.g. Content-Type and Content-Length in POST requests). Your program has to generate legal HTTP headers according to HTTP 1.0 (including Content-Type). It should use a configuration file (mime-config) that will store mappings between file extensions and MIME types. It should use these mappings to determine the desired Content-Type for content, which is referenced by the URL (in your case, file path) specified in the GET or POST request. You will have to support basic path translation—all static URLs will have to be defined relative document root. This also means that your server will need at least a basic general configuration file (see Apache)—at least it should be possible to specify the server root, and both the document root and the cgi-bin directory relative to the server root.

17. Implement HTTP 1.1 support for the mini-server from Exercise 16. Your program should be able to take the port number as its command-line parameter and listen on this port

for incoming HTTP/1.1 requests (remember that backward compatibility requirement is part of HTTP/1.1—this means support for HTTP/1.0 and HTTP/0.9). Your server should support parallel processing of multiple requests. Upon receiving a request, your server should start a new thread for processing that request and keep listening on the same port. The new thread should generate a proper HTTP response, send it back to the browser, and terminate. The server should be able to initiate processing of new requests while old requests are still being processed.

You have to send HTTP/1.1 responses for HTTP/1.1 requests, HTTP/1.0 responses for HTTP/1.0 requests, and HTTP/0.9 responses for HTTP/0.9 requests. Minimal level of compliance is acceptable. Minimal level of compliance implies the following:

- HTTP/1.0 and HTTP/0.9 requests must be processed as before
- The server must check for presence of the Host header in HTTP/1.1 requests, and return 400 Bad Request if the header is not present; the server must accept both absolute and relative URI syntax
- The server must either maintain persistent connections, or include Connection: close in every response
- The server must include the Date header (date always in GMT) in every response
- The server has to support If-Modified-Since and If-Unmodified-Since headers
- Following methods are defined in HTTP/1.1: GET, HEAD, POST, PUT, DELETE, OPTIONS, and TRACE. You have to support GET, HEAD, and POST, return 501 Not Implemented for other defined methods, and 400 Bad Request for undefined methods

The result of this exercise should be a program that would receive legal HTTP/1.1 requests, and send legal HTTP/1.1 responses back. It should function as an HTTP/1.0 server in response to HTTP/1.0 requests.

BIBLIOGRAPHY

Castro, E. (2001) *Perl and CGI for the World Wide Web*. Peachpit Press.

Kopparapu, C. (2002) *Load Balancing Servers, Firewalls and Caches*. John Wiley & Sons.

Luotonen, A. (1997) *Web Proxy Servers*. Prentice Hall.

Hall, M. (2002) *More Servlets and Java Server Pages*. Prentice Hall.

Rajagopalan, S, Rajamani, R., Krishnaswamy, R. and Vijendran, S. (2002) *Java Servlet Programming Bible*. John Wiley & Sons.

Thomas, S. (2000) *SSL & TLS Essentials: Securing the Web*. John Wiley & Sons.

Yeager, N. and McGrath, R. (1996) *Web Server Technology*. Morgan Kaufmann.

5 Web Browsers

In this chapter, we go over the fundamental considerations in designing and building a Web browser, as well as other sophisticated Web clients. When discussing Web browsers, our focus will not be on the graphical aspects of browser functionality (i.e. the layout of pages, the rendering of images). Instead, we shall concentrate on the issues associated with the processing of HTTP requests and responses. The value of this knowledge will become apparent as we proceed to our discussion of more sophisticated Web applications.

It may seem to some that the task of designing a browser is a fait accompli, a foregone conclusion, a done deal, a known problem that has already been 'solved'. Given the history and progress of browser development—from the original *www* browser, through Lynx and Mosaic, to Netscape, Internet Explorer, and Opera today—it might seem a futile endeavor to 'reinvent the wheel' by building a new browser application.

This is hardly the case at all. The desktop browser is the most obvious example of a Web client, and it's certainly the most common, but it's far from the only one. Other types of Web clients include *agents*, which are responsible for submitting requests on behalf of a user to perform some automated function, and *proxies*, which act as gateways through which requests and responses pass between servers and clients to enhance security and performance. These clients need to replicate much of the functionality found in browsers. Thus, it is worthwhile to understand design principles associated with browser architecture.

Furthermore, there are devices like handheld *personal digital assistants*, cellular phones, and *Internet appliances*, which need to receive and send data via the Web. Although many of them have browsers available already, they are mostly primitive with limited functionality. As the capabilities of these devices grow, more advanced and robust Web clients will be needed.

Finally, who said that today's desktop browsers are perfect examples of elegant design? The Mozilla project is an effort to build a better browser from the ground up (from the ashes of an existing one, if you will). Today's desktop browsers may be (relatively) stable, and it would be difficult if not impossible to develop and market a new desktop browser at this stage of the game. Still, there will be ample opportunities to enhance and augment the functionality of existing desktop browsers, and this effort is best undertaken with a thorough understanding of the issues of browser design.

The main responsibilities of a browser are as follows:

1. Generate and send requests to Web servers on the user's behalf, as a result of following hyperlinks, explicit typing of URLs, submitting forms, and parsing HTML pages that require auxiliary resources (e.g. images, applets).

2. Accept responses delivered by Web servers and interpret them to produce the visual representation to be viewed by the user. This will, at a bare minimum, involve examination of certain response headers such as Content-Type to determine what action needs to be taken and what sort of rendering is required.

3. Render the results in the browser window or through a third party tool, depending on the content type of the response.

This, of course, is an oversimplification of what real browsers actually do. Depending on the status code and headers in the response, browsers are called upon to perform other tasks, including:

1. *Caching*: the browser must make determinations as to whether or not it needs to request data from the server at all. It may have a cached copy of the same data item that it retrieved during a previous request. If so, and if this cached copy has not 'expired', the browser can eliminate a superfluous request for the resource. In other cases, the server can be queried to determine if the resource has been modified since it was originally retrieved and placed in the cache. Significant performance benefits can be achieved through caching.

2. *Authentication*: since web servers may require authorization credentials to access resources it has designated as secure, the browser must react to server requests for credentials, by prompting the user for authorization credentials, or by utilizing credentials it has already asked for in prior requests.

3. *State maintenance*: to record and maintain the state of a browser session across requests and responses, web servers may request that the browser accept *cookies*, which are sets of name/value pairs included in response headers. The browser must store the transmitted cookie information and make it available to be sent back in appropriate requests. In addition, the browser should provide configuration options to allow users the choice of accepting or rejecting cookies.

4. *Requesting supporting data items*: the typical web page contains images, Java applets, sounds, and a variety of other ancillary objects. The proper rendering

of the page is dependent upon the browser's retrieving those supporting data items for inclusion in the rendering process. This normally occurs transparently without user intervention.

5. *Taking actions in response to other headers and status codes*: the HTTP headers and the status code do more than simply provide the data to be rendered by the browser. In some cases, they provide additional processing instructions, which may extend or supersede rendering information found elsewhere in the response. The presence of these instructions may indicate a problem in accessing the resource, and may instruct the browser to *redirect* the request to another location. They may also indicate that the connection should be kept open, so that further requests can be sent over the same connection. Many of these functions are associated with advanced HTTP functionality found in HTTP/1.1.

6. *Rendering complex objects*: most web browsers inherently support content types such as text/html, text/plain, image/gif, and image/jpeg. This means that the browser provides native functionality to render objects with these contents *inline*: within the browser window, and without having to install additional software components. To render or play back other more complex objects (e.g. audio, video, and multimedia), a browser must provide support for these content types. Mechanisms must exist for invoking external *helper applications* or internal *plug-ins* that are required to display and playback these objects.

7. *Dealing with error conditions*: connection failures and invalid responses from servers are among the situations the browser must be equipped to deal with.

5.1 ARCHITECTURAL CONSIDERATIONS

So, let's engage in an intellectual exercise: putting together requirements for the architecture of a Web browser. What are those requirements? What functions must a Web browser perform? And how do different functional components interact with each other?

The following list delineates the core functions associated with a Web browser. Each function can be thought of as a distinct module within the browser. Obviously these modules must communicate with each other in order to allow the browser to function, but they should each be designed atomically.

- *User Interface*: this module is responsible for providing the interface through which users interact with the application. This includes presenting, displaying, and rendering the end result of the browser's processing of the response transmitted by the server.

- *Request Generation*: this module bears responsibility for the task of building HTTP requests to be submitted to HTTP servers. When asked by the *User*

Interface module or the *Content Interpretation* module to construct requests based on relative links, it must first resolve those links into absolute URLs.

- *Response Processing*: this module must parse the response, interpret it, and pass the result to the *User Interface* module.

- *Networking*: this module is responsible for network communications. It takes requests passed to it by the *Request Generation* module and transmits them over the network to the appropriate Web server or proxy. It also accepts responses that arrive over the network and passes them to the *Response Processing* module. In the course of performing these tasks, it takes responsibility for establishing network connections and dealing with proxy servers specified in a user's network configuration options.

- *Content Interpretation*: having received the response, the *Response Processing* module needs help in parsing and deciphering the content. The content may be encoded, and this module is responding to decode it. Initial responses often have their content types set to `text/html`, but HTML responses embed or contain references to images, multimedia objects, JavaScript code, applets, and style sheet information. This module performs the additional processing necessary for browser applications to understand these entities within a response. In addition, this module must tell the *Request Generation* module to construct additional requests for the retrieval of auxiliary content such as images, applets, and other objects.

- *Caching*: caching provides web browsers with a way to economize by avoiding the unnecessary retrieval of resources that the browser already has a usable copy of, 'cached' away in local storage. Browsers can ask Web servers whether a desired resource has been modified since the time that the browser initially retrieved it and stored it in the cache. This module must provide facilities for storing copies of retrieved resources in the cache for later use, for accessing those copies when viable, and for managing the space (both memory and disk) allocated by the browser's configuration parameters for this purpose.

- *State Maintenance*: since HTTP is a *stateless protocol*, some mechanism must be in place to maintain the browser *state* between related requests and responses. Cookies are the mechanism of choice for performing this task, and support for cookies is in the responsibility of this module.

- *Authentication*: this module takes care of composing authorization credentials when requested by the server. It must interpret response headers demanding credentials by prompting the user to enter them (usually via a dialog). It must also store those credentials, but only for the duration of the current browser session, in case a request is made for another secured resource in what the server considers to be the same security 'realm'. (This absolves the user of the need to re-enter the credentials each time a request for such resources is made.)

- *Configuration*: finally, there are a number of configuration options that a browser application needs to support. Some of these are fixed, while others are user-definable. This module maintains the fixed and variable configuration options for the browser, and provides an interface for users to modify those options under their control.

5.2 PROCESSING FLOW

Figure 5.1 shows the processing flow for the creation and transmission of a request in a typical browser. We begin with a link followed by a user. Users can click on hyperlinks presented in the browser display window, they might choose links from lists of previously visited links (history or bookmarks), or they might enter a URL manually.

In each of these cases, processing begins with the *User Interface* module, which is responsible for presenting the display window and giving users access to browser functions (e.g. through menus and shortcut keys). In general, an application using a *GUI* (graphical user interface) operates using an *event model*. User actions—clicking on highlighted hyperlinks, for example—are considered *events* that must be interpreted properly by the *User Interface* module. Although this book does not concentrate on the user interface-related functionality of HTTP browsers, it is crucial that we note the events that are important for the *User Interface* module:

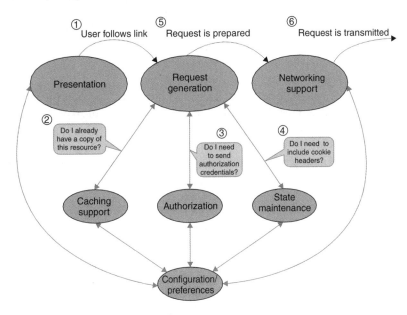

Figure 5.1   Browser request generation

- *Entering URLs manually*: usually, this is accomplished by providing a text entry box in which the user can enter a URL, as well as through a menu option (**File→ Open**) that opens a dialog box for similar manual entry. The second option often interfaces with the operating system to support interactive selection of local files.

- *Selecting previously visited links*: the existence of this mechanism, naturally, implies that the *User Interface* module must also provide a mechanism for maintaining a history of visited links. The maximum amount of time that such links will be maintained in this list, as well as the maximum size to which this list can grow, can be established as a user-definable parameter in the *Configuration* module. The 'Location' or 'Address' text area in the browser window can be a *dropdown* field that allows the user to select from recently visited links. The 'Back' button allows users to go back to the page they were visiting previously. In addition, users should be able to save particular links as "bookmarks", and then access these links through the user interface at a later date.

- *Selecting displayed hyperlinks*: there are a number of ways for users to select links displayed on the presented page. In desktop browsers, the mouse click is probably the most common mechanism for users to select a displayed link, but there are other mechanisms on the desktop and on other platforms as well. Since the *User Interface* module is already responsible for rendering text according to the specifications found in the page's HTML markup, it is also responsible for doing some sort of formatting to highlight a link so that it stands out from other text on the page. Most desktop browsers also change the cursor shape when the mouse is 'over' a hyperlink, indicating that this is a valid place for users to click. Highlighting mechanisms vary for non-desktop platforms, but they should always be present in some form.

Once the selected or entered link is passed on to the *Request Generation* module, it must be *resolved*. Links found on a displayed page can be either absolute or relative. Absolute URLs are complete URLs, containing all the required URL components, e.g. `protocol://host/path`. These do not need to be resolved and can be processed without further intervention. A relative URL specifies a location relative to:

1. the current location being displayed (i.e. the entire URL including the path, up to the directory in which the current URL resides), when the HREF contains a relative path that does not begin with a slash, e.g.: `<A HREF="some_directory/ just_a_file_name.html">`), or

2. the current location's web server root (i.e., only the host portion of the URL), when the HREF contains a relative path that *does* begin with a slash, e.g. `<A HREF="/root_level_directory/another_file_name.html">`.

```
Current URL:   http://www.myserver.com/mydirectory/index.html
<A HREF ="anotherdirectory/page2.html">...</A>
        → http://www.myserver.com/mydirectory/anotherdirectory/page2.html
<A HREF ="/rootleveldirectory/homepage.html">...</A>
        → http://www.myserver.com/rootleveldirectory/homepage.html


Current URL:   http://www.myserver.com/mydirectory/anotherpage.html
<A HREF ="anotherdirectory/page2.html">...</A>
        → http://www.myserver.com/mydirectory/anotherdirectory/page2.html
<A HREF ="/yetanotherdirectory/homepage.html">...</A>
        → http://www.myserver.com/yetanotherdirectory/homepage.html


Current URL:   http://www.myserver.com/mydirectory/differentpage.html
<BASE HREF ="http://www.yourserver.com/otherdir/something.html">
<A HREF ="anotherdirectory/page2.html">...</A>
        → http://www.yourserver.com/otherdir/anotherdirectory/page2.html

<A HREF ="/yetanotherdirectory/homepage.html">...</A>
        → http://www.yourserver.com/yetanotherdirectory/homepage.html
```

Figure 5.2   Resolution of relative URLs

The process of resolution changes if an optional <BASE HREF ="..."> tag is found in the HEAD section of the page. The URL specified in this tag replaces the current location as the "base" from which resolution occurs in the previous examples.

Figure 5.2 demonstrates how relative URLs must be resolved by the browser.

Once the URL has been resolved, the *Request Generation* module builds the request, which is ultimately passed to the *Networking* module for transmission. To accomplish this task, the *Request Generation* module has to communicate with other browser components:

- It asks the *Caching* module *"Do I already have a copy of this resource?"* If so, it needs to determine whether it can simply use this copy, or whether it needs to ask the server if the resource has been modified since the browser cached a copy of this resource.

- It asks the *Authorization* module *"Do I need to include authentication credentials in this request?"* If the browser has not already stored credentials for the appropriate domain, it may need to contact the *User Interface* module, which prompts the user for credentials.

- It asks the *State Mechanism* module *"Do I need to include* Cookie *headers in this request?"* It must determine whether the requested URL matches domain and path patterns associated with previously stored cookies.

The constructed request is passed to the *Networking* module so it can be transmitted over the network.

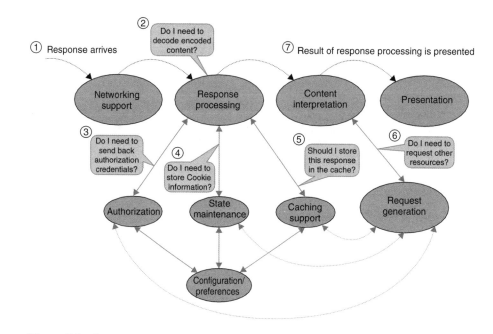

Figure 5.3 Browser response processing

Once a request has been transmitted, the browser waits to receive a response. It may submit additional requests while waiting. Requests may have to be resubmitted if the connection is closed before the corresponding responses are received. It is the server's responsibility to transmit responses in the same order as the corresponding requests were received. However, the browser is responsible for dealing with servers that do not properly maintain this order, by delaying the processing of responses that arrive out of sequence. Figure 5.3 describes the flow for this process. A response is received by the *Networking* module, which passes it to the *Response Processing* module. This module must also cooperate and communicate with other modules to do its job. It examines response headers to determine required actions.

- If the status code of the response is `401 Not Authorized`, this means that the request lacked necessary authorization credentials. The *Response Processing* module asks the *Authorization* module whether any existing credentials might be used to satisfy the request. The *Authorization* module may, in turn, contact the *User Interface* module, which would prompt the user to enter authorization credentials. In either case, this results in the original request being retransmitted with an `Authorization` header containing the required credentials.

- If the response contains `Set-Cookie` headers, the *State Maintenance* module must store the cookie information using the browser's persistence mechanism.

Next, the response is passed to the *Content Interpretation* module, which has a number of responsibilities:

- If the response contains `Content-Transfer-Encoding` and/or `Content-Encoding` headers, the module needs to *decode* the body of the response.

- The module examines the `Cache-Control`, `Expires`, and/or `Pragma` headers (depending on the HTTP version of the response) to determine whether the browser needs to cache the decoded content of the response. If so, the *Caching* module is contacted to create a new cache entry or update an existing one.

- The `Content-Type` header determines the MIME type of the response content. Different MIME types, naturally, require different kinds of content processing. Modern browsers support a variety of content types natively, including HTML (`text/html`), graphical images (`image/gif`, and `image/jpeg`), and sounds (`audio/wav`). Native support means that processing of these content types is performed by built-in browser components. Thus, the *Content Interpretation* module must provide robust support for such processing. Leading edge browsers already provide support for additional content types, including vector graphics and XSL stylesheets.

- For MIME types that are not processed natively, browsers usually provide support mechanisms for the association of MIME types with *helper applications* and *plug-ins*. Helper applications render content by invoking an external program that executes independent of the browser, while plug-ins render content within the browser window. The *Content Interpretation* module must communicate with the *Configuration* module to determine what plug-ins are installed and what helper application associations have been established, to take appropriate action when receiving content that is not natively supported by the browser. This involves a degree of interaction with the operating system, to determine system-level associations configured for filename extensions, MIME types, and application programs. However, many browsers override (or even completely ignore) these settings, managing their own sets of associations through the *Configuration* module.

- Some content types (e.g. markup languages, applets, Flash movies) may embed references to other resources needed to satisfy the request. For instance, HTML pages may include references to images or JavaScript components. The *Content Interpretation* module must parse the content prior to passing it on to the *User Interface* module, determining if additional requests will be needed. If so, URLs associated with these requests get resolved when they are passed to the Request Generation module.

As each of the requested resources arrives in sequence, it is passed to the *User Interface* module so that it may be incorporated in the final presentation. The *Networking* module maintains its queue of requests and responses, ensuring that all requests have been satisfied, and resubmitting any outstanding requests.

All along the way, various subordinate modules are asked questions to determine the course of processing (including whether or not particular tasks need to be performed at all). For example, the *Content Interpretation* module may say '*This page has IMG tags, so we must send HTTP requests to retrieve the associated images,*' but the *Caching* module may respond by saying '*We already have a usable copy of that resource, so don't bother sending a request to the network for it.*' (Alternatively, it may say '*We have a copy of that resource, but let's ask the server if its copy of the resource is more recent; if it's not, it doesn't need to send it back to us.*') Or the *Configuration* module may say '*No, don't send a request for the images on this page, this user has a slow connection and has elected not to see images.*' Or *the State Maintenance* mechanism may jump in and say '*Wait, we've been to this site before, so send along this identifying cookie information with our requests.*'

The rest of this chapter is devoted to a more detailed explanation of the role each of these modules plays in the processing of requests and responses. As mentioned previously, we shall not focus on the *User Interface* module's responsibility in rendering graphics, as this is an extensive subject worthy its own book. However, we will concentrate on the interplay between these modules and how to design them to do their job.

We begin by going over the basics of request and response processing, following that with details on the more sophisticated aspects of such processing, including support for caching, authentication, and advanced features of the HTTP protocol.

5.3 PROCESSING HTTP REQUESTS AND RESPONSES

Let us examine how browsers build and transmit HTTP requests, and how they receive, interpret, and present HTTP responses. After we have covered the basics of constructing requests and interpreting responses, we can look at the more complex interactions involved when HTTP transactions involve caching, authorization, cookies, request of supporting data items, and multimedia support.

Not Just HTTP

Browsers should do more than just communicate via HTTP. They should provide support for Secure HTTP (over Secure Sockets Layer). They should be able to send requests to FTP servers. And they should be able to access local files. These three types of requests correspond to URLs using the `https`, `ftp`, and `file` protocols, respectively. Although we shall not cover these protocols here, it is important to note that HTTP requests and responses are not the only kinds of transactions performed by browsers.

5.3.1 HTTP requests

The act of sending an HTTP request to a web server, in its most trivial form, consists of two basic steps: constructing the HTTP request, and establishing a connection to transmit it across the Internet to the target server or an intermediate proxy. The construction of requests is the responsibility of *the Request Generation* module. Once a request has been properly constructed, this module passes it to the *Networking* module, which opens the socket to transmit it either directly to the server or to a proxy.

Before the *Request Generation* module has even begun the process of building the request, it needs to ask a whole series of questions of the other modules:

1. *Do I already have a cached copy of this resource?*
   If an entry exists in the cache that satisfies this same request, then the transmitted request should include an If-Modified-Since header, containing the last modification time associated with the stored cache entry. If the resource found on the server has *not* been modified since that time, the response will come back with a 304 Not Modified status code, and that cache entry can be passed directly to the *User Interface* module. (*Caching Support*)

2. *Is there any additional information I need to send as part of this request?*
   If this request is part of a series of requests made to a particular web server, or if the target web server has been visited previously, it may have sent "state" information (in the form of Set-Cookie headers) to the browser. The browser must set and maintain cookies according to the server instructions: either for a specified period of time or for the duration of the current session. In addition, the set of saved cookies must be examined prior to sending a request to determine whether cookie information needs to be included in that request. (*State Maintenance*)

3. *Is there any other additional information I need to send as part of this request?*
   If this resource is part of an authorization realm for which the user has already supplied authentication credentials, those credentials should be stored by the browser for the duration of a session, and should be supplied with requests for other resources in the same realm. (*Authorization*)

User preferences may modify the nature of the request, possibly even eliminating the need for one entirely. For example, users may set a preference via the *Configuration* module telling the browser not to request images found within an HTML page. They can turn off Java applet support, meaning that requests for applets need not be processed. They can also instruct the browser to reject cookies, meaning that the browser does not need to worry about including Cookie headers in generated requests.

In the chapter devoted to the HTTP protocol, we described the general structure of HTTP requests, and provided some examples. To refresh our memories, here is the format of an HTTP request:

```
METHOD /path-to-resource  HTTP/version-number
Header-Name-1: value
Header-Name-2: value

[ optional request body ]
```

An HTTP request contains a *request line*, followed by a series of *headers* (one per line), followed by a blank line. The blank line may serve as a separator, delimiting the headers from an optional *body* portion of the request. A typical example of an HTTP request might look something like this:

```
POST /update.cgi HTTP/1.0
Host: www.somewhere.com
Referer: http://www.somewhere.com/formentry.html

name=joe&type=info&amount=5
```

The process of constructing an HTTP request typically begins when a web site visitor sees a link on a page and clicks on it, telling the browser to present the content associated with that link. There are other possibilities, such as entering a URL manually, or a browser connecting to a default home page when starting up, but this example allows us to describe typical browser activity more comprehensively.

Constructing the request line

When a link is selected, the browser's *User Interface* module reacts to an *event*. A GUI-based application operates using an event model, in which user actions (e.g. typing, mouse clicking) are translated into events that the application responds to. In response to a mouse click on a hyperlink, for example, *the User Interface* module determines and resolves the URL associated with that link, and passes it to the *Request Generation* module.

Filling Out the Form

In the case of a user entry form, where the user has entered data into form fields and clicked a 'Submit' button, it may be more than just the URL that is passed to the Request Generation module. The entered data must be included as well.

> As we mentioned in the chapter covering HTTP processing, the data is converted into name/value pairs that are *URL-encoded*. The GET method includes the encoded data in the URL as a *query string*, while the POST method places the encoded data in the body of the request.

At this point, the *Request Generation* module begins to construct the request. The first portion of the request that needs to be created is the *request line*, which contains a 'method' (representing one of several supported *request methods*), the '/path-to-resource' (representing the *path* portion of the requested URL), and the 'version-number' (specifying the version of HTTP associated with the request).

Let's examine these in reverse order. The 'version-number' should be either HTTP/1.1 or HTTP/1.0. A modern up-to-date client program should always seek to use the latest version of its chosen transmission protocol, unless the recipient of the request is not sophisticated enough to make use of that latest version. Thus, at the present time, a browser should seek to communicate with a server using HTTP/1.1, and should only 'fall back' to HTTP/1.0 if the server with which it is communicating does not support HTTP/1.1.

The 'path-to-resource' portion is a little more complicated, and is in fact dependent on which version of HTTP is employed in the request. You may remember that this portion of the request line is supposed to contain the "path" portion of the URL. This is the part of the URL following the host portion of the URL (i.e. "http://hostname"), starting with the "/".

The situation is complicated when the browser connects to a proxy server to send a request, rather than connecting directly to the target server. Proxies need to know where to forward the request. If only the path-to-resource portion is included in the request line, a proxy would have no way of knowing the intended destination of the request.

HTTP/1.0 requires the inclusion of the entire URL for requests directed at proxy servers, but forbids the inclusion of the entire URL for requests that get sent directly to their target servers. This is because HTTP/1.0 *servers* do not understand requests where the full URL is specified in the request line. In contrast, HTTP/1.0 *proxies* expect that incoming requests contain full URLs. When HTTP/1.0 proxies reconstruct requests to be sent directly to their target servers, they remove the server portion of the request URL. When requests must pass through additional proxies, this reconstruction is not performed, and the requests remain unchanged. HTTP/1.1 is more flexible; it makes the inclusion of the entire URL on the request line acceptable in all situations, irrespective of whether a proxy is involved. However, to facilitate this flexibility, HTTP/1.1 requires that submitted requests all include a "Host" header, specifying the IP address or name of the target server. This header was originally introduced to support virtual hosting, a feature that allows a web server to service more than one domain. This means that a single Web server program could be running on a server machine, accepting requests associated with many different domains. However, this header also provides sufficient information to proxies so that they can properly forward requests to other servers/proxies. Unlike HTTP/1.0 proxies, HTTP/1.1 proxies do not need to perform any transformation of these requests.

The 'method' portion of the request line is dependent on which request method is specified, implicitly or explicitly. When a hyperlink (textual or image) is selected and clicked, the GET method is implicitly selected. In the case of HTML *forms*, a particular request method may be specified in the <FORM> tag:

```
<FORM ACTION ="http://www.somewhere.com/update.cgi" METHOD ="POST">
   ...
</FORM>
```

As mentioned in the chapter on the HTTP protocol, the GET method represents the simplest format for HTTP requests: a request line, followed by headers, and no body. Other request methods such as POST and PUT make use of a request body that follows the request line, headers, and blank line. (The blank line serves as a separator delimiting the headers from the body.) This request body may contain parameters associated with an HTML form, a file to be uploaded, or a combination of both.

In any case, we are still working on the construction of the request line. The 'method' portion will be set to "GET" by default: for textual or image-based hyperlinks that are followed, and for forms that do not explicitly specify a METHOD. If a form *does* explicitly specify a METHOD, that method will be used instead.

Constructing the headers

Next, we come to the headers. There are a number of headers that a browser should include in the request:

```
Host: www.neurozen.com
```

This header was introduced to support virtual hosting, a feature that allows a web server to service more than one domain. This means that a single Web server program could be running on a server machine, accepting requests associated with many different domains. Without this header, the Web server program could not tell which of its many domains the target of the request was. In addition, this header provides information to proxies to facilitate proper routing of requests.

```
User-Agent: Mozilla/4.75 [en] (WinNT; U)
```

Identifies the software (e.g. a web browser) responsible for making the request. Your browser (or for that matter *any* Web client) should provide this information to identify itself to servers. The conventions are to produce a header containing the name of the product, the version number, the language this particular copy of the software uses, and the platform it runs on: `Product/version.number [lang] (Platform)`

```
Referer: http://www.cs.rutgers.edu/~shklar/index.html
```

If this request was instantiated because a user selected a link found on a web page, this header should contain the URL of that referring page. Your Web client should keep track of the current URL it is displaying, and it should be sure to include that URL in a `Referer` header whenever a link on the current page is selected.

```
Date: Sun, 11 Feb 2001 22:28:31 GMT
```

This header specifies the time and date that this message was created. All request and response messages should include this header.

```
Accept: text/html, text/plain, type/subtype,...
Accept-Charset: ISO-8859-1, character_set_identifier,...
Accept-Language: en, language_identifier,...
Accept-Encoding: compress, gzip,...
```

These headers list the MIME types, character sets, languages, and encoding schemes that your client will 'accept' in a response from the server. If your client needs to limit responses to a finite set, then these should be included in these headers. Your client's preferences with respect to these items can be ranked by adding relative values in the form of `q` =*qvalue* parameters, where *qvalue* is a digit.

```
Content-Type: mime-type/mime-subtype
Content-Length: xxx
```

These *entity headers* provide information about the message body. For POST and PUT requests, the server needs to know the MIME type of the content found in the body of the request, as well as the length of the body.

```
Cookie: name=value
```

This *request header* contains cookie information that the browser has found in responses previously received from Web servers. This information needs to be sent back to those same servers in subsequent requests, maintaining the 'state' of a browser session by providing a name-value combination that uniquely identifies a particular user. Interaction with the *State Maintenance* module will determine whether these headers need to be included in requests, and if so what their values should be. Note that a request will contain multiple `Cookie` headers if there is more than one cookie that should be included in the request.

```
Authorization:   SCHEME encoded-userid:password
```

This *request header* provides authorization credentials to the server in response
to an authentication challenge received in an earlier response. The scheme (usually
'basic') is followed by a string composed of the user ID and password (separated by
a colon), encoded in the base64 format. Interaction with the *Authorization* module
will determine what the content of this header should be.

Constructing the request body

This step of the request construction process applies only for methods like POST
and PUT that attach a message body to a request. The simplest example is that
of including form parameters in the message body when using the POST method.
They must be URL-encoded to enable proper parsing by the server, and thus the
Content-Type header in the request must be set to application/x-www-form-
urlencoded.

There are more complex uses for the request body. File uploads can be performed through forms employing the POST method (using multipart MIME types),
or (with the proper server security configuration) web resources can be modified
or created directly using the PUT method. With the PUT method, the Content-
Type of the request should be set to the MIME type of the content that is being
uploaded. With the POST method, the Content-Type of the request should be set
to multipart/form-data, while the Content-Type of the individual parts should
be set to the MIME type of those parts.

This Content-Type header requires the "boundary" parameter, which specifies
a string of text that separates discrete pieces of content found in the body:

```
...
Content-Type: multipart/multipart_subtype; boundary="random-string"

--random-string
Content-Type: type/subtype of part 1
Content-Transfer-Encoding: encoding scheme for part 1

content of part 1

--random-string
Content-Type: type/subtype of part 2
Content-Transfer-Encoding: encoding scheme for part 2

content of part 2
```

Note that each part specifies its own `Content-Type`, and its own `Content-Transfer-Encoding`. This means that one part can be textual, with no encoding specified, while another part can be binary (e.g. an image), encoded in Base64 format, as in the following example:

```
...
Content-Type: multipart/form-data; boundary="gc0p4Jq0M2Yt08jU534c0p"

--gc0p4Jq0M2Yt08jU534c0p
Content-Type: application/x-www-form-urlencoded

&filename=...&param =value

--gc0p4Jq0M2Yt08jU534c0p
Content-Type: image/gif
Content-Transfer-Encoding: base64

FsZCBoYWQgYSBmYXJtCkUgSST2xkIE1hY0Rvbm
G1zIGZhcm0gaGUgaGFkBFIEkgTwpBbmQgb24ga
IHKRSBJIEUgSSBPCldpdGggYSNvbWUgZHVja3M
BxdWjayBoZXJlLApFjayBxdWFhIHF1YWNrIHF1
XJlLApldmVyeSB3aGYWNrIHRoZVyZSBhIHF1YW
NrIHF1YWNrCEkgTwokUgSSBFI=
```

SOAP Opera

One increasingly popular usage of the request body is as a container for Remote Procedure Calls (RPC). This is especially true now that there are XML-based implementations of RPC, including the aptly named XML-RPC and its successor, SOAP (Simple Object Access Protocol). When using SOAP over HTTP, the body of a request consists of a SOAP payload, which is an XML document containing RPC directives including method calls and parameters. We will discuss this in greater detail in a later chapter.

Transmission of the request

Once the request has been fully constructed, it is passed to the *Networking* module, which transmits the request.

This module must first determine the target of the request. Normally, this can be obtained by parsing the URL associated with the request. However, if the browser is configured to employ a proxy server, the target of the request would be that proxy server. Thus, the *Configuration* module must be queried to determine the actual target for the request. Once this is done, a socket is opened to the appropriate machine.

5.3.2 HTTP responses

In the request/response paradigm, the transmission of a request anticipates the receipt of some sort of a response. Hence, browsers and other Web clients must be prepared to process HTTP responses. This task is the responsibility of the *Response Processing* module.

As we know, HTTP responses have the following format:

```
HTTP/version-number  status-code  message
Header-Name-1: value
Header-Name-2: value


[ response body ]
```

An HTTP response message consists of a *status line* (containing the HTTP version, a three-digit *status code*, and a brief human-readable explanation of the status code), a series of *headers* (again, one per line), a blank line, and finally the *body* of the response. The following is an example of the HTTP response message that a server would send back to the browser when it is able to satisfy the incoming request:

```
HTTP/1.1 200 OK
Content-Type: text/html
Content-Length: 1234
  ...

<HTML>
<HEAD>
<TITLE>...</TITLE>
</HEAD>
<BODY BGCOLOR="#ffffff">
<H2 ALIGN="center">...</H2>
  ...
</H2>
</BODY>
</HTML>
```

In this case, we have a *successful* response: the server was able to satisfy the client's request and sent back the requested data. Now, of course, the requesting client must know what to do with this data.

When the *Networking* module receives a response, it passes it to the *Response Processing* module. First, this module must interpret the status code and header information found in the response to determine what action it should take. It begins by examining the *status code* found in the first line of the response (the *status line*). In the chapter covering the HTTP protocol, we delineated the different classes of status codes that might be sent by a Web server:

- *informational* status codes (1*xx*),

- *successful response* status codes (2*xx*),

- *redirection* status codes (3*xx*),

- *client request error* status codes (4*xx*), and

- *server error* status codes (5*xx*).

Obviously, different actions need to be taken depending on which status code is contained in the response. Since the successful response represents the simplest and most common case, we will begin with the status code "200".

Processing successful responses

The status code "200" represents a successful response, as indicated by its associated message "OK". This status code indicates that the browser or client should take the associated content and render it in accordance with the specifications included in the headers:

```
Content-Transfer-Encoding: chunked
Content-Encoding: compress | gzip
```

The presence of these headers indicates that the response content has been encoded and that, prior to doing anything with this content, it must be *de*-coded.

```
Content-Type:  mime-type/mime-subtype
```

This header specifies the MIME type of the message body's content. Browsers are likely to have individualized rendering modules for different MIME types. For example, text/html would cause the HTML rendering module to be invoked, text/plain would make use of the plain text rendering module, and image/gif would employ the image rendering module. Browsers provide built-in support for a limited number of MIME types, while deferring processing of other MIME types to *plug-ins* and *helper applications*.

```
Content-Length:  xxx
```

This optional header provides the length of the message body in bytes. Although it is optional, when it *is* provided a client may use it to impart information about the progress of a request. When the header is included, the browser can display not only the amount of data downloaded, but it can also display that amount as a *percentage* of the total size of the message body.

```
Set-Cookie:  name=value; domain=domain.name;
   path=path-within-server; [ secure ]
```

If the server wishes to establish a persistent mechanism for maintaining session state with the user's browser, it includes this header along with identifying information. The browser is responsible for sending back this information in any requests it makes for resources within the same domain and path, using `Cookie` headers. The *State Maintenance* module stores cookie information found in the response's `Set-Cookie` headers, so that the browser can later retrieve that information for `Cookie` headers it needs to include in generated requests. Note that a response can contain multiple `Set-Cookie` headers.

```
Cache-Control: private | no-cache |...
Pragma: no-cache
Expires: Sun, 11 Feb 2001 22:28:31 GMT
```

These headers influence caching behavior. Depending on their presence or absence (and on the values they contain), the *Caching Support* module will decide whether the content should be cached, and if so, for how long (e.g. for a specified period of time or only for the duration of this browser session).

Once the content of a successful response has been decoded and cached, the cookie information contained in the response has been stored, and the content type has been determined, *then* the response content is passed on to the *Content Interpretation* module. This module delegates processing to an appropriate submodule, based on the content type. For instance, images (`Content-Type: image/*`) are processed by code devoted to rendering images. HTML content (`Content-Type: text/html`) is passed to HTML rendering functions, which would in turn pass off processing to other functions. For instance, JavaScript—contained within `<SCRIPT>` block tags or requested via references to URLs in `<SCRIPT SRC =...>` tags—must be interpreted and processed appropriately. In addition, stylesheet information embedded in the page must also be processed. Only after all of this processing is complete is the resulting *page* passed to the *User Interface* module to be displayed in the browser window. (Auxiliary requests for additional resources are explained in the section on *Requesting Supporting Data Items* later in this chapter.)

There are other status codes that fit into the 'successful response' category (`2xx`) including:

"`201 Created`": a new resource was created in response to the request, and the `Location` header contains the URL of the new resource.

"`202 Accepted`": the request was accepted, but may or may not be processed by the server.

"204 No Content": no body was included with the response, so there is no content to present. This tells the browser not to refresh or update its current presentation as a result of processing this request.

"205 Reset Content": this is usually a response to a form processed for data entry. It indicates that the server has processed the request, and that the browser should retain the current presentation, but that it should clear all form fields.

Although these status codes are used less often than the popular 200 OK, browsers should be capable of interpreting and processing them appropriately.

Processing of responses with other status codes

Aside from the successful status code of 200, the most common status codes are the ones associated with redirection (3xx) and client request errors (4xx).

Client request errors are usually relatively simple to process: either the browser has somehow provided an invalid request (400 Bad Request), or the URL the browser requested couldn't be found on the server (404 Not Found). In either of these cases, the browser simply presents a message indicating this state of affairs to the user. Authentication challenges that are caused by the browser attempting to access protected resources (e.g. 401 Not Authorized) are also classified as 'client error' conditions.

Some Web servers may be configured to provide custom HTML presentations when one of these conditions occurs. In those situations, the browser should simply render the HTML page included in the response body:

```
HTTP/1.1 404 Not Found
Content-Type: text/html

<HTML>
<HEAD>
<TITLE>Whoops!</TITLE>
</HEAD>
<BODY BGCOLOR="#ffffff">
<h3>Look What You've Done!</h3>
You've broken the internet!
<P>
(Just kidding, you simply requested an invalid address on this site.)
</BODY>
</HTML>
```

Security Clearance

There is another type of client error that is not quite so simple to process: 401 Not Authorized and 403 Forbidden responses. Servers send responses with the 401 status code when authorization credentials are required to access the resource being requested, and send responses with the 403 status code when the server does not want to provide access at all. The latter may happen when the browser exceeds the server limit for unsuccessful authentication challenges. The methods for dealing with authorization challenges will be discussed later in this chapter.

Redirection status codes are also relatively simple to process. They come in two varieties: 301 Moved Permanently and 302 Moved Temporarily. The processing for each of these is similar. For responses associated with each of these status codes, there will be a Location: header present. The browser needs to submit a further request to the URL specified in this header to perform the desired redirection.

Some Web servers may be configured to include custom HTML bodies when one of these conditions arises. This is for the benefit of older browsers that do not support automatic redirection and default to rendering the body when they don't recognize the status code. Browsers that support redirection can ignore this content and simply perform the redirection as specified in the header:

```
HTTP/1.1 301 Moved Permanently
Location: http://www.somewhere-else.com/davepage.html
Content-Type: text/html

<HTML>
<HEAD>
<TITLE>Dave's Not Here, Man!</TITLE>
</HEAD>
<BODY BGCOLOR="#ffffff">
<h3>Dave's Not Here, Man!</h3>
Dave is no longer at this URL.  If you want to visit him,
click <A HREF="http://www.somewhere-else.com/davepage.html">here</A>.
</BODY>
</HTML>
```

This response should cause the browser to generate the following request:

```
GET /davepage.html HTTP/1.1
Host: www.somewhere-else.com
  ...
```

The difference between the `301` and `302` status codes is the notion of 'moved permanently' versus 'moved temporarily'. The `301` status code informs the browser that the data at the requested URL is now *permanently* located at the new URL, and thus the browser should always automatically go to the new location. In order to make this happen, browsers need to provide a persistence mechanism for storing relocation URLs. In fact, the mechanism used for storing cookies, authorization credentials, and cached content can be employed for this purpose as well. In the future, whenever a browser encounters a request for a relocated URL, it would automatically build a request asking for the new URL.

5.4 COMPLEX HTTP INTERACTIONS

Now that we covered the basics of request and response processing, let us move on to situations where the interplay of requests and responses yields more sophisticated functionality.

The areas we mentioned earlier were caching, authorization, cookies, the request of supporting data items, and the processing of other complex response headers (including advanced HTTP functionality). Let us examine how the modules in our browser architecture interact to provide this functionality.

5.4.1 Caching

When we speak of *caching*, we are referring to the persistence in some storage mechanisms of generated and retrieved server resources to improve the performance of the response generation process.

There is *server-side caching*, which relieves the server of the responsibility of regenerating a response from scratch in appropriate situations. When resources (such as HTML responses or dynamically generated images) are stored in a server-side cache, the server does not need to go through the process of building these responses from the ground up. This can yield an enormous performance benefit, provided the stored response is still deemed usable (i.e. has not *expired*). This variety of caching is application-specific and goes beyond the scope of providing support for HTTP standards. (This is discussed further in the chapter on Web applications).

More relevant to our concerns in designing a browser is *client-side caching*. Client-side caching can relieve the client of the responsibility for re-requesting a response from the server, and/or relieve the server of the responsibility for re-sending a response containing an already requested resource. This can yield enormous savings in data transmission time. To support client-side caching, Web clients must store retrieved resources in a client-side cache. Subsequent requests for the same resource (i.e. the response generated by a request to the same URL with the same parameters) should examine the cache to see if that resource already has been stored in the cache and is still valid (i.e. has not expired). If it has expired, the client should ask the server to send back a copy of the resource only if it has changed since the last time it was requested.

Support for browser caching requires three components:

1. Mechanism for including appropriate headers in requests to support caching (part of *the Request Generation* module),

2. Examination of response headers for directives regarding the caching of the response (part of the *Response Generation* module), and

3. Mechanism for saving retrieved resources in some persistent storage mechanism (memory or disk) until the specified expiration date.

The third item is a module in and of itself: the *Caching* module, which does the bulk of the decision making regarding how to construct requests to support caching, and how to deal with potentially cacheable content found in the response.

Before an HTTP request is generated for a resource, the *Request Generation* module should query the *Caching Support* module to determine whether a saved copy of this resource exists and has not yet expired. If there is such a copy, it can be used to satisfy the request, rather than requiring the browser to transmit an explicit request to a server and wait for a response to be transmitted back. Even if the copy has 'expired', the request for the resource can be sent with an If-Modified-Since header. If the resource has not changed since the time it was originally retrieved, the server can respond with a 304 Not Modified status code, rather than sending a new copy of the resource in the response.

If there is no local copy stored in the cache, the *Request Generation* module does not include the conditional header in the request. The content of the response should be considered as a candidate object to be stored in the cache. If there are no directives in the headers indicating that this item should *not* be cached, the item can be stored in the cache, along with any associated expiration information. The *Response Processing* module must perform the necessary examination of response headers and pass the content of the response to the *Caching* module if appropriate. The caching module determines whether or not the content should be stored in the cache.

Here we see an example of an HTTP response specifying that the content should not be cached. Subsequent requests for this same resource would result in its repeated transmission from the server:

```
HTTP/1.1 200 OK
Date: Sun, 13 May 2001 12:36:04 GMT
Content-Type: image/jpeg
Content-Length: 34567
 ...
Cache-Control: no-cache
Pragma: no-cache


 ...
```

An example of an HTTP response with the defined expiration date is shown below. This entry would expire one day after the original request was made:

```
HTTP/1.1 200 OK
Date: Sun, 13 May 2001 12:36:04 GMT
Content-Type: image/jpeg
Content-Length: 34567
Cache-Control: private
Expires: Mon, 14 May 2001 12:36:04 GMT
Last-Modified: Sun, 13 May 2001 12:36:04 GMT

 ...
```

The next time this particular resource is desired, the cached copy may be used, at least until the specified expiration date.

When a copy of a resource is stored in the cache, the *Caching* module maintains other information (metadata) about the cache entry, namely its expiration date and its last modification date. This information is useful in optimizing the use of cache entries to satisfy requests.

For example, let's say a full day passes from the point in time at which this resource was cached. According to the expiration date specified in the Expires header, the cache entry will have expired by then. At this point, the *Request Generation* module could simply submit a request for a fresh copy of the resource, telling the *Caching Support* module simply to dispose of the expired cache entry. But this may not be necessary. If the content of the resource has not changed since it was originally retrieved, the stored copy is still usable. So, why not use it?

There are several ways to determine whether a resource has been modified since it was last accessed. Prior to HTTP/1.1, the most economical way to do this was to make use of the HEAD method associated with HTTP requests. The HEAD method returns the same results as a GET request, but without the response's body. In other words, only the headers are sent in the response. The browser could simply look at the Last-Modified header in the response, and compare it to the last modification date associated with the cache entry. If the date specified in the header was less than or equal to the date found in the cache entry, the cache entry can still be used. Otherwise, the cache entry is deleted and a request is made for a new copy of the requested resource.

HTTP/1.1 provides a simpler way to accomplish the same goal. Requests can include a new header, If-Modified-Since, that would specify the last modification date found in the cache entry. If the date specified in the header is *greater than or equal to* the last modification date associated with the requested resource, the server will send back a response with a status code of 304 Not Modified. This tells the browser that the cache entry can still be used. Otherwise, the server sends the new copy of the requested resource, and the browser deletes the cache entry. With this new feature of HTTP/1.1, what used to take (potentially) two sets of HTTP requests and responses now can be accomplished in one.

Thus, when the *Caching* module informs the *Request Generation* module that a cache entry exists but may have expired, the *Request Generation* module can add the If-Modified-Since header to its request. The *Response Processing* module, upon receiving a 304 Not Modified response, will then make use of the cache entry.

History Repeats

An awkward situation that occurs in even the most sophisticated browsers is the history anomaly. Users can employ the 'Back' button to see for a second time the presentation of pages they have already visited. The history mechanism within the browser often stores, not only a reference to links, but also the presentations associated with those links, regardless of any caching directives (e.g. Cache-Control: no-cache) that the server may have included in the original response headers!

What browsers need to do is treat the 'Back' button event as a request for new content, making the decision to re-use the presentation only after examining caching directives associated with the original response.

When it comes to pages with form fields, even within the scope of this anomaly, browsers do not act consistently. Internet Explorer 5 seems to present the page again, but with all form fields empty. Older browsers frequently left form fields filled in with whatever values had been entered on the previous visit to the page.

You may have noticed that some sites take precautions against this, explicitly taking action to clear form fields on the page as the form is being submitted. To do this, they must engage in 'stupid JavaScript tricks', copying entered fields into another form with hidden fields, resetting the form with the visible fields, and submitting the hidden form.

5.4.2 Cookie coordination

HTTP is a stateless protocol, but *cookies* are a mechanism for maintaining state during a browser session even though a stateless protocol is being used. The principle is simple: in responses sent to browsers, servers can include key/value pairs (cookies), which the clients are responsible for remembering. Every time the client sends a request back to a server for which it has received a cookie, it must include it in the request. This helps servers to *identify* specific browser instances, allowing them to associate sets of otherwise disjoint requests with particular users. These requests, taken together, do not comprise an actual session in the traditional network connectivity sense, but rather a *logical* session.

Servers transmit cookies to browsers via the `"Set-Cookie"` response header. This header provides a name-value combination that represents the cookie itself. In addition, this header contains information about the server's domain and the URL path with which the cookie is to be associated. It also can contain the secure keyword, which instructs the browser to limit the transmission of accompanied cookies to secure connections (e.g. using HTTPS, which is no more than HTTP over SSL).

The *domain* parameter of the `Set-Cookie` header can be a fully qualified host name, such as `ecommerce.mysite.com`, or a pattern such as `.mysite.com`, which corresponds to any fully qualified host name that *tail-matches* this string (e.g. for `domain=.mysite.com`, `ecommerce.mysite.com` and `toys.ecommerce.mysite.com` match, but `mysite.com` does not). The value of this parameter server must be a domain that the server sending the cookie belongs to. In other words, `ecommerce.mysite.com` could set a cookie with a domain parameter with a value of `ecommerce.mysite.com`, or `.mysite.com`, but not `catalog.mysite.com`.

The *path* parameter designates the highest level of a URL path for which the cookie applies. For instance, if a path parameter with a value of `/` is included in a `Set-Cookie` header sent by a server in a response, the browser should include the value of that cookie in requests for *all* URLs on the server. If the path parameter is set to `/cgi-bin/`, then the cookie need only be sent by the browser in requests for URLs within the `/cgi-bin/` directory subtree on the server.

Browsers send identifying cookies back to appropriate servers by including the `Cookie` header in requests to those servers. The content of this `Cookie` header is simply a set of key/value pairs originally sent by the server, which the browser has stored for future reference:

```
Cookie: key1=value1; key2=value2; ...
```

5.4.3 Authorization: challenge and response

As with any sophisticated mechanism employed within HTTP requests and responses, the authorization mechanism associated with *basic HTTP authentication* is an ongoing interchange. If we start at the *very* beginning, it would be when a simple HTTP request is made for a resource that just happens to be 'protected.'

Mechanisms exist on virtually all web servers to 'protect' selected resources. Usually, this is accomplished through a combination of IP address security (ranges of addresses are explicitly allowed or denied access to the resources) and some form of *Access Control List* (ACL) delineating the identifiers and passwords for users that are allowed to access the resources. ACLs are generally associated with *realms*, which is an abstract classification that a Webmaster can use to organize secure resources into discrete categories. The Webmaster associates groups of resources (usually directory subtrees) with specific realms.

In the chapter on Web servers, we discussed the design of services that implement both IP address security and ACL-based security. Here we will cover the mechanisms that browsers and other Web clients need to employ to interact with these services.

Let's start with a Web client request for a protected resource. The request looks like (and is) a perfectly normal HTTP request, because the client may not even realize that this resource is protected:

```
GET /protected/index.html HTTP/1.1
Host: secret.resource.com
```

The Web server, however, knows that the resource is protected (and is associated with a particular realm), and sends an appropriate response, with the `401 Not Authorized` status code:

```
HTTP/1.1 401 Not Authorized
Date: Sun, 11 Feb 2001 22:28:31 GMT
WWW-Authenticate: Basic realm ="Top Seekrit"
Content-type: text/html

  ...
```

This response is the *authentication challenge*. At this point, the client must answer the challenge by providing *authorization credentials*.

First, before it does anything else, the client should look in its own data storage to see if it has, during the current session, already provided credentials for this realm to this particular server. If it has, it does not need to obtain or derive these credentials anew, it can simply retransmit the stored credentials in its response. But we're getting ahead of ourselves: our scenario involves a *first* request to a server for protected resources.

The Web browser would obtain authorization credentials by prompting the user. Normally, this is accomplished by displaying a dialog box asking the user to enter a userid and password for the realm associated with the requested resource.

Once the browser has obtained these credentials, it must include them in a resubmitted HTTP request for the same resource:

```
GET /protected/index.html HTTP/1.1
Host: secret.resource.com
Authorization: Basic  encoded-userid:password
```

If the credentials do not match the userid and password in the ACL, it sends another response with a `401 Not Authorized` status code, causing the browser to re-prompt for valid credentials. If the user elects to stop trying (e.g. by choosing the 'Cancel' option), the browser will present a message to the user, or alternatively, it will present the HTML content (if any) provided with the `401` response. Most servers will give up after a certain number of exchanges with the browser, changing the `401` status code to `403` (`Forbidden`).

If the credentials provided *do* match the userid and password in the ACL, the Web server will then finally transmit the contents of the requested resource. At the same time, the browser should save the credentials so that the next time a request is made for a resource within the same realm on the same server (during the same session), the user need not be prompted for those credentials again.

5.4.4 Re-factoring: common mechanisms for storing persistent data

Note that there are many similarities between the mechanisms provided for storing cached content, cookie information, and authorization credentials. They can all be thought of as a form of *persistence*, since they all represent efforts to store similarly structured information that will be reused later on. It is probably a good idea to build a generalized persistence mechanism into your browser, and to use that mechanism for all of these purposes. This mechanism would need to support both in-memory persistence (where persisted information is saved only for the duration of the browser session and never stored permanently), and long-term persistence (where persisted information may be placed in some form of permanent data storage so that it lasts beyond the end of the browser session). Obviously, there *are* differences in the ways this mechanism would be used for each of these functions, as summarized in Table 5.1.

- For caching, the decision to store the data in the cache is based on response headers that the *Caching* module must interpret. The *key* used for addressing a cache entry is the requested URL (along with, potentially, any query string, POST content, and URL parameters associated with the request). Cache entries should be stored with an expiration date. If one is provided in an `Expires` header, then that should be used. If the date provided is in the past, then this indicates that this entry should only be cached for the duration of the browser session, meaning they should be flushed from the cache when the session ends. In addition, there should

Table 5.1 Browser mechanisms for storing persistent data

	Decision to store	Access key	When to delete	Storage mechanism
Cache	Depends on response headers	URL associated with request	At expiration date or when cache is full	Memory and/or disk
Cookies	Depends on user settings	Domain and path parameters in cookie	At expiration date, or at end of session if no date provided	Memory for cookies that expire at end of session, disk for persisted cookies
Authorization credentials	Always	Server address and authentication realm	At end of session!!	Memory only (never store on disk)

be a mechanism in the *Configuration* module for establishing the maximum cache size. If that size is exceeded (or approached), the *Caching* module should flush the oldest entries found in the cache.

- For cookies, the decision to store the cookie information found in a response's Set-Cookie header is based on only one factor: whether or not the user has elected (via the interface to the *Configuration* module) to accept cookies. This should be the default behavior in a browser (i.e. users should have to take explicit action to reject cookies). The key for addressing a cookie is the domain and path information specified in the Set-Cookie header. Cookies also have an expiration date. If none is specified, or if the date specified is in the past, the cookie information should only be stored for the duration of the current browser session, and flushed when the session ends. The browser can provide limits on the amount of space available for storage of cookies; it is not required to store all cookies indefinitely.

- For authorization credentials, there is no decision to be made: this information should always be retained. However, authorization credentials are *always* flushed when the session ends and are *never* kept beyond the end of the browser session. Thus they should be kept in memory and never written to stable storage. The key for addressing authorization credentials is the IP address (or name) of the server, and the name of the *realm* with which the server associates the requested resource.

Information that is required only for the duration of the browser session should be kept in memory, while information that must be persisted beyond the end of the session must be recorded using permanent data storage. This can be as simple as a text file (as Netscape does with cookies) or a directory subtree (as most browsers do for cached content), but more sophisticated mechanisms can be used as well.

5.4.5 Requesting supporting data items

Even the simplest web page is not 'self-contained'. Most pages at the very least contain references to images found at other URLs. In order to support graphical page rendering properly, a browser must make supplementary requests to retrieve supporting resources.

To accomplish this, the browser needs to parse HTML markup and find additional resources that are specified on the page. The *Content Interpretation* module is responsible for performing this analysis. Once it has determined which additional resources are desired, it must tell the *Request Generation* module to construct and transmit HTTP requests to obtain these resources (Figure 5.4).

Step 1: Initial user request for `"http://www.cs.rutgers.edu/~shklar/"`

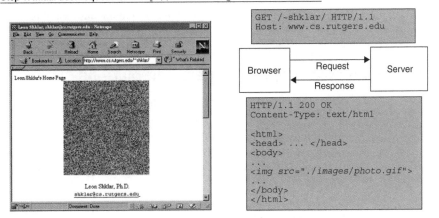

Step 2: Secondary browser request for `"http://www.cs.rutgers.edu/~shklar/images/photo.gif"`

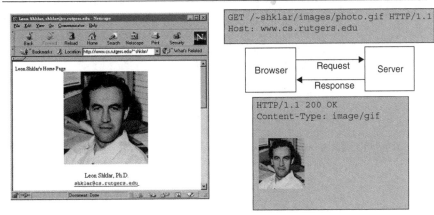

Figure 5.4 Browser steps for requesting supporting data items

> **Keep the Connection Open!**
>
> These resources (e.g. images) are often found on the same server as the HTML
> page itself. Prior to the advent of HTTP/1.1, this would mean that a browser would
> repeatedly open and close connections to the same server to get all the resources
> it needed.
>
> Fortunately, HTTP/1.1 by default supports persistent connections. This means that,
> unless otherwise specified, the browser will keep the connection to a server open so
> that supplemental requests can be made without additional overhead.

Remember that caching comes into play when making supplemental requests. A
well-organized site is likely to use the same images on many different pages. If the
server indicates that these images are cacheable and if a reasonable expiration date
is specified, the browser may not need to make additional requests for some of these
images: it may already have them in the cache!

5.4.6 Multimedia support: helpers and plug-ins

From the beginning, browsers provided integrated support for many different types
of data. Obviously, they rendered HTML (as well as plain text). When it came
to graphics, support for GIF and JPEG images was practically ubiquitous by the
early browsers like Mosaic and Netscape, and support for animated GIFs followed
soon thereafter. The `<IMG SRC="...">` tag was included in the very earliest versions
of HTML.

HTML, plain text, GIF and JPEG are supported "natively" by pretty much all of
the modern desktop browsers. There are exceptions: for example, text-only browsers
like Lynx, and browsers for handheld devices of limited bandwidth and screen size,
do not include support for images. Apart from images, there are other popular types
of data presented via the Web. The most prominent example is that of multimedia
objects (audio and video), but there are also proprietary formats such as Adobe
Acrobat PDF and Macromedia Flash.

To enable the presentation of these data objects, browsers can do one of three
things: they can provide native support for the format, they can allow the invocation
of *helper* programs to present the object, or they can provide support for *plug-ins*.
Plug-ins are program modules closely integrated with the browser, which enable the
rendering/presentation of particular kinds of objects within the browser window.

The first option can be overwhelming. There are many multimedia data formats out there, and supporting even the most popular ones through embedded
code within the browser is a daunting task. Furthermore, proprietary formats like
Flash and PDF are subject to frequent change, as vendors keep implementing more
advanced versions of these formats. It surely seems a far better idea to offload

support for these formats onto the people best capable of providing that support: the vendors themselves.

This leaves the choice between *helper* applications and *plug-ins*. Helper application support is relatively simple to implement. As we know, all of these different formats are associated with particular MIME types. Browsers can be configured to defer presentation of objects whose formats they do not support natively to programs that are specifically intended for presentation of such objects. A browser may create a mapping of MIME types to helper applications (and give users control over which applications should be invoked as helpers), or it can take the simpler route of using the mapping between MIME types and file extensions to defer the choosing of applications to the operating system.

The downside of this approach is that these objects are rendered or presented outside of the browser window. A separate application is started to access and present the object, sometimes obscuring the browser window entirely, but at the very least abruptly shifting the user's focus from the browser to another application. This can be very confusing and can negatively impact the user's impression of the Web presentation.

What's more, this approach is limited to usage with links pointing directly at the object, e.g. `<A HREF="flashmovies/mymovie.swf">`. In many cases, page designers want to embed an object directly into the current page, rather than forcing users to click on a link so that the object can be presented to them.

This leaves us with the plug-in approach. This approach makes use of `<EMBED>` and `<OBJECT>` HTML tags to tell the browser to render an embedded object. The `<EMBED>` tag has been deprecated in favor of the `<OBJECT>` tag. In fact, the W3C sees the `<OBJECT>` tag as a generalized approach to embedding multimedia objects.

The browser must maintain a table defining what actions should be taken to present each defined MIME type. This table should specify whether support for the MIME type is built into the browser, whether there is an installed plug-in, or whether the browser should launch a helper application. Although the browser should provide explicit plug-in specifications in this table (so that it knows which plug-in to use), it need not do this for helper applications. If it does not designate specific helper applications for MIME types, it defers the responsibility of choosing a helper application to the operating system. In any case, the *Configuration* module should provide a mechanism for users to customize these associations.

This table must also associate MIME types with filename extensions (suffixes). These associations are needed when the browser attempts to present local files, and when it attempts to present responses that do not contain a properly formatted `Content-Type` header. Such responses violate HTTP protocol requirements, but browsers can use this table of associations to infer a MIME type from the filename suffix found in the URL.

Browsers should be designed not to be *too* clever in this regard: some versions of Internet Explorer tried to infer a response's MIME type by examining the content. If it 'looked like' HTML, it would try to present it with a `Content-Type` of `text/html`. But webmasters sometimes want HTML content to be explicitly presented as `text/plain` (e.g. to show what the unprocessed HTML associated with a page fragment actually looks like). With this in mind, browsers should only engage in heuristic practices to infer the MIME type if all else fails (i.e. if there is no `Content-Type` and no known URL filename suffix).

Great Moments in MIME History

The notion of associating MIME types with designated applications dates back to the earliest uses of MIME. Remember that MIME was originally intended for use with e-mail attachments. (You may recall that MIME stands for Multimedia Internet Mail Extensions.) UNIX systems made use of a `.mailcap` file which was basically a table, associating MIME types with application programs. From the earliest days of the Web, browsers made use of this capability. Early browsers on UNIX systems often used the `.mailcap` file directly, but as technology advanced and plug-ins got added into the mix, other browsers (e.g. Netscape) started to use their own MIME configuration files.

5.5 REVIEW OF BROWSER ARCHITECTURE

Table 5.2 reviews the browser modules discussed in this chapter, and summarizes their responsibilities:

Table 5.2 Browser modules and their responsibilities

Module	Function	Responsibilities
User Interface	Providing user interface. Rendering and presenting end result of browser processing.	1. Displays browser window for rendering the content received from *Content Interpretation* module. 2. Provides user access to browser functions through menus, shortcut keys, etc. 3. Responds to user-initiated events: — selecting/entering URLs — filling in forms — using navigation buttons (e.g. 'Back') — viewing page source, resource info, etc. — setting **Configuration** options 4. Passes request information to *Request Generation* module.
Request Generation	Constructing HTTP requests.	1. Receives request information from **User Interface** module or *Content Interpretation* module, resolving relative URLs. 2. Constructs request line and basic headers: — `Content-Type:`/`Content-Length:` (if body included in request)

Table 5.2 (*continued*)

Module	Function	Responsibilities
		— `Referer:` (passed from *User Interface* module) — `Host:` — `Date:` — `User-Agent:` — `Accept-*:` 3. Asks *Caching* module if usable cache entry exists: — passes the entry to the *Content Interpretation* module if unexpired, — or adds `If-Modified-Since` header to force the server to only send back newer content. 4. Asks *Authorization* module if this is a domain/path for which we have credentials: — if so, adds `Authorization` header to provide credentials to server, — if not, tells *User Interface* module to prompt the user. 5. Asks *State Maintenance* module if this is a domain/path for which we have cookies? — if so, adds `Cookie` header to transmit cookies to server. 6. Passes fully constructed request to the **Networking** module.
Response Processing	Analyzing, parsing, & processing HTTP responses.	1. Receives responses from *Networking* module. 2. Checks for 401 status code (Not Authorized): — Asks *Authorization* module for credentials for realm named in `WWW-Authenticate` header: **yes**—resubmit request with saved credentials, **no**—prompt user for credentials and resubmit request. 3. Checks for request redirection status codes (301/302/307): — Resubmit request to URL specified in `Location` header. — If 301, store new location in persistent lookup table (so browser relocates automatically when URL is visited again). 4. Checks for `Set-Cookie` headers: — Stores cookies using browser's persistence mechanism. 5. Passes result to *Content Interpretation* module.
Networking	Interfacing with operating system's network services, creating sockets to send requests and receive responses over the network, and maintaining queues of requests and responses.	1. Receives requests from *Request Generation* module and adds them to transmission queue. 2. Opens sockets to transmit queued requests to server. — Connection kept open as additional requests are received. — Connection can be closed explicitly with last resource. 3. Waits for responses to queued requests, which are passed to *Response Processing* module. 4. **Queries Configuration** module to determine proxy configuration and other network options.

(*continued overleaf*)

Table 5.2   (*continued*)

Module	Function	Responsibilities
Content Interpretation	Content-type specific processing (images, HTML, JavaScript, CSS, XML, applets, plug-ins, etc.)	1. Receives content from *Response Processing* module (in some cases, from the *Caching* module). 2. Examines encoding headers (if present, decode content) — `Content-Encoding:` — `Content-Transfer-Encoding:` 3. Passes decoded content to MIME-type-specific submodule based on `Content-Type` header. 4. If content has references to other resources, passes URLs to *Request Generation* module to get auxiliary content. 5. Passes each resource as it is processed to the *User Interface* module.
Caching	Creating, keeping track of, and providing access to cached copies of web resources.	1. *Request Generation* module asks whether appropriate cache entry exists: — If it does, add `If-Modified-Since` header to request containing last modification time of cached entry. 2. *Response Processing* module requests caching of retrieved resource (when appropriate).
State Maintenance	Recording cookie information from response headers, and including cookie information in request headers when appropriate.	1. *Response Processing* module checks for Set-Cookie headers and requests recording of cookie information using browser's persistence mechanism. 2. *Request Generation* module examines stored cookie information and includes Cookie headers when appropriate.
Authorization	Providing mechanisms for submitting authorization credentials, and keeping track of supplied credentials so that users do not have to keep resubmitting them.	1. *Response Processing* module checks for responses with `"401 Not Authorized"` status code. — If browser has stored credentials for the realm defined in `WWW-Authenticate` header, resubmit request with added `Authorization` header containing credentials. — If not, *User Interface* module prompts user for credentials. (Credentials are stored for duration of browser session *only*, so that resources in same realm will not ask for credentials again.) 2. *Request Processing* module checks to see if any stored credentials match the domain/path of the request URL. If so, add `Authorization` header containing credentials.
Configuration	Providing persistence mechanism for browser settings. Providing interface for users to modify customizable settings.	Queried by all modules to determine what action is to be taken based on user-specified preferences.

5.6 SUMMARY

In the previous two chapters, we have examined design considerations for both Web servers and Web clients (specifically browsers). We discussed their module structure and operation, as well as the reasoning behind key design decisions. Given the proliferation of different devices, you just might end up having to implement your own server or browser. Even if you don't, the knowledge and understanding of Web agents and their operation will give you the edge in building and troubleshooting sophisticated Internet applications.

5.7 QUESTIONS AND EXERCISES

1. What main steps does a browser go through to submit an HTTP/1.1 request?
2. What main steps does the browser go through in processing an HTTP/1.1 response?
3. Is it possible for the browser not to support persistent connections and still be compliant with the HTTP/1.1 specification? Why or why not?
4. What is the structure of a POST request? What headers have to be present in HTTP/1.0 and HTTP/1.1 requests?
5. What functionality would be lost if browsers did not know how to associate file extensions with MIME types?
6. What functionality would be lost if browsers did not know how to associate MIME types with helper applications?
7. Consider an html document (say, http://www.cs.rutgers.edu/~shklar/): How many connections would an HTTP/1.0 browser need to establish in order to load this document? What determines the number of connections? How about an HTTP/1.1 browser? What determines the number of connections in this case? What would be the answer for you own home page?
8. Describe a simple solution for using HTTP protocol for submitting local files to the server through your browser. How about the other way around? Use the POST method for transmitting files to the server and the GET method for transmitting files from the server. Make sure to describe file transfer in both directions separately and to take care of details (e.g. setting the correct MIME type and its implications, etc.). Do you need any server-side applications? Why or why not?
9. There was an example from Chapter 3 where the server returned a redirect when a URL pointing to a directory did not contain a trailing slash. What would happen if the server did not return a redirect but returned an index.html file stored in that directory right away? Would it create a problem for browser operation? Why?
10. Suppose we installed a server application at this URL: http://www.vrls.biz/servlet/xml. The servlet supports two ways for passing arguments—as query string and as path info (e.g. http://www.vrls.biz/servlet/xml?name =/test/my.xml and http://www.vrls.biz/servlet/xml/test/my.xml). It is designed to apply a default transformation to the referenced XML file that is located at the server, generate an HTML file, and send it back to the browser. Something is wrong, and even though the servlet generates exactly the html in both

scenarios, the browser renders it as HTML in the first example and as XML in the second. Moreover, when we compare HTTP responses (including status codes, headers, and bodies) in these two cases, it turns out that they are identical. How is this possible? What is the problem with the servlet? Why does the browser behave differently when the HTTP response is exactly the same? How do we fix this problem?

BIBLIOGRAPHY

Gourley, D. and Totty, B. (2002) *HTTP: The Definitive Guide*. O'Reilly & Associates.
Stanek, W. (1999) *Netscape Mozilla Source Code Guide*. Hungry Minds.

6 HTML and Its Roots

One of the original cornerstones of the Web is HTML—a simple markup language whose original purpose was to enable cross-referencing of documents through hyperlinks. In this chapter, we will discuss HTML and its origins as an application of the Standard Generalized Markup Language (SGML). We shall cover SGML fundamentals, and show how HTML is defined within the framework of SGML. We then cover selected details of HTML as a language, and discuss related technologies.

It is important to know HTML's origins to understand its place in the overall evolution of markup languages. Admittedly, SGML is a niche language, though it is certainly one with an extensive history. Thus, it may not be of interest to every reader. We believe that knowledge of SGML is useful both from a historical perspective, and to better understand the advantages of XML. However, readers who want to get through the material quickly can skip directly to Section 6.2, bypassing the details of our SGML discussion.

The eXtensible Markup Language known as *XML* is the cornerstone of a new generation of markup languages, which are covered in the next chapter. For now, it is important to understand the relationship of SGML and HTML with XML, XHTML, and related technologies.

Both SGML and XML are meta-languages for defining specialized markup languages. Figure 6.1 illustrates that XML is a subset of SGML. As you can see, both HyTime and HTML are SGML applications, while XHTML, SOAP, SMIL, and WML are XML applications. Since XML is a subset of SGML, it is theoretically possible to construct SGML specifications for these languages, but since they are much easier to define using XML, you are not likely to find SGML specifications for them. We will come back to this discussion in the next chapter.

6.1 STANDARD GENERALIZED MARKUP LANGUAGE

HTML did not just appear out of the void. It was defined as an application of the *Standard Generalized Markup Language* (SGML)—a language for defining markup

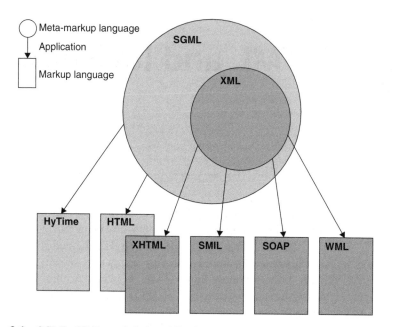

Figure 6.1   SGML, XML, and their applications

languages. SGML was created long before the advent of the World Wide Web. It was designed to define annotation and typing schemes that were jointly referred to as *markup*. Such markup schemes were originally intended to determine page layouts and fonts. Later, they were extended to cover all kinds of control sequences that get inserted into text to serve as instructions for formatting, printing, and other kinds of processing.

SGML was *not* the first attempt at digital typesetting—people have been using *latex, troff*, and other programs that produced all kinds of incompatible proprietary formats. This caused tremendous pains and gave birth to a great number of conversion programs that never did the job right. SGML *was* the first attempt to create a language for creating different specialized but compatible markup schemes. In a sense, this makes SGML a meta-markup language.

An interesting effect is that while there is a huge legacy of latex and other documents, it became quite easy to convert them to HTML and other SGML applications. In fact, as soon as it became clear that only few converters are really important, and that converters to different SGML markups can share quite a bit of code, it became much easier to achieve decent results.

An SGML application (e.g. HTML) consists of four main parts that all have separate roles in defining syntax and semantics of the control sequences:

1. The *SGML declaration* that specifies characters and delimiters that may legally appear in the application.

2. The *Document Type Definition* (DTD) that defines valid markup constructs. The DTD may include additional definitions such as numeric and named character entities (e.g. " or ").

3. A specification that describes the semantics to be ascribed to the markup. This specification is also used to impose additional syntax restrictions that cannot be expressed within the DTD.

4. Document instances containing content and markup. Each instance contains a reference to the DTD that should be used to interpret it.

In this section, we discuss elements of sample SGML applications. Our examples will center mainly on the HTML specification, providing a link to the rest of the chapter.

> **DTDeja Vu**
>
> Many among you may already have encountered DTDs and other related constructs in the context of XML. Do not get confused—this chapter does not talk about XML. DTDs first got introduced in SGML and found their way into XML much later. We shall discuss the commonalities and differences between SGML and XML DTDs in the next chapter. For now, keep an open mind, and do not overreact when you see DTDs that look just a little different than what you may be used to.

6.1.1 The SGML declaration

The role of the SGML declaration is to set the stage for understanding DTDs that define valid markup constructs for SGML applications. The declaration has to specify the character set, delimiters, and constraints on what may and may not be specified in a DTD.

The document character set

The problem of defining a proper character set normally becomes apparent when you face a screen full of very odd characters that were perfectly readable when you composed your document on another system. That is normally when it occurs to you that 'A' is not always an 'A'—it may be something totally incomprehensible if interpreted by a program that has a different convention for representing characters. The two most commonly used conventions for representing text are ASCII (American Standard for Coded Information Interchange) and EBCDIC (Extended Binary-Coded Decimal Interchange Code). The first is most probably the one you have encountered—it is used on most personal computers. Within both systems, many permutations depend on the country or the application domain.

What is needed is a way to associate the bit combination used in the document for a particular character to that character's meaning. It is too verbose to define character meanings directly, which is why SGML allows them to be defined as modifications to standard character sets. For example, the EBCDIC system represents capital letters C and D using bit combinations B'11000011' (decimal 195) and B'11000100' (decimal 196). Suppose that we need to represent these characters in the seven-bit character-encoding standard known as ISO 646. Characters 'C' and 'D' are encoded in this standard using bit combinations B'01000011' (decimal 67) and B'01000100' (decimal 68). The SGML declaration for this association looks like the example shown in Figure 6.2.

In this example, ISO 646 is used as the base character set. On top of this base set we define two additional characters that get mapped to characters 'C' and 'D' of the base set. In addition, we state that the EBCDIC capital letter E (decimal 197) does not occur in the document—a bit strange but this may make sense in some bizarre cases.

Figure 6.3 contains the real character set definition for HTML 4. As we can see, except for the unused characters, the HTML 4 character set maps directly into an

```
CHARSET
      BASESET "ISO 646:1983//CHARSET
            International Reference Version (IRV)//ESC 2/5 4/0"
      DESCSET 195  2  67 -- Map 2 document characters starting at
                            195(EBCDIC C and D)to base set characters
                            67 and 68(ISO 646 C and D)
```

Figure 6.2   Sample SGML character set definition for EBCDIC characters

```
CHARSET
      BASESET "ISO Registration Number 177//CHARSET
            ISO/IEC 10646-1:1993 UCS-4 with
            implementation level 3//ESC 2/5 2/15 4/6"
      DESCSET 0        9        UNUSED
              9        2        9
              11       2        UNUSED
              13       1        13
              14       18       UNUSED
              32       95       32
              127      1        UNUSED
              128      32       UNUSED
              160      55136    160
              55296    2048     UNUSED
              57344    1056768  57344
```

Figure 6.3   SGML character set definition for HTML 4

ISO-defined base set. Characters that are mapped to 'UNUSED' (e.g. two characters starting with decimal 11, or eighteen characters starting with decimal 14) should not occur in HTML 4 documents.

The concrete syntax

The SGML language is defined using the so-called 'delimiter roles' rather than concrete characters. SGML always refers to delimiters by their role names. Once it comes to defining the concrete syntax for the application, roles get associated with character sequences. For example, even though most SGML applications use the '</' character sequence as a delimiter, this sequence is not part of SGML. What is the part of SGML is the role 'etago' indicating the start of the end tag. This role is often associated with '</' in syntax declarations but of course it may be associated with '[*[/' or another bizarre sequence.

It is important to make a clear distinction between the SGML language and the *reference concrete syntax* that is also included in the SGML specification. For example, while SGML makes use of the delimiter roles, the reference implementation associates these roles with most commonly used character sequences ('<', '</', '>', '/>', etc.). SGML applications can defer to definitions included in the reference concrete syntax for convenience.

Syntax declarations also include the following components:

- Characters that should not be used in documents ('shunned' characters).

- Bit combinations that are mapped to the function characters (SPACE, record start, etc.).

- Characters that can be used in names and other naming rules.

- Reserved keywords that are used within SGML (e.g. PCDATA).

- Additional constraints (e.g. the maximum name length, etc.).

Figure 6.4 contains the partial syntax definition for HTML 4. It starts with the enumeration of binary codes for characters that should be avoided in HTML documents. Format of the BASESET and DESCSET sections is the same as that used in defining the character set for legal documents (Section 6.1.1.1) but here it applies to characters that may be used for syntax references. The FUNCTION section defines bit combinations for characters that denote *record start, record end, space*, and *tab* functions. The NAMING section does not provide for any additional name start characters (apart from the defined minimum set—lower and upper case letters), but defines additional characters—'.', '-', '_' and ':'—that may occur elsewhere in names. Finally, the DELIM section defines delimiters by deferring to the reference implementation with the only override which is defined for the HCRO role.

```
SYNTAX
     SHUNCHAR CONTROLS 0 1 2 3 4 5 6 7 8 9 10 11 12 13 14 15 16
              17 18 19 20 21 22 23 24 25 26 27 28 29 30 31 127
     BASESET "ISO 646IRV:1991//CHARSET International Reference Version
              (IRV)//ESC 2/8 4/2"
     DESCSET 0 128 0


     FUNCTION
              RE            13
              RS            10
              SPACE         32
              TAB SEPCHAR    9


     NAMING  LCNMSTRT " "
             UCNMSTRT " "
             LCNMCHAR ".-_:"
             UCNMCHAR ".-_:"
             NAMECASE GENERAL YES
                      ENTITY  NO


     DELIM   GENERAL  SGMLREF
             HCRO "&#38;#x" -- 38 is the number for ampersand -
             SHORTREF SGMLREF
```

Figure 6.4 SGML syntax specification for HTML 4

Feature usage

SGML provides a lot of flexibility in defining markup minimization features. For example, the DATATAG feature of the declaration allows the DTD to specify character strings, which cause an end tag to be implied. In other words, it allows data to be treated both as data and as markup. This may arguably provide some convenience, but does not help with parsing the data and can potentially introduce ambiguities. Other examples include SHORTTAG that makes it possible to omit the tag's closing delimiters, and OMITTAG that makes it possible that certain start and/or end tags may be omitted. These features are the telling evidence of SGML's lineage. As mentioned earlier, SGML originates with library sciences, which had priorities other than computational properties.

Later, we come back to these examples to illustrate differences in philosophy between SGML and XML.

6.1.2 Document Type Definition

The purpose of the Document Type Definition (DTD) is to define the syntax of markup constructs. It may also include additional definitions (e.g. numeric and named

```
<!ENTITY % head.misc "SCRIPT | STYLE | META | LINK">
<!ENTITY % heading "H1 | H2 | H3 | H4 | H5 | H6">
<!ENTITY % attrs "%coreattrs %i18n %events">
<!ENTITY attrs "substitution text">
```

Figure 6.5 Sample entity definitions

character entities). In this section, we discuss how to define elements, attributes and entities, and illustrate these discussions using HTML examples.

Entity definitions

The DTD for HTML 4 begins with entity definitions. Entity definitions can be thought of as text macros. It is important to remember that by now we have already defined the concrete syntax, so we are not trying to define SGML entities, but rather macros that may be expanded elsewhere in the DTD. When the macro is referenced in the DTD, it is expanded into the string that appeared in the entity definition.

In the first two examples in Figure 6.5, %head.misc is defined to expand to the partial enumeration of elements that may occur within the HEAD element— SCRIPT | STYLE | META | LINK—while %heading is defined to expand to the enumeration of elements denoting section and block headings. In the third example, %attrs is defined to expand the sequence of other entities that would get expanded recursively.

Notice the difference between the so-called *parameter entities* that are a matter of convenience for the DTD specification itself, and general entities (last example in Figure 6.5). General entities become a part of the language that is being defined by a DTD and are referenced using the ampersand (e.g. &attrs). General entities are not important for HTML, but remember about them when we get to XML.

Elements

An SGML DTD defines *elements* that represent structures or behaviors. It is important to make the clear distinction between elements and tags. It is not uncommon for people to erroneously refer to elements as tags (e.g. 'the P tag'). An element typically consists of three parts: a start tag, content, and an end tag (e.g. test). It is possible for an element to have no content, and it is for such empty elements that notions of the *element* and the *tag* coincide (e.g. the HTML line break element—
).

An element definition has to specify its name, structure of its content (if any), and whether the end tag is optional or required. For example, the ordered list element is defined in Figure 6.6 to have the name OL, to require both the start tag and the end tag (first and second dashes), and to contain at least one LI element as its content. The line break element is defined to have the name BR, and to not require the end tag. This element is defined not to have any content.

The DTD mechanism was designed to specify verifiable constraints on documents, so it has to express relatively sophisticated relationships between different elements.

```
<!ELEMENT OL - - (LI)+>
<!ELEMENT BR - O EMPTY>
<!ELEMENT OPTION - O #PCDATA>
<!ELEMENT TABLE - - (CAPTION?, (COL* | COLGROUP*), THEAD?, TFOOT?,
                     TBODY+) >
```

Figure 6.6 Sample element definitions

Such relationships are expressed by defining content models. Very simple examples of such models are the empty body, body composed of one or more LI elements, and the body that can only contain document text (#PCDATA) but not other elements (see the first three examples in Figure 6.6). More generally, content models make it possible either to specify forbidden elements or to enumerate allowed elements or text, their sequence, and number of occurrences.

The last example in Figure 6.6 defines the TABLE element. As you can see, no text is allowed directly within TABLE, which is not to say that it cannot be specified within one of its contained elements. Element CAPTION has to appear first within the TABLE element. It may or may not be present as indicated by '?', a so-called *quantifier* indicating that CAPTION may appear exactly 0 or 1 times. Another quantifier, '*', that is applied to elements COL and COLGROUP indicates that they may appear any number of times or not appear at all—this is almost the same as '+' except that '+' requires that the element appears at least once. According to the definition of TABLE, a TABLE element should contain at least one TBODY but may or may not contain other elements.

Another interesting observation relates to grouping COL* and COLGROUP* constructs using parenthesis. The '|' operator indicates that the constructs may appear in any order and one of them may not appear at all. The '&' operator is very similar except that both constructs have to appear. Of course, if the constructs themselves are defined using quantifiers that allow 0 occurrences (e.g. '?' or '*'), there will be no practical difference between these operators (e.g. the COL*|COLGROUP* and COL* & COLGROUP* expressions). Another operator is ',' which indicates the fixed order. In the example, the CAPTION element may or may not occur within TABLE (due to the '?' quantifier), but if it does it has to occur first because expressions separated by the ',' operator impose fixed order.

Both table specifications shown in Figure 6.7 are valid because close tags for elements THEAD, TFOOT, and TBODY are optional, and it is perfectly legal for the TFOOT element to be absent. However, the table in Figure 6.8 is not valid because order imposed by the ',' operator in the HTML DTD (Figure 6.6) is violated—the TFOOT element occurs after the TBODY element. Now, the fact that the HTML fragment in Figure 6.8 is invalid does not necessarily mean that your browser will not display it correctly—desktop browsers are designed to be somewhat tolerant of bad HTML. However, writing invalid HTML is a bad habit that may cause problems when errors accumulate, or when your HTML is served by non-desktop browsers.

```
<TABLE>
        <THEAD>
            <TR>Table 1
        </THEAD>
        <TFOOT>
            <TR>December 2001</TR>
        </TFOOT>
        <TBODY>
            <TR><TD>1</TD><TD>2</TD><TD>3</TD>
            <TR><TD>6</TD><TD>8</TD><TD>5</TD>
        </TBODY>
        <TBODY>
            <TR><TD>23456</TD><TD>12345</TD>
        </TBODY>
</TABLE>
<TABLE>
        <THEAD><TR>Table 2
        <TBODY><TR><TD>1<TD>2<TD>3
             <TR><TD>6<TD>8<TD>5
        <TBODY><TR><TD>23456</TD><TD>12345</TD>
</TABLE>
```

Figure 6.7   Valid HTML fragment—sample HTML tables

```
<TABLE>
        <THEAD><TR>Table 2
        <TBODY><TR><TD>1<TD>2<TD>3
             <TR><TD>6<TD>8<TD>5
        <TFOOT><TR>December 2001</TR>
</TABLE>
```

Figure 6.8   Invalid HTML fragment (TFOOT occurs after TBODY)

Attributes

An element may allow one or more attributes that provide additional information to processing agents. For example, the SRC=url attribute of the HTML SCRIPT element instructs the browser the retrieve the script from the specified URL instead of the body of the SCRIPT element.

An attribute definition begins with the keyword ATTLIST and is followed by the element name (e.g. TABLE in the example in Figure 6.9) and a list of attribute definitions. An attribute definition starts with the name of an attribute (e.g. width or cols), and specifies its type and default value. Sample types shown in Figure 6.9 include NUMBER that represents integers and CDATA that represents document text. Other frequently used types include NAME and ID—both representing character sequences that start with a letter and may include letters, digits, hyphens, colons and periods; ID represents document-wide unique identifiers.

```
<!ENTITY % TAlign "(left|center|right)">
...
<!ATTLIST TABLE          -- table element --
  width        CDATA      #IMPLIED -- table width relative to window --
  cols         NUMBER     #IMPLIED -- used for immediate display mode -
  align        %TAlign;   #IMPLIED -- table position relative to window --
>
<!ATTLIST TH
  rowspan      NUMBER     1
  colspan      NUMBER     1
>
```

Figure 6.9   Sample attribute definitions for the TABLE element

Notice the use of a DTD entity in defining the `align` attribute. This entity—
`Talign`—is defined in the same example to expand to (left|center|right); its
use is simply the matter of convenience. Either way, the domain of the `align`
attribute is defined as the enumeration of `left`, `center`, and `right`.

When the attribute is defined as `#IMPLIED`, its value is supplied by the processing
agent (e.g. browser). The keyword `#REQUIRED` indicates that the attribute should
always be defined with its element. Alternatively, an attribute may be defined as
a fixed value, as in the `rowspan` and `colspan` attributes for the table header cell
element `Th` in Figure 6.9.

6.2 HTML

Our SGML discussion does not attempt to teach you all the details of designing
SGML applications. However, it is important that you understand the roots of HTML
and its upcoming replacement—XHTML. Later in the book, when it is time to talk
about XML, we will look back at SGML declarations and DTDs and think about
how to make use of them in the XML world. Understanding this connection between
SGML and XML is a critical prerequisite to understanding the relationship between
HTML, XML, and XML applications.

For now, let us be concerned with HTML—both syntactic constraints imposed
on HTML documents by HTML declarations and DTDs, and HTML semantics.
This is why we used HTML examples throughout the SGML discussion. Speaking
of which, you probably noticed that SGML declarations and DTDs do not help
with assigning semantics to HTML tags—HTML semantics is defined in HTML
specifications using plain English. It is the responsibility of implementers of HTML
agents (e.g. desktop or cable box browsers) to read, understand, and follow the
specification. By now, there are quite a few versions of such specifications around;
we will have to spend at least a little time sorting it all out. Once we do, we

can discuss the more interesting HTML constructs, paying special attention to the relationship between these constructs and the HTTP protocol.

6.2.1 HTML evolution

As you should have noticed from our SGML discussion, HTML syntax is rather flexible. The syntax of HTML tags is set in stone, but the structure of HTML documents is relatively unconstrained. For example, many HTML elements have optional closing tags, which in practice are commonly omitted. To make things worse, real HTML documents often violate even the liberal constraints imposed by the HTML specification because commercial browsers are tolerant of such violations. Nevertheless, bad HTML, even if it is being rendered properly at the moment, causes all kinds of problems over the lifetime of the document. A simple modification may add just enough insult to the injury to break rendering through a forgiving browser. It gets worse if it becomes important to re-purpose the same markup to non-desktop devices—non-desktop browsers that support HTML are much less tolerant to bad syntax.

Over the last ten years, the HTML specification has gone through a number of transformations. The common theme for all of these transformations is the tightening of the syntax. The latest and final revision of HTML (HTML 4.01) was released in December 1999. It soon became apparent that future developments would be hard to achieve in the context of SGML. The major additional burden is the need to maintain backward compatibility. HTML 4.01 partially addresses this problem by providing both 'strict' and 'transitional' specifications. It is now clear that HTML 4.01 will remain the final specification of the language, with all new development centering on its successor—XHTML.

Rendering modules of early HTML browsers associated fixed behavior with every HTML element. The only way to modify such behavior was through browser-global settings. Even at that time the HTML 2 specification made early attempts at abstraction. For example, it was not recommended to use the `<B>` element to indicate bold text. Instead, it was recommended to use the `<strong>` element for the same purpose, leaving it up to the rendering engine to load a meaning for `<strong>` that by default mapped to `<B>` anyway. Unfortunately, very few web designers actually followed such recommendations.

By the time HTML 4 came out, this simple abstraction developed into a mechanism for style sheets that make it possible to control rendering of HTML elements. HTML 4 also includes mechanisms for scripting, frames, and embedding objects. The new standard mechanism supports embedding generic media objects and applications in HTML documents. The `<OBJECT>` element (together with its predecessors `<IMG>` and `<APPLET>`) supports the inclusion of images, video, sound, mathematical expressions, and other objects. It finally provides document authors with a consistent way to define hierarchies of alternate renderings. This problem has been around since Mosaic and Lynx (early graphical and command-line browsers) that needed alternate ways for presenting images.

Another important development that is represented in HTML 4 is internationalization. With the expansion of the Web it became increasingly important to support different languages. HTML 4 bases its character set on the ISO/IEC:10646 standard (as you remember, SGML gives us the power to define the character set). ISO/IEC:10646 is an inclusive standard that supports the representation of international characters, text direction, and punctuation, which are all crucial in supporting the rich variety of world languages.

6.2.2 Structure and syntax

As already mentioned, it is important not to be mislead by high tolerance to HTML syntax and structure violations that characterizes commercial desktop browsers. HTML specification is the only common denominator for diverse commercial tools, and compliance to this specification is the best way to avoid problems over the lifetime of your documents.

According to the specification, an HTML 4 document must contain a reference to the HTML version, a *header* section containing document-wide declarations, and the *body* of the document. Figure 6.10 contains an example of a compliant HTML document.

As can be seen, the version declaration names the DTD that should be used to validate the document. HTML 4.01 defines three DTDs—the strict DTD that is designed for strict compliance and the other two, one of which supports deprecated elements excluding frames and the other supports frames as well.

HTML header

The *header* section starts with the optional <HEAD> element and includes document-wide declarations. The most commonly used header element is the <TITLE> that

```
<!DOCTYPE HTML PUBLIC "-//W3C//DTD HTML 4.01//EN"
    "http://www.w3.org/TR/html4/strict.dtd">
<HTML>
  <HEAD>
    <TITLE>Sample HTML Document</TITLE>
  </HEAD>
  <BODY>
    <P>I don't have to close the <P> tag.
  </BODY>
</HTML>
```

Figure 6.10 Sample HTML 4.01 compliant document

```
<META name="Author" content ="Leon Shklar">
<META name="Author" content ="Rich Rosen">
<META name="Publisher" content="Wiley Computer Publishing">
<META http-equiv="Expires" content="Sun, 17 Feb 2002 15:21:09 GMT">
<META http-equiv="Date" content="Tue, 12 Feb 2002 08:05:22 GMT">
```

Figure 6.11 Sample META elements

dates back to early versions of HTML. Most browsers display the value of this element outside of the body of the document. In a way, it is an early attempt to specify document metadata. It is widely used by search agents that normally assign it higher weight than the rest of the document.

The recently added <META> element provides a lot more flexibility in defining document properties and providing input to browsers and other user agents. Figure 6.11 shows examples of defining the 'Author' and 'Publisher' properties using the <META> element.

The <META> element may also be used to specify HTTP headers. The last two examples in Figure 6.11 tell the browser to act as if the following two additional HTTP headers were present:

```
Expires: Sun, 17 Feb 2002 15:21:09 GMT
Date: Tue, 12 Feb 2002 08:05:22 GMT
```

You can use this syntax to define any HTTP header you want, but you should not be surprised if some of them affect processing and some don't. No surprise here: some headers have to be processed by the browser before the HTML document is parsed, and therefore cannot be overridden using this method. For example, to start parsing the HTML document, the browser must have already established (from the headers) that the Content-Type of the body is text/html. Thus, the Content-Type cannot be modified using an instance of the <META> element in this way. The browser would not have been able to process the <META> element in the first place unless it had already known the Content-Type. It follows that Content-Type headers defined in the HTML <META> tag, as well as Content-Encoding and Content-Transfer-Encoding headers, would be ignored.

There are advantages to embedding HTTP headers in HTML files. The main reason why we are discussing it in such detail is that it illustrates an important link between different Web technologies. Embedding HTTP-based logic in HTML files may be invaluable in building applications that are very easy to install and distribute across different hardware and software platforms. Whenever you desire to employ this mechanism, you should consider different processing steps that occur prior to parsing the markup, to decide whether your <META> element would have

```
<STYLE type="text/css">
H1 {border-width: 1; border: solid; text-align: center}
</STYLE>
```

Figure 6.12   Sample STYLE element

any effect. This decision may depend on your processing agent—a browser or a
specialized intelligent proxy. Going back to the previous example, the proxy may
use the value of the `Content-Type` header defined in the `<META>` element, to set
the `Content-Type` of the response prior to forwarding it to the browser.

Other elements that are defined in the HTML header section include `<STYLE>` and
`<SCRIPT>`. The `<STYLE>` element is designed to alter the default browser behavior
when rendering the body of the markup. In the example shown in 6.12, we override
the default rendering of the `<H1>` element, telling the browser to center its value in a
box with a solid border. The syntax of the style instructions is defined to comply with
the Cascading Style Sheets (CSS) specification. It is not necessary to include the
style specification in the header section. In fact, it is far more common to reference
a standalone style document using the 'src' attribute of the `<STYLE>` element. This
way, it is possible to completely change the look and feel of HTML documents
simply by changing the 'src' attribute. We shall return to the CSS specification
later in the chapter.

The `<SCRIPT>` element, in combination with event handlers that may be referenced from the body of the document, is designed to provide access to browser
objects that get created when processing HTTP responses. Figure 6.13 illustrates

```
<script language="JavaScript">
function setMethod(form) {
    if (navigator.appName == "Netscape" &&
        navigator.appVersion.match(/^\s*[1-4]/)) {
        form.method = "get";
    } else {
        form.method = "post";
    }
    form.submit();
}
</script>
...
<body>
...
<form action="http://www.neurozen.com/s ervlet/markupTest"
name="testForm"
...
<input type="BUTTON" value="Next" onClick="setMethod(testForm)">
</form>
</body>
```

Figure 6.13   Sample SCRIPT element

using the `<SCRIPT>` element to define a sample JavaScript function, which takes the JavaScript `Form` object as an argument, sets the HTTP method to `GET` for Netscape 4.x and earlier browsers and to `POST` for other browsers, and submits the request. A brief discussion of JavaScript is provided later in this chapter.

HTML body

Content of an HTML document is included within the `<BODY>` element. We refer you to the HTML specification and a rich selection of HTML textbooks for descriptions of different formatting elements that occur in HTML documents. The most commonly used ones include `<TABLE>`, headings (`<H1>`, `<H2>`, etc.), ordered and unordered lists, and other elements designed to control screen layout.

Other important elements include anchors that reference documents or locations within documents, and image elements (check out the `<a href=...>` and `<img src=...>` elements in Figure 6.14). There is a very important difference between the two elements—the anchor is representing a hyperlink that only gets evaluated on request, while requests for loading images are generated automatically when attempting to render the page. Of course, this only applies to rendering agents that support images.

Content accessibility

An interesting observation about the `<img>` element in Figure 6.14 has to do with the use of the ALT attribute and element content. The value of the ALT attribute

```
<html>
<title>Leon Shklar, shklar@cs.rutgers.edu</title>
<base href="http://www.cs.rutgers.edu/~shklar/">
<body bgcolor="#ffffff">
<font size=-1>Leon Shklar's Home Page</font>
<center>
<img src="images/photo_small.gif" align=absmiddle alt="photo">
Photo
</img>
<p>Leon Shklar, Ph.D.</p>
<a href="mailto:shklar@cs.rutgers.edu">
<code>shklar@cs.rutgers.edu</code>
</a>
</center>
<p>
<em>One of these days I will find time and make my pages look cool...
</em>
<a href="classes/476">Here is a link to class notes ...</a>
</body>
</html>
```

Figure 6.14 Simple HTML page

gets displayed by browsers that support up-to-date HTML specifications but do not render images. Examples of command line browsers include Lynx and browsers for text-based mobile devices. The body of the <img> element would only be displayed by a browser that does not fully support current specifications and does not recognize the <img> element. Such a browser would ignore open and close image tags and display content of the <img> element as if it was open text. This example conveys an important point that is applicable to many HTML elements that control rendering—it is important to provide for design pages that can render in a wide variety of browsers that vary in their level of compliance with HTML specifications.

HTTP requests

Most browsers provide a number of options for generating HTTP requests. The most obvious are following a hyperlink, or specifying a URL (by typing it in, selecting a bookmark or a history entry, etc.). The less obvious option is initiating requests through HTTP headers or HTTP-EQUIV constructs. In all of those cases, the browser uses its own discretion in generating the request. We refer you to the browser chapter for gory details of request generation.

Let us take a quick look at request generation controls that are available in HTML. The most direct controls are available through HTML forms that provide support for selecting a URL, an HTTP method, the request type, and some HTTP headers. The example in Figure 6.15 illustrates using an HTML form for file transfer. Notice the use of the 'enctype' attribute to set the Content-Type header of the request. This was not necessary (except as an illustration) because the browser is supposed to default to "multipart/form-data" when transmitting files.

In the example, the first <input> element references a file—most browsers render it as a file selector dialog. Second and third <input> elements represent attribute-value pairs for specifying file name and location on the target system. The final <input> element represents the submission button that, when pressed, initiates the request.

```
<FORM action="http://www.nerozen.com/sendFile" method="post"
    enctype="multipart/form-data">
  <P>
  <LABEL for="select">Choose local file: </LABEL>
  <INPUT type="file" id="localpath"><BR>
  <LABEL for="filename">Target file name: </LABEL>
  <INPUT type="text" id="filename"><BR>
  <LABEL for="location">Target location: </LABEL>
  <INPUT type="text" id="location"><BR>
  <INPUT type="submit" value="Send"> <INPUT type="reset">
  </P>
</FORM>
```

Figure 6.15 File submission form

```
POST http://www.neurozen.com/sendFile HTTP/1.1
Host: www.neurozen.com
Content type: multipart/form-data;
boundary=----------------7d2202e1903de
User-Agent: Mozilla/4.0 (compatible; MSIE 6.0; Windows NT 5.0)
Locale: en_US

----------------7d2202e1903de
Content-Type: text/plain
Content-Length: 1A

This is my test text file.
----------------7d2202e1903de
Content-Type: application/x-www-form-urlencoded
Content-Length: 27

filename=mytestfile.txt&location=/leon/
----------------7d2202e1903de
```

Figure 6.16 Sample file transfer request

The browser needs a multipart MIME message to combine file content with information about the target location. A sample file transfer message is shown in Figure 6.16. It is a multipart message, the first part of which contains the file, and the second part contains form information pertaining to the target location of the submitted file. It is assumed that http://www.neurozen.com/sendFile is either a servlet or some other server-side executable that is capable of parsing the message to extract the file and its target location, and to save it at that location relative the document root.

This example illustrates HTML elements that control the formation of HTTP requests submitted by the browser. HTML provides many other controls that are not discussed in this book—the important part is to understand the idea of such controls and to know what to look for when implementing a specific task.

6.3 HTML RENDERING

As mentioned in the previous section, the only way to modify rendering of HTML elements in older browsers was through browser-global settings. However, early HTML specifications attempted to put stakes in the ground towards rendering abstractions to be achieved in the future (e.g. the distinction between <b> and <strong>). As previously mentioned, it did not make much practical difference, since very few HTML designers made such distinctions, since they had no immediate impact on the look and feel of their pages. Things changed when initial abstractions developed into style sheets that made it possible to exhibit fine-grained control over the rendering of HTML documents.

6.3.1 Cascading Style Sheets

Cascading Style Sheets (CSS) is a mechanism for controlling style (e.g. fonts, colors, spacing) for HTML. A style sheet is made up of rules, each of which applies to an HTML element and controls a certain aspect of its rendering. There are various ways of associating these style rules with HTML documents, but the easiest is to use the HTML <STYLE> element, which is placed in the document HEAD and contains style rules for the page (Section 6.2.2.1).

Figure 6.17 demonstrates sample rules for rendering default fonts within a paragraph (the <P> element). In the first rule font properties are defined through the 'font' argument, while in the second rule they are defined through the 'font-size' argument. The latter makes it possible to define that subset of properties that could be defined through the 'font' argument.

Another observation is that the same element property may be defined with a different level of abstraction. In the first rule, size is defined in absolute units that are independent of browser-global properties. Such a setting means that you are willing to ignore personal preferences, which is rarely a good idea. In the second rule, the font size is defined in terms that depend on browser-global properties but not the element context. In other words, 'medium' may mean '10pt' or '14pt' depending on browser settings, but within the same page and the same browser window, the paragraph would always be rendered exactly the same way. Similarly, the font color may be defined either by using absolute RGB (Red-Green-Blue) units (e.g. "#0000F0" in the first rule), or by using symbolic names that might map to different RGB combinations.

Finally, in the third rule, the font size is defined relative to the context—'larger' may translate into different absolute sizes within the same page, depending on the default font size in the element context where the <p> element is included.

As you can see from our example, CSS rules associate groups of properties with a particular HTML element. Properties that may be defined using style sheet rules include *font, color* and *text* groups. Font properties include font family, weight, size, height, and style, while color properties describe fonts and backgrounds. Text properties are a bit more complex and control word and letter indentation, text decoration (e.g. underline) and alignment, and even simple transformations (e.g. to all lower case or all upper case letters).

```
P { font: italic bold 12pt/14pt Times, serif; color: #0000F0  }
P { font-size: medium; color: blue }
P { font-size: larger }
```

Figure 6.17   Sample CSS rules

```
BODY { margin-top: 0 }
DT { margin-bottom: 2em }
A:visited { border: thin dotted #800080 }
P { display: list-item }
```

Figure 6.18 Sample *box* and *classification* properties

Other interesting groups include *box* and *classification* properties. Sample box properties are shown in the first three rules in Figure 6.18. The first rule serves to eliminate the top margin of a page, while the second rule sets the bottom margin of <DT> elements to two font heights, and the third one describes the border for visited links. The fourth rule defines a sample classification property. According to this rule, paragraphs would be shown not only with preceding and trailing line breaks, but also with the list-item marker.

6.3.2 Associating styles with HTML documents

Let us recall that the main purpose of Cascading Style Sheets is to separate rendering instructions from the markup instructions. (We are deliberately avoiding the overused 'content vs. presentation' comparison because we want to reserve it for server-side processing.) With this in mind, we are ready to consider alternatives for associating full style sheets and style elements with HTML pages and their fragments.

The approach that provides the highest degree of separation between HTML markup and style-based rendering is based on linking HTML documents with external style sheets, which do not contain any HTML markup, only style commands. This is accomplished through yet another HTML header element—<LINK>. Figure 6.19 contains examples of using this element to define the associations. Here, the REL attribute defines the relationship with the associated file and the TYPE attribute specifies the MIME type for the stylesheet (later on, we will learn about other kinds of stylesheets). The HREF attribute carries the expected meaning—it references the location of the stylesheet file. Finally, the MEDIA attribute defines the rendering media, which could be, for example, a regular desktop browser ('screen'), a speech synthesizer ('aural'), a printer ('print'), or other devices.

```
<LINK REL="StyleSheet" HREF="mystyle.css" TYPE="text/css"
      MEDIA="screen">
<LINK REL="StyleSheet" HREF="main.css" TYPE="text/css" MEDIA="screen"
      TITLE="Default Style">
<LINK REL="Alternate StyleSheet" HREF="alt.css" TYPE="text/css"
      MEDIA="screen"
      TITLE="Alternate Style">
<LINK REL="StyleSheet" HREF="audio.css" TYPE="text/css"
      MEDIA="aural">
```

Figure 6.19 Using the HTML <LINK> element to associate styles

The optional 'TITLE' attribute is only present when you need to support alternate stylesheets. Its absence, as in the first example, indicates that no style sheet alternation is supported. Style sheet alternation may have different forms, but would normally involve user interaction. The second and third examples represent the default stylesheet that gets applied at rendering time, and the alternative that has to be explicitly selected by the user. The last example in Figure 6.19 is similar to the first example except that the rendering device is assumed to be a speech synthesizer.

Our next example demonstrates the use of a style sheet embedded in an HTML document (Figure 6.20). It is similar to the example that we used to illustrate our discussion of HTML headers (Figure 6.12). One distinction is the use of the HTML comment syntax that would get ignored by browsers that support <STYLE> elements, but would help older browsers to avoid confusion. The second distinction is the use of the import statement. Use of the <STYLE> element in combination with the @import instruction is equivalent to the first example in Figure 6.19. The embedded syntax also makes it possible to override parts of imported styles with local definitions (e.g. the local definition of the <H1> element in Figure 6.20). This approach does violate the principle of separating markup and rendering but is borderline acceptable since the main style specification still comes from a separate file.

Yet another alternative (illustrated in Figure 6.21) employs inline style using the STYLE attribute that may be applied to most body elements (including <BODY> but excluding <SCRIPT>, <PARAM>, and <FONT>). It allows for the definition of style attributes for a single instance of a tag within a page, but it results in the mixing of style and markup. If you think you have valid reasons to use it anyway, you are supposed to define a single style sheet language for the whole document by including the proper header in the HTTP response (e.g. Content-Style-Type: text/css), though most browsers default to using CSS when processing STYLE attributes within tags. Alternatively, you can achieve the same result by using the HTML <META> element with the HTTP-EQUIV attribute (Section 6.2.2.1).

```
<STYLE type="text/css" media="screen">
<!--
@import url(mystyle.css);
H1 {border-width: 1; border: solid; text-align: center}
-->
</STYLE>
```

Figure 6.20   An embedded style sheet

```
<H1 STYLE="border-width: 1; border: solid; text-align:
center">Chapter 1
</H1>
```

Figure 6.21   Inline styles

```
<SPAN style="text-align: center">DRAFT</SPAN>
<DIV style="font-size: smaller">
        <TABLE><TR><TD>Column 1</TD><TD>Column 2</TD><TR>...</TABLE>
</DIV>
```

Figure 6.22 Associating styles with portions of HTML documents

If you feel that there needs to be a middle ground between document-wide and inline styles, you are not alone. Such middle ground can be achieved by using inline styles with <SPAN> and <DIV> elements, which were introduced for the express purpose of associating styles with portions of HTML documents. While <SPAN> is an inline element, which is used in a manner similar to <STRONG> and <EM>, <DIV> may contain blocks that include paragraphs, tables, and, recursively, other <DIV> elements (Figure 6.22).

6.4 JAVASCRIPT

Markup languages serve their purpose of providing formatting instructions for the static rendering of content. HTML, especially in combination with style sheets, is quite good at performing this function. The HTTP server sends a response to the requesting browser containing an HTML page as its body, which is rendered by the browser. HTML lets you control page layout, combine text with graphics, and support minimal interactive capabilities through links and forms.

The problem is that the presentation is static: there is no way to modify it programmatically once the page is rendered. The rendered page just stays there until the next request. Even a simple operation (e.g. validation of a form entry) requires server-side processing, which means an extra connection to the server.

One of the most noticeable trends in the evolution of HTML has been the introduction of new elements and attributes that make it possible to go beyond static rendering and to control browser behavior in a programmatic fashion. For example, it is possible to automate the submission of certain new requests by the browser by using the <META> element in conjunction with the HTTP-EQUIV attribute. This approach can only take you so far, and is not a replacement for programmable behavior. Something more was needed to provide programmatic functionality within the browser.

The solution was to introduce an object-oriented programming language, *JavaScript*, that includes built-in functionality for accessing browser objects (e.g. page elements, request generation modules, etc.), and to introduce HTML attributes that enable mapping of JavaScript methods to user events.

But I thought we were talking about markup languages!

Although this is a chapter devoted to markup languages, it behooves us to talk about JavaScript here. The HTML specification has evolved to define handlers for browser events, assuming that those handlers are implemented using a browser-supported scripting language that interfaces with the page's document object model. JavaScript was designed with this purpose in mind; it was intended as a browser-side programming/scripting language. It is not possible to completely separate HTML from JavaScript, which is why JavaScript deserves a place in this discussion.

JavaScript was initially developed for Netscape Navigator but is now supported by most desktop browsers, including Internet Explorer. Browsers process JavaScript statements embedded in HTML pages as they interpret bodies of HTTP responses that have their `Content-Type` set to `text/html`. The thing to remember is that with all cross-browser support, there are subtle differences in JavaScript implementations for different browsers. It is possible to write JavaScript programs that work consistently across different browsers, but even if you are using relatively simple JavaScript functionality, consistent cross-browser implementation often becomes an iterative trial-and-error process.

Another important consideration is that not all JavaScript processing is performed at the same time. Some statements are interpreted prior to rendering the HTML document, or while the document is being rendered. These statements are usually contained within script blocks as we shall see shortly. Other statements are grouped into event handlers that are associated with browser events through HTML tag attributes. Let us take a look at the example in Figure 6.23 that makes use of two JavaScript functions, which are defined using the `<SCRIPT>` element in the page header.

The *setMethod* function takes the *form* object as an argument and sets its HTTP request method to POST unless the browser is an early version of Netscape Navigator (versions 1.x through 4.x). The *setMethod* function is used by the *adminAction* function, which gets invoked through an event handler at the click of a button. Note that the association between buttons and event handlers is defined through the `onClick` attribute of the `<INPUT>` element.

The example makes use of the *Navigator, Form*, and *Button* objects, which are available through the JavaScript processor. Other objects associated with HTML elements include *Frame, Image, Link*, and *Window*, to name a few. In addition, JavaScript processors include general-purpose objects that may be used in the language statements, including *RegEx* for regular expressions, as well as *Math* for simple computations, *Number* for manipulating numeric values, and *Date*. Control flow constructs similar to those found in Java are supported as well.

Server-Side JavaScript

In the early years of the Web, there were attempts to use JavaScript on the server, but they did not generate an extensive following. There are a number of open source

JavaScript interpreters (e.g. Rhino[1]), which could be used for server-side processing, but they generally do not contain objects or methods for manipulating HTML documents.

JavaScript is not the right language for implementing sophisticated logic. Apart from making your pages entirely unreadable, and violating the principle of separating content and presentation, complex JavaScript constructs often lead to inconsistencies in the way different desktop browsers behave. To compensate for this, designers

```html
<html>
<head>
<title>JavaScript Example</title>
<script language="JavaScript">
function setMethod(form) {
    if (navigator.appName == "Netscape" &&
        navigator.appVersion.match(/^\s*[1-4]/)) {
        form.method = "get";
    } else {
        form.method = "post";
    }
}
function adminAction(button) {
    setMethod(button.form);
    if (button.name == "Exit") {
        button.form.action = "/test/servlet/action/invalidate";
    } else if (button.name == "New") {
        button.form.action = "/test/servlet/action/process/next";
    }
    button.form.submit();
}
</head>
<body>
...
<form name="admin" action=" ">
<input name="New" type="button" value="New"
onClick='adminAction(New)'>
<input name="Exit" type="button" value="Exit"
onClick='adminAction(Exit)'>
</form>
...
</body>
</html>
```

Figure 6.23 JavaScript example

_____

[1] http://www.mozilla.org/rhino/

often feel the need to add browser-dependent JavaScript code, tailored to work properly in specific browsers. (More accurately, tailored to work in specific *versions* of specific browsers!) This makes it very difficult to achieve consistency across different desktop browsers, let alone different devices. Complex JavaScript is one of the main reasons why some pages would render properly, for example, only through Internet Explorer.

Still, JavaScript is invaluable for field validation and event handling, but it is best to defer the more complex processing to the server. If you've ever seen a page where HTML tags are thoroughly mixed together with a combination of Java code, JavaScript event handlers, and `document.write` statements used to dynamically generate HTML as the page is rendered, then you know what *not* to do!

JavaScript is a little bit like an organic poison—it would kill you in large doses but may be an invaluable cure if you use it just right.

6.5 DHTML

Dynamic HTML (*DHTML*) is often talked about as if it were some new version of the HTML specification, with advanced functionality above and beyond HTML itself.

In reality, DHTML is just a catch-all name used to describe existing features in HTML, JavaScript and CSS that are used to provide engaging forms of page presentation. While HTML by itself provides a static presentation format, the coupling of HTML tags with JavaScript directives (event handlers) and CSS style specifications offers a degree of interactive control over page presentation. It is dynamic in the sense that the presentation of a given page may change over time through user interaction, in contrast to dynamic Web applications that generate entire page presentations.

It is not our intention to provide a DHTML primer in this chapter. Many good books are devoted to describing the intricacies of DHTML, but we believe it is worthwhile to understand the principles associated with DHTML presentation techniques. With this in mind, we describe simple examples illustrating the most common uses of DHTML.

6.5.1 'Mouse-Over' behaviors

JavaScript provides mechanisms to perform actions when the mouse pointer is 'over' an area specified as a hyperlink (e.g. presenting different images associated with a given hyperlink depending on the position of the mouse pointer). The `onMouseOver` and `onMouseOut` directives can be added to an HTML anchor tag (`<A HREF="..."`>) to make this happen.

This image swap technique shown in Figure 6.24 demonstrates the most common mouse-over behavior used by page designers. Note that the `IMG` tag is identified through

```
<A HREF="... "
   onMouseOver="document.images['picture1'].src = 'images/pic1a.gif';"
   onMouseOut="document.images['picture1'].src = 'images/pic1.gif';"
>
   <IMG NAME="picture1" SRC="images/pic1.gif">
</A>
```

Figure 6.24   Sample implementation of `onmouseOver` behavior

its NAME attribute, making it possible to reference the image directly. The SRC attribute
of the IMG tag is set to the relative URL of the default image (`images/pic1.gif`).
JavaScript code to change the image's location (its `src` attribute) to a different URL
is invoked `"onMouseOver"` (when the mouse pointer is over the image), causing
a different image (`images/pic1a.gif`) to be displayed. Similar code is invoked
`"onMouseOut"` (when the mouse pointer leaves the area occupied by the image) to
redisplay the original image. The two code fragments are JavaScript *event handlers*
that are invoked when the respective events occur. (Note that real-world event handlers
perform image swapping by invoking JavaScript functions defined within a script block
or in an external JavaScript source file.)

Similarly, CSS can be used to define styles associated with the mouse-over behavior. Figure 6.25 illustrates the highlighting of links and the addition or removal of
underlining through the A:hover *pseudo-class*. Here, hyperlinks are normally displayed in a shade of green (#009900) with no underlining, but when the mouse
pointer is over a link it becomes underlined, its text color switches to black, and its
background color is transformed to a shade of yellow (#ffff99).

6.5.2 Form validation

Some degree of client-side form validation can be performed using JavaScript,
obviating the need for a potentially time-consuming request/response 'roundtrip'
to perform server-side validation. This is accomplished through the FORM tag's
onSubmit event handler, which is executed prior to the submission of the form.
If the code returned by the event handler evaluates to the boolean value true, the
HTML form has passed validation and an HTTP request is generated to submit it to

```
<STYLE TYPE="text/css">
A
   { color: #009900 ; text-decoration: none }
A:hover
   { background-color: #ffff99; color: black;
     text-decoration: underline }
</STYLE>
```

Figure 6.25   Usage of CSS A:hover pseudo-class for mouse-over link highlighting

```
<HTML>
<HEAD>
<SCRIPT>
function validate(form) {
    var errors = " " ;
    if (form.firstname.value.length < 3) {
        errors += "\nFirst name must be at least 3 characters long." ;
    }
    if (form.lastname.value.length < 5) {
        errors += "\nLast name must be at least 5 characters long." ;
    }
    if (errors.length > 0) {
        alert("Please correct the following errors:" + errors) ;
        return false ;
    }
    else {
        return true ;
    }
}
</SCRIPT>
</HEAD>
<BODY BGCOLOR="#ffffff">
<FORM NAME="form1" METHOD="post" ACTION="... "
    onSubmit="return validate(this)">
<TABLE CELLPADDING=5 BORDER=0>
<TR>
<TD ALIGN="right">First Name:</TD>
<TD ALIGN="left"><INPUT TYPE="text" NAME="firstname"></TD>
</TR>
<TR>
<TD ALIGN="right">Last Name:</TD>
<TD ALIGN="left"><INPUT TYPE="text" NAME="lastname"></TD>
</TR>
<TR>
<TD COLSPAN=2 ALIGN="center">
<INPUT TYPE="submit" VALUE=" Submit "></TD>
</TR>
</TABLE>
</FORM>
</BODY>
</HTML>
```

Figure 6.26   Example of client-side form validation using JavaScript

the server. Otherwise, in the case of validation errors, the code evaluates to `false` and no submission takes place. It is good practice for the event handler to display a JavaScript alert box describing any validation errors that have been detected.

Figure 6.26 demonstrates how client-side form validation can be accomplished using JavaScript. The form contains two fields, and the FORM tag calls for the execution of a JavaScript function, `validate()`, when the form is submitted. This function examines the values entered in the two form fields and determines whether they are valid. If either value is unacceptable, an appropriate error message is appended to the String variable `errors`. If the length of this variable is greater than zero after all the fields in the form have been checked by the `validate()` function, a JavaScript alert box is displayed containing the error messages, and the function returns `false`. Otherwise, the function returns `true`, causing the form to be submitted to the server.

Note that this approach starts the validation process when the form is submitted. It is possible to validate on a per-field basis, by using the `onChange` or `onBlur` JavaScript event handlers in the `INPUT` tags associated with individual form fields. Since the displaying of alert boxes as data is being entered can become overwhelming and confusing to users, and since the acceptability of entered field values is often dependent on what has been entered in other form fields, the 'holistic' approach of validating on submission is preferred.

Client-side form validation is useful in 'pre-validating' field values before the form is submitted to the server. Validations that are dependent on comparisons to data values available only on the server (e.g. user authorization credentials) require server-side validation.

6.5.3 Layering techniques

A page can be divided into 'layers' that occupy the same coordinates on the screen. Only one layer is visible at a time, but users are able to control which layer is visible through mouse clicks or other page interactions. This functionality is often used by page designers to provide tabbed panes and collapsible menus.

The term 'layers' was originally Netscape-specific, referring to the proprietary `<LAYER>` tag understood only by the Netscape browser. The term is now used in DHTML to describe the use of CSS *positionable elements* to support this functionality in a browser-neutral way. This is usually accomplished by specifying co-located blocks of text on the page as `<DIV>` elements with CSS style attributes that determine their position and visibility.

In Figure 6.27, CSS styles are explicitly defined for 'layer 1' and 'layer 2'. JavaScript functions to change the visibility attribute of page elements are also defined. Hyperlinks give users the option to see either 'layer 1' (which is visible when the page loads) or 'layer 2' (which is initially hidden).

The `setVisibility` JavaScript function shown here is somewhat oversimplified. Describing how to implement it in a truly cross-browser compatible manner is too complex for a short overview. Suffice to say that cross-browser compatibility when using CSS positionable elements is difficult but by no means impossible, thanks to the availability of cross-browser JavaScript APIs such as Bob Clary's *xbDom* and *xbStyle* (available at `http://www.bclary.com/xbProjects`).

```
<HTML>
<HEAD>
<STYLE TYPE="text/css">
    #layer1 { position: absolute; z-index: 1; visibility: visible; }
    #layer2 { position: absolute; z-index: 2; visibility: hidden; }
</STYLE>
<SCRIPT LANGUAGE="javascript">
function show(objectID) {
        setVisibility(objectID,'visible') ;
}

function hide(objectID) {
        setVisibility(objectID,'hidden') ;
}

function setVisibility(objectID, state) {
        var obj = document.getElementById(objectID).style ;
        obj.visibility = state ;
}
</SCRIPT>
</HEAD>
<BODY BGCOLOR="#ffffff">
<A HREF="javascript:show('layer1');hide('layer2');">Show Layer 1</A>
<A HREF="javascript:show('layer2');hide('layer1');">Show Layer 2</A>
<DIV ID="layer1">
        Text that will appear when layer1 is visible
</DIV>
<DIV ID="layer2">
        Text that will appear when layer2 is visible
</DIV>
</BODY>
</HTML>
```

Figure 6.27 Example of CSS positionable elements used for layering

Our examples barely scratch the surface in describing the capabilities of DHTML. Readers are invited to pursue referenced sources and explore on their own the possibilities that arise from the interaction of JavaScript, CSS, and HTML.

6.6 SUMMARY

In this chapter, we have discussed HTML and related technologies; we have also established the necessary foundation for the upcoming discussion of XML. We discussed SGML, its DTD syntax, and using it to define HTML as an SGML application. We further discussed the HTML markup language, concentrating on its features that influence HTTP interactions, as well as features that enable the separation of markup and rendering.

We again stress that it is important to distinguish between the separation of markup and rendering, and the separation of content and presentation. The former is accomplished through stylesheets, while the latter is the function of proper application design. The CSS language discussed in this chapter is only the first step in stylesheet evolution. In the upcoming XML chapter, we will refer to CSS as the starting point for our stylesheet discussion.

No matter how many specialized HTML elements and attributes are introduced into the language, there is still an expressed need for a programming language that can be used to introduce simple processing for input validation and event handling. JavaScript does fulfill this role, and numerous interfaces to JavaScript functions are now part of the HTML specification. But beware—using JavaScript to implement complex logic not only makes your applications difficult to debug, it almost always creates browser dependencies as well.

6.7 QUESTIONS AND EXERCISES

1. What is the relationship between HTML, XML, SGML, and XHTML? Explain.
2. What HTTP headers will be ignored when specified using the HTTP-EQUIV mechanism? What headers will not be ignored? Provide examples. Explain.
3. Describe options for using HTML to generate HTTP requests. Can you control the 'Content-Type' header for browser requests? What settings are imposed by the browser and under what circumstances?
4. Put together a simple HTML form for submitting desktop files to the server using POST requests. Remember to provide information about the target location of the file after transmission. What will be the format of the request?
5. What is the purpose for introducing CSS? What are the alternatives for associating styles with HTML documents?
6. What is the relationship between HTML and JavaScript? What is the role of event handlers?
7. What is DHTML? Describe the most common DHTML use patterns and technologies that are used to implement these patterns.
8. How difficult would it be to implement an HTML parser? Why? How would you represent semantics of HTML elements?

BIBLIOGRAPHY

Flanagan, D. (2001) *JavaScript: The Definitive Guide*. O'Reilly & Associates.

Livingston, D. (2000) *Essential CSS and DHTML for Web Professionals*, 2nd *Edition*. Prentice Hall.

Maler, E. and El Andaloussi, J. *Developing SGML DTDs*. Prentice Hall PTR, 1995.

Meyer, E. (2000) *Cascading Style Sheets: The Definitive Guide*. O'Reilly & Associates.

Musciano, C. and Kennedy, B. (2002) *HTML and XHTML, The Definitive Guide*. Fifth Edition. O'Reilly & Associates.

Teague, J. C. (2001) *DHTML and CSS for the World Wide Web: Visual Quickstart Guide*. Second Edition. Berkeley, California: Peachpit Press.

7 XML Languages and Applications

For all its power, SGML has remained a niche language. It originated in the 1970s and enjoyed very strong following in the text representation community. However, the price for the power and flexibility of SGML was its complexity. Just as the simplicity of HTTP gave birth to the brave new World Wide Web, something a lot simpler than SGML was needed in the area of markup languages. The initial approach was to create a targeted SGML application, HTML, which worked relatively well during the early years of the Web. However, it was neither sufficiently powerful and flexible, nor rigorous enough for the information processing needs of sophisticated Web applications.

The solution was to define a relatively simple subset of SGML that would retain the most critical features of the language. Such a subset, called the *eXtensible Markup Language* or XML, was designed to serve as the foundation for the new generation of markup languages. By giving up some of the flexibility (e.g. SGML character set and concrete syntax declarations) and imposing additional structural constraints, it became possible to construct a language that is easy to learn and conducive to the creation of advanced authoring tools.

XML was designed as a subset of SGML, but it did not stay that way. The very simplicity of the language lent itself to the evolution that was not practical for SGML. While XML DTDs are simply a subset of SGML DTDs, XML Schema is the new generation language for defining application-specific constraints. Moreover, entirely new mechanisms have emerged, such as XPath to address fragments of XML documents and XSLT to define document transformations. XML is proving to provide much more than a replacement for SGML-derived HTML. XML applications include specialized markup languages (e.g. MathML), communication protocols (e.g. SOAP), and configuration instructions (e.g. configuration files for HTTP servers and J2EE containers).

In the rest of this chapter, we will discuss XML and related languages that either stand on their own (e.g. XML DTD and XPath), or are defined as XML applications (e.g. XSL and XML Schema). We will also discuss the relationship between SGML and HTML on one side, and XML and XHTML on the other. Finally, we will provide a brief overview of other XML applications.

7.1 CORE XML

As you will recall, the first steps in defining SGML applications were to define the character set and the concrete syntax. XML syntax is relatively rigid—the character set is fixed, and there is a limited number of tag delimiters ('<', '>', '/>', and '</'). There is no need to define *concrete syntax*, which is perfectly all right—XML was designed for a much narrower set of applications than SGML. After all, there cannot be an XML application without the all too familiar angle brackets.

The DTD that defines markup constructs is still required. However, XML DTD specifications have to be less expressive than SGML DTDs, to make it impossible to define element structures that violate constraints on element nesting.

XML Schemas are the next generation replacement for DTDs. The XML Schema language (unlike DTD) is itself defined as an XML application, so that developers do not have to use a different syntax (and different tools) for creating documents and defining document constraints.

Another very important notion is that of a namespace, which makes it possible to use qualified names to distinguish between elements that belong to different XML applications and may have different semantics. Interestingly enough, there is a close relationship between namespaces and XML schemas.

7.1.1 XML documents

XML documents are composed of declarations, elements, tags, comments, character references, and processing instructions. Every document has a single root element, for which neither its start tag nor its end tag are in the context of another element; all other elements have to be properly nested within each other. XML entities are syntactically very similar to HTML escape sequences, but apart from built-in entities (< > & ' and "), it is possible to define new entities through a DTD or an XML Schema. An XML document is *well formed* if it includes document declaration, satisfies element nesting and other syntactic constraints, and does not include undefined entities. A well-formed XML document is *valid* if it satisfies constraints as specified in the associated DTD or a Schema. Of course, only a well-formed document may be valid.

The sample XML document in Figure 7.1 starts with an XML declaration that is followed by a comment, the DTD reference, and a combination of tags and character sequences that satisfy constraints for well-formed XML documents.

```
<?xml version ="1.0" standalone ="yes"?>
<!-- XML example for the Web Architecture book -->
<!DOCTYPE books SYSTEM "books.dtd">
<books>
<book status ="In Print">
<title>Web Application Architecture</title>
<subtitle> Principles, protocols and practices</subtitle>
<author firstName ="Leon" lastName ="Shklar"/>
<author firstName ="Rich" lastName ="Rosen"/>
<info>
<pages count ="500"/>
<price usd ="45" bp ="27.50"/>
<publication year ="2003" source ="&jw;"/>
</info>
<summary>An in-depth examination of the basic concepts and general
principles associated with Web application development.
</summary>
</book>
<!--
<book><TBD>
</book>
-->
<notes><![CDATA[
&lt; !-- This is our CDATA example that hides syntactically incorrect
comments and XML fragments -->
<books><book>
]]>
</notes>
</books>
```

Figure 7.1 Sample XML document

XML comment syntax is similar to HTML comments. Comments can only appear after the XML declaration. They may not be placed within a tag, but may be used to surround and hide individual tags and XML fragments that do not contain comments (e.g. the second `<book>` element).

In addition to comments, XML possesses an even stronger mechanism for hiding XML fragments—CDATA sections. CDATA sections exclude enclosed text from XML parsing—all text is interpreted as character data. It is useful for hiding document fragments that contain comments, quotes, or '&' characters. For example, the CDATA section in Figure 7.1 hides the improperly formatted comment and two XML tags from the XML parser. The only character sequence that may not occur in the CDATA section is ']]>', which terminates the section.

As you can see from the example, XML elements can be represented with two kinds of tags. Non-empty elements use open and close tags that have the same syntax as HTML tags (e.g. `<book>...</book>` and `<summary>...</summary>`).

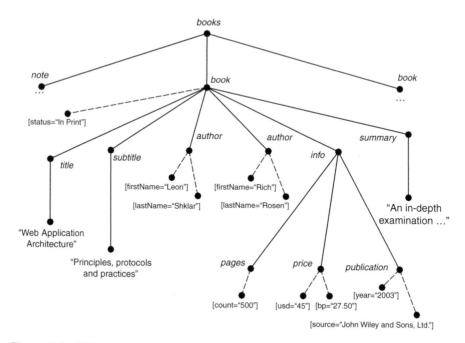

Figure 7.2   XML element tree for the example in Figure 7.1

Empty elements are represented with single tags that are terminated with the '/>' sequence (e.g. <pages.../> and <price.../>). An element may or may not have attributes, which, for non-empty elements, have to be included in open tags (for empty elements, there is only one tag, so there is not much choice).

The document in Figure 7.1 contains sample entities in the body of the second <book> element. Both < and > are references to built-in entities that are analogous to escape sequences in HTML. Since HTML is an SGML application, it already has a DTD, so there is no way to define new escape sequences. XML is a subset of SGML, so it is possible to define new entities using XML DTDs (or schemas). An example of a reference to a newly defined entity is &jw;. Since jw is not a built-in entity, it should be defined in the 'books.dtd' file for the document to be considered well formed. Note that the < character sequence that occurs within the CDATA section is not an entity reference—as we discussed, CDATA sections exclude enclosed text from XML parsing.

Figure 7.2 is a graphic representation of the XML document in Figure 7.1. Here, internal nodes represent elements, solid edges represent the containment relationship, dashed edges represent the attribute relationship, and leaf nodes—either attributes or element content. For example, element <info> is represented as the combination of elements <pages>, <price>, and <publication>, while elements <title> and <subtitle> are represented with their character content. Attribute names and values are shown in brackets, and attribute value edges are represented with equal signs (e.g. [firstName="Leon"]).

Processing an XML document often involves traversing the element tree. There is even a special specification for the traversal paths. It is discussed later in this chapter (Section 7.4.1).

7.1.2 XML DTD

The meaning of XML tags is in the eye of the beholder. Even though you may be looking at the sample document and telling yourself that it makes sense, it is only because of semantics associated with the English language names of elements and attributes.

Language semantics are of course inaccessible to XML parsers. The immediate problem for XML parsers, thus, is validation. A human would most likely guess that the value of the usd attribute of the <price> element is the book price in dollars. It would come as a surprise if for one of the books the value of this attribute is the number 1000 or the word 'table'. Again, this surprise would be based on language semantics and not on any formal specification that is required to perform automated validation.

The second problem is even more complex. How do we make XML documents useful for target applications? It is easy with HTML—every tag has a well-defined meaning that is hard-coded into browser processing and rendering modules. XML elements do not have assigned meaning, though a particular XML application (e.g. XHTML) may have predefined meaning for individual elements.

Let us attempt to address the validation problem using XML DTD (Figure 7.3). Notice that the XML DTD syntax for element definitions is simpler than SGML syntax (see SGML DTD fragment in Figure 7.4). Even if we add more element definitions to the example in Figure 7.4, we would still notice that all of them have pairs of dashes indicating that both an open and a close tag are required. There is no reason to keep this part of the SGML DTD syntax—all XML elements always require both open and close tags.

Similar to the SGML DTD examples in Chapter 6, the XML DTD specification in Figure 7.3 defines the nesting and recurrence of individual elements. The root element is defined to contain at least one <book>, which, in turn, contains exactly one <title>, at least one <author>, and may or may not contain <subtitle>, <info>, and <summary> elements.

XML DTDs provide simple mechanisms for defining new entities, which are very similar to those of SGML DTDs. For example (Figure 7.3), the entity "jw" is defined to expand to 'John Wiley and Sons, Ltd.'; it is used in the sample document in Figure 7.1. An obvious reason for defining names of publishers as entities is their applicability to multiple book entries. Another example in Figure 7.3 is the entity 'JWCopyright', which is defined as a reference to an HTTP resource.

```
<?xml version ="1.0" encoding ="UTF-8"?>
<!ELEMENT books (book+, notes)>
<!ATTLIST books
          status CDATA #IMPLIED
>
<!ELEMENT book (title, subtitle?, author+, info?, summary?)>
<!ELEMENT title (#PCDATA)>
<!ELEMENT subtitle (#PCDATA)>
<!ELEMENT author EMPTY>
<!ATTLIST author
          firstName NMTOKEN #REQUIRED
          lastName  NMTOKEN #REQUIRED
>
<!ELEMENT info (pages, price, publication)>
<!ELEMENT pages EMPTY>
<!ATTLIST pages
          count CDATA #REQUIRED
>
<!ELEMENT price EMPTY>
<!ATTLIST price
          usd   CDATA #REQUIRED
          bp    CDATA #IMPLIED
          euro  CDATA #IMPLIED
>
<!ELEMENT publication EMPTY>
<!ATTLIST publication
          year   CDATA #REQUIRED
          source CDATA #REQUIRED
>
<!ELEMENT summary (#PCDATA)>
<!ELEMENT notes (#PCDATA)>
<!ENTITY jw "John Wiley and Sons, Ltd.">
<!ENTITY JWCopyright SYSTEM "http://www.wiley.com/xml/copyright.xml">
```

Figure 7.3   The books.dtd file—XML DTD for the sample document in Figure 7.1

```
...
<!ELEMENT book  - - (title, subtitle?, author+, info?, summary?>
<!ELEMENT title - - (#PCDATA)>
...
```

Figure 7.4   Fragment of an SGML DTD for the sample document in Figure 7.1

DTDs do not provide easy ways of defining constraints that go beyond element nesting and recurrence. Similarly, while it is easy to associate elements with attributes and to define basic constraints on attribute types (e.g. predefined name token constraints, or enumeration), more complex cases are often an exercise in futility. And of course, DTD is no help in trying to define semantics.

7.1.3 XML Schema

XML Schema is a relatively new specification from the W3C. It does not have an analog in the SGML world. XML Schema was designed as an alternative to the DTD mechanism; it adds stronger typing and utilizes XML syntax. XML Schema contains additional constructs that make it a lot easier to define sophisticated constraints.

XML Schema supports the so-called 'complex' and 'simple' types. Simple types are defined by imposing additional constraints on built-in types, while complex types are composed recursively from other complex and simple types. Built-in types available in the XML Schema are much richer and more flexible than those available in the DTD context. This is very important because it means that the XML Schema makes it possible to express sophisticated constraints without resorting to application logic, which must be coded using a procedural language (e.g. Java) and is much more expensive to maintain.

XML syntax for referencing schemas is shown in Figure 7.5. XML schema specification does not provide for defining entities, so entity definitions have to be included in the document using the DTD syntax.

In the example in Figure 7.6, we demonstrate the brute force approach to defining an XML schema. This pattern is sometimes called the 'Russian Doll Design', referring to the wooden 'matreshka' dolls that are nested inside each other. Here, every type is defined in place, there is no reuse, and the resulting schema is relatively difficult to read. Nevertheless, it is a good starting point for our analysis.

We begin with defining the element <books> by associating it with the complex type that is defined using the 'sequence' *compositor*. Sequence compositors impose the sequential order; they are equivalent to commas when defining constraints on an element nesting in the DTD syntax. Other compositors include 'all', which does not impose an order as long as every enumerated element (or group of elements) is present in accordance with the occurrence constraints, and 'choice', that requires the presence of exactly one element or group of elements.

```
<?xml version ="1.0" encoding ="UTF-8"?>
<!DOCTYPE books [
<!ENTITY jw "John Wiley and Sons, Ltd.">
<!ENTITY JWCopyright SYSTEM "http://www.wiley.com/xml/copyright.xml">
]>
<books xmlns:xsi ="http://www.w3.org/2001/XMLSchema-instance"
       xsi:noNamespaceSchemaLocation ="books1.xsd" status ="In Print">
...
</books>
```

Figure 7.5 Changes to the sample XML document in Figure 7.1 (required for schema-based validation)

```
<?xml version ="1.0" encoding ="utf-8"?>
<xs:schema xmlns:xs ="http://www.w3.org/2001/XMLSchema">
<xs:element name ="books">
  <xs:complexType>
  <xs:sequence>
  <xs:element name ="book" minOccurs ="1" maxOccurs ="unbounded">
    <xs:complexType>
    <xs:sequence>
    <xs:element name ="title" type ="xs:string"/>
    <xs:element name ="subtitle" type ="xs:string"
                minOccurs ="0" maxOccurs ="1"/>
    <xs:element name ="author" minOccurs ="1" maxOccurs ="unbounded">
      <xs:complexType>
      <xs:attribute name ="firstName" type ="xs:string"
                    use ="required"/>
      <xs:attribute name ="lastName" type ="xs:string"
                    use ="required"/>
      </xs:complexType>
    </xs:element>
    <xs:element name ="info" minOccurs ="0" maxOccurs ="1">
      <xs:complexType>
      <xs:sequence>
      <xs:element name ="pages">
        <xs:complexType>
        <xs:attribute name ="count" type ="xs:integer"/>
        </xs:complexType>
      </xs:element>
      <xs:element name ="price">
        <xs:complexType>
        <xs:attribute name ="usd" type ="xs:decimal"
                      use ="required"/>
        <xs:attribute name ="bp" type ="xs:decimal"/>
        <xs:attribute name ="euro" type ="xs:decimal"/>
        </xs:complexType>
      </xs:element>
      <xs:element name ="publication">
        <xs:complexType>
        <xs:attribute name ="year" type ="xs:integer"
                      use ="required"/>
        <xs:attribute name ="source" type ="xs:string"
                      use ="required"/>
        </xs:complexType>
      </xs:element>
      </xs:sequence>
      </xs:complexType>
    </xs:element>
  <xs:element name ="summary" type ="xs:string"
              minOccurs ="0" maxOccurs ="1"/>
```

Figure 7.6   The books1.xsd file—XML Schema for the sample document in Figure 7.1

```
          </xs:sequence>
          </xs:complexType>
        </xs:element>
      <xs:element name="notes"type="xs:string" minOccurs="0"
                    maxOccurs="1"/>
      </xs:sequence>
      <xs:attribute name="status"type="xs:string"/>
      </xs:complexType>
    </xs:element>
    </xs:schema>
```

Figure 7.6 (*continued*)

Here, the complex type for the <books> element is defined as the sequence of <book> and <notes> elements. In this design, types are defined in the depth-first manner, and it is often difficult to see all elements of the sequence when reading the schema. The <book> element is, in turn, associated with the complex type that is also defined as the sequence, etc.

XML Schema syntax for defining element quantifiers (number of occurrences) differs from the DTD syntax, but semantically both possibilities are the same. For example, the number of occurrences for the element <author> is defined to be at least one, which is the same as '+' in the DTD syntax; the element <subtitle> is defined as optional (zero or one occurrences), which is the same as '?' in the DTD syntax. Just as in DTDs, the number of occurrences, if unspecified, defaults to exactly one.

Attributes can be defined only for complex types. It is quite a relief that unlike DTDs, schemas support the same built-in types for attributes as they do for elements. By default, attributes are optional, but may be made required, as in the case of the 'usd' attribute for the <price> element.

Our next step is to improve on the design in Figure 7.6. The new schema in Figure 7.7 uses named types to make the schema more readable and easy to maintain. Instead of defining complex types in place, as in the old design, we start by defining complex types that can be composed out of simple types and attribute definitions, and proceed in order of increasing complexity.

For example, complex types authorType and infoType in Figure 7.7 are first defined and then referenced by name in the definition of bookType. The result is the XML schema composed of simple reusable definitions.

The primary purpose of the schema is to support document validation. It remains to be seen if we can improve the quality of this validation by defining additional constraints. We have done our job in defining element quantifiers and nesting constraints. However, it would be great to impose useful constraints on simple types.

For example, we can assume that a name should not be longer than thirty two characters, and that the price of a book should be in the range of 0.01 to 999.99, whether we are using dollars, pounds, or euros. In Figure 7.8, we define two new

```xml
<?xml version="1.0" encoding="utf-8"?>
<xs:schema xmlns:xs="http://www.w3.org/2001/XMLSchema">

<xs:complexType name="authorType">
   <xs:attribute name="firstName" type="xs:string" use="required"/>
   <xs:attribute name="lastName" type="xs:string" use="required"/>
</xs:complexType>

<xs:complexType name="priceType">
   <xs:attribute name="usd" type="xs:decimal" use="required"/>
   <xs:attribute name="bp"  type="xs:decimal"/>
   <xs:attribute name="euro" type="xs:decimal"/>
</xs:complexType>

<xs:complexType name="pagesType">
   <xs:attribute name="count" type="xs:integer"/>
</xs:complexType>

<xs:complexType name="publicationType">
   <xs:attribute name="year" type="xs:integer" use="required"/>
   <xs:attribute name="source" type="xs:string" use="required"/>
</xs:complexType>

<xs:complexType name="infoType">
   <xs:sequence>
      <xs:element name="pages" type="pagesType"/>
      <xs:element name="price" type="priceType"/>
      <xs:element name="publication" type="publicationType"/>
   </xs:sequence>
</xs:complexType>

<xs:complexType name="bookType">
   <xs:sequence>
      <xs:element name="title" type="xs:string"/>
      <xs:element name="subtitle" type="xs:string"
                  minOccurs="0" maxOccurs="1"/>
      <xs:element name="author" type="authorType"
                  minOccurs="1" maxOccurs="unbounded"/>
      <xs:element name="info" type="infoType"/>
      <xs:element name="summary" type="xs:string"
                  minOccurs="0" maxOccurs="1"/>
   </xs:sequence>
</xs:complexType>

<xs:complexType name="booksType">
   <xs:sequence>
   <xs:element name="book" type="bookType"
               minOccurs="1" maxOccurs="unbounded"/>
```

Figure 7.7   Improved schema design for the sample document in Figure 7.1

```
        <xs:element name="notes" type="xs:string" minOccurs="0"
                    maxOccurs="1"/>
        </xs:sequence>
        <xs:attribute name="status" type="xs:string"/>
    </xs:complexType>

    <xs:element name="books" type="booksType"/>

    </xs:schema>
```

Figure 7.7 (*continued*)

```
        <xs:simpleType name="nameBaseType">
          <xs:restriction base="xs:string">
            <xs:maxLength value="32"/>
          </xs:restriction>
        </xs:simpleType>

        <xs:simpleType name="priceBaseType">
          <xs:restriction base="xs:string">
            <xs:pattern value="[0-9]{1,3}(\.[0-9]{2})?"/>
          </xs:restriction>
        </xs:simpleType>
```

Figure 7.8 Defining constraints on simple types

simple types—nameBaseType and priceBaseType—by imposing constraints on
the base string type. In the first case, the new constraint is maximum length, while
in the second it is the pattern—one to three digits possibly followed by the decimal
point and another two digits. Of course, we have to go back to the schema in
Figure 7.7 and make changes to the type references to take advantage of these new
constraints (Figure 7.9).

XML schemas provide extensive capabilities for defining custom types and utilizing them for document validation. Moreover, XML schemas are themselves XML

```
    <xs:complexType name="authorType">
      <xs:attribute name="firstName" type="nameType" use="required"/>
      <xs:attribute name="lastName"  type="nameType" use="required"/>
    </xs:complexType>

    <xs:complexType name="priceType">
      <xs:attribute name="usd"  type="priceBaseType" use="required"/>
      <xs:attribute name="bp"   type="priceBaseType"/>
      <xs:attribute name="euro" type="priceBaseType"/>
    </xs:complexType>
```

Figure 7.9 Changes to the type definitions in Figure 7.7

documents, and may be validated as well, which serves as a good foundation for building advanced tools. However, advanced validation is not a solution for associating semantics with XML elements, which remains a very difficult problem. Some partial solutions to this problem will be discussed further in this chapter.

7.2 XHTML

As discussed in Chapter 6, the structure of HTML documents is relatively unconstrained. For example, closing tags for many HTML elements are optional and are often omitted. Real-world HTML documents often violate even the liberal constraints imposed by the HTML specification because commercial browsers are implemented to be extremely tolerant of such violations.

XHTML is a reformulation of HTML 4.0 (the last HTML specification) as an XML application. Migration to XHTML not only makes it possible to impose strict structural constraints, but also to dispose with the legacy support for bad syntax. Even commercial browsers do not have to exhibit tolerance when validating documents that claim to implement the XHTML specification.

Differences between the sample HTML document from the previous chapter, and the sample XHTML document in Figure 7.10, include the use of lower case element names, and the presence of the `</p>` tag. Apart from the document declaration, the document in Figure 7.10 is both valid XHTML and valid HTML. Many XHTML constraints do not break HTML validation, including the required close tags and the requirement to enclose attribute values within quotes. Unfortunately, this is not true for all XHTML constructs that occur in real documents.

For example, adding the `<br>` tag after words "I do have to close" would not affect HTML validation, but would constitute a syntactic violation for XHTML. Replacing the `<br>` tag with the `<br/>` tag would produce the reverse effect. However, using the `<br></br>` construct would not break either HTML or XHTML validation

```
<?xml version ="1.0" encoding ="UTF-8"?>
<!DOCTYPE html
     PUBLIC "-//W3C//DTD XHTML 1.0 Strict//EN"
     "http://www.w3.org/TR/xhtml1/DTD/xhtml1-strict.dtd">
<html xmlns ="http://www.w3.org/1999/xhtml"
     xml:lang ="en" lang ="en">
   <head>
     <title>Sample HTML Document</title>
   </head>
   <body>
     <p>I do have to close the &lt;p&gt; tag.</p>
   </body>
</html>
```

Figure 7.10 Sample XHTML document

```
...
<p>I have to close the &lt;p&gt; tag.</p>           <!-- HTML + XHTML -->
<p>I have to close<br> the &lt;p&gt; tag.</p>        <!-- HTML -->
<p>I have to close<br/> the &lt;p&gt; tag.</p>       <!-- XHTML -->
<p>I have to close<br></br> the &lt;p&gt; tag.</p>   <!-- HTML + XHTML -->
...
```

Figure 7.11   HTML and XHTML validation

```
<script type="text/javascript">
<![CDATA[
...
]]>
</script>
```

Figure 7.12   XHTML script syntax

(Figure 7.11). It is fair to mention that the last construct, while valid in both HTML and XHTML contexts, is likely to cause problems for some XML tools.

On the surface, there is not a difference between HTML escape sequences and the XHTML use of references to pre-defined entities, but the real story is more complicated. The nature of XML processing is to recognize and process entity references in #PCDATA context. Elements that are defined to have character content (e.g. <style> and <script>), are vulnerable to the presence of such entity references. For example, < would be resolved to the '<' sign and considered the start of markup. To avoid this problem, in XHTML, bodies of <script> and <style> elements have to be included in CDATA sections (Figure 7.12). Of course, the CDATA syntax breaks HTML validation, and the only solution is to use external script and style documents (on occasions when this problem arises).

As already mentioned, XHTML is the reformulation of HTML as an XML application. XHTML elements have the same well-defined semantics as corresponding HTML elements. Element semantics are defined in the XHTML specification and is hard-coded into presentation modules of browsers that support XHTML.

HTML 4.0 is a deprecated specification. There will be no more new versions of HTML in the future. With the release of new versions of XHTML, differences between HTML and XHTML are likely to accumulate. At some point, it may become impossible to generate valid XHTML that is also valid according to the last HTML specification.

7.3 WML

The Wireless Markup Language (WML) is just as much an XML application as XHTML. By necessity, WML contains elements enabling page structures that are

```
<?xml version ="1.0" encoding ="UTF-8"?>
<!DOCTYPE html PUBLIC "-//WAPFORUM//DTD WML 2.0//EN"
    "http://www.wapforum.org/dtd/wml20-flat.dtd">
<html xmlns ="http://www.w3.org/1999/xhtml"
    xmlns:wml ="http://www.wapforum.org/2001/wml">
    <head>
        <title>Book Info</title>
    </head>
    <wml:card id ="subject" title ="Subject">
        <wml:do type ="accept" label ="Year">
            <wml:go href ="#scope"/>
        </wml:do>
        <p>
        Select:
        <select name ="book" title ="Subject:">
                <option value ="webarch">Web Architecture</option>
                <option value ="xml">XML</option>
                <option value ="jxml">Java and XML</option>
                <option value ="wml">WML</option>
        </select>
        </p>
    </wml:card>
    <wml:card id ="scope" title ="Year:">
        <wml:do type ="accept" label ="Selection">
            <wml:go href ="#selection"/>
        </wml:do>
        <p>
        Enter Year: <input type ="text" name ="year"/>
        </p>
    </wml:card>
    <wml:card id ="selection" title ="Selection:">
        <p>
        You entered:<br/>
        Subject ID: $(book)<br/>
        Year: $(year)<br/>
        </p>
    </wml:card>
</html>
```

Figure 7.13 Sample WML document

quite different from XHTML. Devices that make use of WML are constrained by their limited display size and lower transmission bandwidth. The amount of content that fills a typical HTML page would be too much to fit on one screen. At the same time, it would be wasteful to require the device to make multiple requests for smaller chunks of data. With this in mind, WML provides constructs that support sequences of individual smaller screens within a single document. WML complies with the DTD maintained by the WAP Forum (see the DOCTYPE definition in Figure 7.13).

This DTD defines a set of elements that combine with XHTML elements to create a WML document.

WML elements can be divided into groups, such as the *Decks* (e.g. `<wml:card>`) and *Events and Navigation* (e.g. `<wml:go>`). A WML document is a *deck* that normally contains multiple *cards*, with only one such card at a time visible to the user. The goal is to avoid new connections when traversing cards (or screens) within the same deck.

The sample WML document in Figure 7.13 is composed of three cards identified as 'subject', 'scope', and 'selection', respectively. The first card presents users with the choice of subjects, the second prompts for additional information (year), and the third card displays user entries (Figure 7.14a—c). Notice that the card id serves as its address within the document (e.g. `<wml:go href="#scope"/>`).

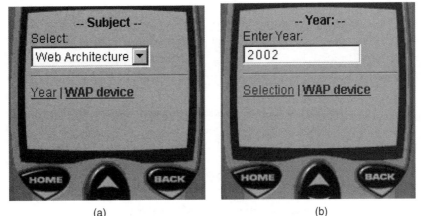

(a)   (b)

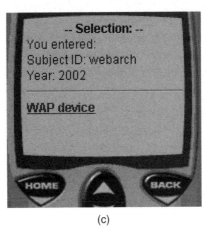

(c)

Figure 7.14 Screen captures for WML cards in Figure 7.13

To support card traversals within a single document, WML makes use of document variables. These variables may be set explicitly using `<wml:setvar>`, or as a side effect of user interaction. For example, the 'name' attribute of `<select>` and `<input>` elements double as variable declarations. In the card 'subject', the value of variable $(book) is set to the 'value' attribute of the selected option, and the value of variable $(year) in the card 'scope' to the input value.

Figure 7.14a shows the 'subject' card that gets displayed first. The result of selecting 'Web Architecture' and following the '#scope' link represented with its label 'Year' is shown in Figure 7.14b. The screen in Figure 7.14c is displayed as the result of the user entering the year and following the '#selection' link. Values 'webarch' and '2002' shown on the last screen come from variables $(book) and $(year) that are set based on user selection and input, respectively.

WML has come a long way from the isolated specification by the WAP Forum. The current specification, WML 2.0, is the language that is compatible with XHTML and extends it with unique WML semantics. Note that the extension is not limited to elements in the WML namespace, which are unique to the language. XHTML elements also obtain additional semantics (e.g. setting document variables).

7.4 XSL

XHTML is an XML-based reformulation of an existing SGML application (HTML) with well-defined semantics. WML is, in turn, a reformulation of XHTML for mobile devices, also with well-defined semantics. What about other XML applications? DTDs or XML Schemas are great for document validation, but neither can bring semantic meaning to XML elements. This is why there are so many different XML application standards. When related applications are using the same XML elements, it becomes possible to encode element semantics in shared application libraries. This is similar to hard-coding XHTML semantics in browser rendering modules.

It is not an attractive prospect—having to change application logic every time we add, change, or delete XML elements. We need both the ability to control application logic, and the ability to perform transformations between XML documents that comply with different schemas. In this way, having defined element semantics for one set of elements, we can use the corresponding schema as the common denominator for a variety of related applications.

The Extensible Stylesheet Language (XSL) serves the dual purpose of transforming XML documents, and of exhibiting control over document rendering. Like XML schemas, XSL programs are well-formed and valid XML documents.

7.4.1 XSLT

The transformation component of XSL, called XSLT, makes it possible to select fragments of XML documents based on patterns, and to apply various transformation operations to these fragments.

```
<?xml version="1.0" encoding="UTF-8"?>
<xsl:stylesheet version="1.0"
  xmlns:xsl="http://www.w3.org/1999/XSL/Transform"
  xmlns:fo="http://www.w3.org/1999/XSL/Format">

<xsl:template match="books">
<html xmlns="http://www.w3.org/1999/xhtml" xml:lang="en" lang="en">
<title>Book List</title>
<h2><xsl:text>Status: </xsl:text><xsl:value-of select="@status"/></h2>

<table border="1">
 <tbody>
    <tr>
       <th>Title</th>
       <th>Authors</th>
       <th>Publisher</th>
       <th>Year</th>
    </tr>
    <xsl:apply-templates select="book"/>
 </tbody>
</table>
</html>
</xsl:template>

<xsl:template match="book">
<tr>
    <td><xsl:value-of select="title"/></td>
    <td><xsl:apply-templates select="author"/></td>
    <td><xsl:value-of select="info/publication/@source"/></td>
    <td><xsl:value-of select="info/publication/@year"/></td>
 </tr>
 </xsl:template>

<xsl:template match="author">
    <xsl:value-of select="@firstName"/>
    <xsl:text> </xsl:text>
    <xsl:value-of select="@lastName"/>
    <br/>
</xsl:template>
</xsl:stylesheet>
```

Figure 7.15   Sample XSLT transformation

The sample XSLT stylesheet in Figure 7.15 serves the purpose of presenting a particular view of the XML document in Figure 7.1. This view contains a simple table of book entries with only some of the properties defined in the original XML document (Figure 7.16).

```
<?xml version ="1.0" encoding ="UTF-8"?>
<html xmlns ="http://www.w3.org/1999/xhtml" xml:lang ="en" lang
="en">
<h2>Status: In Print</h2>
<table xmlns:fo ="http://www.w3.org/1999/XSL/Format" border ="1">
<tbody>
<tr>
<th>Title</th>
<th>Authors</th>
<th>Publisher</th>
<th>Year</th>
</tr>
<tr>
<td>Web Application Architecture</td>
<td>Leon Shklar<br/>Rich Rosen<br/></td>
<td>John Wiley and Sons, Ltd.</td>
<td>2003</td>
</tr>
</tbody>
</table>
</html>
```

Figure 7.16 Result of applying the transformation in Figure 7.15 to the document in
Figure 7.1

You can see that the sample stylesheet is composed of three <template> elements. A template is analogous to a function though the invocation mechanisms are
quite different. The mechanism used in the example is based on matching templates
against elements in the document hierarchy. The first template is invoked when the
XSL processor encounters the <books> element in the target document (Figure 7.1).
As you would expect in template processing, it retains all elements except for those
with the 'xsl:' prefix. The latter are XSLT directives defined in the XSL schema.

XSL processing always occurs in the context of the current element node. On
entering the first template, the current element node is 'books', so <xsl:value-of
select="@status"/> returns the value of the 'status' attribute of the 'books'
node. The <xsl:apply-templates select ="book"/> directive instructs the
XSL interpreter to locate the template defined to match 'book' (second template
in Figure 7.15), and repeatedly evaluate it for every child 'book' element. Since the
target XML document only contains one <book> element, the interpreter evaluates
the second template only once.

The <xsl:value-of select="title"/> instruction in the second template is
evaluated to the content of the <title> element of the target XML document, which
is the direct descendant of the element <book>. The evaluation of <xsl:value-of
select="info/publication/@source"/> and <xsl:value-of select="info/
publication/@year"/> is performed by traversing the element tree from the current

element `<book>` down to `<info>`, then further down to `<publication>`, and, through attribute edges, to attributes 'source' and 'year' correspondingly.

Similar to `<xsl:apply-templates select="book"/>`, the `<xsl:apply-templates select="author"/>` directive instructs the interpreter to locate the template defined to match 'author' (third template in Figure 7.15), and repeatedly evaluate it for every `<author>` element reachable via the child edge from the then-current `<book>` element. Since there are two occurrences of the `<author>` element, the interpreter evaluates the third template twice and generates output for both authors (Figure 7.16).

Traversal expressions used in XSLT instructions (e.g. `title`, `@status`, `info/ publication/@year`) comply with the XPath specification—yet another XML-related standard. XPath is a simple query and traversal language for XML element trees. As you can infer from our examples, every '/' represents an edge (the first '/' is implied). By default, an edge leads to the child element with the specified name, but may lead to other kinds of nodes. For example, the '`@`' sign in '.../`@year`' denotes the 'year' attribute of the element node reached by traversing the preceding part of the XPath expression.

7.4.2 XSL Formatting Objects

XSL Formatting Objects (XSLFO) is a markup language describing the rendering vocabulary designed to support pagination. XSLFO specification is the descendant of Cascading Style Sheets long used by Web browsers to control rendering. It defines generic rendering objects associated with elements of the XSLFO vocabulary, including `<block>`, `<inline>`, `<page-sequence>`, `<footnote>`, as well as style objects (e.g. `<font>`). Most importantly, XSLFO stylesheets define the semantics of formatting information for paginated presentation.

XSLT transformations are unique to XML and serve the purpose of transforming XML documents to an alternate representation. One approach to rendering an XML document is to transform it to a target with well-defined presentation semantics (e.g. XHTML). The target XHTML document may contain a reference to a CSS stylesheet to control browser rendering (Figure 7.17).

XSLFO provides a superset of CSS functionality, except that while CSS supports browser rendering, XSLFO is designed to support print layouts. Semantically,

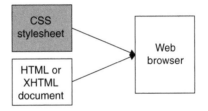

Figure 7.17   Using CSS stylesheets to render HTML and XHTML documents

controls for rendering individual components are very similar, though the variation in syntax is significant. As we discussed in the previous chapter, CSS has its own syntax, while XSLFO is an XML application:

```
P { font: italic bold 12pt/14pt Times, serif; color: #0000F0  }
```

```
<fo:block font-size="12pt" font-weight="bold">content</fo:block>
```

XSL processors can produce XML output, but can also take advantage of styling and pagination information provided by the Formatting Objects to generate PDF, postscript, or another form of print-oriented output. Figures 7.18 and 7.19 illustrate two different paths for creating print-friendly representations. Here, grey circles denote the XSLT processor, and black circles the XSLFO processor. Given that the target of the XSLT transformation is the XSLFO vocabulary, the output of the XSLT processor may serve as input to the XSLFO processor.

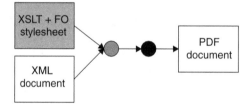

Figure 7.18   Using XSL stylesheets to print XML documents

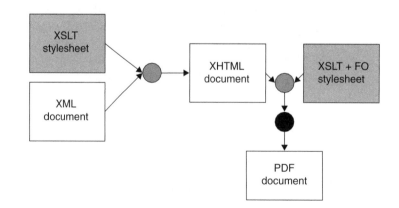

Figure 7.19   Alternate pattern for using XSL stylesheets to print XML documents

The obvious solution for creating a printer-friendly presentation is to implement an XSLT transformation from the desired XML format to the one based on the XSLFO vocabulary. It is also necessary to define Formatting Objects for the desired pagination, layout, and rendering (Figure 7.18). That it is quite a bit of work, and we may already have a rich XSLT library for transforming our documents to XHTML. Since XHTML is ubiquitous, there already exist libraries of easy to parameterize XSL-based transformations from XHTML to PDF, which means that we can render to print with very little work (Figure 7.19).

Our example in Figure 7.20 is a variation on the XSL Stylesheet from Figure 7.15. It implements the direct transformation to the XSLFO vocabulary and looks a lot more complicated than the original. The complexity is due only to the use of XSLFO as the target format. The template structure and the transformation instructions in the two stylesheets are virtually identical, but the 'fo:' elements replaced XHTML constructs.

Sometimes replacements are trivial (e.g. `<fo:table>` instead of `<table>`), but when it comes to table elements, the structure of the target markup is quite different—table columns are defined up front, so the XHTML's `<td>` is replaced with `<fo:table-cell>` and not with `<fo:table-column>`. Notice that every textual component is encapsulated within `<fo:block>` elements. XSLFO block is one of the most basic constructs that controls text positioning—lines, fonts, etc.

You have probably noticed that we glossed over two very important constructs that are evident in the example—the `<xsl:include>` elements and 'xsl:use-attribute-sets' attributes. The former include the pagination control file (Figure 7.21) and the attribute set definitions (Figure 7.22) that parameterize document rendering, and the latter reference attribute sets defined in the 'attributes.xsl' file. This simple design pattern helps to separate the presentation and rendering logic. In fact, you may accumulate a rich library of attribute definitions and page layouts, reusable in different contexts.

In combination with the approach shown in Figure 7.19, which assumes the conversion of original XML files to XHTML, this pattern is even more useful, making it possible to reduce XSLFO programming to a configuration exercise in a properly organized development environment. Note however, that no solution is good for all cases, and conversion to XHTML may result in losing semantics, which are important, for example, for exhibiting control over pagination. Nevertheless, even if the intermediate format ends up being some XHTML+, the idea remains the same—define a simple intermediate format that allows for the best reuse of existing transformation and formatting libraries.

Getting back to our XSLFO example, pagination controls in Figure 7.21 define a single master page that is referenced by name ('testMaster') in `<fo:page-sequence>`. Real applications are likely to require multiple different master pages used in different contexts. To further promote reuse, master pages may be defined in separate stylesheets, and included in page layout stylesheets using `<xsl:include>`. The `<fo:flow>`

```
<?xml version ="1.0" encoding ="UTF-8" ?>
<xsl:stylesheet version ="1.0"
    xmlns:fo ="http://www.w3.org/1999/XSL/Format"
    xmlns:xsl="http://www.w3.org/1999/XSL/Transform">
<xsl:output method="xml" version="1.0" indent="yes"/>
<xsl:include href="attributes.xsl"/>
<xsl:include href="pagelayout.xsl"/>
<xsl:template match="books">
<fo:block xsl:use-attribute-sets ="ablock">Status: <xsl:value-of
select ="@status"/></fo:block>
<fo:block>
<fo:table xsl:use-attribute-sets ="table.info">
    <fo:table-column xsl:use-attribute-sets="table.info.td"/>
    <fo:table-column xsl:use-attribute-sets="table.info.td"/>
    <fo:table-column xsl:use-attribute-sets="table.info.td"/>
    <fo:table-column xsl:use-attribute-sets="table.info.td"/>
    <fo:table-header xsl:use-attribute-sets="table.info.th">
        <fo:table-row>
            <fo:table-cell>
            <fo:block xsl:use-attribute-sets ="cblock">
               Title</fo:block>
            </fo:table-cell>
            <fo:table-cell>
            <fo:block xsl:use-attribute-sets ="cblock">
               Authors</fo:block>
            </fo:table-cell>
            <fo:table-cell>
            <fo:block xsl:use-attribute-sets ="cblock">
               Publisher</fo:block>
            </fo:table-cell>
            <fo:table-cell>
            <fo:block xsl:use-attribute-sets ="cblock">
               Year</fo:block>
            </fo:table-cell>
        </fo:table-row>
    </fo:table-header>
    <fo:table-body>
        <xsl:apply-templates select ="book"/>
    </fo:table-body>
</fo:table>
</fo:block>
</xsl:template>
<xsl:template match ="book">
<fo:table-row>
    <fo:table-cell>
    <fo:block xsl:use-attribute-sets ="cblock">
        <xsl:value-of select ="title"/>
    </fo:block></fo:table-cell>
```

Figure 7.20 XSLFO version of the XSL Stylesheet from Figure 7.15

```
        <fo:table-cell><xsl:apply-templates select="author"/>
</fo:table-cell>
    <fo:table-cell> <fo:block xsl:use-attribute-sets="cblock">
        <xsl:value-of select="info/publication/@source"/>
    </fo:block>
    </fo:table-cell>
    <fo:table-cell>
    <fo:block xsl:use-attribute-sets="cblock">
        <xsl:value-of select="info/publication/@year"/>
    </fo:block>
</fo:table-cell>
</fo:table-row>
</xsl:template>
<xsl:template match="author">
    <fo:block xsl:use-attribute-sets="cblock">
    <xsl:value-of select="@firstName"/>
    <xsl:text> </xsl:text>
    <xsl:value-of select="@lastName"/>
    </fo:block>
</xsl:template>
</xsl:stylesheet>
```

Figure 7.20   (*continued*)

```
        <?xml version="1.0" encoding="UTF-8"?>
        <xsl:stylesheet version="1.0"
            xmlns:xsl="http://www.w3.org/1999/XSL/Transform"
            xmlns:fo="http://www.w3.org/1999/XSL/Format">
        <xsl:template match="/">
            <fo:root>
            <fo:layout-master-set>
              <fo:simple-page-master master-name="testMaster"
                  page-height="29.7cm" page-width="21cm"
                  margin-top="1cm"
                  margin-bottom="2cm" margin-left="2.5cm"
                  margin-right="2.5cm">
                <fo:region-body margin-top="2cm"/>
                <fo:region-before extent="2cm"/>
                <fo:region-after extent="1.5cm"/>
              </fo:simple-page-master>
            </fo:layout-master-set>
            <fo:page-sequence master-reference="testMaster">
              <fo:flow flow-name="xsl-region-body">
                  <xsl:apply-templates select="books"/>
              </fo:flow>
            </fo:page-sequence>
            </fo:root>
        </xsl:template>
        </xsl:stylesheet>
```

Figure 7.21   The pagelayout.xsl file referenced from the XSL Stylesheet in Figure 7.20

```
<?xml version ="1.0" encoding ="UTF-8"?>
<xsl:stylesheet version ="1.0"
xmlns:xsl ="http://www.w3.org/1999/XSL/Transform"
xmlns:fo ="http://www.w3.org/1999/XSL/Format">
<xsl:attribute-set name ="ablock">
   <xsl:attribute name ="font-size">18pt</xsl:attribute>
   <xsl:attribute name ="background-color">black</xsl:attribute>
      <xsl:attribute name ="color">white</xsl:attribute>
   <xsl:attribute name ="text-align">left</xsl:attribute>
</xsl:attribute-set>
<xsl:attribute-set name ="cblock">
   <xsl:attribute name ="font-size">14pt</xsl:attribute>
   <xsl:attribute name ="text-align">center</xsl:attribute>
</xsl:attribute-set>
<xsl:attribute-set name ="table.info">
    <xsl:attribute name ="table-layout">fixed</xsl:attribute>
    <xsl:attribute name ="space-before">10pt</xsl:attribute>
    <xsl:attribute name ="space-after">10pt</xsl:attribute>
</xsl:attribute-set>
<xsl:attribute-set name ="table.info.th">
    <xsl:attribute name ="background-color">#EEEEEE</xsl:attribute>
    <xsl:attribute name ="font-family">sans-serif</xsl:attribute>
    <xsl:attribute name ="border-style">solid</xsl:attribute>
    <xsl:attribute name ="border-width">1pt</xsl:attribute>
    <xsl:attribute name ="padding-start">0.3em</xsl:attribute>
    <xsl:attribute name ="padding-end">0.2em</xsl:attribute>
    <xsl:attribute name ="padding-before">2pt</xsl:attribute>
    <xsl:attribute name ="padding-end">2pt</xsl:attribute>
</xsl:attribute-set>
<xsl:attribute-set name ="table.info.td">
    <xsl:attribute name ="border-style">solid</xsl:attribute>
    <xsl:attribute name ="border-width">1pt</xsl:attribute>
    <xsl:attribute name ="padding-start">0.3em</xsl:attribute>
    <xsl:attribute name ="padding-end">0.2em</xsl:attribute>
    <xsl:attribute name ="padding-before">2pt</xsl:attribute>
    <xsl:attribute name ="padding-end">2pt</xsl:attribute>
</xsl:attribute-set>
</xsl:stylesheet>
```

Figure 7.22   The attributes.xsl file referenced from the XSL Stylesheet in Figure 7.20

element encapsulates rendering components that get generated by XSLT instructions in Figure 7.20, which get invoked when the XSL processor evaluates `<xsl:apply-templates name ="books"/>` in Figure 7.21.

Target XSLFO elements in Figure 7.20 make extensive use of the 'xsl:use-attribute-sets' attribute. Named attribute sets are defined in 'attributes.xsl' (Figure 7.22), to make it easier to parameterize the XSL Stylesheet in Figure 7.20. It is very easy to provide tools for editing simple stylesheets, similar to 'attributes.xsl', for use by graphic designers with little or no knowledge of XSL.

As we showed in Figures 7.18 and 7.19, applying an XSL Stylesheet containing XSLT instructions and designed to target the XSLFO vocabulary is a two-step process. The first step is performing the XSLT transformations. The output of the XSLT engine when applying transformations in Figure 7.20 to the XML document in Figure 7.1 is shown in Figure 7.23. It is an XML document satisfying the XSLFO schema. It contains XSLFO elements, including pagination elements defined in the 'pagelayout.xsl' file. As you can see, the style parameters originate in the 'attributes.xsl' file.

The XSLFO document in Figure 7.23 serves as input to the FO engine that can produce the variety of outputs, including postscript and pdf (Figure 7.24). You do not have to generate the intermediate representation in Figure 7.23. Most FO engines would accept either the file in Figure 7.23, or files in Figures 7.1 and 7.23. In the latter case, the FO engine would simply invoke the XSLT engine and then process the output.

7.4.3 What is so important about XSL?

The XSL specification has had quite a number of twists and turns in its relatively short but eventful history. At this time, it is a combination of two well-defined components—XSLT and XSLFO. The former is the transformation language that enables translations between XML documents that satisfy different schemas, and the latter is the style language that supports page layouts. There is still a plethora of style languages compatible with XHTML (e.g. CSS, CSS2, and other style languages), which are not integral parts of XSL, even though XHTML *is* an XML application.

More twists and turns may still be ahead of us. The desirable direction is for browsers to provide integrated support for XSLFO, which may be sufficient to deprecate other style languages. Once it is practical to express XHTML semantics using the XSLFO vocabulary, the former would become no more than a shortcut notation. Such a development would be very conducive to building advanced tools and simplifying presentation components.

XSLT is now the technology of choice for building applications that target multiple end user devices and presentation formats. It allows for a 'raw' XML representation of a document that can be personalized and transformed into various target formats (e.g. XHTML, WML, SMIL).

Historically, it was common for application developers to jump through many proprietary hoops to create print versions of legal documents, financial statements, etc. XSLFO extends the list of devices and formats to include those that require pagination. This extension has the potential of streamlining application architecture and simplifying both the development and maintenance. XSLFO has already started gaining momentum after its release as a W3C recommendation in 2002.

```xml
<?xml version="1.0" encoding="UTF-8"?>
<fo:root xmlns:fo="http://www.w3.org/1999/XSL/Format">
<fo:layout-master-set>
<fo:simple-page-master master-name="only">
<fo:region-body region-name="xsl-region-body"
        margin="0.7in"/>
<fo:region-before region-name="xsl-region-before"
        extent="0.7in" display-align="before"/>
<fo:region-after region-name="xsl-region-after"
        display-align="after" extent="0.7in"/>
</fo:simple-page-master>
</fo:layout-master-set>
<fo:page-sequence master-reference="only">
<fo:flow flow-name="xsl-region-body">
<fo:title>Book List</fo:title>
<fo:block>Status: In Print</fo:block>
<fo:block>
<fo:table table-layout="fixed" space-before="10pt"
        space-after="10pt">
<fo:table-body>
<fo:table-row>
<fo:table-header background-color="#EEEEEE" border-style="solid"
        border-width="1pt" padding-start="0.3em" padding-end="2pt"
        padding-before="2pt">
Title
</fo:table-header>
<fo:table-header background-color="#EEEEEE" border-style="solid"
        border-width="1pt" padding-start="0.3em" padding-end="2pt"
        padding-before="2pt">
Authors
</fo:table-header>
<fo:table-header background-color="#EEEEEE" border-style="solid"
        border-width="1pt" padding-start="0.3em" padding-end="2pt"
        padding-before="2pt">
Publisher
</fo:table-header>
<fo:table-header background-color="#EEEEEE" border-style="solid"
        border-width="1pt" padding-start="0.3em" padding-end="2pt"
        padding-before="2pt">
Year
</fo:table-header>
</fo:table-row>
<fo:table-row>
<fo:table-column border-style="solid" border-width="1pt"
        padding-start="0.3em" padding-end="2pt"
        padding-before="2pt">
Web Application Architecture
</fo:table-column>
```

Figure 7.23 Output of the XSLT processor

```
<fo:table-column border-style="solid" border-width="1pt"
        padding-start="0.3em" padding-end="2pt"
        padding-before="2pt">
<fo:block>Leon Shklar</fo:block>
<fo:block>Rich Rosen</fo:block>
</fo:table-column>
<fo:table-column border-style="solid" border-width="1pt"
        padding-start="0.3em" padding-end="2pt"
        padding-before="2pt">
John Wiley and Sons, Ltd.
</fo:table-column>
<fo:table-column border-style="solid" border-width="1pt"
        padding-start="0.3em" padding-end="2pt"
        padding-before="2pt">
2003
</fo:table-column>
</fo:table-row>
</fo:table-body>
</fo:table>
</fo:block>
</fo:flow>
</fo:page-sequence>
</fo:root>
```

Figure 7.23 (*continued*)

Status: In Print			
Title	Authors	Publisher	Year
Web Application Architecture	Leon Shklar Rich Rosen	John Wiley and Sons, Ltd.	2003

Figure 7.24 Output of the FO processor

7.5 SUMMARY

In terms of its speed of adoption and ever-growing momentum, XML rivals both the HTTP protocol and HTML. This is not surprising, since XML applications transcend the worlds of desktop computers and even mobile devices. XML advanced from the markup language to the implementation platform. Not only do XML and XSL provide the next generation basis for browser applications—they are critical in large-scale application integration, including messaging and Web services.

XML is the combination of related technologies, including XML Schema, XSL, APIs for accessing XML parse trees, and rich library of XML applications. This chapter barely scratched the surface—there is a lot more to these technologies than what we have discussed here. The purposes that XML is being used for are as varied as the myriad tasks performed by architects, designers, developers, and users.

It is important at different stages of the application lifecycle. XML is used at the application design stage as the representation medium for Universal Modeling Language (UML) diagrams, at implementation time to control and coordinate development, testing, and versioning tools, and at run-time as the universal 'glue' for application components.

XML is used to define presentation languages for a variety of target formats. In addition to XHTML and WML, there is also MathML for describing mathematics, Scalable Vector Graphics (SVG) for describing two-dimensional graphics, Synchronized Multimedia Integration Language (SMIL) used to control the sequencing and layout of multimedia presentations, and many other specialized languages.

There is also the XML Linking Language (XLink) for linking resources, XML Query Language (XQuery) for querying XML elements, and other important technologies that have become strategic in the Internet world. Such technologies include the Simple Object Access Protocol (SOAP) designed to support XML messaging and its companion Web Service Definition Language (WSDL) that implements descriptions for componentized services.

You can find a large selection of XML books that cover the details of all aspects of XML and related technologies. The key to making the right choices and to understanding the details when you need them is the knowledge of underlying principles. The main objective of this chapter was to discuss the core technologies, and to provide you with the understanding you need to choose and understand other resources.

7.6 QUESTIONS AND EXERCISES

1. What makes an XML document well-formed? Is every well-formed document valid? Why? Is every valid document well-formed? Why?
2. Are there documents that are both HTML and XHTML documents? Is every HTML document also an XHTML document? Is every XHTML document also an HTML document? Explain.
3. Are there constraints that can be expressed using XML Schema but not DTD? Provide examples.
4. What is XSLFO? What is the relationship between XSLFO and CSS? What is the relationship between XSLFO and XSLT?
5. Name all XML *applications* that were mentioned in this chapter. Separately, name all XML *specifications* that were mentioned in this chapter.
6. Let us design our own 'CarML' language. Define your XML tags for describing your car and your friends' cars using these tags. Think about what properties should be defined as attributes and what properties are best described as elements. Make sure your documents are well-formed.

7. Define an XML DTD for CarML. You may want to revisit XML documents you defined in the previous exercise and rethink the element and attribute structure as you are defining the DTD. In the end, all your car specifications should be valid XML documents.

8. Define an XML Schema equivalent to the XML DTD from the previous exercise. Compare the two.

9. Strengthen the XML Schema to apply additional constraints. Discuss new simple types that would be introduced in this context? Are there any changes to the complex types as well? Why or why not?

10. Implement an XSLT transformation to convert CarML documents to XHTML. Can your XHTML documents qualify as valid HTML documents as well? If not, can you make changes to your XSLT transformation to ensure that the output qualifies as both valid XHTML and valid HTML? Explain.

11. Implement an XSLT transformation to convert CarXML documents to WML. Re-factor your XSLT implementation from the previous exercise to share as many components as possible with the WML transformation.

12. Extend your XSLT implementation to support conversions of CarXML documents to WML, XHTML, or PDF documents.

BIBLIOGRAPHY

Harold, E. R. (2001) *XML Bible*, 2nd *Edition*. John Wiley & Sons.

Harold, E. R. (2002) *Processing XML with Java: A Guide to SAX, DOM, JDOM, JAXP, and TrAX*. Addison Wesley.

Mangano, S. (2002) *XSLT Cookbook*. O'Reilly & Associates.

Musciano, C. and Kennedy, B. (2002) *HTML and XHTML, The Definitive Guide*. Fifth Edition. O'Reilly & Associates.

Pawson, D. (2002) *XSL FO*. O'Reilly & Associates.

Tennison, J. (2001) *XSLT and XPath: On The Edge*. John Wiley & Sons.

Walmsley, P. (2001) *Definitive XML Schema*. Prentice Hall.

8 Dynamic Web Applications

In the last few chapters, we covered the inner workings of both Web clients and Web servers. Now we examine the nature of *Web applications*: custom applications that operate within the context of a Web server environment, communicating with other Web applications, servers, and clients.

Our first step is to define the notion of a 'Web application'. We then take a look at the processing flow that occurs in a Web application, making a clear distinction between steps that are the responsibility of the application and steps that are 'taken care of' by the Web server and/or the application framework. We will examine typical application functions, along with the recommended best practices for implementing those functions. Finally, we shall go over design and development issues specifically related to applications that interact with database management systems.

8.1 HISTORICAL PERSPECTIVE

Before we discuss the nature of 'Web applications,' we need to put that term in its proper perspective. In the past, an 'application' was defined as a program (such as Microsoft Word or Adobe Photoshop), an instance of which executes on a single system. That definition changed as the technology evolved.

8.1.1 Client-server applications

Client-server applications are groups of distributed programs running on networked computers, and interacting over known communication protocols. Rather than performing all the processing on a single system and transmitting formatted results to 'dumb' terminals, client-server applications distribute processing between dedicated server and client machines. This architecture was facilitated by the proliferation

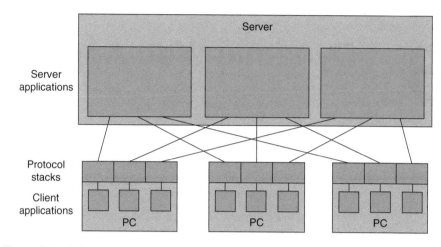

Figure 8.1   Client-server applications that use fat clients

of personal computers, whose additional processing power allowed some of the complex processing to be offloaded from servers down to the clients.

Over time, some proprietary client-server application platforms (e.g. PowerBuilder) grew to be very complex, and their configuration and maintenance became a nightmare. With each new version, the size and complexity of the client platform base seemed to increase by another order of magnitude, resulting in what were referred to as *fat clients*. This application bloat became a serious problem, especially as the number of fat clients installed on a single PC grew as well, as shown in Figure 8.1.

8.1.2 Web applications

A Web application is a client-server application that (generally) uses the Web browser as its client. Browsers send requests to servers, and the servers generate responses and return them to the browsers. They differ from older client-server applications because they make use of a common client program, namely the Web browser, as illustrated in Figure 8.2.

There are important advantages to using Web browsers as clients:

1. Web browsers are ubiquitous. They are present on virtually every desktop and can be used to interact with many different Web applications. There is no need to install several specialized client programs on the desktop, dramatically reducing maintenance headaches.

2. Browsers provide mechanisms to securely download and execute more complex clients (e.g. applets, ActiveX components, and Flash movie players) when additional functionality that browsers alone cannot provide is required

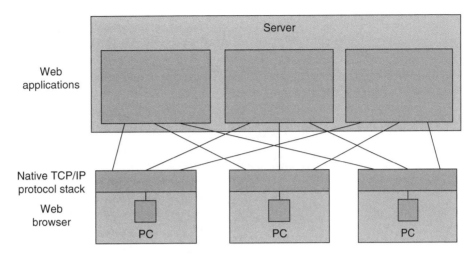

Figure 8.2   Web applications that use a single client application (browser) and a single protocol stack

8.1.3 Multi-tier Web applications

Although Web applications fit into the client-server paradigm, they go beyond it. The interaction between browsers and servers is not all there is to a Web application. The Web servers themselves operate as 'clients' when they interact with other back-end servers, including databases and legacy systems. Thus, the architecture of most Web applications is better described as the *multi-tier* architecture. While simpler client-server applications have only two tiers with distinct roles (the client and the server tiers), multi-tier applications have (as the name implies) multiple tiers, each of which can act as both client and server when communicating with its neighbors.

In multi-tier applications, each tier represents an application layer (browser, web server, application server, database/legacy system, etc.). The bottom layer is the Web client (usually a browser or an intelligent agent) that initiates processing by submitting a request to a Web server. Every set of adjacent tiers represents a pairing of a client and a server, and every intermediate tier may act as either client or server, depending on which of its neighbors it is interacting with. For example, just as the browser connects to the Web server to make a request, the portion of the application executing on the Web server may connect to a business logic or data model layer, acting as a client for that layer's services.

8.2 APPLICATION ARCHITECTURE

Let's take a look at the processing flow associated with a Web application, and the functionality required to perform that processing (Figure 8.3):

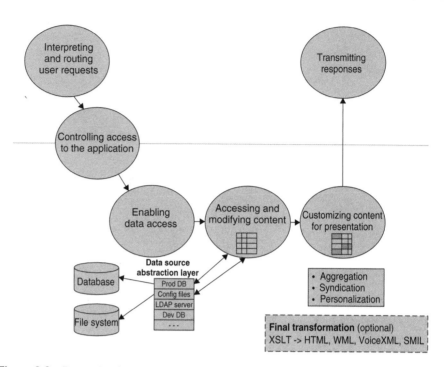

Figure 8.3 Processing flow in a typical Web application (Above the grey line—Web server; below the grey line—Web application)

- *Interpreting and routing user requests*: during this step, the Web server takes responsibility for determining what action needs to be taken to process the request. This action could be the simple retrieval of a static HTML file, the execution of a CGI script, or the invocation of a specialized processing module (e.g. a servlet engine), which in turn may perform complex functions associated with a full-blown Web application.

- *Controlling access to the application*: unless you are dealing with an unrestricted Web site, you need access control mechanisms. This involves more than just support for simple authentication. Some application functions may be available to everyone. Others may be available only to registered customers. Still others (e.g. internal site maintenance functions) may be restricted to application administrators.

- *Enabling data access*: whether your users need to view product information from a catalog or read articles from your online library, your application must gain access to the actual data.

- *Accessing and modifying content*: in addition, to accessing and displaying content, the application may be responsible for performing content updates. Such updates may be the result of an explicit user action, or they may take place automatically based on application logic (e.g. updating a hit counter or tracking user page visits). Discrete groups of interdependent modifications may be organized into *transactions* where all the modifications are treated as a unit that will either be 'committed' (accepted) or 'rolled back' (discarded) as a whole.

- *Customizing responses*: it may be necessary to transform generated responses to facilitate customized presentation for the originating user. These transformations may support customization on a per-user basis (personalization), or on a site referrer basis (co-branding and syndication). They may also customize responses to account for capabilities and limitations of different browsers and devices.

- *Transmitting formatted responses*: in older Web applications, once the appropriate content transformations have been performed, an HTML response containing a formatted presentation was sent back to the originating client. More sophisticated applications (e.g. those that make use of XML) may go through a final device-specific or browser-specific transformation using an XSL stylesheet before the response is transmitted. The result could be an HTML page, a WML document targeted for wireless devices, a VoiceXML document used by a telephony application, or some other target format.

- *Recording and logging application activity*: as the application is used, it is important to keep records of its usage. For example, execution of internal administrative functions should be recorded in an audit trail that records changes and the context in which they were made.

8.2.1 Interpreting and routing client requests

When a user attempts to access a Web application, the browser first submits an HTTP request to a Web server. The information associated with the request (often called the *request context*, see Figure 8.4) includes the information found in the URL itself (e.g. the query string), request headers, and the message body. It also includes *session* information, which preserves the application 'state' across successive requests. (This information is either transmitted with every request, or it is maintained on the server and referenced through a unique id.)

It is the responsibility of the Web server to accept requests and to route them to appropriate processors. Depending on the mechanisms available within the Web server, this processing could take a number of different forms:

- It could result in a response whose contents are obtained from a static file (along with appropriate HTTP headers).

- It could result in the execution of a CGI script.

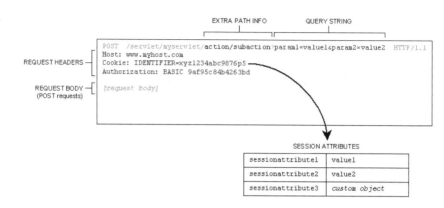

Figure 8.4   Components of the request context

- It could result in the processing of a template or other custom page-generation module (e.g. PHP script, Cold Fusion module, ASP page, Java servlet, JSP page).

- It could make use of a built-in server infrastructure that supports sophisticated Web applications.

> As we've mentioned repeatedly, HTTP is a stateless protocol, meaning that it does not provide for the persistence of state information across requests. However, we know that there are mechanisms for maintaining state across successive HTTP requests from the same user, and these mechanisms (i.e., the session services provided by the Web server or application framework) are critical to any advanced Web application.
>
> The HTTP protocol supports the transmission of authorization information used to manage access to the application (basic authentication using the `Authorization` header). In practice, basic authentication is too limiting, so most applications make use of session services to provide application-controlled authentication.
>
> It is, to a large degree, this usage of an application's state that is maintained across requests which distinguishes a 'Web site' from a 'Web application.'

After evaluating the request context (HTTP headers, URL parameters, form fields and session information), the Web server determines what action needs to be taken in response to the request, and directs the request to the appropriate application function or service.

In the case of static file deliveries, the Web server maps the path portion of the URL to a directory and file name within its local file system. It then builds a response by setting appropriate HTTP headers (e.g. `Content-Type`) and appending the file's content. Finally, it transmits the response back to the requestor. Static file delivery can be thought of as a 'trivial' Web application, built into every Web server by design.

Web servers provide functionality for mapping requests to Web applications and other request processors installed on the server. This is accomplished by analyzing the URL. The path and the file name extension are both used by the Web server to determine the target processor for a given request. HTTP headers may also play a part in determining the target processor.

In the case of CGI scripts and auxiliary server processing modules, this is often accomplished by examining the file name extension at the end of the path portion of the URL. Web servers can be configured to map specific extensions to 'server-side MIME types' that require server-side processing prior to transmission. URLs whose paths end with .cgi might be routed to the CGI processor, while URLs whose paths end with .php, .cfm, or .asp might be routed to the processing modules associated with PHP, Cold Fusion, and Active Server Pages (assuming such modules are installed and mapped to the proper file extensions). It is assumed that the Web server should provide either built-in functionality for these processing modules, or mechanisms to install, register and invoke them.

Other path elements also may control the selection of a server processing module. URLs of the form http://host/cgi-bin/... may tell the server to use the CGI processor if the /cgi-bin path fragment is associated with the CGI processing module. Likewise, URLs of the form http://host/servlet/myservlet/... may tell the server that the request is to be processed by the servlet runner, which would, hopefully, recognize 'myservlet' as the name of a registered servlet. Again, it is assumed that the Web server provides mechanisms for the configuration and recognition of associated processing modules, as shown in Table 8.1.

J2EE Webapps

The J2EE definition of a Web application is somewhat more complex. Web servers that support J2EE Web Applications (often referred to as *'webapps'*) generally designate a directory where webapp directory subtrees and/or *web application archives* (.war files) reside. Web application archives are simply compressed files whose contents have the same directory structure.

Each webapp directory has a predefined structure, containing a 'hidden' sub-directory (WEB-INF) that holds supporting application program files and an XML configuration file (web.xml) for the application.

We shall come back to the subject of webapps when we examine the J2EE approach to building web applications.

The routing of a request does not end when it is associated with a particular Web application. The Web application may further examine the request context to route it to a specific function. This approach is known as the *Front Controller* pattern and is employed in the Apache Project framework known as *Struts*. In the Struts framework, Web applications are configured by defining a set of performable *actions*

Table 8.1 Selection of server processing modules

Approach	Configuration	URL Examples
CGI	1. Server provides mechanism for defining CGI path mappings. 2. Server provides mechanism to map URL file name extensions to CGI processing.	`http://host/`<u>`cgi-bin`</u>`/`*`script`*`?...` `http://host/.../`*`script.`*<u>`cgi`</u>`?...`

Auxiliary processing modules (scripting, template, hybrid)	1. Server provides mechanism for registering processing modules for files with predefined name extensions.
	2. Native support may be built into server (e.g., ASP on IIS).
		`http://host/.../`*`modulename.`*<u>`php`</u>`?...`
		`http://host/.../`*`modulename.`*<u>`cfm`</u>`?...`
		`http://host/.../`*`modulename.`*<u>`asp`</u>`?...`

J2EE Webapp	1. Server provides mechanism for defining application path mappings.
	2. Server provides mechanism to map URL file name extensions to be processed as JSP pages.
		`http://host/`<u>`servlet`</u>`/`*`servletname`*`/...`
		`http://host/`*`webappname`*`/`*`servletname`*`/...`
		`http://host/`*`webappname`*`/`*`modulename.`*<u>`jsp`</u>`?...`
		`http://host/anotherjsp.jsp`

in an XML configuration file. Actions are mapped to custom Java classes that extend the base action class. (We examine Struts in more detail in Chapter 9.)

8.2.2 Controlling user access to the application

Naturally, you would want to control access to your application, except for Web sites that are designed to be open to the general public. When Web applications are secure (i.e. when functions within the application are meant to be used only by authorized users), users must be authenticated prior to accessing these functions. This is usually accomplished by requiring the user to 'log in' prior to accessing secured areas.

Remember that large portions of a Web application may be open and accessible to everyone. You probably don't want to restrict access to the general information pages on a Web site, for example. And of course, if you restrict access to the sign-up page, where new visitors can identify themselves and become registered users, you won't be getting any new users!

Example

A real estate broker's Web site might contain general information about the company's services on the site's front page. This page might contain links to e-mail and telephone contact information, as well as some 'teaser' pictures of properties that might be of interest to a visitor. Naturally, all of this content is publicly accessible. Having been sufficiently attracted by the teasers, users may want to see details about the displayed properties, but in order to do so they must be signed up as registered users. In the sample page displayed in Figure 8.5, links in the navigation bar enable users to login, sign up, search, or display contact information. The dropdown box allows users to visit pages that display lists of properties for different regions, but details about each displayed property are accessible only after users have signed in. The pictures are links to property details for authenticated users, but unauthenticated users following those links get redirected to the registration page.

Using secure connections for user authentication

Both login and signup functions should make use of a secure connection for transmitting user identification data discreetly. This usually means using the SSL (Secure Sockets Layer) connection to a secure server (usually identified by its use of the HTTPS scheme in the URL). To ensure application security and user privacy, the form through which a user provides personal information should be submitted using a secure connection as well. This much is probably obvious. But a common application design mistake is to assume that the page displaying this form need not be sent to the user over a secure connection.

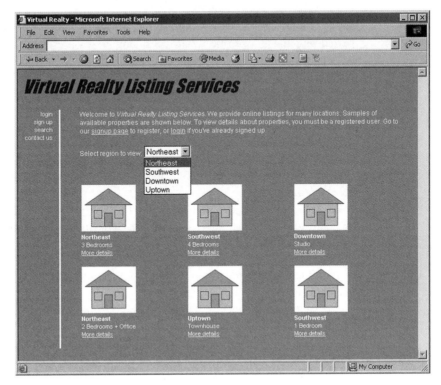

Figure 8.5   Home page for Virtual Realty web application

Consider the situation where an existing user is seeking to *modify* previously recorded personal information: the form is sent to the user with fields already filled in. Even in the initial signup scenario, the form may be redisplayed with some information already filled in (e.g. because some information in the initial submission was omitted, incomplete, or invalid). Thus, both the signup and login processes should be configured within a Web application to operate over the secure connection. (Of course, any transactions involving other personal information, such as addresses and credit card numbers, should also be transmitted over secure connections.)

Example

When signing up on the real estate broker's Web site, users may be prompted for a variety of personal information. If a user omits some information or leaves some entries incomplete, the application would send a response back to the user with the partially completed form, asking the user to correct missing or incomplete entries and resubmit the form. The partially completed response contains at least some personal information, and thus should always be transmitted over a secure connection. This is especially true where the form asks for credit card numbers, social security numbers, and other private information (Figure 8.6).

As we discussed earlier, the application's login function can make use of basic HTTP authentication, which is defined in the HTTP protocol specification. It is supported directly by Web browsers via dialog boxes presented to users so that they can enter authorization credentials whenever the browser receives a security challenge (an HTTP response with the `401 Not Authorized` status code). The browser encodes the credentials entered by the user and includes them in the `Authorization` header for all subsequent requests to the same security realm. Care must be taken to configure the Web application so that related secured resources belong to the same security realm. (It should be noted that the encoding of credentials in the `Authorization` header is not the same as *encryption*; the decoding of these credentials is a trivial process, thus the encoded credentials in this header cannot be considered secure.)

In practice, most applications use more flexible forms-based authentication, where authentication information is entered through an HTML form. This approach is far more common in sophisticated Web applications, because it provides capabilities above and beyond those of basic HTTP authentication. Web applications are responsible not only for authenticating users, but also for explicitly maintaining the authentication information across requests.

As mentioned in Section 8.2.1, maintaining this information across requests is usually accomplished through the use of sessions. Most commonly, information that belongs to a particular 'session' (e.g. user ID, list of items in shopping cart) is recorded on the server, and is accessible to the application only if a key identifying a specific user's session is supplied. The key is usually supplied via a cookie, whose value is a unique session identifier. The actual mechanisms for storing and accessing

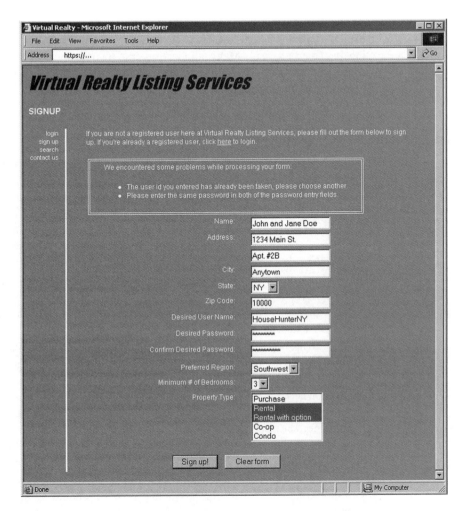

Figure 8.6 Registration page with errors

session information depend on the application framework being employed. Some frameworks (e.g. the Servlet API) have built-in support for sessions, while others require that developers 'roll their own' sessions.

Once the user is authenticated, the authentication information may be added to the session. If the current session for the requesting browser does not exist, a new session is created and its identifier is transmitted to the browser in the Set-Cookie header. Depending on the URL prefix defined in the Set-Cookie header, subsequent requests to the same server would include a Cookie header containing the session identifier.

Assuming that your framework provides built-in support for sessions, it is dangerous to bypass the session mechanism and set cookies containing authentication information directly, since it results in repeated transmission of state information over the wire. Another reason is that users may elect to disable cookie processing in their browsers. Many application frameworks include mechanisms for the automatic detection of cookie support and for ensuring the transmission of session identifiers even without cookies (e.g. via URL rewriting), but these mechanisms are not available if you use cookies directly.

Using cookies for user identification and session management

As already mentioned, cookies should *not* contain authentication information (neither the user name nor the password) but rather unique identifying strings that act as session identifiers. The application makes use of session services provided by the processing environment (e.g. servlet runner, template processor) to maintain persistent information about the identity of the authenticated user for the duration of the user's session. The Web application can make decisions about when to invalidate the session, e.g. after a specified period of user inactivity (time during which the user has not made any requests), or even after a fixed period of time regardless of user activity.

Note that not every processing environment provides session management services. For example, the CGI mechanism does not provide any support for session management, though some optional CGI packages do provide these services.

There are cases when it is justified to use the cookie mechanism directly. One example is persisting user identities beyond the end of the session, so that users would not need to identify themselves the next time they visit the site. However, the application should *never* presume to make decisions about the use of such functionality for the user. Since some computers are shared amongst many users (e.g. at an Internet café or public web kiosk), you wouldn't want to store a cookie that enables automatic authentication—unless the user explicitly expresses a desire to do this. In other words, if you intend to provide automatic authentication functionality, you should let the user to decide whether or not it should be used. This is usually done with a checkbox in the registration and/or login form. (MSN's Hotmail application provides for three levels of safety that a user can choose, ranging from the strictest ('public/shared computer'), which tells Hotmail not to use any persistent cookies to identify users, to the most lenient, which tells Hotmail to use a persistent cookie to always automatically identify users and sign them in.

Example

When signing up to the real estate broker's Web site, you may be asked (via a checkbox on the form) whether or not you want to keep a persistent cookie on your computer, which will automatically identify you to this Web application in the future (Figure 8.7). If you don't check this box, no persistent cookie will survive the termination of your current session, and every time you visit the site, you will be prompted for your user name and password. If you do check this box, your browser will transmit the persistent identifier

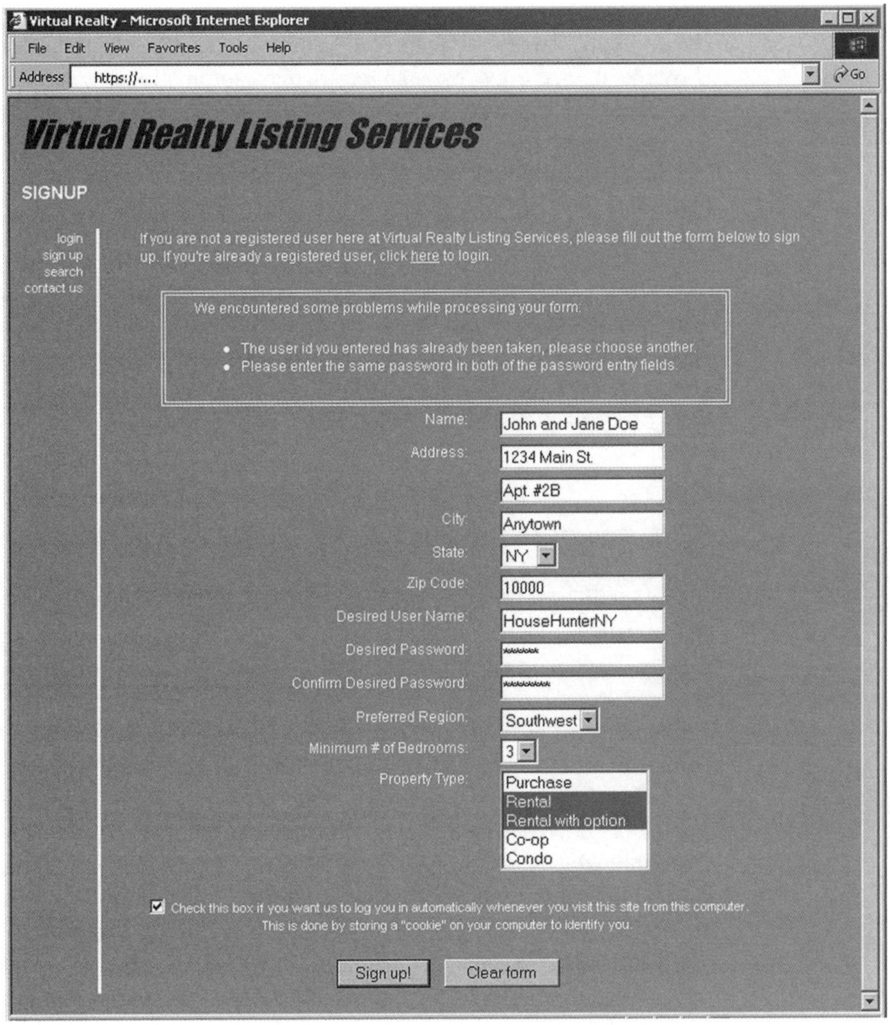

Figure 8.7 Signup page with checkbox to allow automatic login via cookie

contained in the cookie each time you visit this Web site, and the Web application will authenticate you automatically.

There are a number of variants on this process. The Web application can store a cookie on your computer that identifies you, but still require you to enter a password when you access the application. In this case, when you visit the site, the Web application would receive a cookie from your browser identifying you. It would then send down the login form, fill in the field that is supposed to contain your user name, but leave the password field blank, requiring you to fill it in. This also provides the opportunity for another authorized user to sign in instead, by overriding the contents of the user name field and entering their own password.

While this is a lot less dangerous than automatic authentication, it exposes the user name of the last person to use the application on this computer. This may or may not be a matter of concern, but remember to consider these issues when deciding how to support user authentication in your application.

Storing user authentication credentials

While the ACL (Access Control List) associated with HTTP basic authentication is normally maintained as part of the server configuration, forms-based authentication requires the application (or the application framework) to maintain its own access control lists. This usually involves a relational database or an LDAP directory that stores user names and passwords encrypted using MD5 or SHA-1 hashes.

Defining user roles

When designing an application, it is important to remember that it can be used in more than one way. A user could be a customer, or an employee responsible for maintaining the application content and configuration. There are multiple *roles* that a user could take on when accessing a Web application. Such different roles may be implemented through separate access control lists. It is important to design the application so that appropriate entry points are exposed to the right audience. For example, the login and registration pages are usually accessible to the general public, but the administrative functions should be hidden from public view, perhaps even hosted on a different server that is only accessible on the local network.

Finally, do not forget the administrative functions associated with maintaining the application and its underlying content. Consider these during the early stages of your application design. Building a Web application that provides user access to a diverse array of functions and content is only the beginning. Web site content usually cannot update itself, and requiring tedious manual intervention to modify such content is a recipe for failure. It increases the likelihood that it would rapidly get out of date, and that users would quickly grow tired of the stagnant unchanging site and stop coming back.

> **Caution**
>
> Remember that simply placing a 'gateway' page between the user and a restricted functional area does not provide real security for your application and its underlying content (Figure 8.8). For example, the real estate broker's Web site might choose not to publicize the URLs associated with details about available properties, since that content is intended only for paid users. They might decide to put a login page on the

site; once users were authenticated through a login form, they could be redirected to a page containing links to static detail pages about all the available properties.

However, if one of these users e-mails those 'hidden' links to others, those others could read the content even though they were not authorized users. This 'security through obscurity' approach does not work if you want to provide true protection for your content and limit access only to authorized users. It is important to always check user authentication credentials prior to presenting content.

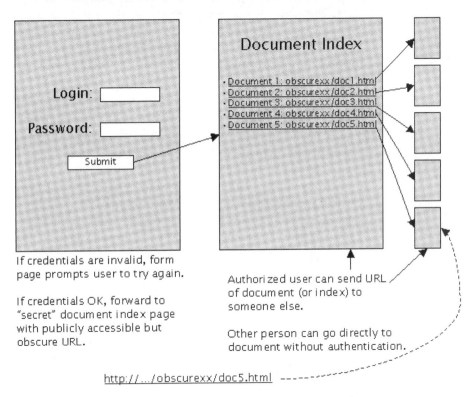

If credentials are invalid, form page prompts user to try again.

If credentials OK, forward to "secret" document index page with publicly accessible but obscure URL.

Authorized user can send URL of document (or index) to someone else.

Other person can go directly to document without authentication.

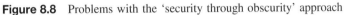

http://.../obscurexx/doc5.html

Figure 8.8 Problems with the 'security through obscurity' approach

Best practices

1. Define in advance the types of users (e.g. general public, authorized subscriber, premium authorized subscriber, free trial access, administrator) who will be accessing the application. *Use Case* analysis is a good method for developing scenarios that describe how the application is to be used.

2. Organize the application architecture into specific functional areas. Identify classes of users that should have access to these areas. Ensure that access to restricted

functional areas is limited only to authorized users by building autonomous authorization checks into each functional area of your application (i.e. avoid 'security through obscurity'!).

3. Authentication should be performed over secure connections. This includes not only the link activated when a login/registration form is submitted, but also the page displaying the form.

4. If you intend to support automated authentication for your users using persistent cookies, be sure to provide them with appropriate options. You might want to give them the choice as to whether or not they *want* to keep authentication credentials on their computer to identify them to your application automatically, or to take the halfway approach and only store user names but not the passwords. Note that, if you employ fully automatic authentication, you need to provide a mechanism for a user to log out, and/or for another user to log in. One common approach is to provide a link (e.g. "If you are not **bob1234**, click here") that invalidates the session and requests new authentication information.

5. Internal administrative functions for the application should be considered early on in the design process. These functions need to be protected from unauthorized users, lest an outsider change the price of a product on your site to zero while you're not looking. Three steps should be taken to secure administrative functions within your application: (1) host these functions on a separate Web server that is not accessible outside your firewall; (2) make that server accessible only through a secure SSL connection even inside the firewall; and (3) allow only explicitly authenticated users to access these functions.

8.2.3 Enabling data access

A sophisticated Web application must enable access to underlying data. This is not an explicit step in the application flow, i.e. it does not happen as requests are being processed. Rather, it is part of the application's configuration, utilized by application tasks that perform data access. These tasks should not access data haphazardly; they should make use of consistent abstractions to data sources. Configuring data access in this manner is a critical part of good Web application architecture.

As mentioned earlier, the simplest form of data access is static file delivery, but this is a trivial service performed by the Web server itself. Once you get beyond static file delivery, you are dealing with a dynamic web application that does more than map a URL to a local file name. You have to consider the *information architecture* of your application.

For example, if the data is contained in a relational database, then the application must have an understanding of the database schema in order to intelligently direct the request. It must have the ability to connect to the database, formulate queries, and interpret the results of those queries.

It is a good idea to have the database schema designed in tandem with the application, so that there is cooperation between the two. Unfortunately, this is not always feasible, e.g. when dealing with existing content that is scattered about the network.

A more sophisticated approach is to abstract the actual mechanics of data access into a separate application layer. This way the portion of the application interpreting user requests does not need to know how to get the data, it only needs to make a request to the dedicated tier, asking it to perform a designated function.

Content sources for Web applications are likely to include:

- ASCII/plain text files (including XML files),

- static pages from other Web servers,

- database management systems,

- content management systems,

- other Web applications.

ASCII/plain text files

The use of ASCII or plain text files as a content source differs from the static file delivery performed by a Web server, in that:

1. The files in question may not be found under the Web server's document root directory.

2. The files are not intended for presentation in their 'raw' unprocessed form.

For example, these files may not be in HTML format at all; they might be encoded as XML, as comma- or tab-separated values, etc. Such files need to be parsed and analyzed, so that their components could be used by your Web application to build the body of the HTTP response.

Example

Your Web application might have to read a CSV file (comma separated values) exported from an Excel spreadsheet by an analyst (Figure 8.9). This file might contain the latest listings provided to real estate brokers, with columns in the spreadsheet representing the address of each property, its price, its size, etc. Naturally, you would not want a file in this format to be directly accessible over the Web, especially since some of the information might not be intended for public consumption.

Your application would have to read this file and parse each line, extracting information from each column, and presenting it in HTML format (e.g. as a row in a table), perhaps with links to an application function that presents detailed information for selected items.

```
1234,Smith,John,green
4567,Jones,Ed,purple
2468,Shklar,Leon,red
3579,Rosen,Rich,blue
```

```
<TABLE>
<TR>
<TD>ID #</TD>
<TD>Last Name</TD>
<TD>First Name</TD>
<TD>Favorite Color</TD>
</TR>
<TR>
<TD>1234</TD>
<TD>Smith</TD>
<TD>John</TD>
<TD>green</TD>
</TR>
<TR>
<TD>4567</TD>
<TD>Jones</TD>
<TD>Ed</TD>
<TD>purple</TD>
</TR>
<TR>
<TD>2468</TD>
<TD>Shklar</TD>
<TD>Leon</TD>
<TD>red</TD>
</TR>
<TR>
<TD>3579</TD>
<TD>Rosen</TD>
<TD>Rich</TD>
<TD>blue</TD>
</TR>
</TABLE>
```

Figure 8.9   Conversion of CSV file to HTML format

It is a good idea to keep files that are not intended for direct viewing *outside* of the Web server document root directory. Thus, in those situations where condition 2 above holds (i.e. where the raw content is not intended for direct viewing), condition 1 should also hold (i.e. files should be placed outside of the Web server document root tree).

Even HTML files might not represent the entire content of an HTML page. They are often either page templates–complete page presentations employing parameter substitution to include dynamic content—or page fragments—common components intended for inclusion in dynamically produced pages (e.g. headers/footers, navigation bars, etc.).

Web servers support mechanisms for the inclusion of page fragments within static files (e.g. SSI—Server Side Includes), but Web applications require more sophistication. For example, you might want to include different headers, footers, navigation bars, and page graphics depending on certain parameters in the request context. Again, it is a good idea to keep these files outside of the Web server document root directory. (We discuss various approaches to this kind of response customization in Section 8.2.5.)

Static pages from other servers

Static and dynamic pages from other servers may be legitimate sources of content for your application. If your application aims to present an entire remote page, then the simplest approach is to generate a response that would redirect the browser to the location of the page. This may not work if the server hosting the page is behind a firewall. It might be accessible to your application but not to outside users. In fact, the purpose of your application might be to provide access to that otherwise hidden content, but only to those authorized to see it. In this situation, your application is responsible not only for retrieving the page, but also for ensuring that users get authenticated and that their privileges are sufficient for viewing the requested content. The aforementioned cautions regarding 'security through obscurity'—routing users to hidden but unprotected URLs as a security mechanism—apply with equal force in this situation.

Dynamic content: databases, content management systems, and other Web applications

Although it is possible that other Web servers might be used as content sources for your Web application, they are not likely to be the main sources of content. They are more likely to be used as fragments that aid in the tailoring and customization of the ultimate response. The bulk of your application's content is going to come from database management systems, content management systems, and other Web applications (accessed through their APIs as opposed to indirectly, through their respective Web servers).

Very few sophisticated commercial Web sites today are maintained as static HTML pages. Most use some sort of content management system, in which *templates* are defined with both common elements and placeholders for dynamic content positioned appropriately within the page.

When we use the term *content management system*, we include commercially available software products for content management, as well as custom applications that rely on homegrown schemas for storing content within relational or object databases (see summary in Table 8.2).

Each has its advantages and disadvantages, of course. Every site has what amounts to a 'content management system,' even if that system is a guy on the third floor who knows the name of the directory where all the Microsoft Word documents are stored. The ideal content management system would allow those who create and modify content to continue to do their job in the same way they always have,

Table 8.2 Content management choices

Content management approach	Usage	Advantages	Disadvantages
Commercially available content management software	• Organizations with large amounts of content requiring complex multi-step approval processes, frequent updates, etc. all managed internally by authorized administrators.	• The bulk of the functionality for content management has been implemented for you. • Added functionality for staging, approval processes, and workflow may also be included in the product.	• Both users and developers must be retrained in the new system. • Migration of existing content into new content repositories. • Significant customization is still required.
Custom content management solution	• Organizations with relatively static content maintained/managed using long-lived procedures. • Desire to leave things as they are: no 'rocking the boat,' no retraining of users	• Content can remain at its original location. • Content providers/maintainers can continue to use the same interfaces. • Added functionality for staging, approval processes, and workflow may also be included in the product.	• Web application must provide its own services to access content. • Web application functionality limited by existing content structure.
Content stored in a database (using custom schema)	• Organizations with very large amounts of content dynamically changing in response to transactions initiated by both users and internal administrators.	• Installation control over content database schema.	• Web application must provide both content access and content maintenance functions.

while giving application developers both search and retrieval interfaces for units of content. Such interfaces are based on descriptive properties associated with the content, often referred to as *metadata* (e.g. title, author, etc.).

Commercially available content management systems may provide an 'out-of-the-box' solution to your content woes, but you still have a lot of configuration, customization, migration, and retraining issues to contend with. Users would need to learn new methods for creating and modifying content, and developers would need to learn custom interfaces for accessing stored content.

Implementing your own content management application provides an opportunity to interface with existing content. You can have direct control over how content is to be created and accessed, and the need to retrain users could be dramatically lessened. The problem is time and resources, since you would be, in essence, reinventing the wheel. Modern content management systems often provide you enough hooks so that you can take advantage of built-in functionality while achieving the flexibility of catering to your own unique needs. It pays to remember that such hooks are often the first victims of backward compatibility issues.

Using a database management system directly as the storage medium for your content is another middle ground option, but there is still plenty of effort that needs to be expended to get such a system up and running, since your application must provide both content access and content maintenance functionality.

Administrative mechanisms must be in place to maintain the content. This includes interfaces for adding new content, as well as for modifying, deleting, and archiving existing content. Mechanisms for performing content modifications are discussed in Section 8.2.4, but in this section we examine the organizing principles associated with content management.

In some situations, the partitioning between 'readers' and 'writers' is clear. For instance, online content providers have end-users that subscribe to their content service. They are able to read the available content through Web applications. Administrators within their organizations are the ones to produce and/or approve additions or changes to the available content.

In other situations, the partitioning is less obvious. For a financial institution application, there would be content available to specific users (e.g. their account balances) that they could not simply modify at their whim (e.g. changing their account balance from −$0.50 to +$1,000,000), but which they can modify in pre-scribed ways (e.g. moving funds between accounts). A database-driven solution is appropriate for these situations.

Most larger Web sites employ a composite approach to content management, using (for example) commercially available content management systems for their global content (e.g. textual articles, site maps, instructions) and database manage-ment systems for volatile and critical content (e.g. account information, customer orders, product catalogues, historical data). Again, some advanced content manage-ment systems support both file-based and database-based storage mechanisms within a single environment.

If you store your content in a database using your own custom schema, you would need to consider the content access interfaces as part of your application design. An administrative user role must be defined, having access to all the necessary content management functionality and the authorization to use that functionality. Follow the guidelines in the Section 8.2.2 when designing the application as a whole, paying attention to the requirements for discrete access to specific content.

If you use a commercial content management system to store your content, a good portion of this task has already been implemented for you—but by no means all of it! There is a significant effort that must be undertaken in migrating data into content repositories used by the new content management system, which may involve the development of an additional application dedicated to this purpose. Some vendors provide tools to aid in the migration, but there is almost always a significant amount of custom coding that needs to be done.

If you build your own custom 'content management system' to access existing content at its original location (e.g. legacy systems, word processing document servers), then your application's responsibilities would not include the actual maintenance of the underlying content. Whatever mechanisms are currently in place would continue to be used. However, your application would need its own mechanisms for determining what content is available, what new content has been created, and what existing content has changed.

Other considerations

You need to consider the administrative/site maintenance functions when designing the application. Mechanisms will be needed for authorized users to add new content, to modify existing content, and to delete or archive outdated content. In addition, provide mechanisms for *classifying* content to support different classes of users. It is a good idea to use the same authentication mechanisms for controlling access to the application as for controlling access to content within the application. It is safer and helps to avoid double authentication.

It is also a good idea to design your application to use centrally administered and configured *datasources* for accessing databases. The *datasource* is an abstraction that allows applications to refer to a logical name rather than an explicit hard-coded location from which data will be accessed. Many Web servers and application frameworks provide mechanisms for associating specific back-end databases with registered names. If the database is physically moved or the network configuration is modified, changing the centrally defined descriptor is all that is needed to keep the application functioning. In the absence of datasources, each application would have to be modified to account for the new location of the database. Figure 8.3 at the beginning of Section 8.2 illustrates how datasource descriptors can be logically configured to point applications to the actual sources of data.

Best practices

1. You may be tempted to keep portions of your dynamically accessed content under the Web server document root directory, but this is not a good idea. Even with a secure site design, it may still expose the content to unauthorized access. If content items are meant to be embedded as page components, it may be inappropriate (or erroneous) to view them outside that context as standalone pages.

2. Don't forget the administrative/site maintenance functions when designing the application. Provide mechanisms for adding new and modifying existing content,

and for deleting or archiving outdated content. In addition, provide mechanisms for *classifying* content to support different classes of users. It is a good idea to use the same authentication mechanisms for controlling access to the application as for controlling access to content within the application. It is safer and helps to avoid double authentication. Our guidelines from the section on *Controlling User Access to the Application* are especially applicable here.

3. Use centrally administered and configured *datasources* for accessing databases. Use mechanisms provided by the Web server or application framework if available. Note that this abstraction need not apply only to databases, but to other back-end content sources as well.

8.2.4 Accessing and modifying content

Once the methodology for maintaining content has been established, the next step is to access that content. Applications may require read-only access, or may need additional privileges for adding, deleting and modifying existing content. Content access privileges should be determined by the authentication and authorization system you have put in place.

If the design involves only the Web client and server tiers, then the Web application, which is responsible for directly accessing (and possibly modifying) the data, uses the Web server's native data access capabilities. (If the request was intended to change back-end data, elements of the request context will determine how the application should modify persistent storage information.)

More sophisticated application architecture defers data access to another tier, allowing the portion of the application residing on the Web server to make abstract requests (e.g. *"Get User Account Information"*) to a tier that understands what actions need to be taken to retrieve back-end data. This design separates responsibility for implementing *business logic* from responsibility for implementing and accessing the *data model*. It is a powerful architectural strategy, since it allows components that use business logic to remain the same when the underlying data model is modified (Figure 8.10).

Read-only applications would only be concerned with reading data. But sophisticated Web applications allow the modification of content as well. There are two types of modifications to content that a Web application is likely to perform. The first type is performed by authorized administrators, who are allowed to make changes to existing content, add new content, or delete/archive old content. The second type occurs in applications where end users are allowed to make changes to site content through functions that are provided by the application. These two types of content modification differ mostly in their scope: options available to end users (even authorized subscribers) are likely to be far more limited than the options available to application administrators.

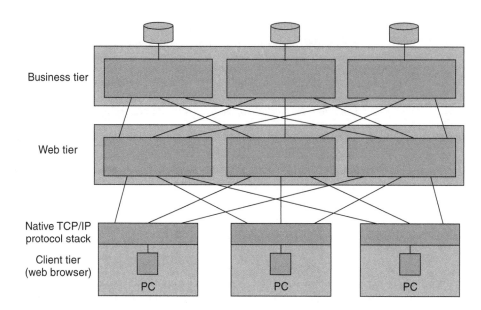

Figure 8.10 Multi-tiered Web application

Example

In our real estate broker application, subscribers would be allowed to make certain modifications to their personal profiles (e.g. name, address, telephone number, type of property being sought), but not to their subscription levels (e.g. free trial, regular subscriber, premium subscriber). On the other hand, an application administrator would be authorized to change the subscription level as well.

Commercially-available content management systems tend to perform these tasks for themselves in a proprietary fashion, so our focus here will be on solutions that must be designed specifically for a custom Web application.

There is always a good deal of work to be done even when using commercially-available content management systems! Although such systems do much of the work of organizing your content and providing interfaces for maintaining that content, there is still a substantial amount of work that you will need to do. Even 'out-of-the-box' solutions require configuration and explicit definition of content formats by administrators before they can be utilized. In addition, these systems employ proprietary APIs that your application must interact with.

Requests for content and the results they produce

Content sources come in a variety of formats, ranging from content repositories and file systems to message servers (e.g. online forums and e-mail) and, of course, databases. Yet all requests for content share a number of common characteristics.

One of these characteristics is the use of *selection criteria* in a content request. Selection criteria are the set of parameters provided to a request to determine which content item(s) should be retrieved. These criteria may be specified in a variety of ways, depending on the nature of the content source. In database queries, selection criteria take the form of a *WHERE clause* which defines the conditions that must be satisfied in order for data to be included in the query result. In LDAP queries, the selection criteria take the form of *search filter strings*. In Web applications, the selection criteria are usually specified via request parameters, such as those that might be included in the URL query string (for GET requests) or in the request body (for POST requests). The application must translate the request parameters into the format for selection criteria that is appropriate for the actual back-end content source.

At the most fundamental level, results returned by a content request take one of the following forms:

1. a set of several content items,

2. a single content item, or

3. no content items.

It is very important to be aware of what might be returned from a content request in your application. If your request should have returned one content item, and instead it returns many, your application is likely to process only the first one (erroneously) or raise an error condition because it doesn't know what to do. If you are not sure, the best approach is to assume that you may see many content items in the response to your content request.

Certain content requests are formulated to return one content item only, by including a unique identifier in the selection criteria that is guaranteed to be associated with only one content item. In database parlance, this is known as the *primary key*. For other content sources, this unique identifier might be a sequence number, a user id, or a combination of multiple fields.

Most initial content requests, however, are expected to return multiple content items. This simply means that the selection criteria associated with the request are potentially satisfied by a number of content items, not necessarily just one.

A common pattern used in both database applications and other content access applications is the *master/detail pattern*. When this pattern is employed, the initial content request returns a set of content items. This set (or a subset of it) should be displayed to the user in a tabular or list format, where each HTML table row or list entry represents a single content item. You have doubtless seen this format on pages containing search engine results, web-based e-mail services, and online account histories. This page is known as the *master page*.

Typically, items on the master page are represented only by relevant identifying information. If there are further details available about a content item, a hyperlink

```
<TABLE>
<TR>
<TD ALIGN="center" VALIGN="center"><B>ID Number</B></TD>
<TD ALIGN="center" VALIGN="center"><B>Name</B></TD>
<TD ALIGN="center" VALIGN="center"><B>Favorite Color</B></TD>
</TR>

<TR>
<TD ALIGN="center" VALIGN="center">
  <A HREF="/app/details?id={ID}">{ID}</A>
</TD>
<TD ALIGN="center" VALIGN="center">
  {LASTNAME}, {FIRSTNAME}
</TD>
<TD ALIGN="center" VALIGN="center">
  {FAVCOLOR}
</TD>
</TR>
</TABLE>
```

Figure 8.11 Sample fragment of a Master page template

within the table row or list entry allows the user to examine those details on a subsequent page, known as the *detail page*. The same base URL is employed for links in every row, with a query string containing selection criteria that uniquely identify the content item whose details are to be displayed.

The HTML fragment in Figure 8.11 is a representation of an HTML table that might be found in a master page, using a notation that might be used for a page template. The block in the middle (bounded by <TR> and </TR>) represents a table row that is to be repeated in the generated HTML response for each row found in the query result set. The text in braces (e.g. {ID}) signifies a substitution variable that refers to the name of a column in the database query that produces the results being displayed, as shown in Figure 8.12.

There are a number of issues associated with the design of user interface for interacting with master and detail pages. If the detail page is presented in the same window occupied by the master page, the user can only traverse to other detail records by hitting the 'back' button to go back to the master page. The detail page could contain a link back to the master page, as well as 'next' and 'previous' links to adjacent content items, which would provide sequential access to the results. One way to achieve additional flexibility is to present the master and detail pages together, as frames within an HTML frameset, or with the detail page opening a new browser window. (Be careful not to design the application to open too many detail windows simultaneously, as this will be distracting to the user and will complicate navigation.) Your application requirements will determine which approach is appropriate.

```
<TABLE>
<TR>
<TD ALIGN ="center" VALIGN ="center"><B>ID Number</B></TD>
<TD ALIGN ="center" VALIGN ="center"><B>Name</B></TD>
<TD ALIGN ="center" VALIGN ="center"><B>Favorite Color</B></TD>
</TR>

<TR>
<TD ALIGN ="center" VALIGN ="center">
  <A HREF ="/app/details?id =1234">1234</A>
</TD>
<TD ALIGN ="center" VALIGN ="center">
  Smith, John
</TD>
<TD ALIGN ="center" VALIGN ="center">
  green
</TD>
</TR>

<TR>
<TD ALIGN ="center" VALIGN ="center">
  <A HREF ="/app/details?id =4567">4567</A>
</TD>
<TD ALIGN ="center" VALIGN ="center">
  Jones, Ed
</TD>
<TD ALIGN ="center" VALIGN ="center">
  purple
</TD>
</TR>
  .
  .
  .
</TABLE>
```

Figure 8.12   The result of interpreting the fragment in Figure 8.11

If the number of content items is sufficiently large, it may be impractical to present all of them on the same master page. In such cases, it may be advisable to segment the results into subsets, presenting only a fixed number of content items per page. A mechanism should be included to provide sequential access to adjacent subsets via 'next' and 'previous' links. There could also be direct access to specific subsets by number (or by range of values within the subset). Sun refers to this within their set of J2EE Blueprint patterns as the *Value List Handler* or *Page-by-Page Iterator* pattern.

Figure 8.13 illustrates a typical master-detail page layout, where the master and detail pages are part of an HTML frameset. The top frame is simply a header

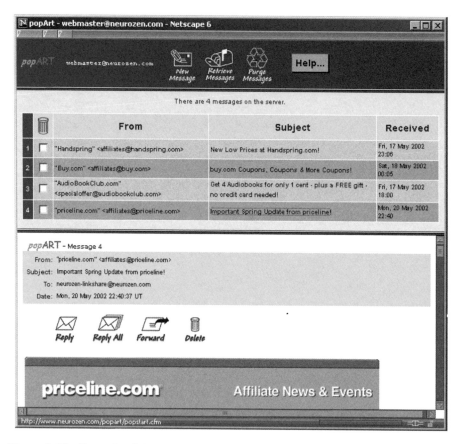

Figure 8.13   Example of the Master-Detail layout

with user identification information and a toolbar. The middle frame is the master page, containing tabular information about e-mail messages available for viewing on a POP3 server. The message number, originator, subject, and transmission date are all cells in an HTML table row for each message. By clicking on any of the displayed fields within a given row, the full text of the e-mail message associated with that row is displayed within the detail frame below. Traversing to other detail records can be accomplished by following links in other rows found in the master frame, refreshing the detail frame with the new content.

As mentioned previously, a content request could return a set of content items, a single content item, or no content items. We refer to this as the *many-one-none pattern* in master-detail processing. If there are many content items returned, you can display the master page with links to details for each item. If there is one content item—either because your content request was specifically formulated to return one item or because it just happened to do so—your application can go directly to a detail page for the unique content item retrieved. If there are no content items, you can present a specialized page that informs the user that the content request has not returned any items.

Careful consideration must be made during the application design phase to determine characteristics associated with master/detail page functionality:

1. *Which attributes associated with an item should be displayed on the master page?* This should be the minimum set of significant but universally readable attributes that uniquely identify an item. (In other words, in an application task devoted to listing a customer's previous orders, use the date, order number, and customer name—but not the customer's credit card number or the individual items ordered—as displayed attributes on the master page.)

2. *Can all the attributes of the data item be viewed? If not, which attributes are viewable by what classes of users?* Establishing the set of attributes associated with the data item that can be displayed by various classes of authorized users is the first step in organizing detail presentation.

3. *Can the data item be edited? If so, which attributes are editable, and by whom?* Designating classes of users that have update access for the data item is only the first part of this process.

4. *Can the data item be deleted? If so, by whom?* Again, defining which classes of users may delete the data item is only the beginning.

5. *Can new data items be inserted? If so, by whom?* Also, assuming the new data item would be stored in a database, what methods are used to create the unique primary key for this new data item?

Content modification

Content can be modified in one of three ways. A new content item can be created, an existing content item can be updated, or an existing content item can be deleted. Content modifications can be implicit, in which case they occur behind the scenes during back-end application processing, or they can be explicit, in which case they occur as a result of direct action taken by a user or site administrator. We concentrate on the latter case here.

Detail pages provide an opportunity not only to display details associated with a particular data item but also to edit and update that data item, depending on the design of the application and the user's authorization level. It is also possible to allow editing on the master page, but this feature should be used judiciously, as it can be overly confusing to users since many items are displayed at once.

The first step is to define classes of users that have update access for the data item. Remember that it is possible to have an authorization schema that allows certain classes of users to edit some attributes, other classes of users to edit other attributes, and still other classes of users to be limited to read-only access to all attributes.

The same detail presentation page could in theory be used for all classes of users as both display and update page, provided the application has the intelligence to display attributes appropriately as read-only text or editable form input items (or not at all) depending on the user's authorization level. (You could also present all detail information initially in read-only format to all users, providing a link to an update page only for those users that are authorized to perform updates.)

The same issues of authorization hold with respect to deletion of data. Depending upon application requirements, the delete functionality could be provided as a button on the detail editing page, or it could be provided on the master page to allow the deletion of multiple data items at the same time (e.g. providing checkboxes for each e-mail message header displayed, providing the option to delete all 'checked' or 'marked' messages by clicking one button).

There are a number of ways that a new data item could be created. A completely new item could be created from scratch; the best way to support this is to provide a blank form to be filled in (and validated) before submission. This could be the same form page used for editing existing data items, but with all the fields left blank. A copy of an existing data item could also be created; in this case, a 'copy' button on the detail page (or on an individual line on the master page) could create a filled-in form that could be modified before submission. In both cases, the same authorization issues continue to hold.

Example

The underlying data associated with a real estate property might include pictures, a floor plan, the address, the price, status (available, sold, or in contract), owner contact information, and the name and phone number of the broker associated with this property. Visitors to the Web site could ask to see all properties in a particular neighborhood (by name or by zip code), resulting in a master page listing of available properties

— Unregistered visitors may only be allowed to see the number of bedrooms and the price of each property, with no opportunity to drill down to further detail.

— Registered users may be allowed to drill down to details for individual properties, so that they can see pictures and floor plans but not the address or other contact information. (This would encourage them to contact a broker to find out more about a particular property.) They would be able to access and modify personal information in their user profiles, but not their access level (e.g. regular vs. premium subscriber).

— Brokers who use the Web site would have additional access so that they could see more private information such as contact information for the owner, the address, etc.

— Only site administrators would be able to add entries for new properties, modify existing entries (e.g. change the price or status of a property), and delete entries (once they are sold or go off the market). They could also modify access levels for users that pay for upgrades (or, conversely, fail to renew).

Best practices

1. When content requests return multiple data items, use the master-detail pattern to organize data presentation. The most common approach is to present each content item as an HTML table row, with the capability to 'drill down' via a hyperlink to detailed information for the item described in that row. If the number of rows is large enough, segment the presentation into subsets, allowing the user to view 'a page at a time' (where a page contains a small fixed number of rows, e.g. 10, 20, 25). Sun refers to this as the *Value List Handler* or *Page-by-Page Iterator* pattern in their *J2EE Blueprints*.

2. When content requests return a single content item (e.g. where a unique item is requested using a primary key), go directly to the detail page. This rule could be applied not only to requests designed to return a unique item, but also to requests that just happen to return a single item this time around. Assuming the focus of the application is access to detail information, why make the user view the single content item on the master page and *then* drill down to the one item available?

3. With this in mind, consider the *many-one-none* pattern when dealing with master-detail processing. A content request could return *many* content items, in which case you display all or some of these items to the requestor with hyperlinks to detail information for each item. The request could return *one* item, in which case you can take the user directly to the detail page. Or it could return *none*, in which case you present a specialized page devoted to conveying this fact to the requestor.

4. Where there are different classes of administrative users with the authority to update different portions of the available content, carefully define the content items (and their attributes) that each class of users can update.

5. Provide a confirmation notice informing users of the success or failure of the update request. You may also want to ask users beforehand whether or not they want to proceed with a request that would modify the back end data.

8.2.5 Customizing content for presentation

The final step in the preparation of the response to be sent to the request originator is the tailoring or customization of that response. The types of customization fall into several broad categories. Your Web application may use one or more of these customization functions in the process of producing the final response. There are a variety of possible customizations that can be made to the retrieved data:

1. *Aggregation*—the presentation could be a *portal*, consisting of an *aggregation* of back end data sources selected by an individual user or a site administrator and presented in a single response.

2. *Syndication*—the presentation could contain content from an outside source (a *content provider*), *co-branded* so that the page layout conforms to the 'look and feel' of your site. (Alternatively, your application may syndicate *your* content to others that you designate as partners or affiliates.)

3. *Personalization*—the presentation could be tailored to the requirements associated with a particular end user, based on user preferences, authorization levels, tracked behaviors, etc.

Aggregation and syndication

Aggregation and syndication can be viewed as two sides of the same coin. Somewhere on the Web, someone is offering up content that registered affiliates (or perhaps *anyone*) can access and embed within their own Web application. Meanwhile, somewhere else on the Web, someone is developing a Web application that could embed syndicated content from different sources. Both kinds of functionality need to be in place for the symbiotic relationship between syndicators and aggregators to work.

Aggregation functionality involves accessing page components (remotely from syndicators and/or locally from your own content sources) and including them within a presented page. The selection and placement of these components can be determined statically by your application. Sometimes, users could be given an opportunity to exercise control over this selection and placement themselves. An application devoted specifically to that sort of personal customization is often called a *portal*. Examples of portals include Yahoo's 'My Yahoo' page, which lets users choose the syndicated components they want to see on their personal home page. While your site may not be intended as a configurable personal portal for its users, it can be enhanced through the use of portal functionality, combining personalization and aggregation capabilities.

A significant development in portal technology is the *Portlet API*, which is already supported by several vendors of commercial server packages, including BEA, IBM, Oracle, and Sun. It is also implemented as part of Jakarta's JetSpeed project. Within this API, a portlet is a specialized servlet designed to run within a portal server. Portlets can be aggregated within the context of a portal page, giving users control over the placement and selection of portlets within their pages, much like the aforementioned 'My Yahoo' page.

Example: Syndication

Suppose you are building an application for what real estate brokers call 'multiple listing services'. Such services make it possible for many different brokers to provide a common set of property listings. Different broker Web sites might use your application to enable visitors to these sites to obtain specific information from these listings. You want visitors to see a page presentation 'branded' to the look and feel of the site they are visiting, rather than the generic look and feel of your application. In the simplest case, they should see the detailed listing information, surrounded by the name and logo for that broker, as well as links back to that broker's Web site. (This functionality, illustrated in Figure 8.14, is often known as *co-branding*.)

This can be accomplished by having your application construct a dynamic response in the following fashion. The first step in producing the response involves accessing the listing information, be it in a static file, a database, or a content management system. The presentation markup (HTML or XML) associated with the listing should be surrounded by custom markup (headings, images, etc.) tailored for the broker whose site the user had been viewing. For many common scenarios, the identity of the referring broker site can be obtained from the HTTP `Referer` header. This header contains the URL of the page where the user found and followed a link to this listing. Based on the host portion of the `Referer` URL, your application can decide dynamically what text, graphics, and links need to be inserted into the body of the response. If the target markup language is XML, the application has the additional opportunity to customize the response by applying XSL transformations.

You can also achieve an added measure of security by allowing only registered affiliate sites to include your content or even to link to one of your syndicated pages. The host portion of the `Referer` URL represents the identity of the affiliate. If it does not represent one of your registered affiliates, the request could be rejected, by having the application return an appropriate response code (e.g. `404 Not Found` or `403 Not Authorized`) to the requestor.

Example: Aggregation

Conversely, you may want your application to embed content from other sites. For instance, once you have determined the regional preferences of a visitor, you might want to present weather or traffic information for their preferred region. You might also want to present local news items associated with that region that are relevant to the real estate market. You might even enable users to choose the external information they want included in the pages they access.

Personalization

Personalization is the creation of customized views for individual users. It can be thought of as an extreme example of content syndication, where the presentation 'branding' is performed on an individual user basis rather than on a syndication affiliate basis. Personalization is enabled through user preferences, which may be either explicitly entered by the users, or be inferred based on collected information about usage patterns (e.g. types of viewed content, preferred selections, etc.). In either case, it is important to remember that user preferences are dynamic, that they are subject to change over time, and that your application needs to react promptly to those changes, whether made explicitly or implicitly.

Perhaps the best-known example of implicit site personalization is Amazon.com. They are the world leaders in the practice of implicit preference gathering. When

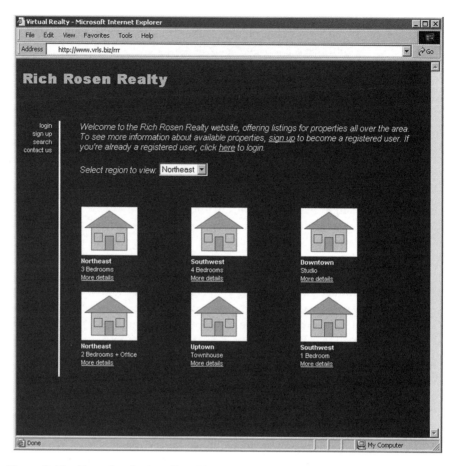

Figure 8.14   Example of cobranding: Virtual Realty site presented with Rich Rosen Realty
look and feel

a site visitor purchases a book, or simply views the page describing that book,
this event is recorded in the database, providing input to customization processes
invoked during subsequent visits to the site by both this visitor and others. The next
time this visitor accesses the Web site, it may display this book again, mentioning
other books that those interested in *this* book purchased, and offering pointers to
user generated suggestion lists that include this book.

Example

Registered users might be interested in real estate properties located in specific geographic
regions, and/or specific types of properties (e.g. rental vs. purchase, houses vs. apartments).
Based on this information about user interests, your application can provide users with
personalized pages. For example, it could display 'hot' properties of the type users are

looking for in their own regions. They would still have access to properties of other types in other areas, using the same mechanisms that are available to unregistered users and/or registered users who have not provided their preferences, explicitly or implicitly.

8.2.6 Transmitting the formatted response

Finally, it is time to send the response back to the originating requestor. Once upon a time, this simply meant wrapping the collected content into an appropriate HTML envelope, adding custom page layout decoration around the content, and transmitting an HTTP response with appropriate headers. By the time step 5 (***Customizing Content for Presentation***) was completed, an application would have all the pieces it needed, fully formatted, ready for inclusion in an HTML-based HTTP response.

Advanced Web applications may require more sophistication. In the spirit of *separating content from presentation*, the content prepared in step 5 might not be HTML. It could be an XML document, a JavaBean, an Active Data Object, a database `RowSet`, or some other generalized container. To ensure their manageability and extensibility for the long term, Web applications need to separate data access decisions from response formatting decisions at execution time.

Moreover, there is no guarantee that the target is expecting an HTTP response with an HTML body. Requests made through Web Services (using SOAP over HTTP) may expect payloads as XML. Other XML vocabularies such as SVG, SMIL, and VoiceXML allow graphical and multimedia content to be included in a response. In addition, requests transmitted by wireless devices may require responses over WAP formatted as CHTML or WML.

With these concerns in mind, the seemingly simple task of building and transmitting a response becomes a bit more complex. Thus, a final transformation is likely to take place just before the response is actually transmitted.

Best practices

1. Do not format any collected content prior to the presentation step. All collected content should be accessible to the response generation process through generic containers (XML, JavaBeans, Active Data Objects, `RowSets`, standard collection objects such as lists or maps), so that it can make choices at execution time about formatting specifics.

2. Employ a uniform format for the results of data access queries/requests. This provides a consistent interface that can be used by page designers when selecting data elements to be included in the presentation.

8.2.7 Logging and recording application activity

Web applications may be responsible for recording the actions taken over the course of request processing. It is this recording that enables applications to track user behaviors, examine trends, evaluate site stickiness, and measure application performance. Do not underestimate the usefulness of logging facilities: as a debugging tool during development, as a monitoring tool while the application is running, and as a tracking tool to facilitate Customer Relationship Management (CRM) based on log analysis.

Accurate logging of user interactions with your application makes possible the kinds of personalization we described in the previous section. If you record not only which products customers have purchased, but also which products they have simply looked at, you can customize the pages they view to display links to similar products (often called *upsells*), or offer them discounts on products they looked at the next time they visit your site.

Most application server environments provide logging services, but if they don't, it behooves you to either build your own or use an available package that performs logging functions. Your system's logging service should enable selective recording and displaying of log messages, so that the recording of lower level messages (e.g. 'debug', or even 'informational') can be skipped. It is a good idea to establish discrete levels of logging information, and to record application events in the log at the appropriate level. For example, messages useful while developing and testing portions of the application should be considered 'debug' messages. On the other hand, normal application initialization messages should be considered 'informational', while serious error messages should be highlighted as 'critical'.

When it comes to operations support, the logging service provides critical information to ensure that the application is operating properly. It should be easy for your operations staff to view the log, either as a console log dumped to a terminal window, as a file that can be browsed, and/or as a dynamically accessible administrative web page (secured so that only operations personnel can view it). Those who view the log, either after the fact or in real time, should be able to notice—preferably at a glance—when something goes wrong (e.g. through highlighting of serious error conditions).

The question comes to mind: what should be logged? The answer to that will depend on your application. Usually, the Web server log would provide an enormous amount of information about requests made to the server, but you might want to keep separate logs of your own to record the comings and goings of your site visitors. Such information could be recorded in its own log and then uploaded to a database periodically so that trends associated with your site, with individual users, and with groups of users, can become apparent by querying the database.

Your application architecture can and should go way beyond the real-time interactions between users and your application. After recording information, batch processes could query the database and the logs, looking for things to do (e.g. sending incentive e-mails to frequent customers, or to those customers that *haven't* visited for an extended period). Reports on which of your products are most (or least) popular could be sent to product managers. Customers who have not visited your site in 60 days may deserve an e-mail reminding them of your company's services, possibly offering a reward for returning to the site. An examination of which areas of your site are most popular could result in a re-engineering of the user experience to emphasize those areas and make them more accessible. With this in mind, it is a good idea to pay attention to keeping track of application activity for posterity.

Best practices

1. Examine the types of activities that take place within your application and determine early on which ones need to be recorded and to what degree. It may seem that only actual financial transactions need to be recorded, but recording user action patterns could prove invaluable over time. With this in mind, it is better to log too much than to log too little.

2. Do not log private information such as credit card numbers 'in the clear' (even in debug mode). Just as it is necessary to encrypt such information when transmitting it over the Web, it is necessary to encrypt it when it is recorded for logging purposes.

3. Establish logging levels and record events at the appropriate level (e.g. 'debug', 'informational', 'critical'). The 'debug' level should be used for messages needed while the application is being developed and tested. Since these messages may be plentiful and since they are usually not needed in a production environment, the logging service should selectively enable and disable the recording of messages associated with lower levels, so that the log is not cluttered.

8.3 DATABASE PROCESSING ISSUES

If your application uses a database management system (DBMS) as one or more of its content sources, there are a number of issues that come to the forefront when designing and developing the application.

Content requests targeting a relational database are called *queries*, and are usually written in SQL (Structured Query Language). Responses to database queries take the form of a *result set*, which contains zero or more *rows* of data that satisfy the query's selection criteria. Certain database queries are intended to produce a result set containing a single row, as the selection criteria associated with the query includes a unique identifier called a *primary key* that accesses one unique row. Where queries produce multiple-row result sets, the *master/detail* pattern described earlier in this chapter is frequently utilized, so that requestors see the set of entries that satisfy their requests (or a subset of that set of entries) on a dynamically generated page.

8.3.1 Configuration

Application designers and developers do not exercise a lot of control in an organization regarding the configuration of databases. Database management systems are generally supported and maintained by database administrators. It is their responsibility to configure database services so that clients (users and other applications) can access the database properly. This situation sometimes leads frustrated developers to seek alternatives, such as the installation of their own open source DBMSs (e.g. MySQL), or even the abandonment of relational databases altogether in favor of custom persistence mechanisms, object databases and in-memory databases. However, most production quality applications need to connect with production databases, and thus it is worthwhile to understand the mechanisms by which these connections are configured.

Security is naturally a primary issue in database configuration. Database administrators and security specialists configure databases to maximize security while allowing proper access to authorized users and client applications. To ensure database security for a Web-based application, a number of steps should be taken.

First, the database management system should be hosted on a separate server not accessible via the Web. Naturally, it is a good idea to keep this database server behind your organization's firewall, but this is not enough. Many installations leave the default user IDs and passwords (set up when the database software is installed) in place. It is a good idea to disable these and replace them with passwords associated with specific roles. Most database management systems have the ability to define roles, associate them with specific privileges, and then associate discrete sets of users with those roles.

Given the tedium associated with connecting to and interacting with a database, it is a good idea to create a reusable mechanism for developers that have to perform these tasks. Database application programming is frequently made more difficult by the complexities of communicating with the database. Providing a service that offers a single point of contact for database communication means that application programmers need not concern themselves with the mundane details of connecting to the database. This single point of contact is often referred to as a *Data Access Object* (DAO). The creation of a DAO is simplified when the data source abstraction is utilized to define named database services, rather than requiring manual specification of a particular address for the database server that is subject to change when the installation configuration is modified.

The use of data sources also helps in implementing *connection pooling*, where a set of pre-established database connections is available for reuse by applications that use the database. Since the cost of opening a connection can be quite high, maintaining a connection pool can dramatically improve performance. The pool can be designed to grow and shrink in size as needed, depending on system activity levels.

8.3.2 Transactions

The application may be required to group its changes to back end data sources into *transactions*, where either all the changes must be 'committed' (saved permanently) at once or else they must all be 'rolled back' (discarded).

Transactional processing is a topic worthy of an entire book all by itself. While in-depth discussion of transactional processing might seem to be outside the scope of a book devoted to the topic of Web application architecture, understanding of transactional processing is critical to the development of sophisticated Web applications. Thus, it behooves us to spend some time here covering this topic.

The properties of transactions are often signified by the acronym **ACID**:

- *Atomic*—the 'all-or-nothing' quality of a transaction: either all the processing steps succeed, or none of them should.

- *Consistent*—the transaction should always leave the underlying data in a consistent state, regardless of the success or failure of individual processing steps.

- *Isolated*—the transaction is isolated from the effects of other transactions that are also being processed by the system.

- *Durable*—once committed, the results of transactions should persist, i.e. they should be recorded permanently, surviving any system failures.

The importance of transactional controls cannot be understated. The obvious example is the transfer of funds between accounts associated with an online banking service. Taking $500 out of one account and putting it into another involves checking that the funds are present, subtracting the $500 from the balance of the source account, and adding $500 to the balance of the target account. The first step (checking the current account balance) is a read-only action, but the remaining steps involve modification of the data associated with the accounts. Success of one of these two modifications without the success of the other is unacceptable: the customer either has funds added to her account erroneously, or she gets shortchanged. Thus the two modifications must be combined into a single transaction, where the only acceptable result is successful completion of both modification processes. Any other result is considered an error and treated accordingly. If one modification completes successfully and the other doesn't, the successful modification must be undone, or 'rolled back.'

Do not be deceived into thinking that read-only actions do not need to participate in transactions. Take, for example, this same situation described above, but this time with both husband and wife accessing their joint account online at the same time. While the wife's transaction to transfer $500 from the checking account into the savings account is processing, the husband could be using the online banking service to send a $2000 mortgage payment, reducing the balance of the account below $500. If the husband submits his request after the step in his wife's transaction where the account balance is being checked, but before the step where the money is actually transferred, the accounts would end up in an inconsistent state after completing both transactions. By the time the wife's transaction begins, there would no longer be sufficient funds in the checking account, but because the balance check has already been performed, the attempt to process the transaction will commence anyway. Including the read-only step within these transactions ensures that the processing of other transactions would not put the data in an inconsistent state. This is achieved by isolating the effects of one transaction from the effects of another (at the cost of resource locks being held for a longer period of time).

How Strict Are Your Transactionality Requirements?

Of course, not all applications have the same rigid requirements associated with online banking. For instance, 'dirty reads' could be considered acceptable. A dirty read occurs when a request to read data is made while a transaction that may be modifying data is processing, e.g. the husband accessing the account balance during the wife's transfer transaction. For a banking application this would clearly be a problem, but in other applications it might not be.

The transactionality requirements associated with an application must be understood and established before it can be developed and deployed. Remember that more stringent transactionality requirements would result in more intensive resource locking and performance penalties.

Database management systems use the notions of *commit* and *rollback* to support transactions. When a database modification occurs, the result is not truly 'committed' to the database until an explicit request to 'commit' the data is issued. Thus, in the money transfer example, the request to subtract $500 from the checking account balance is processed first, then the request to add $500 to the savings account balance. After both requests have been successfully processed, the results are committed. However, if for some reason the first request succeeds but the second one fails, a request is made to roll back the results to their original unmodified state.

This scenario becomes more complicated if transactions have to operate across multiple database systems. Since commit and rollback operations only work within the scope of a single database system, they are not enough to support distributed transactions. A higher-level transactional controller that provides coordinated transactions across multiple database systems is needed. This controller may take the form of a teleprocessing monitor like CICS or Tuxedo, or be provided by an application layer such as an EJB container. One of the functions that this controller must provide is the so-called *two-phase commit*.

To illustrate the two-phase commit, let's assume that the account transfer transaction we described earlier utilizes two distinct database systems, one for the checking account and one for the savings account. We cannot employ a single commit statement to cover both modifications, since each database system must be told to commit individually. Two-phase commit comes into play to coordinate the commit status of each database system participating in the transaction. If both modification operations succeed, only then should they remain committed. If the first commit request succeeds while the second one fails, the transactional coordinator must take explicit action to roll back the first modification even if its database has committed the change.

> **AUTOCOMMIT**
>
> Note that many database management systems offer a processing option called *AUTO-COMMIT*, where each modification to the database is committed automatically, without the need for an explicit commit request. Where each modification is atomic, this setting might be acceptable, but if more complex transactions are involved, we strongly recommend that you turn the AUTOCOMMIT setting off to ensure that your application has control over the processing of transactions.

Another option available to support transactional processing is the *stored procedure*, which is a native database program that performs a set of requests as an atomic operation. Stored procedures are implemented so that they can be invoked by larger applications. In addition to providing a mechanism for enforcing atomicity and consistency of transactions, stored procedures often provide an additional benefit: speed. Because they are implemented in a language specific to the underlying database management system, they execute within the scope of that system as a single operation. They are frequently compiled or at the very least pre-processed, which drastically decreases processing time. The use of stored procedures also means that the application developer need not be as concerned with underlying database schema details, because these are taken care of by the stored procedure. Programmers can simply invoke stored procedures within their code, rather than requiring them to compose SQL queries to interact with the database.

8.3.3 Best practices

1. When using a relational database management system as your content repository, host the database on a separate server not accessible via the Web.

2. Placing the database server behind the firewall is a good start for securing your database, but pay attention to database security issues. Do not use default userid's and passwords for database access. Even in a protected database environment, this is asking for trouble. Arrange to use separate datasource configurations (using

separate userid's) for read-only vs. update access. For example, pages devoted to providing end user access for reading data from a product catalog should use a different datasource from internal pages used for maintaining the database.

3. Carefully analyze the transactional requirements of your application, and establish transactional boundaries when deploying the application. Be sure to turn off any 'autocommit' settings that may be associated with your application, during both development and deployment. If transactional requirements cross over database system boundaries, utilize transactional controllers such as teleprocessing monitors or EJB containers rather than trying to implement this functionality within your application. Stored procedures, if available, can also help to ensure proper transactional processing.

4. Create a reusable direct mechanism for applications to connect to and interact with the database. This functionality, often referred to as a *DAO* or *Data Access Object*, is made simpler through the use of datasources.

5. Where possible, the database communication service should make use of *connection pooling*, creating a set of pre-established reusable database connections.

8.4 SUMMARY

In this chapter we have covered a lot of ground. After explaining the nature of Web applications from both a structural and historical perspective, we examined the functionality associated with a typical Web application, and differentiated between tasks that are performed by the server and tasks that must be performed by the application and the application framework. These include application security, content source configuration, data access, customization and transmission of responses, and the recording of application activity. We then went over issues specifically related to the development of applications that use database management systems as content sources.

In the next chapter, we will show how popular approaches to Web application development attempt to organize application functionality into a manageable and extensible component-based architecture.

8.5 QUESTIONS AND EXERCISES

1. While older client/server applications used a variety of proprietary protocols and clients, Web applications use a common client program (the browser) and a common protocol (HTTP). This resolved the problems associated with maintaining and supporting multiple clients and protocols on the desktop, but in what sense do today's Web applications still have similar problems? In what sense are today's complex web clients (applets, Flash

movies, etc.) different from those older client/server applications? Given the nature of HTTP requests and responses and how they processed by Web browsers, what advantage is there in using such complex clients over browser-based applications?

2. What are the differences between using HTTP authentication and forms-based authentication? Where does responsibility lie for each, in the server or in the application? Why is it important to have the application obtain authentication credentials over a secure HTTP connection?

3. Explain the problem that arises when Web sites provide a login page as a 'gateway' but do not explicitly protect the content found behind that gateway.

4. What are the four things, aside from delivering content, that a content management system must be able to do? In what sense is a message forum or weblog application different from a traditional publishing application that makes use of a content management system?

5. Why is it a bad idea to keep dynamically accessed content under the Web server document root directory?

6. What is the *master/detail* pattern and how is it used in Web applications? Explain how the *many-one-none* pattern and the *Value List Handler* pattern work in conjunction with master/detail processing?

7. We described how the HTTP `Referer` header can identify which 'partner' is associated with a request, so that the response can be presented with a look and feel associated with that partner. What are the limitations on this approach to co-branding? What other methods can be used to support co-branding functionality?

8. What are the advantages of consolidating data access functionality into a single *Data Access Object*?

9. Give an example of an application that would tolerate 'dirty reads' during transaction processing?

10. Why is two-phase commit necessary for distributed database transactions?

BIBLIOGRAPHY

Gamma, E., Helm, R., Johnson, R. and Vlissides, J. (1995) *Design Patterns*. New York, NY: Addison-Wesley.

Alur, D., Crupi, J. and Malks, D. (2003) *Core J2EE Patterns*. Upper Saddle River, NJ: Prentice-Hall.

Date, C. J. (2003) *An Introduction to Database Systems*. New York, NY: Addison-Wesley.

Hunter, J. (2000) The Problems with JSP. Servlets.com, January 2000. <http://www.servlets.com/soapbox/problems-jsp.html>

Davis, M. (2001) Struts, an open-source MVC implementation. IBM DeveloperWorks, February 2001. <http://www-106.ibm.com/developerworks/library/j-struts/>

9 Approaches to Web Application Development

It is not practical to design and develop every new Web application from the ground up. We would have to keep building the same functional components that accept and interpret user requests, authenticate and authorize the requestors, access and transform requested data, and construct and transmit final responses. Many of these components would be identical across different applications. Web servers provide application developers with well-defined endpoints—the acceptance of requests and transmission of responses. Some servers also lay the simple groundwork for building and deploying Web applications (as we discussed in Chapter 4). In practice, such groundwork is not enough: what is needed is the additional infrastructure to facilitate Web application development and deployment.

Web application *approaches* take advantage of the Web server foundation, providing functional components that are reusable across most Web applications. Not every approach to Web application development is an example of a Web application *framework*. A true Web application framework provides a consolidated approach to building dynamic Web applications. It should give developers and page designers a consistent architecture for building and accessing request context elements that can be embedded within the presented page. It should include support for state and session management and authentication, as well as data access and transformation.

Web application frameworks aim to achieve that fleeting goal of good Web application architecture—separation of content from presentation—by making developers responsible for program logic and access to content, while giving creative page designers control over presentation formatting. Ideally, these distinct functions should reside in separate source objects, so that designers and developers do not 'collide' with each other while doing their respective jobs.

In this chapter, we shall examine various approaches to Web application development. We look at the evolution of such approaches from the early years of the Web through to the present day.

The spectrum of Web application approaches can be divided into four broad categories:

1. scripting or programmatic approaches,

2. template approaches,

3. hybrid approaches, and

4. frameworks.

Although there is some overlap (as well as some debate about where certain approaches belong in this categorization scheme), most established approaches fit into one of these categories. The differences lie in the objects designated to contain the 'source' for the generated pages, and in the degree of support provided by the infrastructure for the development of advanced, scalable applications.

9.1 PROGRAMMATIC APPROACHES

In *scripting* or *programmatic approaches*, the source associated with the page object consists predominantly of code written in Perl, Python, Tcl or a high-level programming language like Java. The code may be interspersed with some degree of formatting constructs. Naturally, such approaches appeal to programmers. The bulk of the page object consists of application logic, while the page formatting (e.g. HTML) is generally produced using output statements in the associated programming language. Among the approaches that fit into this category are *CGI* scripts and *Servlets*, which were covered in Chapter 4.

Limitations

The biggest problem with programmatic approaches to Web application development is the code-centric nature of the development paradigm. HTML (along with other formatting constructs) is embedded within program logic. It is produced using output statements (e.g. 'print') associated with the source programming language. This limits the creative input that Web designers can have into the layout of the final page. Web designers can 'mock up' pages, but these pages must then be translated into statements that must be integrated into the script or program. Programmer intervention is required to modify virtually any aspect of the generated page, whether it is related to program logic or presentation layout.

9.1.1 CGI

Since the CGI approach is 'code-driven,' it fits into the category of programmatic approaches. It provides a structure for writing programs that generate dynamic Web pages. CGI gives programmers access to request context information, including headers and URL parameters. Support for higher level abstractions, including state and session management, evolved into specialized packages for C, Perl, and other languages used in CGI development. These packages often provide added functionality in other areas including database access.

One of the major deficiencies of the CGI mechanism is the overhead associated with creating a new process for every request. Various approaches (e.g. FastCGI, mod_perl) arose to eliminate this problem, but none developed a following large enough to rise out of obscurity.

9.1.2 Java Servlet API

The *Java Servlet API* implements the server-side Java approach for dynamic page generation. Like CGI, it provides access to request and response information. Unlike CGI, a servlet is loaded and initialized at server startup time (or with the initial request made for the servlet). There is no overhead of process creation and initialization for each request.

Servlet programmers get access to the *servlet context* (e.g. servlet initialization parameters, server information) as well as scoped environment variables (request, response, and page). The Servlet API has evolved to provide high-level support for state and session management.

An example of a simple servlet that makes use of a diverse selection of servlet functionality is displayed in Figure 9.1. When loaded, the servlet enumerates the set of initialization parameter names and stores them in a member variable as a Map. For each request, it gets the name of the 'user agent' from request headers, and determines the value of the session attribute called 'title.' It then sets the MIME type of the response to 'text/html' and outputs the collected information in HTML format via the 'writer' associated with the response.

The Servlet API took dynamic page generation to the next level. It transcended many of the inadequacies associated with standard CGI processing, but did not get us past our dependence on code-centric approaches to dynamic page generation. However, it did set the stage for important advancements toward that goal.

9.2 TEMPLATE APPROACHES

The *template approach* utilizes a source object (the template) that consists predominantly of formatting structures, with limited embedded constructs that add programmatic power. The focus of the source object is on formatting, not programming logic. Naturally, this approach appeals to Web page authors and graphic designers much more than the scripting/programmatic approach.

```
import javax.util.* ;
import javax.io.* ;
import javax.servlet.* ;
import javax.servlet.http.* ;

public class MyServlet extends HttpServlet {

  private Map _initParams = new HashMap() ;

  public void init() throws ServletException {

      Enumeration enum = getServletConfig().getInitParameterNames() ;
      while (enum.hasMoreElements()) {
            String initParamName = (String) enum.nextElement() ;
            _initParams.put(initParamName,
                getServletConfig().getInitParameter(initParamName)) ;
      }
  }

    public void doGet(HttpServletRequest req, HttpServletResponse resp)
      throws ServletException, IOException {

      PrintWriter out = resp.getWriter() ;
      String browser = req.getHeader("User-Agent") ;

      HttpSession session = req.getSession() ;
      String title = (String) session.getAttribute("title") ;
      resp.setContentType("text/html") ;
      out.println("<HTML><HEAD><TITLE>") ;
      out.println(title) ;
      out.println("</TITLE></HEAD><BODY>") ;
      out.println("<H1>" + title + "</H1>") ;
      out.println("Your browser: " + browser) ;
      out.println("<H3>Initialization Parameters:</H3>") ;
      Iterator i = _initParams.keySet().iterator() ;
      while (i.hasNext()) {
            String initParamName = (String) i.next() ;
            out.println(initParamName + " = " +
                  _initParams.get(initParamName)) ;
      }
      out.println("</BODY></HTML>") ;
      out.close() ;
  }
}
```

Figure 9.1   Servlet example

As mentioned in the previous section, scripting/programmatic approaches are code-centric, and the source objects associated with page generation are scripts or program modules. Template approaches, on the other hand, revolve around the page structure and the formatting tags, not around the code. The source objects are page templates, consisting mostly of HTML coupled with embedded constructs that support conditional processing, iterative result presentation, and parameter substitution.

SSI (Server-Side Includes) was an early mechanism for adding simple template functionality to Web pages. Among other well-known template approaches are Allaire's *Cold Fusion* and *WebMacro/Velocity*.

Relative Power

Some would argue that the presence of processing constructs makes the template approach no different than the scripting/programmatic approach. They say that it is, by virtue of these constructs, a programming language of sorts, albeit less powerful than other programming languages commonly used to produce CGI scripts and other applications. Comparing the two approaches this way, it would seem that scripting/programmatic approaches 'should' win out over template approaches, because ('clearly') they provide more programmatic power! You can do much more with a programmatic approach than with a template approach, owing to the power of its native programming language.

But the question arises: who is it that could 'do much more' with a programmatic approach? It has to be a programmer/developer. The page designer, operating from a very different perspective, would probably be able to do much *less* with a programmatic approach. Page designers would have to depend on programmers to modify source objects in order to reflect their design changes.

The whole idea behind template approaches is to put presentation objects in the hands of presentation specialists, namely page designers, while putting control of program logic in the hands of programmers. With this in mind, a comparison of scripting/programmatic approaches with template approaches based on the power associated with their respective languages misses the point. It is a *good* thing to have only a minimal set of logic constructs within templates, because it is designers, not programmers, who 'own' these templates. The goal of the template approach is to accomplish that fleeting goal associated with good Web application architecture: the separation of content from presentation. (As we will see, few if any of the existing template approaches genuinely achieve that goal. In fact, most template approaches still confuse the issue of who 'owns' the template—the designer or the developer.)

9.2.1 Server-Side Includes (SSI)

The *Server-Side Includes (SSI)* mechanism was a popular adjunct to CGI scripts in many early Web applications. The simple syntax for SSI directives (which look like HTML comments) allowed page designers to embed dynamically produced output into HTML pages (as shown in Figure 9.2), including:

```
<!--#include virtual="/common/include.html" -->
<!--#config timefmt="%B %e, %Y - %I:%M:%S" -->
It is currently <!--#echo var="DATE_LOCAL" -->
This page was last modified on <!--#echo var="LAST_MODIFIED"-->
```

Figure 9.2 SSI example

- results of executing various system commands,

- results of executing a CGI script,

- CGI environment variables associated with the request,

- other environment variables associated with the file and/or the server, and

- date and time.

The Apache version of SSI also provided simple conditional constructs for including portions of HTML pages selectively based on the value of environment variables.

The combination of CGI scripts with server-side includes offered additional power to the Web page designer, but ultimately not enough to support more robust dynamically generated pages, especially for database-driven applications. The problem with accessing the database from a CGI script and invoking that script from an SSI template is that the script is responsible for all formatting of query results and provides designers with no control over the look and feel of these results.

9.2.2 Cold Fusion

Cold Fusion represents one of the first commercial template approaches to dynamic server-side page generation, providing a set of tags that support the inclusion of external resources, conditional processing, iterative result presentation, and data access. Cold Fusion owes much of its success to two features:

1. Queries are very simple to create and use, and

2. Every form of data access acts just like a query.

Database queries are constructed using the <CFQUERY> element, referencing an ODBC datasource with the SQL code embedded between the opening <CFQUERY> and the closing </CFQUERY> tags. The results can be iteratively traversed using the <CFOUTPUT> element, with each column available for variable substitution (Figure 9.3).

In addition to <CFQUERY> for talking to databases, Cold Fusion provides elements for accessing other sources of data, including POP3 e-mail servers, FTP servers, and the local file system. Each of these elements utilizes the same method for accessing and presenting iterative results through variable substitution (Figure 9.4).

```
<CFQUERY DATASOURCE="oracle-prod" NAME="dbquery1">
    SELECT NAME, ADDRESS, PHONE
      FROM CUSTOMERS
      WHERE LAST_PURCHASE_DATE < '2001-01-01';
</CFQUERY>
    ...
<TABLE>
<TR>
    <TD ALIGN="center"><B>Name</B></TD>
    <TD ALIGN="center"><B>Address</B></TD>
    <TD ALIGN="center"><B>Phone</B></TD>
<TR>
<CFOUTPUT QUERY="dbquery1">
    <TD>#NAME#</TD>
    <TD>#ADDRESS#</TD>
    <TD>#PHONE#</TD>
</CFOUTPUT>
</TR>
</TABLE>
```

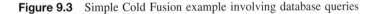

Figure 9.3   Simple Cold Fusion example involving database queries

Like the Servlet API, Cold Fusion provides access to scoped environment variables (e.g. query string parameters, URL components, and session data). It also allows for the creation of custom tags (much like the JSP custom tags that we will discuss later).

As the Cold Fusion platform evolved, it succumbed to the pressure to provide scripting capabilities within templates. Although this capability need not be used (and is not used by most deployed Cold Fusion applications), it makes it too easy to create that clumsy mixture of code and formatting within the same source object.

```
<CFPOP USERNAME="userid" PASSWORD="*****"
        SERVER="pop3.email.com" NAME="email">
 ...
<TABLE>
<TR>
<CFOUTPUT QUERY="email">
    <TD>#MSGNUMBER#</TD>
    <TD>#FROM#</TD>
    <TD>#SUBJECT#</TD>
</CFOUTPUT>
</TR>
</TABLE>
```

Figure 9.4   Another Cold Fusion example using <CFPOP>

Although Cold Fusion offers many of the features associated with a solid template approach to Web application development, it has serious deficiencies. Most importantly, it is a proprietary software product, and the Cold Fusion Markup Language (CFML) is the intellectual property of Macromedia. This is a matter of serious concern, since Cold Fusion tags represent a proprietary approach to Web application development. The irony is that many of the tag specifications in Sun's *Java Standard Tag Library*, which we will discuss later in this chapter, are semantically similar to Cold Fusion tags. Although this does not eliminate the problem, it is a sign that Cold Fusion may have been on the right track regarding tag functionality.

In addition, there are performance, scalability, and stability issues with Cold Fusion, especially on non-Windows platforms. The Cold Fusion engine was originally designed for Windows, and efforts to port the engine to UNIX and other environments have met with mixed success. Still, it offers a good deal of functionality, and has a significant following among Web developers, who use it to get an application up and running quickly. It may be acceptable if you are developing a simple application with a small number of users that does not require the power and performance of a robust framework.

9.2.3 WebMacro/Velocity

WebMacro is a true template-based approach to dynamic page generation. Using a small set of logic constructs to support iteration, conditional processing, and the inclusion of external resources, it provides the functionality needed by page designers to build dynamic Web pages without scattering code fragments and related clutter throughout the page. Although by itself it is not fully compliant with the *Model-View-Controller* (*MVC*) design pattern (described in detail in Section 9.4.1), it does fit into the MVC paradigm. *Velocity* is the Apache/Jakarta project's open source implementation of WebMacro.

```
#set ($message = "Blah blah blah!")

#if ($x == $y)
Here is your message: $message
#end


    ...


#include filename.wm


    ...


<TABLE>
#foreach ($row in $dbquery.results)
<TR>
<TD>$name</TD>
<TD>$address</TD>
<TD>$phone</TD>
</TR>
#end
</TABLE>
```

Figure 9.5 Simple example of Velocity template

Figure 9.5 shows a fragment from a sample *Velocity Template Language* (VTL) template. The VTL directives illustrated include a conditional construct (a message that is only displayed if $x is equal to $y), an inclusion of an external file (`file-name.wm`), and the iterative construct that maps the result set produced by the database query stored in a previously defined variable (`$dbquery`) to the HTML table.

As in other template (and hybrid) approaches, Velocity templates depend on the request context that is established by a controlling servlet. This makes it possible to provide template designers with access to content that has been transformed into an appropriate data model by an MVC-compliant controller.

There are a couple of outstanding issues with the WebMacro/Velocity template language. The first is its emphasis on the UNIX-style parameter substitution, which shows a bias towards programmers rather than page designers. The `$variable` notation is obvious and intuitive to UNIX users and Perl programmers, but probably not so obvious and intuitive to page designers. The same variable boundary issues that arise in UNIX shells come into play in WebMacro/Velocity templates as well. They are resolved by providing a 'formal' notation for variables (`${variable}`) to alleviate confusion (e.g. by replacing `$variableness` with `${variable}ness`).

The second issue is XML compliance. Template directives, which begin with '#', are obviously not XML-compliant. WebMacro/Velocity functionality is not impaired by the lack of XML compliance (which is also absent in older approaches, e.g. Cold Fusion and ASP), but it would be very nice indeed to see XML compliance in a future version of Velocity.

9.3 HYBRID APPROACHES

Hybrid approaches combine scripting elements with template structures. They have more programmatic power than pure templates because they allow embedded blocks containing 'scripts'. This would seem to offer the benefit of a page-oriented structure combined with additional programmatic power. Examples of this approach include *PHP*, Microsoft's *Active Server Pages* (ASP) and Sun's *Java Server Pages* (JSP).

Is this really the 'best of both worlds,' or a Web developer's worst nightmare?

The intermixing of script blocks with presentation formatting represents a serious violation of the principle of separating content from presentation. The issue of who 'owns' the source object becomes very muddled. The frequent contention that page designers can easily learn to work around the embedded code constructs is not borne out by experience. Once again, designers and developers must work on the same source objects, leading to conflicts and collisions when code changes break the HTML formatting, or when changes made by designers inadvertently introduce bugs into the embedded code.

Most of these systems have been designed to translate the hybrid source objects into code. The systems have evolved significantly since their inception, but their origins still expose serious issues with these approaches.

9.3.1 PHP

PHP is a recursive acronym that stands for *PHP Hypertext Preprocessor*. It allows developers to embed code within HTML templates, using a language similar to Perl and UNIX shells. The source object is structured as an HTML page, but dynamic content generation is programmatic. For example, the PHP fragment:

```
<B><?php if ($xyz >= 3) { print $myHeading; }
   else {
?>DEFAULT HEADING<?php
   }
?></B>
```

gets translated into:

```
print "<B>";
if ($xyz >= 3) { print $myHeading; }
else { print "DEFAULT HEADING"; }
print "</B>"
```

In other words, text embedded within `<?php ... ?>` blocks is processed using the native PHP language, while text *outside* of these blocks is treated as arguments passed to 'print' statements.

While other template-based approaches provide several distinct elements designed to perform specific tasks, in PHP there is one—`<?php ... ?>`—which serves as a 'container' for PHP code. Although PHP scripts are often referred to as templates, being dependent on code to perform most of the work associated with dynamic page generation makes PHP closer to a scripting approach than a template approach, putting it beyond the reach of the average page designer as a tool for building dynamic Web pages.

9.3.2 Active Server Pages (ASP)

By the late 1990s, many companies produced their own proprietary server-side processing solutions. Netscape offered LiveWire (which evolved into Server Side Javascript). Other companies, including Allaire (ColdFusion), NetDynamics (now rolled into SunOne) and Art Technology Group (Dynamo), also developed products to support their own approaches for building dynamic Web applications.

Microsoft entered the fray with *Active Server Pages* (ASP). ASP combined server-side scripting capabilities with access to the wide variety of OLE and COM objects in the Microsoft arsenal, including ODBC data sources. Bundled with Microsoft's free Internet Information Server, ASP quickly gained popularity among Visual Basic programmers who appreciated the VB-like syntax and structure of ASP scripts. Unfortunately, that syntax and structure are ill suited to modern Web applications. ASP pages contain references to obscurely named COM objects, intermixed with HTML formatting. Unlike object-oriented languages like Java or C++, the language used within ASP pages is flat, linear, and strictly procedural.

In the ASP example in Figure 9.6, there are two 'script blocks' embedded within the page. The first block, which appears before the start of HTML markup, sets up the page context by creating a database connection, opening it with appropriate credentials, creating a result set, associating it with the connection, and populating it with the results of the database query. The second block is inserted in the middle of HTML table markup; it contains procedural code that writes an HTML table row whose cells contain values associated with columns in the result set.

Like PHP, ASP's structure is simple: blocks delimited with the `<%` and `%>` character sequences contain script code to be executed by the server at response generation time, while text found outside such blocks is treated as 'raw' HTML. Thus, as with PHP, the page is simply divided between discrete blocks of code and HTML. (Note the presence of page directives in ASP, e.g. `<%@LANGUAGE = VBScript %>`.)

The fact that ASP is bundled with Microsoft's IIS Web server makes it an attractive option for those installations that employ Microsoft-only solutions. ASP *is* popular enough to have been ported to other platforms besides Microsoft's IIS.

```
<% @LANGUAGE = VBScript %>
<%
  Set conn = Server.CreateObject("ADODB.Connection")
  conn.open("Data Source=mydata;User ID=myname;Password=*****")
  Set results = Server.CreateObject("ADODB.RecordSet")
  Set results.ActiveConnection = conn
  query = "SELECT X, Y, Z FROM TABLE1 WHERE X > 23"
  results.Open query
%>
<HTML>
<HEAD><TITLE>Active Server Page</TITLE></HEAD>
<BODY BGCOLOR="#ffffff">
<TABLE>
 <TR>
  <TD ALIGN="center">X</TD>
  <TD ALIGN="center">Y</TD>
  <TD ALIGN="center">Z</TD>
 </TR>
<%
 While Not results.EOF
   Response.Write "<TR>"
   Response.Write "<TD>" & results("X") & "</TD>"
   Response.Write "<TD>" & results("Y") & "</TD>"
   Response.Write "<TD>" & results("Z") & "</TD>"
   Response.Write "</TR>"
 Wend
%>
</TABLE>
</BODY>
</HTML>
```

Figure 9.6   ASP example

This is probably good for the future of ASP, given the security holes and other problems associated with IIS. As with Cold Fusion, its benefits are mostly in the area of speeding up the deployment of relatively simple Web applications.

Microsoft's *.NET* offering purports to be a 'framework' that alleviates many of the limitations of ASP. In reality, it is ASP on steroids: a set of extensions to the existing ASP infrastructure that offer many of the convenience features found in the Java language, coupled with the option to create pages using a variety of languages (e.g. VB.NET and the new language C#). There is a lot of additional power provided in .NET, but there are still limitations in scalability, flexibility, and reusability of components.

9.3.3 Java Server Pages

Java Server Pages (JSP) was Sun's answer to Microsoft's ASP. As with PHP, JSP support was implemented through a pre-processor that turned page objects

```
<%@ page import="java.io.*" %>
<%!
        private CustomObject myObject ;
%>
<h1>My Heading</h1>

<%
        for(int i = 0; i < myObject.getCount(); i++) {
%>
        <P>Item #<%= i %> is '<%= myObject.getItem(i) %>'.</P>
<%
        }
%>
```

Figure 9.7 Sample JSP page

with embedded code blocks into servlet source code. For example, the sample JSP page in Figure 9.7, would be translated into servlet code similar to that shown in Figure 9.8.

The first line of the JSP fragment in Figure 9.7 is the page directive to import classes in the `java.io` package. The next three lines represent a variable declaration. Java code blocks are delimited with '<%' and '%>' character sequences. HTML outside of these delimiters is translated into 'print' statements as shown. The entire page is translated into a complete Java class that is compiled by the server.

JSP represents yet another approach to convert hybrid page-like structures into code that is then compiled and executed. (In the case of JSP, the code is translated into a Java servlet that is compiled and executed by the Web server's servlet engine.) The vestiges of such origins can be found in the structure of a typical JSP page (e.g. page directives, declarations, and—in pages that fail to satisfy strict design constraints—clumsy intermixing of 'scriptlets' and HTML formatting). However, JSP evolved over time, providing new powerful features that allow it to transcend its roots.

Among these features is the JSP *taglib*. A taglib is a library of custom JSP tags that can abstract functionality that would otherwise have required the inclusion of an embedded scriptlet containing complex Java code. These tags are a step towards XML compliance in the JSP world, since they are specified using XML namespaces and defined in XML configuration files. Two of the most commonly used tags are `<jsp:useBean>` and `<jsp:getProperty>`. The `<jsp:useBean>` tag allows page designers to embed a *JavaBean* (constructed and populated by the application and perhaps stored as a session variable) within a JSP page. They can also access and possibly modify properties within that JavaBean using the `<jsp:getProperty>` and `<jsp:setProperty>` constructs. These constructs are translated by the process that JSPs go through prior to compilation and execution. For example:

```
package jsp._myapp ;
import java.io.* ;
import java.util.* ;
import javax.servlet.* ;
import javax.servlet.http.* ;
import javax.servlet.jsp.* ;

public class _mypage extends HttpJspBase {

 private CustomObject myObject;

 public void _jspService(HttpServletRequest req, HttpServletResponse
 resp)
 {
     ServletConfig config = getServletConfig() ;
     ServletContext application = config.getServletContext() ;
     Object page = this ;
     PageContext pageContext =
       JspFactory.getDefaultFactory().getPageContext(this, req, resp,
         null, true, 8192, true) ;
     JspWriter out = pageContext.getOut() ;
     HttpSession session = request.getSession(true) ;

     out.print("<h1>My Heading</h1>") ;

     for(int i = 0; i < myObject.getCount(); i++) {
         out.print("<P>Item #" + i + " is '" +
             myObject.getItem(i) + "'.</P>") ;
     }
 }
}
```

Figure 9.8   Translation output for the JSP page in Figure 9.7

```
<jsp:usebean id="myBean" class="mypackage.MyBean" scope="session"/>
    ...
<P>The value of the 'thing' property
    is '<jsp:getProperty name="myBean" property="thing"/>'.</P>
```

is translated into:

```
MyBean myBean = (MyBean) session.getAttribute("myBean") ;
out.print("<P>The value of the 'thing' property is '" +
   myBean.getThing().toString() + "'.</P>" ;
```

Note the syntactic complexities associated with variable substitution in the JSP environment. To access a property from a JavaBean, the `<jsp:getProperty>` tag must be included. (The alternative—to use the `<% = object.variable %>` syntax—is no less complex.) In addition, despite the claims that these tags make JSP XML-compliant, variable substitutions may actually force violations of XML formatting requirements. Take, for example, this attempt to use a JavaBean property to specify the SRC parameter for an IMG tag:

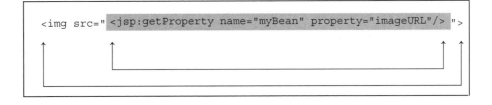

The text with the grey background above is a `<jsp:getProperty>` tag embedded within an HTML `<img>` tag. Not only is this difficult to read, but it violates XML tag formatting constraints (i.e. that tags can not be embedded within one another). JSP provides workarounds to produce the same result in an XML-compliant way, but a more friendly mechanism for parameter substitution is desirable, especially if JSPs are intended for manipulation by page designers.

9.4 SEPARATION OF CONTENT FROM PRESENTATION

Ultimately, none of these approaches fulfils one of the primary requirements of a good Web application framework: the true separation of content from presentation. It is like the Holy Grail, sought out by all the various Web application development approaches. Essentially, it boils down to understanding that (1) there is content or data (often called the *model*), (2) there is the way in which that data is presented (often called the *view*), and (3) these are two separate things.

Why is it so important to keep the two separate?

9.4.1 Application flexibility

When people talk about 'confusing the map and the territory,' they are describing exactly the same problem that occurs when the distinct natures of content and presentation are confused. The map is not the territory; it is a representation of that territory in one of many possible ways. A map could be a street map, showing the highways and roads found in a region. It could be a topographical map, describing the surfaces and elevations of that region. A map might not even be graphical: a set of explicit verbal directions to get from one place to another is also a representation of the territory and thus a kind of map. We have the flexibility of representing the territory in a number of different ways, using a variety of different maps.

In Web applications, the 'territory' is the actual data or content. The 'map' is the view—the organization and layout of the content in the desired format. The content can be represented in many different ways. The choice of presentation mode should be separate from the choices made to access the data, so that any 'territory' can be represented as any kind of 'map' (HTML, WML, VoiceXML, etc.). The 'map' can be personalized, co-branded, embedded, or otherwise customized in a variety of ways.

It does not matter whether your content was read from a file, extracted from a database via a query, requested from an online directory service, or downloaded as a list of messages from an e-mail server. What matters is that the data model should be open-ended so that it is usable by a variety of views, and that some controlling mechanism should be the glue that hooks up retrieved content with the appropriate presentation format—hence, the *Model-View-Controller* or *MVC* design pattern.

In Figure 9.9, the Controller receives a user request, constructs the Model that fulfils this request, and selects a View to present the results. The View communicates

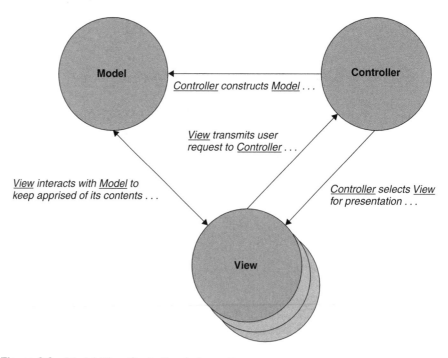

Figure 9.9   Model-View-Controller design pattern

with the Model to determine its content, and presents that content to the user in the desired format. The View also serves as the interface for transmitting further requests from the user to the Controller.

This pattern, designed to facilitate true separation of content from presentation, enables the development of applications that can dynamically tailor and customize presentations based on user preferences, device capabilities, business rules, and other constraints. The data model is not tied to a single presentation format that limits the flexibility of the application.

9.4.2 Division of responsibility for processing modules

There is one other reason why separation of content from presentation is critical: the people responsible for these two aspects of an application have very different skill sets and agendas. Presentation specialists are page designers whose skills center on formatting languages such as HTML, page design tools such as Macromedia Dreamweaver and Microsoft Frontpage, and possibly XML with XSLT. They are not programmers, thus their expertise is not in the area of coding and application logic. Content access is the responsibility of application developers and/or database specialists. It may require elaborate conditional logic and complicated queries to obtain the desired data. Just as you would not ask a page designer to code up your SQL stored procedures, you would not want an application developer to design and implement the layout of your pages.

Some approaches, including Cold Fusion, ASP, and JSP, offer a great deal of power by combining presentation formatting with application/data access logic. But who is responsible for ASP or JSP page development? Who 'owns' the Cold Fusion module that accesses the database and presents the tabular results to the user? The application developer? The database specialist? The page designer? What happens when the page designer's modifications break the JSP developer's embedded Java code? What happens when a database specialist alters the query in a Cold Fusion page, inadvertently altering the HTML layout? (And don't get us started about ASP!)

This is one of the most prominent (though least emphasized) reasons why separation of content from presentation is so important: to ensure the division of responsibility between those who access and process content and those who present it. Few if any people have *all* the skills necessary to perform *all* the tasks associated with dynamic page generation. The issue of page ownership cannot be understated. Designers and developers have different orientations, different skill sets, and different requirements. Collisions between the efforts of designers and developers modifying the same page modules occur all too frequently.

When allowing the intermixing of programmatic code blocks within the page markup, the temptation to turn the entire page into one contiguous block of code (like a CGI script) is enormous. Anyone who has worked heavily with PHP, ASP, or JSP can attest to this. What's more, the intermixing gets ugly, so that the page modules become extremely difficult for both designer and developer to read.

An MVC-based approach makes it possible to combine application flexibility with the appropriate division of responsibility. Developers are responsible for the *controller* component. This is often a lightweight module, which delegates processing to appropriate subordinate tasks, also created by developers. These tasks are responsible for accessing data and building the *model*. Presentation specialists are responsible for building the *views*. The tasks (and/or the *controller*) can determine dynamically which *view* will present the data associated with the *model*.

Notice that we are no longer talking about encapsulating a page in a single module; we are now talking about a complex set of interactions between components. This degree of complexity requires that conventions and standards for these interactions are well defined and easily understood. When a Web application development approach reaches this level of sophistication, it can justifiably be called a *framework*.

9.5 FRAMEWORKS: MVC APPROACHES

9.5.1 JSP 'Model 2'

JSP Model 2 (as distinguished from Sun's Java Server Pages version 2.0) is Sun's attempt to wrap JSP within the *Model-View-Controller* (MVC) paradigm. It's not so much a product offering (or even an API) as it is a set of guidelines, that go along with Sun's packaging of Java-based components and services under the umbrella of *J2EE* (Java 2 Enterprise Environment).

The general structure of a Web application using the JSP Model 2 architecture is:

1. User requests are directed to the *controller* servlet.

2. The controller servlet accesses required data and builds the *model*, possibly delegating the processing to helper classes.

3. The controller servlet (or the appropriate subordinate task) selects and passes control to the appropriate JSP responsible for presenting the *view*.

4. The view page is presented to the requesting user.

5. The user interacts with the controller servlet (via the view) to enter and modify data, traverse through results, etc.

Data access and application logic should be contained entirely within the controller servlet and its helper classes. The controller servlet (or the helper class) should select the appropriate JSP page and transfer control to that page object based on the request parameters, state, and session information. The availability of this information to the controller servlet offers a number of customization options. Based on user identification information, the controller servlet can retrieve user preferences, select JSP pages, and let selected pages personalize the response. For example, the referring URL may help to perform content co-branding. By examining the request, it is possible to learn about the User Agent, infer the type of the device making the request, and choose different formatting options (HTML, WML, VoiceXML, etc.) appropriately.

One of the major advances that came along with JSP Model 2 is Sun's specification of the *Java Standard Tag Library* (JSTL). It specifies the standard set of tags for iteration, conditional processing, database access, and many other formatting functions. The Jakarta project (part of the Apache Software Foundation that gave us the Apache Web Server) includes a subproject that is focusing on JSP taglibs. This subproject has developed a reference implementation for JSTL.

In addition to the guidelines associated with JSP Model 2, Sun also provided a set of *blueprints* for building applications using the MVC paradigm. These blueprints were eventually renamed the *J2EE Core Patterns*. They are too numerous and complex to examine in detail here, but some of the more important patterns are described below:

- *Front Controller*—a module (often a servlet) acting as the centralized entry point into a Web application, managing request processing, performing authentication and authorization services, and ultimately selecting the appropriate view.

- *Service-to-Worker* and *Dispatcher View*—strategies for MVC applications where the front controller module defers processing to a *dispatcher* that is selected based on the request context. The dispatcher can be a part of the front controller, but normally it is a separate task, selected by the controller module based on the request context.

  In the *Dispatcher View* pattern, the dispatcher performs static processing to select the ultimate presentation view. In the *Service-to-Worker* pattern, the dispatcher's processing is more dynamic, translating logical task names into concrete task module references, and allowing tasks to perform complex processing that determines the ultimate presentation view.

- *Intercepting Filter*—allows for pluggable *filters* to be inserted into the "request pipeline" to perform pre- and post-processing of incoming requests and outgoing responses. These filters can perform common services required for all or most application tasks, including authentication and logging.

- *Value List Handler*—a mechanism for caching results from database queries, presenting discrete subsets of those results, and providing iterative traversal through the sequence of subsets.

- *Data Access Object (DAO)*—a centralized mechanism for abstracting and encapsulating access to complex data sources, including relational databases, LDAP directories, and CORBA business services. The DAO acts as an adapter, allowing the external interface to remain constant even when the structure of the underlying data source changes.

The structures and guidelines defined by JSP Model 2 form the foundation for a number of tightly integrated frameworks.

9.5.2 Struts

The *Struts* framework provides a robust infrastructure for Model 2 application development. Developed within the open source Apache Jakarta project, Struts makes use of the *Model-View-Controller, Front Controller*, and *Service-to-Worker* patterns to provide a true framework for Web application development.

A Struts application generally consists of the following components:

- *Controller*—generally, the `org.apache.struts.action.ActionServlet` class that comes with Struts is flexible enough to work for most applications, though it is possible to extend this class if required. This servlet class represents the entry point for user requests.

- *Dispatcher*—again, the `org.apache.struts.action.RequestProcessor` class that comes with Struts is flexible enough to work for most applications, though it is possible to extend this class if required.

- *Request handlers* (custom)—these are application-specific classes, often called *actions*, that extend the `org.apache.struts.action.Action` class and override its `execute()` method to perform the processing required by the application.

- *View helpers* (custom)—for Struts, this functionality are contained in the `org.apache.struts.action.ActionForm` class. Custom subclasses that extend this abstract class are Java Beans that mediate between the Model and the View, providing getter and setter methods for form fields and implementing custom validation if desired.

- *Views* (custom)—the Struts framework is platform-neutral with regard to views: your view components can be JSPs, Velocity templates, or any other mechanism that can access the servlet runtime context.

The main attraction of the Struts framework is that developers can make use of configurable application components (e.g. the controller servlet) that come with the Struts distribution, instead of having to implement these components themselves.

The whole application comes together through the XML configuration file named `struts-config.xml` that is located in the application's WEB-INF directory (Figure 9.10):

```
<struts-config>
  <controller processorClass="myapp.controller.MyRequestProcessor">
  <form-beans>
    <form-bean name="loginForm" type="myapp.view.LoginForm"/>
       :
       :
  </form-beans>
  <action-mappings>
    <action path="/myapp/login"
        type="myapp.controller.LoginAction"
        name="loginForm" scope="request">
          <forward name="success" path="/myapp/success.jsp"/>
          <forward name="failure" path="/myapp/failure.jsp"/>
    </action>
       :
       :
  </action-mappings>
</struts-config>
```

Figure 9.10   Sample struts-config.xml file

1. The <action-mappings> section of the file tells the dispatcher (RequestPro-cessor) which request handler (Action) should process an incoming request, based on the path portion of the request URL.

2. The <action> element in the example maps the/myapp/login URL (the action's 'logical name') to the name of the Java class implementing the request handler to be invoked. It also references the form processing bean by its logical name (as defined in a <form-bean> element elsewhere in the file) and establishes the scope of the action to be that of the current request.

3. A separate <form-bean> element maps the logical name of the form processing bean referenced in the <action> element to the Java class implementing the form processing bean.

4. In addition, <forward> elements (nested within <action> elements) can further define processing components by mapping names (e.g, success and failure) to URL paths associated either with views, or with other processing components. The execute() method of the Action class returns an ActionForward object. The name associated with the returned ActionForward object determines what the application does next after this action has been performed.

Notice that there is no need to implement a new Java class for every processing component. It is possible to define just a few generic components and control their behavior through the <action> configuration. Decisions about the generality of application-specific action classes, form beans, and other components are part of the application design.

Using a small set of extensible, reusable components, along with a well-organized structure hooking those components together, Struts provides a viable platform for serious Web application development. Add to this the Struts JSP taglibs that make it easier to format pages that make use of `ActionForm` beans, and you have a powerful framework. And to top it all off: it's open source.

Still, it is not the 'be all and end all' of Web application frameworks. In fact, there are a number of other competing Jakarta projects working on alternatives to Struts (e.g. Turbine), and Craig McClanahan (creator of Struts and primary developer of Tomcat 4) is now working with Sun on a framework called *Java Server Faces* (JSF). MVC frameworks are still relatively young, and it is too early to say which framework (if any) will win out.

9.6 FRAMEWORKS: XML-BASED APPROACHES

A number of approaches to Web application development make use of *XML* as the foundation for their data models. (See Chapter 7 for additional information about XML.) In these approaches, an XML skeleton selected or constructed by the controller module serves as the data model. It may contain request context elements that are exposed to page designers to help them 'flesh out' the skeleton. *XSLT* is the common approach for transforming this data model into an appropriate presentation format (XHTML, WML, SMIL, VoiceXML, etc.).

Tidying Up HTML Pages

XPath expressions (used to specify the set of elements to process in XSL stylesheets) can be employed independently of XSLT, simply as a mechanism for identifying and extracting portions of an XML document. This can even be used on existing HTML documents retrieved from a Web server, provided the proper precautions are taken. Most HTML documents are not XHTML-compliant, and thus cannot be used as-is to generate an XML DOM tree.

But there is a solution. Tidy—a parser that converts an HTML page into a compliant XHTML document—can be used to produce a valid DOM tree from most HTML documents found on the Web. From this DOM tree, fragments identified via XPath expressions can be extracted from the page. HttpUnit (the open source Web site testing tool) makes use of this method to analyze and extract portions of HTML pages.

As this book is being written, there are a few competing XML-based approaches, including another Apache/Jakarta project, *Cocoon*. None seems robust enough to upset the applecart as a true next generation Web application framework. Nonetheless, this approach has a lot of merit, since XML provides so much flexibility, but there are a number of issues with both existing approaches and with the concept in general. Among the most prominent of these is the complexity of XSL.

While it is claimed that XSL transformations are within the grasp of the average page designer, once again, this is not borne out by experience. XSL is yet another example of a failure to *keep simple things simple* in order to provide the most flexibility. There is, however, no reason why the power of XSLT cannot be enclosed in more user-friendly 'wrappers' that make application-specific functions more accessible to page designers.

9.7 SUMMARY

It would seem that the most viable approach to building a durable and flexible Web application is to make use of the MVC paradigm in conjunction with the power of XML. At the moment, the most viable approach that satisfies these requirements is the Struts framework. In the next chapter, we will design our simple real estate broker application using Struts.

Before we move on, let us compare the existing Web application development approaches, side by side (Table 9.1). Even though the MVC-oriented architecture may be the ideal, no existing framework (including Struts) achieves all the goals of that architecture. In real life, we do not always get to choose the best platform for our application development. With this in mind, it behooves us to know the capabilities—and limitations—of a variety of Web application development approaches.

Table 9.1 Web application development approaches compared

Name	Approach	Availability	Advantages	Drawbacks
CGI	scripting	open standard	1. Portable across all Web servers. 2. Simple programming paradigm. 3. Modules available to augment base language functionality. 4. Open standard.	1. All HTML formatting performed programmatically. 2. Overhead of process creation and initialization for each request. 3. Programmatic approach puts it beyond grasp of average page designer
SSI	template	open standard	1. Simple syntax. 2. Open standard.	1. Not enough power by today's standards. 2. Security holes.
PHP	scripting	open source	1. Structural change from code focus to page focus. 2. Modules available to augment base language functionality. 3. Open source.	1. Intermixing of code and formatting. 2. Who is the target audience? Page designers? Programmers?

(continued overleaf)

Table 9.1   (*continued*)

Name	Approach	Availability	Advantages	Drawbacks
Servlet API	scripting	Sun specification (open source implementations available)	1. Portable across all Web servers that support servlets. 2. Access to full power and extensibility of the Java language (JDBC, JNDI, RMI, EJB) 3. Though proprietary, uses open specification with community participation.	1. Programmatic approach puts it beyond grasp of average page designer. 2. HTML formatting still performed programmatically.
Cold Fusion	template/ hybrid	Macromedia proprietary	1. Portable across all Web servers supporting CGI. 2. Simple programming paradigm. 3. Modules available to augment base language functionality. 4. Quick way to get a Web application up and running.	1. Program logic and data access *still* embedded within the page structure. 2. Simpler than most programmatic approaches, but out of reach for most page designers. 3. Proprietary
ASP	hybrid	Microsoft proprietary (has been ported to non-Microsoft environments)	1. Direct access to COM and ActiveX objects, ODBC databases. 2. "Free" (with Microsoft IIS). 3. Quick way to get a Web application up and running.	1. Abrupt intermixing of code and formatting. 2. Visual Basic code orientation not sophisticated and structured enough for advanced scalable Web applications. 3. Too complex for page designers to create without programmer assistance. 4. Proprietary
JSP	hybrid	Sun specification (open source implementations available)	1. Power of servlets within a page-oriented framework. 2. The `<jsp:useBean>` tag allows direct access to named scoped JavaBeans and their accessible properties. 3. Custom taglibs provide extensibility. 4. Though proprietary (like servlets), uses open specification with community participation.	1. Does nothing to prevent or even discourage intermixing of formatting and code. 2. Variable substitution is unnecessarily ornate, and is difficult to read. 3. The claim that JSP is 'accessible' to page designers does not hold up under scrutiny, given the complexity of JSP tags (no improvement over ASP).

Table 9.1   (*continued*)

Name	Approach	Availability	Advantages	Drawbacks
WebMacro/ Velocity	template	open source	1. True template approach. 2. Limits code infestation within templates to iteration and conditional processing constructs. 3. Works well within MVC architecture.	1. UNIX orientation for parameter substitution—is it friendly/intuitive? 2. Not XML-compliant
Struts	framework	open source	1. Full fledged MVC framework. 2. Infrastructure includes dynamic dispatching, form validation, custom taglibs. 3. Flexibility in selecting presentation views (JSP, Velocity template, etc.).	1. Careful design is required to reap full benefits.
XML-based (e.g. Cocoon)	framework	open source	1. DOM allows encapsulation of all sorts of data. 2. XPath expressions can be used to extract elements (or sets of elements) from the DOM structure. 3. XSLT is a very powerful mechanism for data transformation. 4. Different stylesheets can be established/dynamically pieced together to build pages.	1. Performance of XSLT transformation (even with caching of preprocessed stylesheets) is slow. 2. Complexity of XSLT beyond the grasp of most page designers.

9.8 QUESTIONS AND EXERCISES

1. What is the difference between a programmatic approach and a template approach? Provide examples. Can we apply this classification to the MVC paradigm? Explain.
2. Give examples of a hybrid approach. Explain.
3. What are the advantages of the Model-View-Controller pattern for Web application development?
4. The Model-View-Controller paradigm provides separation of content from presentation, which means that the same model can be presented using many different views. Give as many reasons as you can why applications might require multiple views.
5. What are the main advantages of the Struts framework?

6. Describe the main components of a Struts application and their operation.
7. What would be the effect of XML and XSLT on different approaches?
8. What was the approach that you used last? Were you satisfied with it? Describe your main concerns with regard to this approach. Can you recommend improvements?

BIBLIOGRAPHY

Birznieks, G., Guelich, S. and Gundavaram, S. (2000) *CGI Programming with Perl.* Sebastopol, California: O'Reilly & Associates.

Converse, T. and Park, J. (2002) *PHP Bible*, 2nd *Edition*. Indianapolis, Indiana: John Wiley & Sons.

Hunter, J. and Crawford, W. (2001) *Java Servlet Programming, Second Edition*. Sebastopol, California: O'Reilly & Associates.

Payne, C. (2002) *Teach Yourself ASP.NET in 21 Days* (2nd *Edition*). Indianapolis, Indiana: Sams Publishing.

Forta, B., Weiss, N., Chalnick, L. and Buraglia, A. C. (2002) *Cold Fusion MX Web Application Construction Kit*. San Francisco, California: Macromedia Press.

Goodwill, J. (2002) *Mastering JSP Custom Tags and Tag Libraries*. New York, NY: John Wiley & Sons.

Spielman, S. (2002) *The Struts Framework: A Practical Guide for Programmers*. San Francisco, California.

10 Application Primer: Virtual Realty Listing Services

In the last two chapters, we discussed guidelines for designing Internet applications. We reviewed application development frameworks that simplify the design and implementation processes. It is time to return to the sample application described in Chapter 8 and go through the process of architecting, building, and deploying it.

To reiterate the nature of that application, Virtual Realty Listing Services (VRLS) is a fictitious online real estate company that supports *multiple listing services*, a cooperative venture that is common in the real estate community. Many brick-and-mortar real estate brokers share listings for properties they want to sell or lease with other brokers, in an attempt to attract customers who want to buy or rent these properties. If a customer goes to one broker and buys or rents a property associated with another, the two brokers split the commission. In this way, there is a greater chance for all brokers to sell or rent their properties.

An online version of this service would link the web sites of several real estate brokerages to a database of shared property listings. Customers locate the VRLS site through links from their real estate broker, online search, print advertisements, or word-of-mouth. On this site, they have access to property listings from many different brokers. They can browse the available listings but need to register in order to see details about particular properties. When customers register, they are associated with the broker whose site referred them to the VRLS registration page. These referring brokers are called *affiliates* or *partners*.

In the sample scenario in Figure 10.1, Jane starts her house search by visiting the 'Why-Kurt' realty web site. While browsing through that site, she comes across a link to the VRLS application and follows it. Upon her initial arrival at the VRLS site, her affiliation is identified based on the referring site (found in the HTTP request's `Referer` header), and she is presented with the welcome page co-branded to the look and feel of 'Why-Kurt.' Jane uses the VRLS application to search for shared listings, but never follows any links to property details and remains an

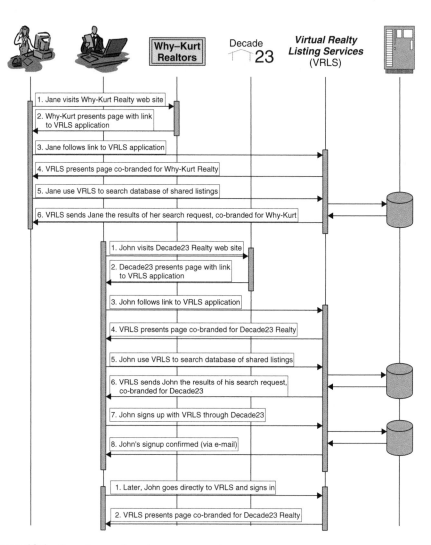

Figure 10.1   Sample search and access scenario

anonymous user. Consequently, her affiliation with 'Why-Kurt' is preserved only for the duration of her session.

Meanwhile, John visits the 'Decade 23' site and follows a link to the VRLS application from there. His affiliation is recognized as well, and he is presented with the welcome page co-branded to the look and feel of 'Decade23'. Just like Jane, John searches for his dream house and finds a listing that on the surface looks interesting. He attempts to retrieve detailed information about the listing, which results in an invitation to either login or register in order to proceed. John registers, receives an email message with his assigned password and logs in. By that time, his affiliation is already stored in his profile. From that point on, whenever he signs in he will be presented with pages co-branded to the look and feel of 'Decade23'.

10.1 APPLICATION REQUIREMENTS

Let us pretend we are building the VRLS application for a real company. Ideally, the client would provide detailed application requirements from the start. Anyone who has worked on real-world projects knows that this rarely happens. More often, application developers get a loosely defined set of objectives, which have yet to be detailed and clarified to serve as the foundation for building the application

Getting clients to construct well-defined requirements is almost an art form, which goes way beyond the scope of this book. Still, developing an application on a foundation of poorly defined requirements is like constructing a building on a foundation of Jell-O™. It may stand, for a while, but it will rarely be stable. Thus, it is important to clarify and refine requirements carefully and methodically.

With that in mind, let us assume that through a process of client interviews, case scenarios, and business process analyses, we have come up with the following simplified set of application requirements:

1. There should be four classes of users for this Web application: *customers, anonymous visitors, partners*, and *administrators*.

2. There should be a mechanism for associating partner brokers with individual requests to the VRLS application. This identification could be either implicit (e.g. identifying the partner using the referring URL), or explicit (e.g. identifying the partner via a query string parameter found in its links to the VRLS site). When unregistered visitors to VRLS arrive from a partner site, they see a view that is customized with partner-specific branding (e.g. a toolbar and company logo) that is applied across all pages of the site.

3. Mechanisms should exist for login by registered customers and for new customer signup.

4. Once they log in, existing customers should see co-branded pages, according to their partner affiliation. Partner identification for existing customers prior to login is on a 'best-effort' basis. If it is not possible to determine the active partner, the application should present a default view.

5. Customers should have the ability to create their personal profiles at registration time, and to modify them in the future. Profile information should include a login name and password, name, address, phone number, e-mail address (used for confirmation), and the identity of the partner. Customers should not be able to modify their system-assigned unique user ids, their login names, or their partner affiliation, but should be able to modify all other profile parameters.

6. After a successful signup, customers should receive a confirmation notice via email, containing a link to the login page and a generated password that can be modified once the customer logs in.

7. Customers should be able to search the available listings for properties that satisfy their search criteria, which could include type of property, number of bedrooms, etc. Search results should include summary information about each listing that satisfies the search criteria.

8. Authenticated customers should be able to retrieve details about a particular property. Anonymous visitors attempting to view property details should be redirected to the login page. There they can identify themselves if they have already registered, or they can follow a link to the signup page.

9. The details page should contain images and additional information about the property, including links for further inquiries.

So far, we have discussed requirements for the customer interface. However, as we mentioned in Chapter 8, the administrative interface is just as important as the interface exposed to the 'outside world.' Let us provide a brief summary of administrative requirements for this application:

1. *Customer administration*: select customer, reset customer password, change customer status (active, suspended, etc.), remove customer.

2. *Partner administration*: add new partner, specify custom markup (logos, background colors, etc.), specify partner selection rules, remove partner.

3. *Listing administration*: add a new listing, modify listing (change summary and detail information, add/remove image), remove listing.

4. *Administrator authentication*: access to the administrative interface should be internal and restricted to IP addresses within the company firewall.

While these requirements are not as detailed as they could be, they can form the starting point for our design and development. In the real world, we would create page mockups to demonstrate workflow scenarios. Next, we would iteratively 'nail down' the precise application requirements. For the purposes of this chapter, we assume that this process did occur and resulted in the workflows and page layouts used in the rest of this chapter.

10.2 APPLICATION DEVELOPMENT ENVIRONMENT

Our goal is to provide a practical demonstration of application design principles. To that end, we want to employ an application development framework that represents state-of-the-art programming practices and paradigms. For this reason, we will implement the VRLS application using *Struts* (the MVC application framework from the Apache Jakarta Project), along with the reference implementation of Sun's *Java Standard Tag Library* (JSTL).

This chapter is not a tutorial on Struts. The focus is on applying the principles of Web application architecture that we have been describing throughout this book. These principles can and should be transferable to other frameworks and approaches that come along in the future.

There are times when application architects are not free to decide on the underlying framework/approach, and it is necessary to make the most of what is available. The hope is that these principles can be applied no matter what platform is used to create an application. Furthermore, Struts is not the be-all and end-all of application frameworks. New frameworks will come along, and these general principles also should be applicable to applications developed using those future frameworks.

Struts is a stable MVC-based framework that is being used successfully in many different production environments on a variety of server platforms. Its action mapping abstraction feature in and of itself is one of Struts' biggest selling points. Even in the simplest Struts application, the use of action mapping makes it possible to keep the exposed URLs unchanged even when the underlying pages (e.g. JSP templates) responsible for producing the view change or move. This remains true even when switching to an entirely new view component architecture (e.g. Velocity templates).

Struts includes its own tag libraries that offer dynamic application functions (e.g. conditional and iterative processing, etc.). In particular, the Struts HTML tag library (`struts-html`) provides a bridge between HTML forms and Struts FormBean classes. However, there exists a project separate from Struts, known as JSTL (JSP Standard Tag Libraries), which is endorsed by Sun and is the most advanced effort to date to simplify JSPs and make them more accessible to page designers. It employs consistent tags and a class-agnostic 'expression language' that is much simpler than embedded Java scriptlets. While struts-html is not part of JSTL, the most recent version of Struts provides a version of the struts-html tag library that supports the very same expression language used in core JSTL tags. It is this version of the struts-html tag library that we will employ in implementing our application.

Since both Struts and JSTL rest on top of J2EE, we chose to use the most up-to-date version of Sun's Java Development Kit (JDK version 1.4) and the J2EE environment (version 1.3, including Servlet API 2.3 and JSP 1.2). We selected the Jakarta Tomcat server to deploy our application. Tomcat is a stable open source server that supports these choices. It is also the official reference implementation of the Java Servlet API and the JSP specification.

Likewise, we use the MySQL relational database management system to support persistence. While MySQL is a fully functional RDBMS, it lacks a number of features common to sophisticated commercial database products, including referential integrity and callable statements (stored procedures). For this reason, both our database schema and our persistence functionality employ the lowest common denominator of RDBMS capabilities. Re-factoring this application for usage with a commercial RDBMS (e.g. Oracle) might involve reworking parts of the schema to employ referential integrity, and to take advantage of stored procedures (which can greatly improve usability and performance) to support persistence.

We are using well-defined and widely accepted standards, which ensure that the application is easily portable to other J2EE servers (e.g. BEA WebLogic, IBM Websphere, SunOne, Macromedia JRun, etc.) and other database management systems (e.g. Oracle, Sybase, PostgresSQL). It should run on any operating system that supports Java (e.g. Solaris, Windows 98/NT/XP/2000, Linux, Mac OS X).

10.3 ANATOMY OF A STRUTS APPLICATION

Although it is not our intention to provide a tutorial on Struts, we will review the main organizing principles of a Struts application.

In an MVC application, the entry point is the *Controller* component. Incoming requests are directed to the Controller, which serves as a 'traffic cop' that determines, based on the request context, which task should be performed next. These tasks are mapped to application use cases. The components that perform these tasks may be part of the core Controller module or distinct processing components in their own right. They include data access functions and additional processing to access and manipulate the *Model*, based on the current state and input parameters associated with the request. When the selected task is complete, the Controller determines whether it is necessary to perform another task, or to generate a response offering a specific presentation (the *View*) to the requestor. The presentation sent to the user may provide links back to the Controller, for further requests to perform additional tasks.

In a Struts application, MVC components are organized as follows:

- The *Model* is comprised of a set of well-defined JavaBeans. In complex applications, a separate business layer (e.g. EJBs) may communicate with back-end data sources to provide access to the Model implementation.

- The *View* components are provided by JSPs, although the Struts framework supports other alternatives (e.g. Velocity templates, etc.). In addition, there are *view helper* classes (subclasses of `org.apache.struts.action.ActionForm`) used to support interaction with HTML forms.

- The *Controller* function is performed by the `ActionServlet`, which is provided with the Struts distribution. The `struts-config.xml` configuration file provides *action mappings* enabling the `ActionServlet` to direct requests to application-specific components (called `Actions`) that implement individual processing tasks.

For each task, an action mapping (defined in the `struts-config.xml` configuration file) specifies its *path*, which is a URL defined relative to the servlet context root, and

```
public class CustomerAuthCheckAction extends VrlsBaseAction {
    public ActionForward performAction(ActionMapping p_mapping,
        ActionForm p_form, HttpServletRequest p_request,
        HttpServletResponse p_response) {
        HttpSession session = p_request.getSession() ;
        if (session.getAttribute("customer") == null) {
            return (p_mapping.findForward("login")) ;
        } else {
            session.setAttribute("customer", null) ;
            return (p_mapping.findForward("logout")) ;
        }
    }
}
```

Figure 10.2 Example of an Action class

its *type*, which is the name of the Java class (a subclass of org.apache.struts. action.Action) associated with it.

The action mapping also specifies a set of *forwards*, which are symbolic names mapped to URL paths (also defined relative to the servlet context root), or to other actions. (Global forwards may be defined and used as possible outcomes for any configured Action.)

When a request reaches the application, the controller servlet examines its URL to determine which Action class is to be executed. Depending on the result of its processing, the Action class selects one of the defined forwards by name. It consequently constructs and returns an instance of the ActionForward class that specifies the context-relative URL associated with the selected forward name.

The controller servlet then routes processing to this URL, either by forwarding or redirecting (depending on the value of the optional *redirect* attribute that may also be specified in the action mapping). Figure 10.2 provides an example of how a simple Action class accomplishes all this.

If an action mapping defines an *input* attribute (Figure 10.3), that attribute represents the context-relative URL of a view component (or the name of a forward, which is mapped to a view component) that is responsible for the display of an HTML form used for data entry. This form's fields correspond to those defined in the subclass of org.apache.struts.action.ActionForm specified by the action mapping's *name* attribute. The data entered by the user in the displayed form will be validated if the action's *validate* attribute is set to 'true,' and if the custom Action-Form class has a validate() method. This method returns an ActionErrors object, which is a collection of every ActionError encountered during validation.

If the returned ActionErrors object is empty, then the Action considers the form fields to have been successfully validated. If it is not empty, then the form has not passed validation, indicating to the controller servlet that it should redisplay this view component to allow correction of invalid data. Messages associated with named errors can be defined in the properties file named in the `application` parameter associated with the Struts controller servlet in the application's `web.xml` file, usually named `ApplicationResources.properties`.

The presence of an *input* attribute tells the controller servlet that the first time an action is processed, it should route processing to the view component directly or indirectly specified by this attribute, typically to display a data entry form. The `validate()` method does not get invoked the first time the form is displayed, because it may consider empty fields to be invalid.

`ActionForm` classes allow for an optional `reset()` method that can be used to provide initial values to be displayed in the data entry form. This method would be used, for example, if you are not entering data for the first time (as you would when entering profile information for a new customer), but instead you are modifying an existing set of data (such as the profile of an already registered customer). In this case, the method would populate the fields of the `ActionForm` from the existing customer profile.

10.4 THE STRUCTURE OF THE VRLS APPLICATION

Our application does not stray far from the general structure of a Struts application:

- The *Controller* is a custom subclass of the `ActionServlet` class distributed with Struts, which performs additional application-specific tasks, including partner identification.

- The *View* makes use of JSPs that do not embed Java code. Instead, they use the core JSTL tags and the new version of the Struts HTML tag library that supports the JSTL Expression Language. The pages that utilize form submission (e.g. login, profile, and search pages) have corresponding form beans (subclasses of `ActionForm`) associated with them.

- The *Model* is a small set of JavaBeans persisted in a relational database. The bean classes implement `CustomerProfile`, `Listing`, and `Partner` interfaces.

The application configuration is defined in the `struts-config.xml` file shown in Figure 10.3. This file contains separate sections for defining form beans, global forwards, action mappings, and properties that tell the controller how to interpret the directives found in this file. For example, the `<set-property>` element found within the `<controller>` element towards the end of this file tells the controller that *input* attributes associated with actions are the names of *forwards* rather than explicit URL paths.

We chose to use the `/action/`*name* URL format for defining actions, so that the URLs are more or less abstract. There is no dependency (at least as far as

```
<?xml version="1.0" encoding="ISO-8859-1" ?>
<!DOCTYPE struts-config PUBLIC
  "-//Apache Software Foundation//DTD Struts Configuration 1.1//EN"
  "http://jakarta.apache.org/struts/dtds/struts-config_1_1.dtd">
<struts-config>
  <form-beans>
     <form-bean name="customerLoginForm"
                type="biz.vrls.struts.form.CustomerLoginForm"/>
     <form-bean name="customerProfileForm"
                type="biz.vrls.struts.form.CustomerProfileForm"/>
     <form-bean name="customerSearchForm"
                type="biz.vrls.struts.form.CustomerSearchForm"/>
     <form-bean name="customerContactForm"
                type="biz.vrls.struts.form.CustomerContactForm"/>
  </form-beans>
  <global-forwards>
     <forward name="notauthorized" path="/authcheck"/>
  </global-forwards>
  <action-mappings>
     <action path="/home"
             type="biz.vrls.struts.action.SuccessAlwaysAction">
        <forward name="success"
                 path="/pages/main.jsp?name=home"/>
     </action>
     <action path="/login"
             type="biz.vrls.struts.action.CustomerLoginAction"
             name="customerLoginForm" scope="request"
             input="failure"
             validate="true">
        <forward name="failure"
                 path="/pages/main.jsp?name=login"/>
     </action>
     <action path="/authcheck"
             type="biz.vrls.struts.action.CustomerAuthCheckAction">
        <forward name="logout"
                 path="/pages/main.jsp?name=logout"/>
        <forward name="login"
                 path="/action/login" redirect="true"/>
     </action>
     <action path="/profile"
             type="biz.vrls.struts.action.CustomerProfileAction"
             name="customerProfileForm" scope="request"
             input="failure"
             validate="true">
        <forward name="success"
                 path="/pages/main.jsp?name=profileConfirm"/>
        <forward name="failure"
                 path="/pages/main.jsp?name=profile"/>
     </action>
```

Figure 10.3   The struts-config.xml configuration file for the VRLS application

```
              <action path="/search"
                      type="biz.vrls.struts.action.CustomerSearchAction"
                      name="customerSearchForm" scope="request"
                      input="failure"
                      validate="true">
                  <forward name="many"
                          path="/action/results" redirect="true"/>
                  <forward name="one"
                          path="/action/details" redirect="true"/>
                  <forward name="failure"
                          path="/pages/main.jsp?name=search"/>
              </action>
              <action path="/results"
                      type="biz.vrls.struts.action.SuccessAlwaysAction">
                  <forward name="success"
                          path="/pages/main.jsp?name=results"/>
              </action>
              <action path="/details"
                      type="biz.vrls.struts.action.CustomerSearchDetailsAction"
                      input="failure">
                  <forward name="success"
                          path="/pages/main.jsp?name=details"/>
                  <forward name="failure"
                          path="/pages/main.jsp?name=listingerror"/>
              </action>
              <action path="/images"
                      type="biz.vrls.struts.action.ImageDisplayAction"/>
              <action path="/contact"
                      type="biz.vrls.struts.action.CustomerContactAction"
                      name="customerContactForm" scope="request"
                      input="failure"
                      validate="true">
                  <forward name="failure"
                          path="/pages/main.jsp?name=contact"/>
                  <forward name="success"
                          path="/pages/main.jsp?name=emailConfirm"/>
              </action>
          </action-mappings>
          <controller>
              <set-property property="inputForward" value="true"/>
          </controller>
      </struts-config>
```

Figure 10.3   (*continued*)

action URLs go) on suffixes like `*.do`, `*.jsp`, etc. When next generation controller and view components, or even entirely new frameworks, come along, URLs
like `http://server/context/action/home` are more reusable than URLs like
`http://server/context/home.do`.

Table 10.1 Action mappings for the VRLS application

Controller		View		Model
Path	Actions and Forwards biz.vrls.struts.action	Page	Forms biz.vrls.struts.form	Java Bean
/action/home — present home page	SuccessAlwaysAction — on success -->	home.jsp		
/action/authcheck — log in or log out depending on state	CustomerAuthCheckAction — on logout --> — on login:/action/login	logout.jsp		
/action/login — identify & authenticate	CustomerLoginAction — on failure (input) --> — otherwise invoke reroute() method	login.jsp	CustomerLoginForm	CustomerProfile
/action/profile — sign up if new user — modify profile if logged-in customer	CustomerProfileAction — on failure (input) --> — on success->	profile.jsp profileConfirm.jsp	CustomerProfileForm	CustomerProfile
/action/search — browse for listings satisfying search criteria	CustomerSearchAction — on none (input) --> — on many:/action/results — on one:/action/details	search.jsp	CustomerSearchForm	
/action/results — view search results	SuccessAlwaysAction — on success -->	results.jsp		List of Listings
/action/details — view listing details	CustomerSearchDetailsAction — on success --> — on unauthorized: /action/login	details.jsp		Listing
/action/contact — send e-mail to realtor	CustomerContactAction — on failure (input) --> — on success -->	contact.jsp emailConfirm.jsp	CustomerContactForm	

Table 10.1 provides a summary of the contents of the `struts-config.xml` file, including action mappings, forwards, form beans, and view components. Note that the names of JSP pages found in this table differ from the names specified in the `struts-config.xml` file. The `<forward>` elements specify URLs that point to a single JSP page, `/pages/main.jsp`, with a query string parameter that provides the name of the target page. In other words, a path of `/pages/main.jsp?name=home` ultimately routes processing to `/pages/partnerName/home.jsp` where `partner-Name` is the name of the active partner associated with this session. The page names in this table are the ultimate target pages (e.g. `home.jsp`).

Since portions of the application are restricted to registered customers, we need a mechanism for identifying and authenticating customers when they access the application. We use forms-based authentication rather than HTTP authentication, because it provides more control and flexibility. Applications can use custom HTML form pages for transmission of credentials, and the persistence mechanism for user credentials is under application control. In our application, user credentials are stored in a relational database as part of the customer's profile. For additional security, the passwords are encrypted as one-way hashes.

Authentication Roles

There are alternative approaches that may make HTTP authentication more attractive for some applications. In version 2.2 and later of the Java Servlet API, the web.xml file can contain <security-constraint> elements. Each <security-constraint> element may contain <web-resource-collection> elements (each defining a resource as a basic unit of authentication) and an <auth-constraint> element (defining who has access to a resource). A <web-resource-collection> element defines a resource by specifying its name and the URL pattern(s) that are associated with it. An <auth-constraint> element may contain any number of <role-name> elements specifying which roles (e.g. enduser, administrator) will be allowed access to the defined resource.

The mechanism for specifying the roles and associating them with users is specific to the application container. For example, Tomcat comes with built-in support for specifying user names, passwords, and role membership via realms, which can be configured either in an XML file (tomcat-users.xml) or in a relational database.

Since our application requirements necessitated the flexibility of forms-based authentication, we did not pursue the usage of this functionality. Additionally, we did not want to introduce dependencies on the usage of a particular application container (i.e. Tomcat). This functionality is worth investigating if you have complex authorization requirements and you are already committed to using a particular application container.

10.4.1 Controller: ActionServlet and custom actions

Our VrlsActionServlet class is a subclass of the org.jakarta.struts. action.ActionServlet class, which is responsible for the initial processing and routing of requests (Figure 10.4). The process() method of this class locates the proper subclass of org.jakarta.struts.action.Action based on the mappings defined in the struts-config.xml file, and passes control to that Action's execute() method.

We did not define our Action classes as direct subclasses of org.apache.struts. action.Action. Instead, they are subclasses of our own biz.vrls.struts. action.VrlsBaseAction class, which is itself a subclass of org.apache.struts. action.Action VrlsBaseAction over-rides the Action class's execute() method to perform common processing functions and then invoke an abstract method, performAction(), which must be defined in subclasses.

Consequently, application-specific functionality that is common to all actions can be specified either in VrlsActionServlet or in VrlsBaseAction. All other things being equal, it is much less intrusive to override Action than it is to over-ride ActionServlet. While creating a custom base Action class is encouraged, creating

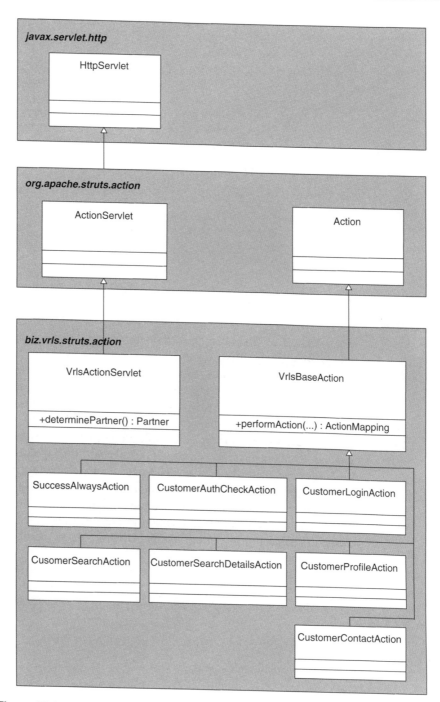

Figure 10.4 Action class hierarchy

```
public class VrlsActionServlet extends ActionServlet
    implements ApplicationConstants {

    protected void process(HttpServletRequest p_request,
                           HttpServletResponse p_response)
    throws IOException, ServletException {
        HttpSession session = p_request.getSession() ;
        if (session.getAttribute("partner") == null) {
        session.setAttribute("partner", determinePartner()) ;
        }
            ...
        super.process(p_request, p_response) ;
    }
    protected Partner determinePartner()
        throws IOException, ServletException {
        ...
    }
}
```

Figure 10.5 Fragment of the VrlsActionServlet class

a custom `ActionServlet` class, though not recommended, is sometimes justified and is not actively discouraged.

This application provided us with circumstances that warranted the creation of a custom `ActionServlet` class. While the `process()` method of the `ActionServlet` class is invoked for every request, the `execute()` method of the custom `Action` is not invoked when initially displaying an input form. This has very practical implications. If we decided to perform partner identification in the `VrlsBaseAction`'s `execute()` method, then whenever a user visited one of the form pages directly before visiting the home page, there would be no chance to identify the partner prior to displaying the form. At best, this would result in a strange user experience—going from a default presentation to a partner-specific one after submitting the form. Consequently, we chose to perform partner identification in the `VrlsActionServlet`'s `process()` method, so that proper partner identification would be performed for all requests (Figure 10.5).

Let us move on to a brief discussion of individual tasks and their action mappings:

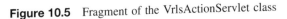
`/action/home: biz.vrls.struts.action.SuccessAlwaysAction`

- Entry page for site.

- Always display welcome page.

- Forwards:
  - `success: /pages/main.jsp?name=home -> /pages/.../home.jsp`

The `performAction()` method for the `SuccessAlwaysAction` class always returns the `ActionForward` associated with 'success.' It is used by actions that have a 'trivial' nature, e.g. always routing to the home page, or always presenting search results.

`/action/authcheck: biz.vrls.struts.action.CustomerAuthCheckAction`

- Invoked when customer selects 'log in' or 'log out' from navigation bar.

- If customer already logged in, returns the 'logout' forward, goes to logout page.

- If customer is not logged in, returns the 'login' forward, performs login action.

- Forwards:
  - `logout: /pages/main.jsp?name=logout -> /pages/.../logout.jsp`
  - `login:  /action/login`

The `CustomerAuthCheckAction` class is designed as a mediator between 'login' and 'logout' actions. If the customer is logged in, its `performAction()` method invalidates the session and returns the `ActionForward` associated with 'logout,' which is mapped to the logout notification. If the customer is not logged in, the `performAction()` method returns the `ActionForward` associated with the name 'login,' which is mapped to `/action/login`.

`/action/login: biz.vrls.struts.action.CustomerLoginAction`

- Invoked either by `CustomerAuthCheckAction` or by actions not supported for anonymous users.

- For input, displays login page.

- User enters user id and password for authentication.

- Validates and checks credentials against user database.

- On authentication failure, redisplays login page with error message(s).

- Once authenticated:
  - Constructs `CustomerProfile` from user database.
  - Updates `CustomerProfile` to reflect the date of the last visit.
  - Maintains `CustomerProfile` object until logout.
  - On success, invokes `reroute()` method from `VrlsBaseAction`, which forwards either to the home page (when invoked by `CustomerAuthCheckAction`), or to the original target (for actions not supported for anonymous users).

- Forwards:
  - `failure: /pages/main.jsp?name=login -> /pages/.../login.jsp`

The `CustomerLoginAction` class uses the `CustomerLoginForm` form bean referenced on the `login.jsp` page, to support specifying user name and password. A user may initiate this action by following a link to 'authcheck,' or the application may perform this action if an anonymous user tries to use a function limited to signed-in registered customers. The input attribute of the action is set to 'failure,' which points to the login page. This page is presented when the action is first invoked, and again as long as the entered credentials do not match those of a registered user. Once the credentials match, the `reroute()` method inherited from the `VrlsBaseAction` class is invoked, to perform the originally intended task that required authentication.

`/action/profile: biz.vrls.struts.action.CustomerProfileAction`

- Invoked when customer selects 'sign up' or 'profile' from navigation bar.

- For input, displays profile page.

- Allows unregistered visitors to sign up by entering new customer profile.

- Allows signed-in registered customers to modify their profiles.

- Provides a blank form to unregistered visitors.

- Provides pre-populated forms containing `CustomerProfile` data for signed-in customers.

- Forwards:
  o `failure:  /pages/main.jsp?name=profile->/pages/.../profile.jsp`
  o `success:  /pages/main.jsp?name=profileConfirm->`
  `                      /pages/.../profileConfirm.jsp`

The `CustomerProfileAction` class serves a dual purpose: to allow new users to enter profile information so that they can become registered customers, and to allow already registered customers to modify their profiles. The profile page contains conditional logic that causes it to present itself differently for each of these situations. The input attribute of the action is set to 'failure,' which routes to the profile page when the action is first invoked, and repeats this presentation until the entered information passes validation. At that point, the action's `performAction()` method returns the `ActionForward` associated with the name 'success,' which results in the presentation of a confirmation page.

`/action/search: biz.vrls.struts.action.CustomerSearchAction`

- Invoked when customers select 'search' from navigation bar.

- Provides data entry form for search criteria.

- If no results found, returns to the input page.

- If multiple results found, routes to 'results' action.

- If one result found, routes directly to the action for displaying details about a single listing.

- Forwards
  - failure: /pages/main.jsp?name=search->/pages/.../search.jsp
  - many: /action/results
  - one: /action/details

The `CustomerSearchAction` class allows users to enter selection criteria for searching the listing database. The input attribute of the action is set to 'failure,' which routes to the search page when the action is first invoked, and again if the search returns no results. If the query produces multiple results, the action's `performAction()` method returns the `ActionForward` associated with the name 'many,' which is mapped to /action/results. If the query produces a single result, the action's `performAction()` method returns the `ActionForward` associated with the name 'one,' which is mapped to /action/details, bypassing the results page.

`/action/details: biz.vrls.struts.action.CustomerSearchDetailsAction`

- Invoked when customers follow a link from `results.jsp`.

- Also invoked when search produces a single result.

- Displays details about a particular listing.

- Uses a request parameter to identify the listing.

- Not supported for anonymous visitors.

- Forwards
  - success: /pages/main.jsp?name=details->/pages/.../details.jsp
  - failure: /pages/main.jsp?name=error->/pages/.../error.jsp
  - notauthorized: /action/login (global forward)

The `CustomerSearchDetailsAction` class is responsible for displaying details about a particular property listing. It may be referenced either explicitly or through the 'search' action. The action's `performAction()` method returns the `ActionForward` associated with the name 'success' if the user is a signed-in registered customer, and if the provided `listingId` parameter corresponds to a valid listing. If the user is not signed-in, the action's `performAction()` method returns the global `ActionForward` associated with the name 'notauthorized,' which is mapped to the URL /action/login.

`/action/images: biz.vrls.struts.action.ImageDisplayAction`

- Invoked through `details.jsp` <IMG> tags to display images for a particular listing.

- Only available to registered users (i.e. a registered user should not be able to send a URL for one of these images to a non-registered person and allow them to see it).

- Displays an image containing an error message to anonymous users.

```
/action/contact: biz.vrls.struts.action.CustomerContactAction
```

- Invoked when customers select 'contact us' from the navigation bar (or the listing details page).

- Provides input form for identifying users and sending messages to realtors.

- Once the form is filled in, e-mail is sent to the partner's e-mail contact address.

- Forwards:
    - o `failure: /pages/main.jsp?name=contact->/pages/.../contact.jsp`
    - o `success: /pages/main.jsp?name=emailConfirm->`
      `/pages/.../emailConfirm.jsp`

The `CustomerContactAction` class allows users to contact the broker to express interest in a particular listing, or simply to request further information about the broker. The input attribute of the action is set to 'failure,' which routes to the contact page when the action is first invoked, and redisplays the contact page on failed validation (i.e. if the e-mail address entered in the form is improperly formatted). If the user is a signed-in registered customer, the e-mail address field on the form is pre-populated with the e-mail address from the `CustomerProfile`. If the user was looking at details for a particular listing when this action was invoked, the subject field is pre-populated with a reference to the listing's ID. Once a valid address has been entered, the action's `performAction()` method sends e-mail to the referring partner's contact e-mail address and displays a confirmation page.

10.4.2 View: JSP Pages and ActionForms

We need the ability to present a number of different pages throughout the application. The home page, search results page and listing details page are designed to display information, while the login, profile, search, and contact pages are interactive forms (Figure 10.6).

We also need the ability to present partner-specific versions of these pages, with each set of pages having a 'look and feel' that reflects that of the partner's own branded Web site. Design alternatives for supporting partner-specific presentations vary greatly. They range from the sharing of all page templates, to maintaining separate sets of page templates for each partner. Sharing templates between partners limits the degree of customization to style sheets (and possibly custom images such as corporate logos). We made the choice to maintain separate sets of templates in

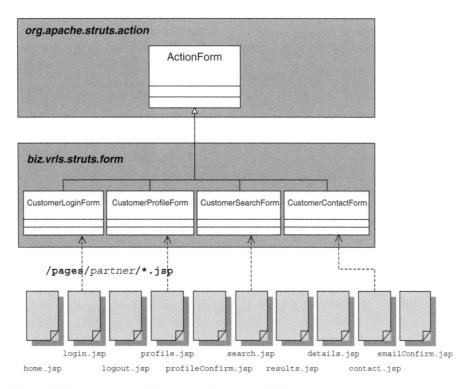

Figure 10.6 `ActionForm` hierarchy and associated JSPs

order to achieve the greatest flexibility, and to enable partners to create and upload their own templates.

All of these pages have a lot in common: they reference the same JSP taglibs, display the same navigation bar (with variations), and have the same general look and feel. Clearly, something needs to be done to reduce redundancy.

Our first step in this direction was to create an `include.jsp` page (Figure 10.8), which is included in all other pages. This page defines tag libraries and initializes shared variables that define commonly referenced URLs and paths used for other shared page components such as the navigation bar.

To support co-branding, our original intent was to create a set of 'root' pages, each of which would embed its corresponding custom page within a directory containing custom pages for a specific partner. The `VrlsActionServlet` would have, by this point, determined who the active partner was and placed the appropriate `Partner` object in the session. In other words, `/pages/home.jsp` would embed `${sessionScope.partner.code}/home.jsp`.

However, as we discovered during the course of implementing this strategy, these root pages were practically identical, and the only difference between them was the name of the custom page to be embedded. Thus, we re-factored our design

```
<%@ include file ="include.jsp" %>
<html>
<head>
<meta http-equiv ="Content-Type" content ="text/html;
      charset=iso-8859-1">
<title><c:out value ="${sessionScope.partner.name} -
   ${param.name}"/></title>
<style type ="text/css">
<c:import url ="${sessionScope.partner.code}/vrls.css"/ >
</style>
</head>
<c:import
   url="${sessionScope.partner.code}/${param.name}.jsp"/>
</html>
```

Figure 10.7 Shared main.jsp file

to use *one* common root page, main.jsp, which determined which custom page should be embedded via the query string parameter name. In other words, a request to /pages/main.jsp?name=profile would embed /pages/abc/profile.jsp, assuming abc was the code associated with the active partner.

The main.jsp page is shown in Figure 10.7. As mentioned previously, it embeds include.jsp. Using JSTL's <c:import> tag, it selects and embeds a partner-specific page based on session information and request parameters, i.e. ${sessionScope.partner.code}/${param.name}.jsp. It also references a partner-specific stylesheet found in the partner directory (${sessionScope.partner.code}/vrls.css).

Every custom page should include a navigation bar, but apart from that, we leave it up to each partner to design their page templates as they see fit. The navigation bar should include the following links:

1. /action/home for the home page,

2. /action/authcheck for the authorization action that eventually routes to the login or logout page (depending on whether the customer is logged in or not),

3. /action/profile for the profile data entry action that routes to the profile page for both new customer profile entry and existing customer profile modification,

4. /action/search for the search form page, and

5. /action/contact for the customer contact page.

It does not make sense for the action that displays search results, /action/results, to be included in the navigation bar, since it should only be accessible through the search page. By convention, each page should not include a link to itself in the navigation bar (which is one reason a common include page or tag for the navigation bar was not implemented).

```
<%@ taglib uri="/WEB-INF/c.tld" prefix ="c" %>
<%@ taglib uri="/WEB-INF/struts-html-el.tld" prefix="html" %>

<c:url var="url_home" scope ="session" value="/action/home"/>
<c:url var="url_authcheck" scope="session"
       value="/action/authcheck"/>
<c:url var="url_profile" scope="session" value="/action/profile"/>
<c:url var="url_search" scope="session" value="/action/search"/>
<c:url var="url_results" scope="session" value="/action/results"/>
<c:url var="url_details" scope="session" value="/action/details"/>
<c:url var="url_contact" scope="session" value="/action/contact"/>
<c:set var="partner_images" scope="session"
       value="${pageContext.request.contextPath}/pages/
              ${sessionScope.partner.code}/images"
/>
```

Figure 10.8 Shared include.jsp file

The labels associated with links in the navigation bar appear to be obvious:
'home' for the home page, 'login' for the login page, 'profile' for the profile page,
etc. However, these labels should depend on the visitor's 'state'—logged in or
logged out. When dealing with an anonymous visitor (someone who has not signed
in), it is appropriate for the authorization link to have a label of 'login,' but the
profile link should say 'sign up,' since the visitor is not modifying an existing profile
(they don't have one yet), but rather signing up for the first time. Likewise, the label
for the authorization link should say 'log in' for an anonymous customer who has
not logged in, but 'log out' for a logged-in customer.

Thus, the set of links in the navigation bar is static, but the set of labels is not.
As you can see in Figure 10.8, the include.jsp page defines the set of links using
the JSTL <c:url> tag as a set of session attributes. This tag is intelligent enough
to create a context-relative link, and to append appropriate parameters to support
URL rewriting when cookie support is not available from the browser.

The set of labels is defined elsewhere, in the VrlsActionServlet class. A custom object, an instance of the biz.vrls.util.AppTextLabels class, is stored as a
session attribute with the name 'navbar.' This class implements the java.util.Map
interface, and maintains two sets of label mappings: one for the logged-in state,
and another for the anonymous state. The set of labels is retrieved from the
ApplicationResources.properties file, where Struts also looks for error
message mappings and other localized application properties. Labels that are supposed to have different values depending on the customer state are defined twice,
once using a 'vanilla' name (e.g. app.navbar.profile), and again adding the
suffix .auth for logged-in customers (e.g. app.navbar.profile.auth), like this:

```
app.navbar.home=home
app.navbar.authcheck=log in
app.navbar.authcheck.auth=log out
app.navbar.profile=sign up
app.navbar.profile.auth=profile
app.navbar.search=search
app.navbar.contact=contact us
```

From these specifications, two Maps are built and maintained by the AppTextLabels class, one for the logged-in state, and one for the anonymous state. The isLoggedIn() method in the biz.vrls.utils.SessionUtils class is invoked to determine which set of label mappings should be displayed.

Let us move on to the discussion of default templates provided as part of the application:

home.jsp

- Acts as a welcome page.

- Personalized to display customer name.

- Contains navigation bar to link to other important application functions.

This simple page displays static information and does not contain a form for interactive data entry.

login.jsp and CustomerLoginForm

- Simple form for authenticating users by entering user name and password.

- Contains the navigation bar to link to other important application functions.

A fragment of this page is shown in Figure 10.9. The CustomerLoginForm bean does *not* directly correspond to a Model component, but refers indirectly to the CustomerProfile object. The CustomerLoginForm's validate() method is invoked on form submission. The page is redisplayed on validation failure. Validation error messages, if any, are requested through the <html:errors/> tag. Note how the struts-config.xml file (Figure 10.3) associates the CustomerLoginForm class with the /login action, which uses the login.jsp page for input.

Note that in our sample application we send these credentials 'in the clear' (over a non-secure connection). In practice, this action should always operate over a secured connection, especially if sensitive personal information is included in the transmission.

```
...
<html:form action="/login" focus="username">
<html:errors/>
   <TABLE>
      <TR>
         <TD COLSPAN=2 VALIGN=top ALIGN=left>
         </TD>
      </TR>
      <TR>
         <TD CLASS=text ALIGN=right VALIGN=top>User ID:</TD>
         <TD ALIGN=left VALIGN=top><html:text
            property="username"/></TD>
      </TR>
      <TR>
         <TD CLASS=text ALIGN=right VALIGN=top>Password:</TD>
         <TD ALIGN=left VALIGN=top><html:password
            property="password"/></TD>
      </TR>
      <TR>
         <TD ALIGN=center COLSPAN=2>
            <html:submit value=" Login "/>  
            <html:reset value=" Clear form "/>
         </TD>
      </TR>
   </TABLE>
</html:form>
...
```

Figure 10.9 Template page fragment for `login.jsp`

`profile.jsp` and `CustomerProfileForm`

- Structure is similar to `login.jsp` and `CustomerLoginForm`.

- Form for entering personal information as part of user registration.

- Also used for modifying personal information in existing customer profiles.

- `CustomerProfileForm` *does* directly correspond to the `CustomerProfile` object, but does not include getters and setters for all of its attributes.

- Contains navigation bar to link to other important application functions.

Note how the `struts-config.xml` file (see Figure 10.3) associates the `CustomerProfileForm` class with the `/profile` action, which uses the `profile.jsp` page for input. Remember that the label text associated with the link to this action depends on whether or not the visitor is logged in.

`profileConfirm.jsp`

- The structure is similar to `home.jsp`.

- Displayed upon 'success' of `/profile` action: confirms successful entry of personal information.

- Contains navigation bar to link to other important application functions.

`search.jsp and CustomerSearchForm`

- The structure is similar to `login.jsp` and `CustomerLoginForm`.

- Form for entering search criteria for browsing the property listings database.

- Contains navigation bar to link to other important application functions.

Note how the `struts-config.xml` file (see Figure 10.3) associates the `Customer SearchForm` class with the `/search` action, which uses the `search.jsp` page for input.

`results.jsp`

- Designed to display search results based on search criteria entered from the `search.jsp` page by iterating over a `List` of `biz.vrls.listing.Listing` objects placed in the session by `CustomerSearchAction` class (associated with the `/search` action).

- Each displayed listing provides a link to the `/details` action, which is implemented by `SearchDetailsAction`, for individual results.

- Contains navigation bar to link to other important application functions.

Note how the `struts-config.xml` file (see Figure 10.3) associates the `Customer SearchForm` class with the `/search` action, which uses the `search.jsp` page for input.

`details.jsp`

- Designed to display details about individual properties.

- Queries an instance of `biz.vrls.listing.Listing` placed on the session by the `SearchDetailsAction` class (associated with the `/results` action) to display attributes of a particular real estate property.

- Contains navigation bar to link to other important application functions.

`contact.jsp, CustomerContactForm, and emailConfirm.jsp`

- Mechanism for customers to contact brokers with general questions or queries about specific listings.

- `emailConfirm.jsp` serves as confirmation page.

- The structure is similar to `profile.jsp`, `CustomerProfileForm`, and `profileConfirm.jsp`.

- If customer is logged in, e-mail address is pre-populated, otherwise anonymous visitors can enter their e-mail addresses manually.

- If reached from a link on the listing details page, subject is pre-populated with mention of specific listing ID.

- Contains navigation bar to link to other important application functions.

Note how the `struts-config.xml` file (see Figure 10.3) associates the `CustomerContactForm` class with the `/contact` action, which uses the `contact.jsp` page for input. The `CustomerContactForm` bean does *not* directly correspond to a Model component.

10.4.3 Model: JavaBeans and Auxiliary Service Classes

Our model (shown in Figure 10.10) includes beans that implement interfaces associated with the three main classes of objects in our application: `CustomerProfile`, `Partner`, and `Listing`. Each of these interfaces extends three common interfaces: `Identifiable`, `Describable`, and `Logged`.

The `CustomerProfile` bean is designed to store information about a customer. Much of this information comes from user input provided during the signup process. The most common use case for this process has a visitor following the 'profile' link in the navigation bar, which routes to `/action/profile`, ultimately displaying the `profile.jsp` page.

As you can tell by looking at the `struts-config.xml` file, the 'profile' action is associated with the `CustomerProfileForm` bean. It may seem reasonable to use the same class for both the model and the form bean, but it is not a good idea. If the `CustomerProfile` bean were used as the form bean, hostile users could figure out the names of bean properties that are not exposed to the outside world, and construct HTTP requests that reset these properties and jeopardize the integrity of our application. In a way, `CustomerProfileForm` acts as a 'firewall' for `CustomerProfile`—users do not have direct access to setter and getter methods on the `CustomerProfile` bean. Without this separation, we would be relying on 'security through obscurity.' which is a very dangerous practice.

The `Partner` bean stores partner-specific information, including partner id and URL prefix that are necessary for inferring partner affiliation for new visitors. Many of its properties are populated through the `PartnerDataForm` bean (which is part of the administrative interface left as an exercise for our readers).

The `Listing` bean is designed to represent individual real estate properties. Details about individual homes are populated interactively, through the `ListingForm` bean

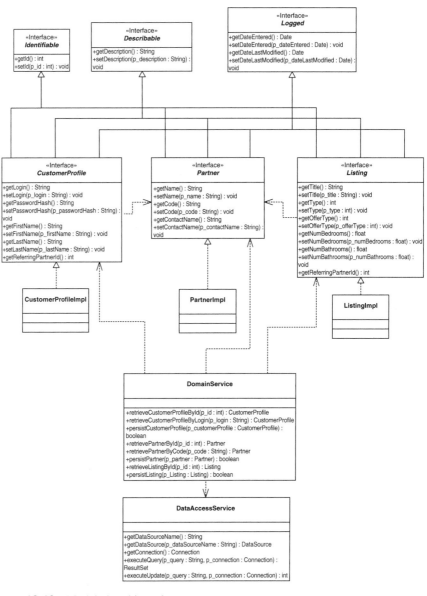

Figure 10.10 Model class hierarchy

that is exposed through the administrative interface. (As we already mentioned, the implementation of the administrative interface is left as an exercise for our readers, though a brief discussion of its design is provided later in this chapter.)

Our design supports model persistence, implemented through auxiliary service classes—`DataAccessService` and `DomainService`—that are discussed in the following section. On successful login, an instance of `CustomerProfile` is populated from the database and stored on the session. This caches customer information for the duration of the browser session. A modification to one or more attributes of the `CustomerProfile` instance causes a 'write through' to the database to maintain data integrity.

The `Partner` bean is populated from the database when a new session is established. The `VrlsActionServlet` has a method (`determinePartner()`) that figures out partner association. This association may be modified on login if the initial inference about partner identity was incorrect. Modifications are handled in the same way as with `CustomerProfile`.

Strictly speaking, it is not necessary to store the `Listing` bean on a session because of its transient nature. We do it to simplify processing in the `details.jsp` page, which refers to this session attribute to determine which listing should be displayed. We also make use of it in the `contact.jsp` page: if this attribute exists and is non-null, its ID is included in the subject of the e-mail to be sent to the partner.

10.5 DESIGN DECISIONS

In the course of building this application, we made a number of critical design decisions. Here we discuss the rationale behind them. In some cases, we also list alternatives and areas where there is room for improvement.

10.5.1 Abstracting functionality into service classes

In designing this application, we abstracted various functions into service classes in the `biz.vrls.services` package. The `DataAccessService` class encapsulates the acquisition of database connections and the execution of SQL queries (for both selection and update). The `DomainService` class provides methods to retrieve and persist the Model components (`CustomerProfile`, `Partner`, `Listing`) associated with the application. The `EmailService` class obtains a `javax.mail.Session` through the Web server's JNDI lookup facilities, and uses it to process e-mail.

Service classes exploit the *singleton* pattern, which ensures that only one instance of a class is present in a system. In Java, this pattern is implemented by providing a static method, `getInstance()`, that is the only way to access an instance of the class. There are no public constructors for the class; the `getInstance()` method returns a static member variable (instantiated using a *private* constructor) that represents the single instance of the class. Applications use methods found in service classes by calling the static `getInstance()` method and invoking instance methods on the returned object, e.g.:

```
DomainService ds = DomainService.getInstance();
Listing listing = ds.retrieveListingById(1234);
        or
Listing listing
   = DomainService.getInstance().retrieveListingById(1234);
```

BENEFITS

1. *Code simplification*—for domain objects, retrieval or persistence is accomplished through a single method call within the `DomainService` class. For other database functions, queries can be executed directly via methods in the `DataAccessService` class with a `RowSet` (a disconnected cacheable implementation of the `java.sql.ResultSet` interface) returned for processing by the calling class. Developers do not need to know the details of how persistence and retrieval take place.

2. *Flexibility*—the Model components are designed explicitly around interfaces rather than concrete implementation classes, and the return values for the methods in these classes are interfaces. This makes the application independent of specific implementations of the Model components.

3. *Extensibility*—since the code for these functions is in one place, instead of being scattered throughout the application, maintenance of this code is also simplified. Any or all of these service classes can be replaced with a new version that performs its operations differently. This opens the door for versions that make use of more sophisticated persistence mechanisms (e.g. EJB, JDO).

ALTERNATIVES/IMPROVEMENTS

1. We could have defined our services as interfaces, and used the Factory pattern to create instances of classes which implement that interface. The particular implementation class to be used can be specified in a properties file, providing flexibility in configuring the application at deployment time.

2. We also could have used *Fulcrum*, a Jakarta project services framework that used to be part of the Velocity template engine but is now a project in its own right. For those implementing complex services, Fulcrum has already laid down a foundation and done a large part of the work.

3. Finally, we could have added smart caching functionality to the `DomainService` class. We shall discuss this further in the next section.

10.5.2 Using embedded page inclusion to support co-branding

The VRLS application supports presentation co-branding based on the referring partner. This means that if a visitor comes to the VRLS application through a particular partner broker's Web site, the pages will have a look and feel that conforms to the layout of that site.

The method is simple. There is one root JSP page, `/pages/main.jsp`, which contains instructions for including common JavaScript files and CSS stylesheets. The 'name' parameter included in the query string specifies the action being invoked—'home,' 'login,' etc. The code associated with the partner (who has already been identified by the `VrlsActionServlet`) provides the name of the directory in which custom pages are to be found. Thus, a visitor who came to the site through a partner whose code is 'partner1,' attempting to access the URL `http://host/context/action/home`, would be routed to `http://host/context/pages/main.jsp?name=home` which would embed `http://host/context/pages/partner1/home.jsp`. Since the root page acts as a 'wrapper' for the embedded page, the latter is assumed to contain only HTML body content (i.e. not the head part of the HTML document).

BENEFITS

1. *Simplicity*—our approach uses a single root JSP page that embeds a custom partner page given a partner directory name and a function. The URL `/pages/main.jsp?name=home` refers directly to `/pages/partnerName/home.jsp`.

2. *Extensibility*—the addition of new partners does not require any modifications to the application. It is simply a matter of adding a partner to the database, creating a directory to hold partner JSPs and images, and creating or uploading those JSPs and images.

ALTERNATIVES/IMPROVEMENTS

1. We could have eliminated virtually all the HTML in the root page and had it simply embed an entire page. This would mean that all inclusion and common functions would need to be replicated in every custom page.

2. Alternatively, we could have created one set of common JSP pages and put placeholders in them to facilitate co-branding customization. The placeholders could have been used to change a small set of common elements like page background color, URL for the logo image, etc., using substitution parameters provided in a partner configuration file or in attributes of the `Partner` object itself. This approach would indeed work if all we wanted was this sort of limited customization capability.

```
partner.bgcolor =#999999
partner.logo =http://partner1.com/images/logo.gif
    ...
<BODY BGCOLOR ="${sessionScope.partner.bgcolor}">
<IMG SRC ="${sessionScope.partner.logo}">
```

3. One other possibility is to use *Tiles*, another Jakarta framework that partners with Struts to provide JSP template functionality. The Tiles framework lets you create JSP templates that define the general page layout as a set of components (known as *tiles*). Other JSPs can use this layout, and specify which external resources should be used to fill in the template components, by including a `<tiles:insert>` tag (functionally similar to a JSP include tag). When used in conjunction with Struts, Tiles layouts (and the URL paths they are associated with) can be configured directly in an XML file. The article referenced at the end of this chapter provides a good introduction to Tiles.

10.5.3 A single task for creation and modification of customer profiles

There are two discrete tasks in this application that were combined into one: the creation of a new customer profile by an anonymous user (during signup), and the modification of an existing customer profile by a registered user. While these tasks are similar, they are obviously not equivalent. For example, the signup process allows users to select a login identifier, but the modification process does not allow them to change this identifier once it has been selected.

We could have chosen to treat each function as its own task, with its own `Action` class and its own view components (JSP pages and `ActionForm` view helper classes). Instead, we chose to concentrate on what these two functions have in common, and create one `Action` class and one set of view components.

The `CustomerProfileAction` class determines whether the user is logged in. If so, it considers this a task that modifies an existing profile. Otherwise, it considers it a task to create a new one. If the task is to modify an existing profile, the HTML form is populated with current profile values, and conditional logic within the JSP page presents the login name as a fixed text field rather than a form input field. If the task is to create a new profile, the form is initially displayed in an unpopulated state, including a form input field for a user-selected login name.

BENEFITS

1. *Minimizes redundancy*—if we created separate tasks and separate sets of view components, there would have been substantial duplication, e.g. two form pages with mostly redundant fields, and two `ActionForm` beans. Our approach emphasizes

what the two processes have in common rather than focusing on what makes them different. In doing so, the number of objects that must be created and maintained is reduced.

ALTERNATIVES

1. We could create separate `Action` classes, `ActionForm` beans, and JSP pages for each of these functions. Whether this is a good idea, depends on how much difference there is between the views and processing for each task. Other applications may have requirements that cross this threshold.

10.6 ENHANCEMENTS

No application is ever complete. Even if you successfully build an application that fulfills all the specified requirements, you can bet that these requirements will change after the application is deployed (probably even before!).

This application is no exception. Since it was designed as a tutorial, some of the requirements were deliberately not implemented, or were implemented only partially. The suggestions described in this section describe enhancements over and above the original requirements, as well as steps necessary to implement those unimplemented and partially implemented requirements.

10.6.1 Administrative interface

Although we strongly emphasized that an application is not complete without an administrative interface, we did not make the implementation of the administrative interface available for download. The application package includes SQL queries for adding partners and listings to the database, but no mechanism (other than manual execution of SQL queries) for updating the database to add partners or listings.

The administrative interface should have its own authentication scheme. In other words, the mechanism used to identify and authenticate administrators must be separate from the one used to identify and authenticate customers. If you want an interface that employs one fixed administrative password shared by all administrators, you can include that (preferably encrypted) in the application resources file. It would be more thorough (and more secure) to provide a database table (similar to `VRLS_CUSTOMER_PROFILE_DATA` used for administrator authentication).

Ideally, the administrative interface should be a separate application, installed with a distinct servlet context that is not associated with the main application. It would naturally require its own set of actions and view components.

Figure 10.11 offers a sample `struts-config.xml` file for the administrative interface. It defines actions to perform login, partner additions and modifications,

```
<?xml version="1.0" encoding="ISO-8859-1" ?>
<!DOCTYPE struts-config PUBLIC
    "-//Apache Software Foundation//DTD Struts Configuration 1.1//EN"
    "http://jakarta.apache.org/struts/dtds/struts-config_1_1.dtd">
<struts-config>
    <form-beans>
        <form-bean name="adminLoginForm"
                   type="biz.vrls.struts.form.AdminLoginForm"/>
        <form-bean name="partnerDataForm"
                   type="biz.vrls.struts.form.PartnerDataForm"/>
        <form-bean name="partnerSelectForm"
                   type="biz.vrls.struts.form.PartnerSelectForm"/>
        <form-bean name="listingForm"
                   type="biz.vrls.struts.form.ListingForm"/>
        <form-bean name="listingSelectForm"
                   type="biz.vrls.struts.form.ListingSelectForm"/>
    </form-beans>
    <global-forwards>
      <forward name="notauthorized"
               path="/pages/error.jsp" redirect="true"/>
    </global-forwards>
    <action-mappings>
        <action path="/home"
                type="biz.vrls.struts.action.SuccessAlwaysAction">
          <forward name="success"
                   path="/pages/home.jsp"/>
        </action>
        <action path="/partner"
                type="biz.vrls.struts.action.PartnerDataAction"
                name="partnerDataForm" scope="request"
                input="failure"
                validate="true">
          <forward name="failure"
                   path="/pages/partnerData.jsp"/>
          <forward name="success"
                   path="/pages/partnerDataConfirm.jsp"/>
        </action>
        <action path="/selectPartner"
                type="biz.vrls.struts.action.PartnerSelectAction"
                name="partnerSelectForm" scope="request"
                input="failure"
                validate="true">
          <forward name="failure"
                   path="/pages/selectPartner.jsp"/>
          <forward name="success"
                   path="/action/partner" redirect="true"/>
        </action>
        <action path="/listing"
                type="biz.vrls.struts.action.ListingAction"
```

Figure 10.11 A sample struts-config.xml for the administrative interface

```
                name="listingForm" scope="request" input="failure"
                validate="true">
            <forward name="failure"
                    path="/pages/listing.jsp"/>
            <forward name="success"
                    path="/pages/listingConfirm.jsp"/>
        </action>
        <action path="/selectListing"
                type="biz.vrls.struts.action.ListingSelectAction"
                name="listingSelectForm" scope="request"
                input="failure"
                validate="true">
            <forward name="failure"
                    path="/pages/selectPartner.jsp"/>
            <forward name="success"
                    path="/action/partner" redirect="true"/>
        </action>
    </action-mappings>
    <controller>
        <set-property property="inputForward" value="true"/>
    </controller>
</struts-config>
```

Figure 10.11   (*continued*)

and listing additions and modifications. There should be mechanisms for selecting partners or listings that need to be modified.

For selecting partners (assuming the number of partners was not huge), there could be a form with a dropdown box to allow partner selection. Since the number of listings can be expected to be much larger, a more sophisticated mechanism is needed for listing selection. The simplest approach would be to allow the administrator to type in a listing ID manually, but this would be prone to error.

The same mechanisms provided for searching in the main application can be transplanted into the administrative interface to serve this purpose. Administrators could enter search criteria via a form on the search page. If the search produced many results, the /results action would present the results page, with links to the /details action for each listing. If the search produced only one result, processing would be routed directly to the /details action which would present the details page for that listing. In contrast to the main application, where the details page is a read-only presentation of information about a listing, the administrative details page is a form that could be used for either modifying an existing listing or entering a new one.

The administrative interface should employ its own base Action class, similar to the VrlsBaseAction class associated with the main application but tailored to the needs of the administrative interface. Since virtually all actions in the administrative interface (with the exception of the login function) require that the administrator be logged in, this base class could return 'unauthorized' whenever a user that is not logged in attempts access, using that global forward to route directly to an error page.

10.6.2 Enhancing the signup process through e-mail authentication

One of the requirements associated with this application was the ability for new users to sign up and create new customer profiles. Our implementation allows users to enter all the information needed to populate a `CustomerProfile` object, including their chosen login name and password.

However, application requirements specify that new users should *not* be allowed to specify their passwords. They should be able to enter all required information, including e-mail addresses, but this information should not include passwords. Instead, once the form has passed validation, the application should send a confirmatory e-mail to the address that was entered, containing a random password automatically generated by the application. The user, upon receiving the e-mail at the specified address, would return to the application, entering their chosen login name and the provided password. Once they have successfully logged in, only then could they change the password to one of their own choosing, using the application's profile modification functionality.

This is a more secure method of enrolling new users than the one we have built into the application. In its current state, the application allows someone to enter an invalid e-mail address, or someone else's valid e-mail address, with impunity. Requiring that new users enter a valid e-mail address, where they will receive a message containing the password they need to log in, ensures that we have verified the identity of our enrolling user.

Currently, the application includes a form field on the signup page in which new users can enter their password of choice. They can then proceed to the login page to provide their login name and password. To make this process more secure, the following steps need to be taken:

1. Remove the password field (and the password confirmation field) from the signup page. Note that these fields are still needed when modifying profiles for existing customers, so the `profile.jsp` page must be modified appropriately to support this.

2. The profile confirmation page that users are routed to after the profile form has been validated (`profileConfirm.jsp`) should provide an indication to the new user that they should expect an e-mail containing their password, which they can change after they connect to the application.

3. After successful form validation (but before routing to the profile confirmation page), the application should use the `EmailService` class to send an e-mail to the provided address. The e-mail should contain the random password generated by the application.

Proper Profile Password Processing

Note also that the right way to perform customer profile modification would be to require the current password to be entered, making it a pre-condition for the processing of changes. Thus, three password fields (all initially blank) would be required on the form for profile modification: one for the current password, one for the desired new password, and one more to provide confirmation of the desired new password. If the current password field is incorrect, the form should fail validation. Otherwise, if the two 'new password' fields are blank, the password should not be changed, but other changes should be processed. Changes to the password should only be processed when the current password is entered correctly and when both new password fields are filled in and match each other.

10.6.3 Improving partner recognition through a persistent cookie

One of the problems with the current design is that customers returning to the application may not have their partner affiliations recognized until after they sign in. Some approaches to partner identification make this process easier (e.g. using a sub-domain strategy to always identify the partner for requests to `http://rrr.vrls.biz` as `rrr`). Using the referring URL for partner identification is more problematic, especially on subsequent visits when the customer comes directly to the site (i.e. there is no referring URL).

Saving a persistent cookie to identify the partner would alleviate this problem. This could be accomplished by having the `VrlsActionServlet` include a `Set-Cookie` header in its generated responses once the user has successfully signed up with a particular partner. This cookie should identify the application's domain and set a value of `partnerCode=abc` (assuming the partner's code is 'abc') and an expiration date far into the future (e.g. six months to a year). Subsequent requests from this customer (from the same browser on the same computer) will include a `Cookie` header providing this name/value pair. The `VrlsActionServlet`'s `determinePartner()` method should be enhanced so that it looks first for this cookie before trying to determine the partner via the `Referer` header.

Note that other information can be persisted in this cookie, including the customer's login name and password, which would cause the customer to be identified and logged in automatically. We *can* do this, but best practices dictate that we do not do so, unless customers have explicitly elected (via a checkbox on the profile page) to keep this information in a persistent cookie so that they can be logged in automatically the next time they visit the site.

10.6.4 Adding caching functionality to the DomainService class

Many different kinds of caching can be used in a Web application. The kind of caching we are talking about here is not Web caching but object caching, using the DomainService class. Methods that store and retrieve instances of CustomerProfile, Partner, and Listing make a database call every time, which may be very costly.

It is relatively simple to cache all retrieved objects in a Map that is maintained as an instance variable in the DomainService class. The key associated with an entry in the Map is the identifying field used to retrieve the object, and the value is the object itself. (For retrieveById methods, the 'id' field is generally an integer, so the key must be converted into an object using the Integer wrapper class, since the java.util.Map interface requires that a key be an object and not a primitive type.) Each retrieval method in the DomainService class should be modified as in the example in Figure 10.12.

Similarly, the persistence methods should update the Map whenever objects are modified by the application. It should be noted, however, that the underlying data source could be modified independently of the application (e.g. through direct database updates). A decision must be made as to whether the application should tolerate this discontinuity or provide a mechanism for clearing the cache to allow updated objects to be refreshed from the database.

```
public CustomObject retrieveCustomObjectById(int p_id) {
    Integer idKey = new Integer(id) ;
    if (m_customObjectCacheMap.contains(idKey)) {
        return (CustomObject) m_customObjectCacheMap.get(idKey) ;
    }
    else {
        CustomObject customObj = null ;
        //perform database retrieval functions from original method
        ...
        if (customObj ! = null) {
            m_customObjectCacheMap.put(idKey, customObj) ;
        }
        return customObj ;
    }
}
```

Figure 10.12   Object caching example

To make this whole process work, the following steps must be taken:

1. Modify the retrieval methods in the DomainService class according to the example in Figure 10.12.

2. Similarly modify the persistence methods to update the Map when persisting new or modified objects.

3. Provide public methods that can be invoked to clear object caches (individually or collectively). The administrative interface should provide a mechanism to invoke these methods directly, so that the cache can be cleared on request when necessary.

10.6.5 Paging through cached search results using the Value List Handler pattern

The result set returned from a search query can be quite large. Rather than displaying the entire result set on one page, the number of results displayed per page should have a predefined limit, and the application should provide a mechanism for customers to page through the discrete result subsets. Sun refers to this as the *Value List Handler* pattern (one of the Core J2EE Patterns). It is also known as the *Paged List* or *Page-by-Page Iterator* pattern.

We have already laid the groundwork for implementing this pattern. Query execution methods in the DataAccessService class return a CachedRowSet, which is a disconnected cacheable implementation of the RowSet interface (which extends the ResultSet interface). Normally, ResultSet objects produced by database queries are inextricably tied to the database Connection. In other words, they are destroyed once the Connection has been closed, and since well-behaved applications close Connections as part of their task cleanup, these ResultSets cannot 'live' across multiple HTTP requests. CachedRowSets are 'disconnected' (not tied to the Connection), thus they can be used across requests, provided they are stored in the HTTP session. Fortunately, the application already does this.

To implement this pattern in our application, the following steps must be taken:

1. Provide a mechanism for defining how many results should be displayed per page. Using a property in the ApplicationResources.properties file makes this parameter configurable.

2. Modify the SearchResultsAction class to acknowledge a request parameter, 'page,' that indicates which page number should be displayed (defaulting to 1). Use this parameter to calculate sequence numbers of the first and last results that should appear on the page, and store these values as page attributes named 'begin' and 'end.' In addition, set two boolean page attributes named 'atBegin' and 'atEnd' that indicate whether this is the first or last page in the result set.

3. Modify the `<c:forEach>` tag on the `results.jsp` page(s) so that it displays only the specified range of results. This is accomplished by adding these attributes:

- `begin="${pageScope.begin}"`

- `end="${pageScope.end}"`

4. Add links to the page to allow forward backward traversal to the next/previous page (e.g. `http://host/context/action/results?page=${request.page+1}`). Place these links within conditional constructs (e.g. `<c:if>` or `<c:choose>` tags) so that the next page link does not appear if this is the last page, and the previous page link does not appear if this is the first page.

10.6.6 Using XML and XSLT for view presentation

The most forward-looking approach to presenting application views is to use XML and XSLT. An incremental approach to adding XSLT functionality would be to modify the existing HTML templates so that they are in XHTML. Once they are in an XML-compliant format, they can be used as an XML source to which XSLT transformations can be applied. These XSLT transformations would serve as a post-processing step that performed final customizations on presented views. This approach is the least intrusive but ultimately the most costly in terms of performance.

A more robust alternative is to construct the model as an XML document and to use XSLT stylesheets to transform the model into an appropriate view. The beauty of this approach is its inherent flexibility. The application can choose a target format (e.g. HTML, WML, SMIL, VoiceXML) based on the type of device or program making the request. It can then select a specific presentation by choosing a custom XSLT stylesheet appropriate for that target format. This technique realizes the promise of MVC fully: the model is completely decoupled from the view, and the number of views that can be made available is limited only by the number of stylesheets that developers can construct.[1]

Two shortcomings to this approach have impeded its acceptance in the Web application development community. The first is the sluggish performance associated with XSLT transformation; the second is the overall complexity historically associated with XML and XSLT processing.

XSLT performance has been dramatically improved through mechanisms that allow the compilation and caching of stylesheets. Still, there is room for improvement, but performance is no longer the impediment to XSLT acceptance that it once was.

---

[1] Even this number is not a true upper limit, since XSLT stylesheets can be constructed from embedded fragments, thus exponentially increasing the number of possible combinations.

The complexity of both XML and XSLT processing has been reduced signifi-cantly. Early adopters of XML and XSLT had to deal with cumbersome configuration issues and inconsistent APIs. Now virtually all commercial frameworks and server products provide native support for XML processing, and native support for XSLT is not far behind. In addition, frameworks like Cocoon simplify the building of applications that publish content using XSLT as their presentation layer.

Perhaps the most radical simplification in XML and XSLT processing can be found in JSTL's XML tags. These tags not only provide the ability to parse XML documents into a DOM tree, but also the ability to perform direct XSLT transfor-mation on a constructed or imported XML document. Assuming that the controller component has constructed an XML document and put it into the session, and assuming that this component (or some other component) has either imported or constructed an appropriate XSLT style sheet and put *it* into the session, then the controller could route processing to a JSP page as follows:

```
<%@ taglib prefix ="x" uri ="http://java.sun.com/jstl/xml" %>
<x:transform xml ="${sessionScope.xmlDocument}"
             xslt ="${sessionScope.styleSheet}"/>
```

XSLT is an extremely powerful mechanism for transforming XML documents into human-readable presentations, but it is also rather complex. It was hoped that Web designers would ultimately be the ones who create XSLT style sheets, Unfortu-nately, most of their tools do not yet support interactive stylesheet creation, and most designers have not taken it upon themselves to learn XSLT (which, given its complexity, is not surprising).

Yet another alternative is to build a DOM tree using the JSTL <x:parse> tag, and access individual elements (or sets of elements) using the <x:out>, <x:set>, and <x:forEach> tags. The select attribute in each of these tags can be set to an XPath expression that may return an individual element or (with the <x:forEach> tag) a node set. Using this approach, the results.jsp page could be rewritten as in fragment in Figure 10.13.

In this fragment, a variable called listings is constructed as an XML DOM tree from the listingsAsXml session attribute using the <x:parse> tag. (In a properly segmented MVC application, a controller component would have built this XML document and stored it in the session.) The <x:forEach> tag selects each element matching the XPath expression /listings/listing and processes it, displaying the values of elements found within it.

As you can see, there are a number of options available for using XML, XSLT, and XPath functionality to make the selection and generation of application views more dynamic and flexible.

```
<x:parse var="listings" xml="${sessionScope.listingsAsXml}"/>
<x:forEach select="$listings/listings/listing">
    <x:set var="listingId" select="id"/>
    <c:url value="/action/details" var="detailURL" scope="page">
        <c:param name="listingId" value="${listingId}"/>
    </c:url>
    <span class="listingTitle">
        <html:link href="${pageScope.detailURL}">
            <x:out select="title"/>
        </html:link>
    </span>
    <br/>Property Type: <x:out select="typeAsString"/>
    <br/>Offer Type: <x:out select="offerTypeAsString"/>
    <br/>Region: <x:out select="region"/>
    <hr/>
</x:forEach>
```

Figure 10.13   Example of parsing XML documents using the JSTL `<x:parse>` tag

10.6.7 Tracking user behavior

Keeping track of user actions and recording them for later analysis is another capability that can be added to our application. For example, when customers visit the search page and enter criteria for browsing the listing database, their entries could be recorded implicitly. When a customer views the details of a particular listing, this fact could also be saved (in a log or in a database table) for future reference.

This recorded data could be used by our application, and other applications, to perform a number of tasks:

1. Sending targeted e-mails based on tracked behaviors about the availability of properties of a particular type.

2. Reminding customers who have not logged in for an extended time about the existence of the application, through a reminder e-mail (especially useful for subscription Web sites, e.g. to notify inactive customers that their subscription or free trial has lapsed or is about to lapse).

3. Personalizing customer home pages by showing thumbnails of new property listings that satisfy their past search criteria.

4. Keeping anonymous statistics about the popularity of individual listings (based on the results of searches, detailed views, and broker inquiries).

To accomplish this, the Action classes need to be modified to record information about tracked events. The least intrusive approach would be simply to record the events we want to track into a log file. Each log entry would need to contain all the relevant information, including timestamps, customer ids (or an indicator denoting an anonymous visitor), listing ids, and source (search, targeted e-mail, etc.). The format of log records should be standardized enough that those records could be browsed and searched later. Our `LoggingService` class simplifies the process of writing records to a log.

A more methodical approach would record tracked events in a database. This means creating tables that would contain records of well-defined events that need to be tracked, e.g. 'customer login,' 'listing view,' 'customer search.' The main advantage of this approach is that it is much easier to perform analysis by querying a database than by parsing log entries from a text file.

10.7 SUMMARY

Our goal in this chapter was to walk through the process of designing and implementing a Web application. On our Web site, we offer this application for non-commercial tutorial purposes, in a package that includes source code, database schema, and configuration instructions. We think that providing a complete working application is a better starting point than having readers build it themselves from the ground up. The enhancements described in Section 10.6 provide readers with the opportunity to start with a working application and build on it.

10.8 QUESTIONS AND EXERCISES

1. Install and deploy the sample application. Follow the instructions found on the Web site, at http://www.WebAppBuilders.com/... (You will need to register and sign in to download the application package.)
2. What changes need to be made to the `DataAccessService` class to allow the application to work in environments that do not support JNDI lookup for datasources? How could this be done in a way that would still provide runtime configuration options (i.e. without hard-coding database connectivity parameters)?
3. In Section 10.4.2, we mention that we did not implement a custom tag or an includable page to display the navigation bar, because the links presented on the navigation bar would be different on every page (i.e. a page should not present a link to 'itself'). Remember, though, that a parameter in the request URL identifies the page that is currently being displayed. Thus, it is possible to build a reusable mechanism for presenting the navigation bar that uses conditional processing to skip the label and link associated with the current page. Implement this functionality using either an included JSP page or a custom tag, and modify embedded pages to refer to it.
4. Formulate a plan for building the administrative interface described in Section 10.6.1. Include a separate database table containing credentials for administrators.

5. Modify the application to provide the enhancements described in Section 10.6.2 (and in its associated footnote). What changes need to be made to the `profile.jsp` page to support this? What other components need to be modified to enable this functionality?

6. Modify the application to provide the enhancements described in Section 10.6.3 to use a persistent cookie for partner identification. Include the functionality that would also enable automatic login if customers indicate this as a preference in their profiles. What changes must be made to the `profile.jsp` page? What other components need to be modified to enable this functionality?

7. Modify the application to provide the enhancements described in Section 10.6.4, providing caching functionality within the service classes. Include the functionality that would clear the cache on request. Which part of the application should expose this function?

8. Modify the application to provide the enhancements described in Section 10.6.5 to provide a mechanism for paging through large result sets using discrete subsets.

9. What difficulties are likely to arise in maintaining an application that makes use of the 'less intrusive' XML support strategy described in the beginning of Section 10.6.6?

10. Modify the application to implement the model as an XML document, and to use XSLT stylesheets to transform the model into an appropriate view, as described in Section 10.6.6. What are the maintainability and performance improvements over the original approach, and over the less intrusive alternative described earlier in that section? What issues does this approach solve?

BIBLIOGRAPHY

Spielman, S. (2002) *The Struts Framework: A Practical Guide for Programmers.* San Francisco, CA.

Husted, T. *et al.* (2002) *Struts in Action: Building Web Applications with the Leading Java Framework.* Greenwich, CT, Manning Publications.

Malani, P. (2002) UI design with Tiles and Struts. JavaWorld, January 2002.
  `<http://www.javaworld.com/javaworld/jw-01-2002/jw-0104-tilestrut.html>`

Bayern, S. (2002) *JSTL in Action.* Greenwich, CT: Manning Publications.

Kolb, M. (2002) JSTL: The Java Server Pages Standard Tag Library. Presentation at Colorado Software Summit 2002.
  `<http://www.taglib.com/blokware/presentations/css2002/JSTL.ppt>`

Yarger, Rees and King. (1999) *MySQL & mSQL.* Sebastopol, CA: O'Reilly & Associates.

Harrison, P. and McFarland, I. (2002) *Mastering Tomcat Development.* New York, NY: John Wiley & Sons.

11 Emerging Technologies

Rapid expansion of Internet technologies has not come without cost. Technological incompatibilities and inconsistencies have put a strain on the Web application development process. Today, after more than a decade of exponential growth, Internet technologies are reaching the point where they are stable, robust, and part of the mainstream. We are seeing encouraging examples of technology convergence. XHTML is supplanting (if not replacing) HTML, WML is being redefined as an extension to XHTML, and the relationship between XSL, XSLT, XSLFO, and other stylesheet specifications is coming into focus. The most recent specifications from the W3C and other standard-setting bodies (e.g. WAP Forum, OASIS, etc.) concentrate on achieving improvements to accepted and emerging technologies, as well as convergence between them, as opposed to dramatic new directions.

This chapter is devoted to a discussion of the most significant of the emerging technologies, including:

- *Web Services* which represent an important architectural advancement in building distributed Web applications.

- *Resource Description Framework (RDF)* which is currently the leading specification for machine-understandable metadata.

- *XML Query* which supports the extraction of data from XML documents, closing an important gap between the Web world and the database world.

We shall also introduce one particular RDF application, *Composite Capabilities/ Preference Profiles (CC/PP)*, which is a promising platform for serving content across multiple devices and formats, followed by a brief overview of the *Semantic Web* that may very well employ RDF as its foundation.

Finally, we present our speculations and suggestions regarding the future of Web application development frameworks.

11.1 WEB SERVICES

Web Services are distributed Web applications that provide discrete functionality and expose that functionality in a well-defined manner over standard Internet protocols to other Web applications. In other words, they are Web applications that fit into the client-server paradigm, except that the clients are not people but other Web applications.

The type of Web application we have discussed throughout the book has employed an architecture in which the data is provided to a human being—an end user—usually via a Web browser. Using a browser, end users submit HTTP requests (consisting of a URL plus query string parameters, headers, and an optional body) to Web servers. Web servers send back HTTP responses (consisting of headers and a body) for browsers to present to users. The body of the response is some human-readable content such as an HTML page, an image, or a sound.

Web Services work similarly, except that the intended recipient of the response is another Web application. Since the recipient is a software program rather than a person, the response should be *machine-understandable*. Consequently, it must conform to protocols that machines (i.e. computers running Web applications) can understand. If you are writing an application, which will only be used within a very limited environment, you can make your own decisions about how it operates. The goal of Web Services is not only to provide inter-application communication, but also to do so in a uniform, well-defined, open, and extensible manner.

Using a broad definition, applications providing Web Services have been around for a long time. As we have mentioned earlier in the book, the 'server side' of a Web application can be a client that transmits its own requests to other applications. Responses generated by those other applications are consumed by the original Web application, which further processes them to deliver a response to the end user.

Today, the term 'Web Services' means something more: it refers to the set of protocols for defining standardized service descriptions, the mechanisms for publicizing their existence, and the construction, transmission, and processing of Web Service requests. Together, these protocols provide uniformity, extensibility, and interoperability, making it possible for Web Services to work across a variety of environments (including Sun's J2EE and Microsoft's .NET).

11.1.1 SOAP

The most popular protocols for Web Service requests and responses are *XML-RPC* (*XML Remote Procedure Call*) and *SOAP* (*Simple Object Access Protocol*), with SOAP having overtaken XML-RPC as the protocol of choice. SOAP is an application layer protocol for constructing and processing Web Service requests and

```
<?xml version ="1.0" encoding ="UTF-8" ?>
<soap:Envelope xmlns:xsi ="http://www.w3.org/2001/XMLSchema-instance"
               xmlns:xsd ="http://www.w3.org/2001/XMLSchema"
               xmlns:soap ="http://schemas.xmlsoap.org/soap/envelope"
               xmlns:soapenc
                  ="http://schemas.xmlsoap.org/soap/encoding">
  <soap:Body>
    <w:getWeather xmlns:w ="http://www.intlweather.com/services">
        <degreeslong xsi:type ="xsd:float">-73.0</degreeslong>
        <degreeslat xsi:type ="xsd:float">40.0</degreeslat>
        <locale xsi:type ="xsd:string">en/us</locale>
    </w:getWeather>
  </soap:Body>
</soap:Envelope>
```

Figure 11.1   Example of a SOAP request with multiple parameters

responses. It can use HTTP, SMTP, and a variety of other protocols (e.g. messaging protocols like JMS and MQ/MSMQ) to transport requests and responses.

Figure 11.1 shows an example of a simple SOAP request with multiple parameters. The request is represented in XML format. In the example, the Web Service returns local weather information. The intent of the request is to retrieve information about New York weather. For that, you must provide the longitude and latitude of the region, as well as locale information (e.g. en/us), which determines not only the language but also the format for the temperature (Celsius or Fahrenheit) and wind velocity (MPH or km/h).

Note the use of different namespaces to disambiguate SOAP envelope elements, references to XML data types, and service-specific elements. The SOAP envelope contains the body element (this example does not contain an optional header). The body contains a single element defining a remote procedure call, by specifying a method (getWeather) and its arguments (degreeslong, degreeslat, and locale).

The envelope is transported to a SOAP server over a protocol such as HTTP or SMTP. In the case of HTTP, the envelope comprises the body of the HTTP request, which follows the request line (e.g. POST /services HTTP/1.1) and associated headers, as shown in Figure 11.2.

After receiving the request, the SOAP server invokes the specified method with the provided arguments, and generates a response for transmission back to the requesting application. In Figure 11.3, the response contains values for pre-defined response elements, which inform the requestor that the temperature in New York is 25° (Fahrenheit), the conditions are partly cloudy, and the wind is from the southeast at 5 MPH. Since the response is transmitted back to the requestor over HTTP, it includes the appropriate HTTP headers.

A SOAP client can translate this response into a human-readable format. This can be accomplished by using one of the available SOAP APIs or toolkits (e.g.

```
POST /services HTTP/1.1
Host: www.intlweather.com
Content-Type: text/xml; charset ="utf-8"
Content-Length: ...

<?xml version ="1.0" encoding ="UTF-8" ?>
<soap:Envelope xmlns:xsi ="http://www.w3.org/2001/XMLSchema-instance"
               xmlns:xsd ="http://www.w3.org/2001/XMLSchema"
               xmlns:soap ="http://schemas.xmlsoap.org/soap/envelope"
               xmlns:soapenc
                  ="http://schemas.xmlsoap.org/soap/encoding">
  <soap:Body>
    <w:getWeather xmlns:w ="http://www.intlweather.com/services">
        <degreeslong xsi:type ="xsd:float">-73.0</degreeslong>
        <degreeslat xsi:type ="xsd:float">40.0</degreeslat>
        <locale xsi:type ="xsd:string">en/us</locale>
    </w:getWeather>
  </soap:Body>
</soap:Envelope>
```

Figure 11.2   The same SOAP request transmitted over HTTP

```
HTTP/1.1 200 OK
Content-Type: text/xml; charset ="utf-8"
Content-Length: ...

<?xml version ="1.0" encoding ="UTF-8" ?>
<soap:Envelope xmlns:xsi ="http://www.w3.org/2001/XMLSchema-instance"
               xmlns:xsd ="http://www.w3.org/2001/XMLSchema"
               xmlns:soap ="http://schemas.xmlsoap.org/soap/envelope"
               xmlns:soapenc
                  ="http://schemas.xmlsoap.org/soap/encoding">
  <soap:Body>
    <w:getWeatherResponse xmlns:b ="http://www.intlweather.com/services">
        <temperature xsi:type ="xsd:int">25</temperature>
        <tempmode xsi:type ="xsd:string">F</tempmode>
        <conditions xsi:type ="xsd:string">partly cloudy</conditions>
        <windvelocity xsi:type ="xsd:int">5</windvelocity>
        <windvelocityunits xsi:type ="xsd:string">MPH</windvelocityunits>
        <winddirection xsi:type ="xsd:string">SE</winddirection>
    </w:getWeatherResponse>
  </soap:Body>
</soap:Envelope>
```

Figure 11.3   The response to the previous SOAP request

Microsoft SOAP Toolkit, JAXM/SAAJ) or by transforming the body of the response using XSLT into a human-readable format (e.g. HTML, WML, or VoiceXML).

11.1.2 WSDL

Defining a SOAP-based Web Service is only a partial step toward true interoperability. Constructing a SOAP request requires knowledge about the service—the name of the method to be invoked, its arguments, and their datatypes, as well as the response semantics. This knowledge could be available through human-readable documentation, but this falls short of the goal of true interoperability. Since Web Services are meant to be machine-understandable, their semantics (and even their existence) should be exposed to Web applications, so that they could discover and make use of them without human intervention.

WSDL and *UDDI* are designed to close the interoperability gap. WSDL (*Web Services Definition Language*) provides a common language for defining a Web Service and communication semantics. (UDDI, which stands for *Universal Description, Discovery, and Integration,* serves as a mechanism for registering and publishing Web Services. It is covered in the following section.)

Let us examine the Web Service definition shown in Figure 11.4 from the bottom up. The <service> element contains a <documentation> element (to give the service a human-readable description) and a <port> element, bound to the <binding> element with the name WeatherServiceBinding, which is in turn associated (through its type attribute) to the <portType> element with the name WeatherServicePortType. The <port> element contains a <soap:address> element whose location attribute defines the URL that can be used to invoke the service.

The <binding> element defines the transport mechanism (SOAP over HTTP) and the names of operations that may be performed using the service as <operation> elements. In this case, there is just one operation, getWeather (which we saw in the previous section). Specifications for the encoding format for the input and output bodies are included here.

The <portType> element lists names of operations as <operation> elements. Since there is only one operation associated with the service, there is only one <operation> element. It contains <input> and <output> elements, which in turn refer to <message> elements (getWeatherInput and getWeatherOutput). The <message> elements specify references to complex data types, weatherRequest and weatherResponse, respectively. The definitions of complex types (which also make use of XML Schema Datatypes, which were covered in Section 7.1.3) specify components for both input messages (requests) and output messages (responses).

This may seem like overkill for a simple Web Service, and indeed, it is. There are a number of ways to simplify this definition. Our example avoids shortcuts to mention some of the more complex aspects of WSDL and demonstrate the available options.

```xml
<?xml version="1.0" ?>
<definitions name="InternationalWeather"
             targetNames pace="http://www.intlweather.com/weather.wsdl"
             xmlns:tns="http://www.intlweather.com/weather.wsdl"
             xmlns:xsd1="http://www.intlweather.com/weather.xsd"
             xmlns:soap="http://schemas.xmlsoap.org/wsdl/soap/"
             xmlns="http://schemas.xmlsoap.org/wsdl/">
  <types>
    <schema targetNamespace="http://www.intlweather.com/weather.xsd"
            xmlns="http://www.w3.org/2000/10/XMLSchema">
      <element name="weatherRequest">
        <complexType>
          <all>
            <element name="degreeslong" type="float"/>
            <element name="degreeslat" type="float"/>
            <element name="locale" type="string"/>
          </all>
        </complexType>
      </element>
      <element name="weatherResponse">
        <complexType>
          <all>
            <element name="temperature" type="int"/>
            <element name="tempmode" type="string">
            <element name="conditions" type="string">
            <element name="windvelocity" type="int">
            <element name="windvelocityunits" type="string">
            <element name="winddirection" type="string">
          </all>
        </complexType>
      </element>
    </schema>
  </types>

  <message name="getWeatherInput">
    <part name="body" element="xsd1:weatherRequest"/>
  </message>
  <message name="getWeatherOutput">
    <part name="body" element="xsd1:weatherResponse"/>
  </message>

  <portType name="WeatherServicePortType">
    <operation name="getWeather">
      <input message="tns:getWeatherInput"/>
      <output message="tns:getWeatherOutput"/>
    </operation>
  </portType>
```

Figure 11.4 Sample WSDL definition for the Weather Service

```
          <binding name="WeatherServiceBinding"
                  type="tns:WeatherServicePortType">
            <soap:binding style="document"
                          transport="http://schemas.xmlsoap.org/soap/http"/>
            <operation name="getWeather">
              <soap:operation soapAction="getWeather"/>
              <input>
                <soap:body use="literal"/>
              </input>
              <output>
                <soap:body use="literal"/>
              </output>
            </operation>
          </binding>

          <service name="InternationalWeatherService">
            <documentation>My first service</documentation>
            <port name="WeatherServicePort"
                  binding="tns:WeatherServiceBinding">
              <soap:address location="http://www.intlweather.com/services"/>
            </port>
          </service>
        </definitions>
```

Figure 11.4 (*continued*)

11.1.3 UDDI

While WSDL provides a common standard for defining Web Service semantics, UDDI provides the last piece to the interoperability puzzle through its mechanisms for registering and advertising Web Services.

UDDI servers provide two functions: inquiry and publishing. Inquiry allows users to look for Web Services that fit into specific categories (e.g. business name, service name, service type) and match specified search criteria. The inquiry request in Figure 11.5 is a query for businesses whose names contain the word 'weather.' You can see that this UDDI request is also a SOAP request (albeit somewhat simpler than the one found in our original Web Service example).

The results from such inquiries are (naturally) SOAP responses (as shown in Figure 11.6). SOAP clients can parse them to derive information about available Web Services that match the provided search criteria. The clients can then choose a Web Service (from those located by the inquiry), access its WSDL definition, and invoke it. Note that, for brevity, we have omitted the businessKey and serviceKey attributes. These are identifying keys assigned by a UDDI registrar when adding a business or service to the registry.

```
<?xml version="1.0" encoding="UTF-8" ?>
<Envelope xmlns="http://schemas.xmlsoap.org/soap/envelope/">
  <Body>
    <find_business xmlns="urn:uddi-org:api" generic="1.0"
    maxRows="50">
      <findQualifiers/>
      <name>weather</name>
    </find_business>
  </Body>
</Envelope>
```

Figure 11.5 Example of a UDDI request from a SOAP client

```
<?xml version="1.0" encoding="utf-8" ?>
<soap:Envelope xmlns:soap="http://schemas.xmlsoap.org/soap/envelope/"
               xmlns:xsi="http://www.w3.org/2001/XMLSchema-instance"
               xmlns:xsd="http://www.w3.org/2001/XMLSchema">
  <soap:Body>
    <businessList generic="1.0" operator="Microsoft Corporation"
                  truncated="false" xmlns="urn:uddi-org:api">
      <businessInfos>
        <businessInfo businessKey="... ">
          <name>International Weather</name>
          <description xml:lang="en">Weather
            information</description>
          <serviceInfos>
            <serviceInfo serviceKey="... " businessKey="... ">
              <name>InternationalWeatherService</name>
            </serviceInfo>
          </serviceInfos>
        </businessInfo>
        <businessInfo businessKey="... ">
          <name>Weatherwax Dog Kennel</name>
          <serviceInfos/>
        </businessInfo>
        ...
      </businessInfos>
    </businessList>
  </soap:Body>
</soap:Envelope>
```

Figure 11.6 Fragment of a UDDI response

The publishing component of UDDI lets a Web Service provider register their service in a UDDI registry (Figure 11.7). The publishing component accepts SOAP requests to add an entry to the registry, allowing the service provider to specify the service name, description, access point (i.e. the URL), and a reference to the *tModel*

```
<?xml version="1.0" encoding="utf-8" ?>
<soap:Envelope xmlns:soap="http://schemas.xmlsoap.org/soap/envelope/"
               xmlns:xsi="http://www.w3.org/2001/XMLSchema-instance"
               xmlns:xsd="http://www.w3.org/2001/XMLSchema">
  <soap:Body>
    <Service>
      <businessService serviceKey="... " businessKey="... ">
        <name>International Weather</name>
        <bindingTemplates>
          <bindingTemplate bindingKey="... " serviceKey="... " >
            <description xml:lang="en">
              Weather information
            </description>
            <accessPoint URLType="http">
              http://www.internationalweather.com/services"
            </accessPoint>
            <tModelInstanceDetails>
              <tModelInstanceInfo tModelKey="... "/>
            </tModelInstanceDetails>
          </bindingTemplate>
        </bindingTemplates>
      </businessService>
    </Service>
  </soap:Body>
</soap:Envelope>
```

Figure 11.7   Example of a request to publish a Web Service in a UDDI registry

(service type) associated with this service. Note again that we have omitted various key attributes for brevity: `businessKey`, `serviceKey`, `bindingKey`, and finally, `tModelKey`—a key that identifies a specific service type definition also maintained in the UDDI registry.

The Chicken or the Egg?

You may have already noticed that there is a Catch-22 situation with respect to UDDI servers: once you know about them, it is easy to make use of them, but how do you discover the existence of UDDI servers in the same way you use UDDI to discover new Web Services?

The problem is not unlike the 'chicken and the egg' situation associated with DNS (Domain Name Service)—for your system to use DNS to translate domain names into IP addresses, your network configuration must know the IP address of a DNS server. Knowing the name of your DNS server (e.g. `dns.myprovider.com`) is useless, since you need DNS to determine the IP address to which this name resolves.

Analogously, there is no way to 'know' about new UDDI servers, without already 'knowing' about them.

Currently, there are only a small number of centralized UDDI servers, so this problem does not yet manifest itself. As the number of Web Services grows, it will become very difficult (if not impossible) for a small number of servers to support UDDI inquiries. Research is already under way to extend the possibilities associated with UDDI service; using distributed servers like those used for DNS and federated servers like those employed in P2P networks.

In a broad sense, any layered Web application makes use of 'Web Services.' Back-end systems provide loosely defined 'services' to other application components. The importance of SOAP, WSDL and UDDI specifications is in providing more formalized and rigorous definitions of Web Services, and methods for locating, accessing and utilizing them. This makes them structured, modular, and reusable for a wide variety of applications. Web Services functionality provides a platform that will allow many other emerging technologies to flourish.

11.2 RESOURCE DESCRIPTION FRAMEWORK

The next wave of technological advances may very well be powered by *machine-understandable metadata*. Metadata technologies have been slow to gain momentum, but now that the base technologies are consolidating, this is already changing. RDF is a standard that was designed to support machine-understandable metadata, and to enable interoperability between metadata-based applications. Early applications of RDF address real problems in the areas of resource discovery, intelligent software agents, content rating, mobile devices, and privacy preferences. RDF is used to construct metadata models that may be understood by processing agents.

Strictly speaking, RDF is not an XML application, even though XML is used to encode and transport RDF models. XML is not the exclusive mechanism for representing RDF models; other representation mechanisms may be available in the future. (Natively, RDF models are defined as sets of *triples*, as described in the next section.)

11.2.1 RDF and Dublin Core

The Dublin Core (DC) metadata standard predates RDF. It was proposed as an element set for describing a wide range of networked resources. DC's initial design goals were very ambitious and not all of them materialized. What emerged was the simple set of fifteen elements, the semantics of which have been established through long and painful negotiations within the international, cross-disciplinary group that included librarians and computer scientists.

The DC elements cover such core notions as 'Title,' 'Creator,' 'Publisher,' 'Date,' 'Language,' 'Format,' and 'Identifier.' Together with qualifiers, the nouns corresponding to these key concepts can be arranged into simple statements, which enable simple 'pidgin-level' communications. DC elements are easy to use but are not up to the task of communicating complex concepts.

The emergence of RDF breathed new life into the DC specification. RDF provides the formal mechanism for describing DC concepts. More importantly, the DC specification provides the necessary 'semantic grounding' for RDF models through its atomic concepts that were designed for describing networked resources.

The most basic RDF concept is that of a resource, which is any entity represented with a URI. An RDF *triple* is the combination of a *subject*, an *object*, and a *property* (also referred to as *predicate*). Both subjects and properties are RDF resources, while objects may be either resources or *literals* (constants). Our example in Figure 11.8 is the simplified RDF model for this book. The meaning of the model is obvious—it describes the book, by specifying authors and the publisher. RDF models are designed to be *machine-understandable*—their meaning may be interpreted and acted upon by computer programs that do not have any built-in knowledge of the matter (in this case, publishing).

The book resource, which is the object of all three triples in Figure 11.8, is identified by its URI—http://purl.org/net/shklar/wabook. The resource identified with http://purl.org/net/shklar represents the first author of the book and is the subject of one of the triples; the 'Creator' property is represented with http://purl.org/dc/elements/1.1/creator. Similarly, the resource identified with http://www.neurozen.com represents the second author of the book and is the subject of the second triple (the property is the same). The subject of the final

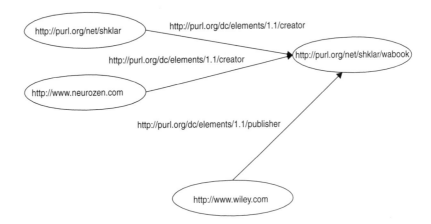

Figure 11.8 Sample RDF model

```
<?xml version="1.0"?>
<rdf:RDF xmlns:rdf="http://www.w3.org/1999/02/22-rdf-syntax-ns#"
         xmlns:dc="http://purl.org/dc/elements/1.1/">

  <rdf:Description rdf:about="http://purl.org/net/shklar/wabook">
      <dc:creator>http://www.neurozen.com</dc:creator>
      <dc:creator>http://purl.org/net/shklar</dc:creator>
      <dc:publisher>http://www.wiley.com</dc:description>
  </rdf:Description>
</rdf:RDF>
```

Figure 11.9 XML Representation of the RDF model in Figure 11.8

triple is the resource representing the 'John Wiley & Sons' publishing company; the 'Publisher' property is represented with `http://purl.org/dc/elements/1.1/publisher`.

The XML representation of the model is shown in Figure 11.9. The DC vocabulary of atomic concepts is identified by its URI—`http://purl.org/dc/elements/1.1/`—and the semantic grounding of RDF properties is achieved by mapping them to DC concepts 'Creator' and 'Publisher.' The triples in Figure 11.8 all relate to the common object represented by the `<rdf:Description>` element. The `<dc:creator>` and `<dc:publisher>` elements represent RDF properties, and the content of these elements represent subjects of their respective triples.

By the nature of XML, the structure in Figure 11.9 is hierarchical, which creates the obvious impedance mismatch problem for arbitrary RDF models. In this example, the hierarchical nature of XML works to our advantage, resulting in the very compact representation. It gets a lot more complicated for complex models.

The same resource may be the subject of one triple, and the object of another. In Figure 11.11, we show the representation of the original model with two additional triples that specify the creation date for both the book and the publisher. The creation date for the book is its publication date, '2003-05.' while the creation date for the publisher is the foundation date of the company='1807'. Notice, that the publisher resource—`http://www.wiley.com`—is the object of the `<dc:publisher>` property and the object of the `<dc:created>` property.

The structure of the XML representation in Figure 11.11 did not change all that much compared to the XML document in Figure 11.9. However, you can recognize the early signs of trouble—the resource identified with `http://www.wiley.com` is referenced in two different places, which is not the case in the model (Figure 11.10). In XML representations of complex models, there may be numerous references to different resources, which is the indication of the impedance mismatch problem we mentioned earlier.

The hierarchical nature of XML makes it impractical to process XML representations of RDF models directly. Instead, RDF processors use such representations

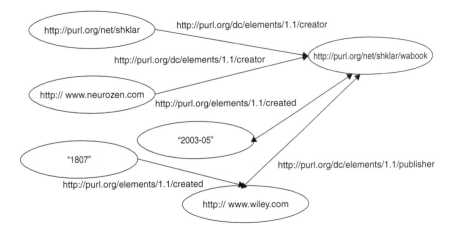

Figure 11.10   Modified RDF model from Figure 11.8

```xml
<?xml version="1.0"?>
<rdf:RDF xmlns:rdf="http://www.w3.org/1999/02/22-rdf-syntax-ns#"
        xmlns:dc="http://purl.org/dc/elements/1.1/">

  <rdf:Description rdf:about="http://purl.org/net/shklar/wabook">
      <dc:creator>http://www.neurozen.com</dc:creator>
      <dc:creator>http://purl.org/net/shklar</dc:creator>
      <dc:publisher>http://www.wiley.com</dc:description>
      <dc:created>2003-05</dc:created>
  </rdf:Description>
  <rdf:Description rdf:about="http://www.wiley.com">
      <dc:created>1807</dc:created>
  </rdf:Description>
</rdf:RDF>
```

Figure 11.11   Adding information about the Publisher to the Model in Figure 11.9

as input for constructing RDF graphs. In other words, RDF is more than another XML application. It is a separate specification based on an entirely different non-hierarchical model. RDF serves the purpose of expressing complex interrelationships between Internet resources. Its long-term goal is to enable automated reasoning in the space of resources, their properties, and relationships.

Persistent URLs

You may have noticed that addresses of Dublin Core elements refer to purl.org. Remember, back in Chapter 3 we discussed that a URI (Uniform Resource Identifier) may be either a URL (Uniform Resource Locator) or a URN (Uniform Resource Name). By definition, URNs do not change when pages move.

URNs used to be a theoretical notion, but `purl.org` is an early attempt to make it practical. The name of the site stands for 'Persistent URL.' It is a public service site, which makes it possible to assign persistent names to Internet resources. (Think of it as an open source/public domain equivalent to AOL's proprietary 'keywords' if you like.)

This is exactly what we did with the book resource—`http://purl.org/net/shklar/wabook`. At the moment, this URI maps to `http://wiley.com/WileyCDA/WileyTitle/productCd-0471486566.html`, which is a transient address. Not to worry—if Wiley decides to reorganize their site, all we need to do is change the mapping on the `purl.org` site and the URN would continue to work. As long as we distribute the URN and not the physical address of the page, and make sure that it stays current, we will be all right.

11.2.2 RDF Schema

The RDF Schema specification aims at constraining the model context by introducing the notion of *model validity*. This is quite different from the validity of XML documents—a valid XML document may represent an invalid RDF model. Remember, XML is just one of many representation vehicles for RDF documents.

RDF Schema enables the definition of new resources as specializations of the ones that already exist. This makes it possible to define new concepts by semantically grounding them to existing specifications. For example, we can take advantage of the Dublin Core 'creator' property and its associated semantic concept in defining two new properties—`firstAuthor` and `secondAuthor` (Figure 11.12).

As you can see, both new properties are defined as specialization of the `dc:creator` property through `rdfs:subclassOf`, which is defined in the RDF Schema specification. The `rdfs:necessity` property, which is also defined in the RDF Schema specification, serves to express occurrence constraints—a book always has at least one author, but may have two or more; only one author may appear in the particular position on the cover. Note that the order of triples representing the `dc:creator` property in Figures 11.9 and 11.11 is arbitrary and not semantically meaningful.

Now that we have defined our new properties and specified the authoritative location of the new schema (`rdfs:isDefinedBy`), we can modify the model in Figure 11.11 to take advantage of the new specification (Figure 11.13). As you see, we introduce the additional name space 'book' and use it to qualify the new properties.

To repeat the obvious, RDF Schema is not an alternative to the XML Schema. Figures 11.13 and 11.14 both represent valid XML documents, but the model in Figure 11.14 is not valid—it violates the `rdfs:necessity` constraint imposed on

```
<?xml version="1.0"?>
<rdf:RDF xmlns:rdf="http://www.w3.org/1999/02/22-rdf-syntax-ns#"
    xmlns:rdfs="http://www.w3.org/2000/01/rdf-schema#"
    xmlns:dc="http://purl.org/dc/elements/1.1/">

<rdf:Property
  rdf:about="http://purl.org/net/shklar/rdfschema/sample/firstAuthor">
    <rdfs:subClassOf
      rdf:resource="http://purl.org/dc/elements/1.1/creator"/>
    <rdfs:necessity
      rdf:href="http://www.w3.org/TR/WD-RDF-Schema#ExactlyOne"/>
    <rdfs:label xml:lang="en-US">First Author</rdfs:label>
    <rdfs:comment xml:lang="en-US">
      The author whose name appears first on the book cover.
    </rdfs:comment>
    <rdfs:isDefinedBy
      rdf:resource="http://purl.org/net/shklar/rdfschema/sample/"/>
</rdf:Property>
<rdf:Property
  rdf:about="http://purl.org/net/shklar/rdfschema/sample/secondAuthor">
  <rdfs:subClassOf
    rdf:resource="http://purl.org/dc/elements/1.1/creator"/>
    <rdfs:necessity
      rdf:href="http://www.w3.org/TR/WD-RDF-Schema#ZeroOrOne"/>
  <rdfs:label xml:lang="en-US">Second Author</rdfs:label>
  <rdfs:comment xml:lang="en-US">
    The author whose name appears second on the book cover.
  </rdfs:comment>
  <rdfs:isDefinedBy
      rdf:resource="http://purl.org/net/shklar/rdfschema/sample/"/>
</rdf:Property>
</rdf:RDF>
```

Figure 11.12 Sample RDF schema

```
<?xml version="1.0"?>
<rdf:RDF xmlns:rdf="http://www.w3.org/1999/02/22-rdf-syntax-ns#"
      xmlns:dc="http://purl.org/dc/elements/1.1/"
      xmlns:book="http://purl.org/net/shklar/rdfschema/sample/">

  <rdf:Description rdf:about="http://purl.org/net/shklar/wabook">
      <book:secondAuthor>http://www.neurozen.com</book:secondAuthor>
      <book:firstAuthor>http://purl.org/net/shklar</book:firstAuthor>
      <dc:publisher>http://www.wiley.com</dc:description>
      <dc:created>2003-05</dc:created>
  </rdf:Description>
  <rdf:Description rdf:about="http://www.wiley.com">
      <dc:created>1807</dc:created>
  </rdf:Description>
</rdf:RDF>
```

Figure 11.13 Taking advantage of the schema in Figure 11.12

```
<?xml version="1.0"?>
<rdf:RDF xmlns:rdf="http://www.w3.org/1999/02/22-rdf-syntax-ns#"
      xmlns:dc="http://purl.org/dc/elements/1.1/"
      xmlns:book="http://purl.org/net/shklar/rdfschema/sample/">

  <rdf:Description rdf:about="http://purl.org/net/shklar/wabook">
    <book:firstAuthor> http://www.neurozen.com</book:firstAuthor>
    <book:firstAuthor>http://purl.org/net/shklar</book:firstAuthor>
    <dc:publisher>http://www.wiley.com</dc:description>
    <dc:created>2003-05</dc:created>
  </rdf:Description>
  <rdf:Description rdf:about="http://www.wiley.com">
    <dc:created>1807</dc:created>
  </rdf:Description>
</rdf:RDF>
```

Figure 11.14   An invalid version of the model in Figure 11.13

the firstAuthor property in Figure 11.12. RDF Schema provides the same service for RDF models as the XML Schema for XML documents—enables specialized applications.

11.3 COMPOSITE CAPABILITY/PREFERENCE PROFILES

One of the early applications of RDF is the *Composite Capabilities/Preference Profiles* (CC/PP) specification, which is the joint effort of W3C and the Wireless Access Protocol (WAP) Forum. The idea is quite simple—let the devices and user agents describe themselves and make those descriptions available to smart services that would tailor their responses accordingly. User agents that run on different platforms may expect different content types (e.g. XML, WML, HTML, etc.) and structures (e.g. different arrangement into tables and cards or different use of graphics).

The flexibility of RDF makes it possible to create self-describing device specifications based on their screen size, keyboard (if any), display characteristics, etc. Devices are represented as composites of features, and properly constructed services do not need to be modified every time a new device comes out. Services can combine information about devices and user agents with information about connection bandwidth and use it dynamically to customize output.

Targeted output transformations lend themselves to the application of XSLT technology. XSLT stylesheets get composed from parameterized feature-specific components. An efficient server would optimize stylesheet construction by caching components as well as intermediate composites. For example, caching device-specific stylesheets that are constructed based on device profiles and combining them with stylesheet components that are determined by the operating system, user agent software, and connection bandwidth.

```
<?xml version="1.0"?>
<rdf:RDF xmlns:rdf="http://www.w3.org/1999/02/22-rdf-syntax-ns#"
         xmlns:prf="http://www.wapforum.org/profiles/UAPROF/ccppschema-
         20000405#">
  <rdf:Description rdf:ID="XYZ 123">
    <prf:component>
      <rdf:Description rdf:ID="HardwarePlatform">
        <rdf:type rdf:resource=
             "http://www.wapforum.org/profiles/UAPROF/ccppschema-
             20000405#HardwarePlatform"/>
        <prf:CPU>Dual: XYZ Special</prf:CPU>
        <prf:Vendor>XYZ Corp.</prf:Vendor>
        <prf:Model>123</prf:Model>
        <prf:Keyboard>PhoneKeypad</prf:Keyboard>
        <prf:ScreenSize>200x240</prf:ScreenSize>
        <prf:ImageCapable>No</prf:ImageCapable>
      </rdf:Description>
    </prf:component>
  </rdf:Description>
</rdf:RDF>
```

Figure 11.15 Sample device description

Figure 11.15 contains a CC/PP-compliant description of the device '123' from the 'XYZ Corporation'. In this example, `rdf` and `prf` prefixes are bound to URIs for 'RDF Syntax' and the WAP Forum's 'User Agent Profile' namespaces, correspondingly. The first element of the specification is `rdf:Description` for our device; it contains only one specification component that describes device hardware. The `rdf:type` element references the schema element that identifies the hardware platform. Next, `prf:CPU` defines the default CPU, `prf:ScreenSize` defines the default screen size, etc.

Figure 11.16 contains CC/PP-compliant descriptions of software for the same device. It includes two separate components that describe the device operating system and the user agent. The OS is our hypothetical 'XYZ-OS,' and acceptable content is limited to `text/plain` and `text/vnd.wap.wml` (`prf:OSName` and `prf:CcppAccept`). The user agent is the particular version of Mozilla that supports tables (`prf:BrowserName`, `prf:BrowserVersion`, and `prf:TablesCapable`).

The semantic grounding of CC/PP concepts is based on existing specifications. For example, acceptable values for `prf:CcppAccept` are MIME types, and acceptable values for `prf:Vendor` and `prf:Model` come from industry registries. This 'by reference' approach to defining semantics is well-suited for the real world. There are a growing number of CC/PP specifications for wireless devices developed and maintained by real world equipment manufacturers.

Individual devices and user agents often differ from default configurations. For example, my personal version of the 'XYZ 123' device may have an optional

```
<?xml version="1.0"?>
<rdf:RDF xmlns:rdf="http://www.w3.org/1999/02/22-rdf-syntax-ns#"
        xmlns:prf=
          "http://www.wapforum.org/profiles/UAPROF/ccppschema-
          20000405#">
  <rdf:Description rdf:ID="XYZ 123">
    <prf:component>
      <rdf:Description rdf:ID="SoftwarePlatform">
        <rdf:type rdf:resource=
            "http://www.wapforum.org/profiles/UAPROF/ccppschema-
            20000405#SoftwarePlatform"/>
        <prf:OSName>XYZ-OS</prf:OSName>
        <prf:CcppAccept>
          <rdf:Bag>
            <rdf:li>text/plain</rdf:li>
            <rdf:li>text/vnd.wap.wml</rdf:li>
          </rdf:Bag>
        </prf:CcppAccept>
      </rdf:Description>
    </prf:component>
    <prf:component>
      <rdf:Description rdf:ID="BrowserUA">
        <rdf:type rdf:resource=
            "http://www.wapforum.org/profiles/UAPROF/ccppschema-
            20000405#BrowserUA"/>
        <prf:BrowserName>Mozilla</prf:BrowserName>
        <prf:BrowserVersion>Symbian</prf:BrowserVersion>
        <prf:TablesCapable>Yes</prf:TablesCapable>
      </rdf:Description>
    </prf:component>
  </rdf:Description>
</rdf:RDF>
```

Figure 11.16   Sample description of device software

screen, and may be image capable. Fortunately, it is possible to incorporate default configurations by reference as in Figure 11.17.

The `prf:Defaults` element references the default profile from Figure 11.15, which we assume to be available from `http://www.xyz-wireless.com/123Profile`. Here, `prf:ScreenSize` and `prf:ImageCapable` override default properties of the device. The resulting profile would be uploaded to the profile registry either when the device first goes online, or after it is modified. The server-side agent that controls automated assembly of the XSLT stylesheet would interpret the profile. Ideally, this stylesheet would produce markup that can take advantage of optional features added to the device.

CC/PP, in combination with XML and XSLT, enables applications that can serve content to the wide variety of desktop and wireless devices. Most importantly,

```
<?xml version="1.0"?>
<rdf:RDF xmlns:rdf="http://www.w3.org/1999/02/22-rdf-syntax-ns#"
        xmlns:prf=
        "http://www.wapforum.org/profiles/UAPROF/ccppschema-20000405#">
  <rdf:Description
    about="http://www.my-wireless-service.com/registry/123675894">
    <prf:component>
     <rdf:Description rdf:ID="HardwarePlatform">
       <rdf:type rdf:resource=
           "http://www.wapforum.org/profiles/UAPROF/ccppschema-
           20000405#HardwarePlatform"/>
       <prf:Defaults
           rdf:resource="http://www.xyz-wireless.com/123Profile"/>
       <prf:ScreenSize>220x280</prf:ScreenSize>
       <prf:ImageCapable>Yes</prf:ImageCapable>
     </rdf:Description>
    </prf:component>
  </rdf:Description>
</rdf:RDF>
```

Figure 11.17   Individual hardware profile

properly constructed applications would require minimal or no modification to
expand support to new and modified devices and software platforms.

11.4 SEMANTIC WEB

The Semantic Web is the major new effort on the part of the World Wide Web
Consortium. It aims to create the next generation Internet infrastructure, where
information has well-defined meaning, making it possible for people and programs
to cooperate with each other. The critical part is to associate data with meaning, and
here the important role belongs to RDF and its descendants. In the long term, we
expect that RDF in conjunction with other standards such as XML, WSDL, SOAP,
and UDDI will serve as the foundation for Semantic Web applications.

When RDF first came out a few years ago, people often thought of the Semantic
Web as a collection of RDF applications. New RDF-based specifications, including the *DARPA Agent Markup Language (DAML)* and the *Ontology Inference Layer
(OIL)*, strengthened the belief that RDF would be the foundation of the Semantic Web.

However, it soon became clear that it is going to be some time until DAML
and OIL applications would be practical. As a result, more and more people are
taking a wider view of the Semantic Web, including the possibility of using existing
standards in conjunction with RDF models for building advanced Web services.

Applications that benefit from the use of machine-understandable metadata range from information retrieval to system integration.

Machine-understandable metadata is emerging as a new foundation for component-based approaches to application development. Web services represent the latest advancement in the context of distributed component-based architectures. Whether applications make use of RDF, or are trying to achieve similar goals by using XML, WSDL, UDDI, SOAP, and XSL, they create fertile grounds for the future.

11.5 XML QUERY LANGUAGE

As the scope and variety of XML applications have grown, so have the integration requirements associated with those applications, and with them the necessity to query XML-structured information. The convergence and consolidation of XML specifications made it practical to define uniform query facilities for extracting data from both real and virtual XML documents, with the ultimate goal to access and query XML information as a distributed database.

The challenge is that XML documents are very different from relational databases. Instead of tables where almost every column has a value, we have to deal with distributed hierarchies, and with optional elements that may or may not be present in a particular document. Relational query languages such as SQL are thus not suited for XML data.

The XML Query language, XQuery, is still being designed by W3C. Even so, there are already numerous implementations based on the early specifications. XQuery combines the notions of query and traversal. The traversal component serves to define the query context, which is determined by the current XML element and its location in the DOM tree. The query component serves to evaluate conditions along different axis (element, attribute, etc.) in the query context. Both components are involved in evaluating an expression.

For example, consider the sample XML document (sample.xml) from Chapter 7 (Figure 7.1). We modified this example to support unique identifiers for individual books by adding the `<isbn>` element (Figure 11.18). We shall make use of the unique identifiers later in this section to demonstrate multi-document queries.

All XQuery expressions in Figure 11.19 are designed to select books written by Rich Rosen. The first expression uses full syntax to define traversal from the document root down to the author element. Notice that the traversal expression is composed of slash-separated axis-selection criteria. Here, 'child::' determines the element axis, 'child::*' means that any element edge should be investigated, and 'child::author' limits the traversal paths to those that lead to `<author>` elements. The predicate enclosed in the pair of square brackets establishes selection conditions, limiting acceptable `<author>` elements to those that have 'firstName' and 'lastName' attributes set to 'Rich' and 'Rosen,' respectively.

```
<?xml version="1.0" standalone="yes"?>
<!-- XML example for the XQuery section of the Web Architecture book
-->
<!DOCTYPE books SYSTEM "books_plus_isbn.dtd">
<books>
<book status="In Print">
<title>Web Application Architecture</title>
<subtitle> Principles, protocols and practices</subtitle>
<author firstName="Leon" lastName="Shklar"/>
<author firstName="Rich" lastName="Rosen"/>
<isbn>0471486566</isbn>
<info>
<pages count="500"/>
<price usd="45" bp="27.50"/>
<publication year="2003" source="&jw;"/>
</info>
<summary>An in-depth examination of the basic concepts and general
principles associated with Web application development.
</summary>
</book>
...
</books>
```

Figure 11.18   Modified sample.xml file from Figure 7.1

```
document("sample.xml")/child::*/child::*/child::author
    [attribute::firstName = "Rich" and
    attribute::lastName = "Rosen"]
document("sample.xml")/*/*/author[@firstName = "Rich" and
    @lastName = "Rosen"]
document("sample.xml")/**/author[@firstName = "Rich" and
    @lastName = "Rosen"]
document("sample.xml")/books/book/author[@firstName = "Rich" and
    @lastName = "Rosen"]
```

Figure 11.19   Sample XQuery expressions

The second expression is identical to the first, except that it makes use of the abbreviated syntax, which includes the default selection of the element axis. The third expression, while producing identical results for 'sample.xml,' has somewhat different semantics—it results in evaluating all paths along the element axis that originate at the document root and lead to the <author> element, regardless of the number of hops.

Finally, the fourth expression contains very explicit instructions for the evaluation engine to only consider element edges through the <books> and <book> element nodes. It is easy to see that as far as performance is concerned, this is the least

```
<?xml version="1.0" standalone="yes"?>
<!-- XML example - sales log -->
<!DOCTYPE books SYSTEM "book_sales_daily_log.dtd">
<records date="05/12/2003">
<record isbn="0471486566"/>
<record isbn="... "/>
...
</records>
```

Figure 11.20   Daily sales log in XML format

expensive option for the evaluation engine, while the third expression is potentially the most expensive option.

Notice that the syntax and semantics of XQuery expressions are closely related to XPath—the simple, specialized query and traversal language that we discussed briefly in the context of XSLT (Section 7.4.1). This is not a coincidence—XQuery designers made every effort to be consistent with existing XML specifications.

Of course, there has to be more to the XML query language than path expressions. The language has to provide ways to express complex conditions that involve multiple documents and path expressions, and to control format of the result.

For example, suppose we want to analyze book sales logs that are collected daily in XML format (Figure 11.20). The sales log, which is stored in the file sales_log.xml has very simple format—the root element <records> contains the 'date' attribute; every individual <record> element corresponds to a single sale and contains the single attribute that serves as ISBN reference. We need a report on the sale of books that reach at least one hundred copies per day.

The query to generate such a sales report is shown in Figure 11.21. The 'for' clause implements iteration through <book> elements in sample.xml. Here, the '$i' variable is always bound to the current element in the set. The 'let' clause defines the join and produces the binding between the <book> element and

```
for $i in document("sample.xml")/*/book
let $s := document("sales_log.xml")/*/record[@isbn = $i/isbn]
where count ($s) > 99
return
<active-book>
    {
        $i/title,
        $i/isbn,
        <sales>{count($s)}</sales>
    }
</active-book>
sortby (sales) descending
```

Figure 11.21   Sample query

<record> elements in the `sales_log.xml` file. The `count($s)` > 99 condition in the 'where' clause eliminates all bindings that do not include at least one hundred sales records.

The 'return' clause, which determines output format, is executed once for every binding that was not eliminated by conditions in the 'where' clause. It produces units of output that are sorted according to the 'sortby' clause. For every execution of the 'return' clause, the '$i' variable is bound to the current <book> element, which provides context for path expressions in the 'return' clause ('$i/title' and '$i/isbn').

XQuery is a very complex language. We did not even scratch the surface in our brief discussion. There are many different kinds of expressions that were not covered, as well as the whole issue of XQuery types and their relationship to the XML Schema. Still, the objective was to provide the flavor of language expressions and query construction.

11.6 THE FUTURE OF WEB APPLICATION FRAMEWORKS

Although Web application frameworks have come a long way during the course of the last few years, there are still outstanding issues with currently available frameworks that aggravate existing problems in Web application development and deployment.

11.6.1 One more time: separation of content from presentation

Foremost among the outstanding issues is the difficulty that arises when content and presentation are mixed. When this mixture occurs, collisions are bound to occur between those responsible for the development and maintenance of a Web application, namely web page designers and programmers. There is still no framework that enforces module-level separation of responsibility. This means that input from both designers and programmers is required to create and modify Web application modules. Depending on the framework, either designers must provide input for code modules, or programmers must provide input for page view modules. Even MVC-compliant frameworks like Struts do not have all the answers. The 'view' component in these frameworks is supposed to be the responsibility of page designers, but the technologies used (e.g. JSPs) are still too complex for non-programmers to handle on their own.

The inefficiency that arises from this situation cannot be understated. The current state of affairs dictates that designers first come up with a page layout based on creative input, which programmers then modify to embed programming constructs. In all probability, such a module becomes a hodgepodge of design elements and programming constructs that neither programmer nor designer has control over. Efforts employed by various frameworks to separate these elements within a module have not been entirely successful. In theory, designers could make direct changes to the module. In practice, a seemingly simple change in page layout made by a designer may require a complete reworking of the module. Programmers must either embed the constructs they need in the new layout all over again, or try to fit new and modified design elements into the existing module.

Since we have been bringing up the issue of separating content from presentation throughout the book, it is probably about time we proposed some solutions. A solution to this problem would require a two-pronged approach. First, the next generation of Web application frameworks would need to enforce a cleaner separation between programming logic modules (application code), which represent the Controller in the MVC model, and presentation modules ('pages'), which represent the View. Application code should establish a page context that determines the set of discrete display components that could be selected for presentation on the page. Secondly, the tools used to develop Web applications, especially front-end design tools, need to catch up with the rest of the technology, and support integration and cooperation with these frameworks.

As we suggested earlier, pages should be structured as templates that use markup languages such as HTML, WML, VoiceXML, and SMIL. Stylesheet technologies like CSS and XSLT should be used to provide flexible formatting. Page templates should be 'owned' and maintained by page designers, who use display components found in the page context. Programmers would be responsible for making these components available to designers through standard uniform interfaces. The display components should support a simple limited set of programmatic constructs for dynamic content generation through iteration, conditional logic and external resource inclusion. The simplicity is important because it is designers, not programmers, who own and maintain the templates.

Designers should be the ones who decide how to present the results, and they should be able to make these decisions without requiring programmer assistance. Making a clean separation in focus between application code and presentation views helps ensure that this will happen.

Keeping Complex Processing Out of the Page

We want to repeat that the page is not the appropriate place for complex business logic, or even for deciding which of several possible views should be presented. If such processing is required, its place is within the application code.

When an application module produces a discrete atomic result, it can be included in the page context as an explicit display component that the designer can use in the presentation. For example, a processing component that determines the 'state' of a transaction performed by the application (e.g. 'completed' or 'in progress') should set the value of a display component in the page context that reports this state. Designers can map different states to messages of their choosing (e.g. 'This transaction is still in progress. Please wait... ') and make use of this in the page layout. (Note that the actual message is not in the realm of application code, so that modifying it does not require a code change.)

On the other hand, when the difference between the possible results of such processing is dramatic enough, the application code should make a choice as to which page should present the results, rather than deferring the decision between coarse-grained presentation alternatives to the page itself. In other words, if the presentation to be employed when the state is 'completed' is radically different from the one desired when the state is 'in progress', it may not be advisable to expose the state to application designers within the page context. Doing this would lead to several complete alternate presentations embedded in one page. Instead, the application code should choose between different templates. Each presentation is an individual template that is the designer's responsibility.

All the aforementioned suggestions are *feasible* but not *enforced* within existing frameworks. We hope to see that changed in next generation frameworks.

11.6.2 The right tools for the job

The second facet of the solution is to make the tools used by page designers functional within these new frameworks. Today, page designers rarely code HTML by hand; they make use of automated page design tools such as Macromedia Dreamweaver and Microsoft FrontPage. For these tools to work properly within the kind of frameworks described above, they would need to provide support for the dynamic constructs that can be embedded within a page.

For example, support for iterative constructs in these tools could be designed to allow creation of a `foreach` block where the substitution variables are populated with data dynamically generated by the tool, so that designers can get an idea of what the final result would look like. A more sophisticated approach would be to integrate the tool with the development environment, so that the tool had knowledge of what substitution variable names were available from the page context, what their data types and likely sizes are, etc. Similar support could be provided for constructs used for conditional logic and external resource inclusion.

Figure 11.22 shows a page fragment using JSTL tags for iterative and conditional processing. Designers need to see the results of their work as they progress, but attempting to preview the JSP fragment shown in Figure 11.22 would not work: browsers would ignore the JSP tags and display the substitution variables (e.g. `${transactiondata.order_number}`) as is (see Figure 11.24).

To enable tighter integration between front-end design tools and back-end application frameworks, the design tools should have a browser preview function that understands the iterative and conditional constructs used in the underlying framework. At

```
<table border="1" align="center">
   <tr>
      <td valign="bottom" align="center"><b>Order<br>Number</b></td>
      <td valign="bottom" align="center"><b>Customer<br>ID</b></td>
      <td valign="bottom" align="center"><b>Total<br>Amount</b></td>
      <td valign="bottom" align="center"><b>Completed?</b></td>
   </tr>
   <c:foreach var="transactiondata"
              items="${sessionScope.transactionResults}">
   <tr>
   <td align="left">${transactiondata.order_number}</td>
   <td align="left">${transactiondata.customer_id}</td>
   <td align="left">${transactiondata.total_amount}</td>
   <td align="center">
      <c:if test="${transactiondata.completed}">*</c:if>
   </td>
   </tr>
   </c:foreach>
</table>
```

Figure 11.22   Example of page fragment using JSTL 'foreach' and 'if' tags

the very least, they should mock up an appropriate page layout, based on heuristic definitions provided for each of the display components, presenting 'dummy' data of appropriate type and length so that the browser preview is meaningful to the designer.

Figure 11.23 is a mockup of a dialog box that could be used in a page design tool, to specify how results from the 'foreach' tag should be presented when the designer previews the page. Sample browser previews of results (with and without framework integration) are shown in Figures 11.24 and 11.25. In a more integrated environment, the design tool might have access to application configuration information so that it can derive these heuristic definitions directly.

Advances in Web application frameworks indicate that we are moving in the right direction. Smarter frameworks already provide intelligence in their iteration constructs (e.g. the 'foreach' directives/tags in Velocity and JSTL) to make them *class agnostic*. In other words, they don't care what kind of object is returned from a data request, as long as it is an object that they can somehow iterate over (e.g. array, `Enumeration`, `Iterator`, `Collection`, `Vector`). This may enable more seamless integration between front-end design tools and the application framework. It would be nice to see these class-agnostic constructs extended to support tabular objects as well (e.g. `RowSets`, collections of JavaBeans, `Lists` of `Map` objects).

11.6.3 Simplicity

Finally, the Web application development world is faced with a more global problem. As developers and designers, perhaps foremost among our cardinal sins is our failure

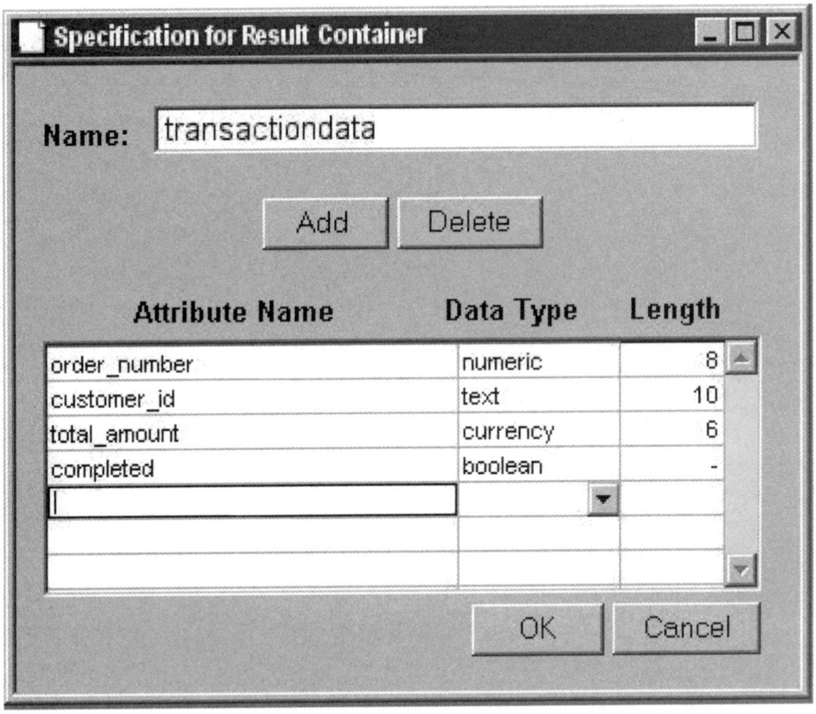

Figure 11.23 Dialog box for specifying content to be displayed by an iterative page construct

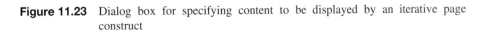

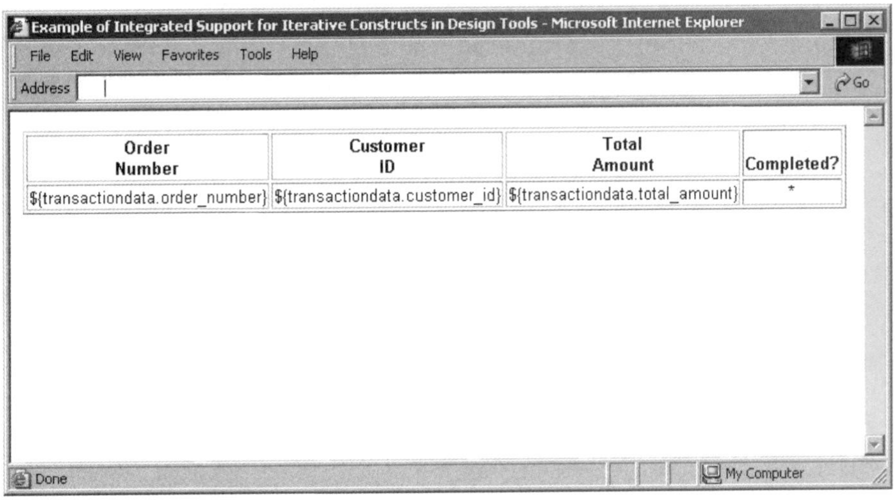

Figure 11.24 Browser preview of the page fragment without framework integration

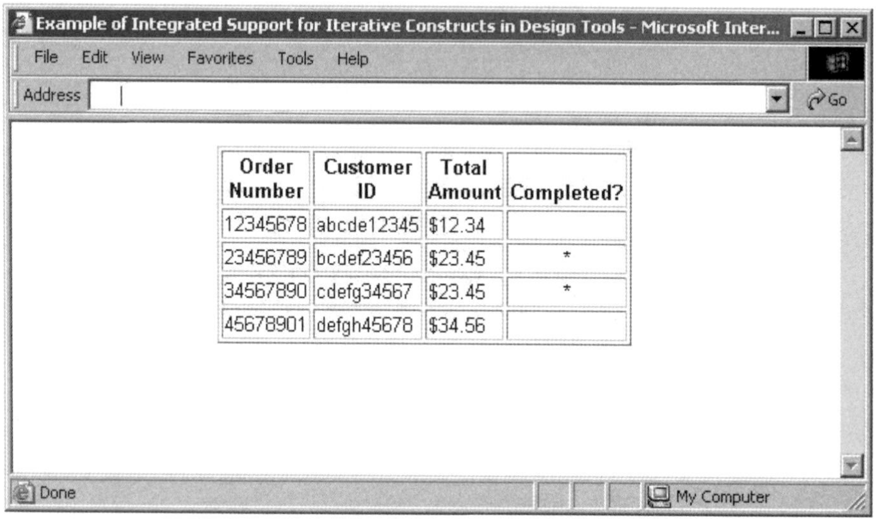

Figure 11.25 Browser preview of the page fragment with framework integration (mockup)

to keep the simple things simple. We want to ensure maximum flexibility, especially when developing APIs and tools that others will use, but we often do so at the cost of providing simple ways of doing simple things. This can make the tools difficult to use by anyone—except perhaps the developers themselves! This has become a major concern in the Web application development community. There have even been online debates among developers about 'civil disobedience' against overly complicated specifications that make it difficult to do simple things in a simple way.

Part of the problem in the Web application framework space is the difference in perspective between developers and the supposed target audience of the presentation-level tools, the page designers. Developers see it as 'no big deal' to 'simply' write a program or script, insert a code snippet, or compile and build a tool. This is why programmatic approaches appeal more to them than to page designers. But the price for using programmatic approaches is that programmers must 'get involved' in the maintenance of the view component. This means that programmers and not designers must implement even the most trivial design changes.

This is an inefficient use of staff resources. Moreover, programmers do not like recurring requests to 'tweak' page layouts. Layout changes requested by creative and business staff may be subtle and significant (to *them*), but to programmers those changes seem trivial, especially when they are called upon to make such changes repeatedly. When the nature of the application development approach requires that programmers be the ones who make such changes, the flexibility and viability of the application suffer, since seemingly trivial tasks wind up being inordinately complex. Page designers (or even site administrators) should be able to make these changes themselves, without programmer intervention.

Using programmers to perform trivial tasks is not just a misapplication of staff resources; it is also an inordinate waste of time for the entire organization. When programmers make changes to code, the code must go through an entire 'build' cycle, where it is recompiled, unit tested, integration tested, packaged for deployment, deployed to a 'test' environment for functional and regression testing, and finally deployed to the production environment. Changes made at the presentation level (or through an administrative interface) can bypass the recompilation, packaging, and unit testing phases. Designers can preview them locally, approve, and deploy to production.

One More Reason

This brings us back to another reason why we do not want programmers creating markup as part of the application code.

Imagine an application that invokes the Weather Service we described earlier in the chapter. Suppose this application provides all the information obtained from the Weather Service in a page fragment that includes formatting, as shown in Figure 11.26. If it were decided by creative or business people that this formatting should be changed (e.g. the temperature should stand out by itself in large red text), this would require a change to the code rather than the page template.

By inserting individual data items associated with the Weather Service into the page context as discrete display components, we bring the layout completely under the control of the page designers, allowing them to change it themselves (as shown in Figures 11.27 and 11.28).

Designers want ready-made, user-friendly tools that do not require them to become programmers. Perhaps the root of this problem is in the question: "Why are people who don't care about simplicity, ease-of-use, and user-friendliness building interfaces and tools for people who do?"

```
<TABLE BORDER="1">
<TR>
<TD ALIGN="right"><B>Temp:</B></TD>
<TD ALIGN="left">28&deg; F</TD>
</TR>
<TR>
<TD ALIGN="right"><B>Conditions:</B></TD>
<TD ALIGN="left">Sunny</TD>
</TR>
<TR>
<TD ALIGN="right"><B>Wind:</B></TD>
<TD ALIGN="left">SE 5 MPH</TD>
</TR>
</TABLE>
```

Figure 11.26 Directly embedded page fragment generated by the Weather Service

```
<TABLE BORDER="1">
<TR>
<TD ALIGN="right"><B>Temp:</B></TD>
<TD ALIGN="left"> ${weather.temp} &deg; ${weather.tempscale} </TD>
</TR>
<TR>
<TD ALIGN="right"><B>Conditions:</B></TD>
<TD ALIGN="left"> ${weather.conditions} </TD>
</TR>
<TR>
<TD ALIGN="right"><B>Wind:</B></TD>
<TD ALIGN="left"> ${weather.winddirection}  ${weather.windvelocity}
                  ${weather.windvelocityunits} </TD>
</TR>
</TABLE>
```

Figure 11.27   Same as Figure 11.26 but using discrete display components in the page context

```
<TABLE BORDER="0">
<TR>
<TD ALIGN="center" VALIGN="center">
    <IMG SRC="/images/weather/ ${weather.conditions} .gif">
        <BR><SPAN CLASS="small"> ${weather.conditions} </SPAN>
</TD>
<TD ALIGN="center" CLASS="bigred" BGCOLOR=#ffff99>
    ${weather.temp} &deg; ${weather.tempscale}
</TD>
</TR>
<TR>
<TD COLSPAN="2" ALIGN="center">
    ${weather.winddirection}
    ${weather.windvelocity}  ${weather.windvelocityunits}
</TD>
</TR>
</TABLE>

<TABLE BORDER="0">
<TR>
<TD ALIGN="center" VALIGN="center">
    <IMG SRC="/images/weather/ Sunny .gif">
        <BR><SPAN CLASS="small"> Sunny </SPAN>
</TD>
<TD ALIGN="center" CLASS="bigred" BGCOLOR=#ffff99>
    28 &deg; F
</TD>
</TR>
<TR>
<TD COLSPAN="2" ALIGN="center">
    SE 5 MPH
</TD>
</TR>
</TABLE>
```

Figure 11.28   An alternate specification of the same page fragment using discrete display components

Many people in the open source community have a disdain for Microsoft and the products they offer. But their products have been successful in the marketplace, at least in part, because they were designed to keep simple things simple (e.g. through user-friendly interfaces called 'wizards'). The argument that these products can *only* do the 'simple things' has some merit. Fortunately, this is not an 'either-or' situation. Tools, APIs, and application development frameworks can be designed to make simple things simple for those who design, develop, deploy, and administer Web applications, while still providing flexibility for those who need more complex functionality. It is not unlike the dichotomy between those who prefer command-line interfaces and those who prefer GUIs. There is no reason both cannot exist side by side, in the same environment, with the individual free to choose which mode they want to work in.

It is easier to keep simple things simple in a Web application when the framework is designed to support such simplicity. Even in the absence of such a framework, it is still the responsibility of Web application architects to employ good design practices, so tasks that *ought to be* easy to perform actually are. They should rigorously analyze and document application requirements upfront, including use case analysis to determine the tasks likely to be performed. The design should facilitate adding support for as many of those tasks as possible without requiring that the entire application be rebuilt. Proper utilization of these practices should ensure that the application is flexible, extensible, and viable.

Such goals can be accomplished within existing frameworks (e.g. Struts), but only by following solid application design and development practices. Existing frameworks do not *enforce* good design practices; the best of them simply provide a platform that enables good design. Hopefully, the next generation frameworks will make it a trivial task to follow these practices, so that Web applications can be more flexible and be developed more quickly.

11.7 SUMMARY

Current trends in the world of Web application development are extremely promising. Recent XML specifications, including XSL, XSLFO, and XQuery further the objective of making XML a mainstream technology. Support for Web Services is now an integrated part of many commercial products.

Due to its complexity, RDF has been relatively slow to gain momentum. However, recent developments show the growing acceptance of this technology. First RDF applications are already taking hold (e.g. CC/PP), and more are under development. It is too early to say whether RDF will be the main power behind the Semantic Web, but it deserves to be watched very closly.

In the J2EE world, JSTL tags also make both XML and SQL processing simpler, and represent a huge step towards making JSPs accessible to page designers. JSP

2.0 raises the bar even higher, incorporating the Expression Language directly into the JSP syntax and opening the door for declarative definition of custom tags.

Alternative approaches to page presentation exist, both open-source (like Velocity) and proprietary (like Macromedia Cold Fusion and Microsoft ASP.NET). The more flexible approaches strive to fit into the widely accepted MVC paradigm, serving as a possible View component architecture for frameworks like Struts.

The next generation of Web application development frameworks are likely to employ the technologies described in this chapter. They should solve many of the pressing problems that currently face developers and designers of Web applications. We hope this book has prepared you, not only to understand the current generation of Web technology, but also to play a part in the development of the next.

11.8 QUESTIONS AND EXERCISES

1. What is SOAP? If SOAP is a protocol, what does it mean that SOAP is an XML application? What is the relationship between SOAP and HTTP? Is it possible to use SOAP with SMTP? Explain.
2. What is a Web Service? What specification is used to define Web service semantics?
3. What is the role of WSDL and UDDI? Why do we need both specifications? How do WSDL, UDDI, and SOAP together support Web Services?
4. What is RDF? What is the purpose of introducing the RDF specification?
5. What is the relationship between RDF and XML? Since an RDF model can be represented in XML, is it not enough to use XML Schema to impose constraints on the model? Why do we need an RDF Schema?
6. What is the relationship between RDF and Dublin Core?
7. What is the purpose of CC/PP? What is the relationship between CC/PP and RDF?
8. Does your cell phone support Web browsing? Can you find or define a CC/PP-compliant description for your cell phone?
9. Let us go back to the CarML markup language and XML documents, which resulted from your exercises in Chapter 7. Define an XQuery-compliant query to retrieve all red cars that have two doors and whose model year is no older than 2000.
10. Suppose that you have access not only to documents describing cars, but to the owner records as well (you can make assumptions about the structure of these records). Can you define a query to retrieve all red cars that have a 6-cylinder engine and that are owned by a person who is less than 25 years old?
11. What future advances do you consider the most important? Explain.

BIBLIOGRAPHY

Alur, D., Crupi, J. and Malks, D. (2003) *Core J2EE Patterns*. Upper Saddle River, NJ: Prentice-Hall.

Glass, G. (2001) *Web Services: Building Blocks for Distributed Systems*. Upper Saddle River, NJ: Prentice-Hall.

McGovern, J, Bothner, P., Cagle, K., Linn, J. and Nagarahan, V. (2003) *XQuery Kick Start*. Sams.

Powers, S. (2003) *Practical RDF*. Sebastapol, CA: O'Reilly & Associates.

Tate, B. A. (2002) *Bitter Java*. Greenwich, CT: Manning Publications.

Index

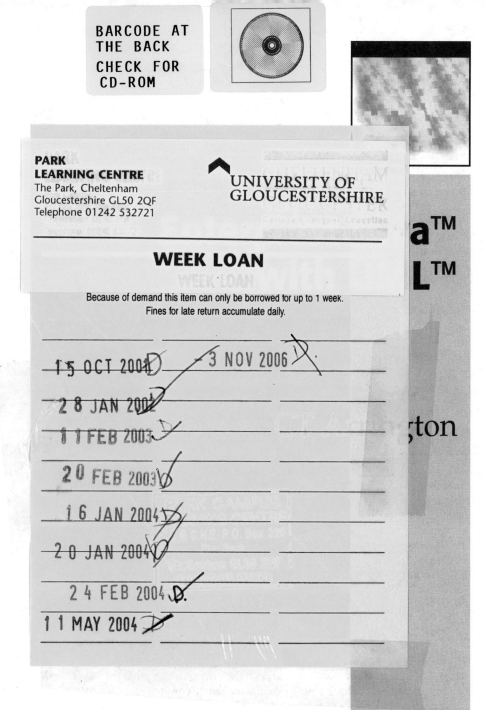
UNIVERSITY OF
GLOUCESTERSHIRE

a™
L™

Wiley Computer Publishing

John Wiley & Sons, Inc.
NEW YORK · CHICHESTER · WEINHEIM · BRISBANE · SINGAPORE · TORONTO

To my beautiful wife Anne, you were sooo worth the wait!

Always and forever,
CT

To Bethany Carleen, our precious daughter, and my
personal trainer.

To Anne Burzawa, my best friend from cradle to grave.

Publisher: Robert Ipsen
Editor: Theresa Hudson
Developmental Editor: Kathryn A. Malm
Managing Editor: Angela Smith
Text Design & Composition: Publishers' Design and Production Services, Inc.

Designations used by companies to distinguish their products are often claimed as trademarks. In all instances where John Wiley & Sons, Inc., is aware of a claim, the product names appear in initial capital or ALL CAPITAL LETTERS. Readers, however, should contact the appropriate companies for more complete information regarding trademarks and registration.

This book is printed on acid-free paper. ∞

This publication is designed to provide accurate and authoritative information in regard to the subject matter covered. It is sold with the understanding that the publisher is not engaged in professional services. If professional advice or other expert assistance is required, the services of a competent professional person should be sought.

Library of Congress Cataloging-in-Publication Data:

ISBN: 0-471-38680-4

Printed in the United States of America.

10 9 8 7 6 5 4 3 2 1